근현대사 주요용어 영문표기 표준화 연구

문화체육관광부 대한민국역사박물관

2015년 1월 20일 1판 1쇄 인쇄
2015년 1월 20일 1판 1쇄 발행

지 은 이 문화체육관광부 대한민국역사박물관
발 행 인 이헌숙
표   지 김학용
발 행 처 생각쉼표 & 주)휴먼컬처아리랑
　　　　 서울특별시 영등포구 여의도동 45-13 코오롱포레스텔 309
전   화 070) 8866 - 2220 FAX • 02) 784-4111
등록번호 제 2009 - 000008호
등록일자 2009년 12월 29일

www.휴먼컬처아리랑.kr
ISBN 979-11-5565-238-1

근현대사 주요용어 영문표기 표준화 연구

문화체육관광부 대한민국역사박물관

대한민국역사박물관
『근현대사 주요용어 영문표기 표준화 연구』

주요연구기관 : (사)전쟁과 평화연구소
연 구 책 임 자 : 이명화(독립기념관 한국독립운동사연구소)
공 동 연 구 원 : 조윤정(이화여자대학교 통번역대학원)
　　　　　　　　박현주(이화여자대학교 통번역대학원)
　　　　　　　　나종남(육군사관학교 역사학과)
　　　　　　　　강창국(혜천대학교 교양교직과)
 검 증 위 원 : 홍석민(연세대학교 서양사과)
　　　　　　　　김마이클(연세대학교 언더우드국제대학)
　　　　　　　　김명섭(연세대학교 정치외교학과)
　　　　　　　　강규형(명지대학교 기록과학전문대학원)
　　　　　　　　김동형(Korea Times기자)
　　　　　　　　이영관(순천향대학교서양사학과)
　　　　　　　　이정은(대한민국역사문화원 원장)

차 례

1. 연구 개요 ··· 9
   1-1 과업명 : 근현대 주요용어 영문표기 표준화 연구 용역
   1-2 연구 배경 및 목적
   1-3 과업 개요
   1-4 과업 내용 및 범위

2. 과업 수행 내용 ·· 10

3. 과업 진행 개요 ·· 11

4. 용어 선정 기준 ·· 12
   4-1 한국근대사 부분
   4-2 한국현대사 부분

5. 근현대사 주요용어 영문번역 표준원칙 ················· 13

6. 근현대사 주요용어 영문표기 ····································· 19

1. 연구 개요

1-1 과업명 : 근현대 주요용어 영문표기 표준화 연구 용역

1-2 연구 배경 및 목적
- 대한민국의 성장, 발전과정과 민주화에 대한 외국인의 인식을 높이고자 한다.
- 한국근현대사 용어를 올바로 영역함으로써 대한민국역사박물관 전시관과 전시물을 관람하는 외국인들에게 한국의 역사문화를 올바르게 인식할 수 있도록 유도한다.
- 대한민국역사박물관 전시 및 각종 조사연구 사업에 활용하기 위한 대한민국 근현대사 관련 주요 용어 영문표기 표준지침 마련하고자 한다.
- 대한민국역사박물관 전시물 및 자료 설명에 필요한 영문명칭 확정으로 외국수요자에게 통일된 정보를 제공한다.

1-3 과업 개요
- 과업기간 : 2012. 04. 06 - 2012. 09. 03
- 사업예산 : 99,800,000원

1-4 과업 내용 및 범위
- 역사용어 분류 및 선정
  - 중·고등학교 한국사·근현대사 교과서 및 역사부도 등 총 38종 46책 참조
  - 국사편찬위원회 '한국역사용어 시소러스' 참조
  - 대한민국역사박물관 전시와 연구에 직접적으로 필요한 역사용어 참조
  - 「한민국역사박물관 전시주제 해설 기초자료 연구 보고서」 소항목 및 핵심어 참조

- 대한민국근대화과정 기초자료 수집 및 DB구축 연구보고서 참조
○ 현행 및 기성 영역 조사 및 검토
○ 용어 영문화 원칙 수립
○ 용어 영문화 원칙에 따른 용어 영역화 작업
○ 검증, 감수 - 통일 및 수정 작업

2. 과업 수행 내용

○ 영문번역 대상 역사용어 선정수량: 총 4,380개
  - 대한민국역사박물관 전시예정 관련 자료명 등 1,500여 개
  - 사건, 지명, 계기 등 선정 1,380여 개
  - 기존 연구소의 소항목 및 핵심어 등 1500여 개
○ 기존 영문화 용어 조사 및 분석
  * 국사편찬위원회 시소러스, 한국학 중앙연구원 영문역사용어, 독립기념관, 전쟁기념관, 서울역사박물관 등 기타 영역작업 비교
○ 제1차 자체 업무회의 개최, 작업 시트지 통일화 논의
○ 제2차 자체 업무회의 개최, 역사용어 영문화 표준원칙 정립
○ 원칙에 의한 용어영문표기 표준화작업
○ 제3회 자체 업무회의 개최 - 과업 수행 중간 점검, 과업 수행상의 문제점 정리
○ 영문용어 시트지 작성(기존 영문용어 수정 시 수정이유 표기)
○ 영문과업 시트지 완성
○ 내용적, 언어적 차원의 감수 시행
○ 제1,2차 검증회의
  - 최종 검증 및 교열 2차 감수
  - 지적사항 수정

3. 과업 진행 개요

진 행 일 자	내　　　용	비　　고
2012. 4. 6	- 근현대사 주요용어 영문표기 표준화 연구 용역 계약 체결	
4. 9	- 착수 보고회 개최	
4. 10	- 1차회의 개최 · 진행 과제의 범위 선정 · 연구 및 용어 선정 방향 논의, 결정	* 자료수집, 용어추출
4. 10 ~ 4. 20	- 국사편찬위원회, 한국학중앙연구원의 역사용어 용례 및 서울역사박물관·독립기념관·전쟁박물관 등 전시 역사용어 실태 조사	* 역사전문가와 영어전문가가 함께 참여하여 용어선정 작업
4. 10 ~ 4. 30	- 기존 영문화 용어 조사 및 분석 · 국사편찬위원회 역사용어 시소러스 작업의 조사, 분석 · 한국학중앙연구원 한국사 용어 용례사전 조사, 분석 · 국사편찬위원회 시소러스와 한국학중앙연구원 영역 작업 비교, 분석 · 조사, 분석 결과의 시트화	* 국사편찬위원회 시소러스, 한국학 중앙연구원 영문역사용어, 기타 영역작업 비교, 시트화
5. 10	- 2차회의 개최 · 역사용어 영문화 표준 번역 원칙 정립 · 번역 원칙 내용의 공유	* 역사 및 영어전문가가 함께 참여 * 외국인 1차 고려, 의미 전달에 주안점을 두는 것으로 번역원칙을 정함
5. 10 ~ 7. 30	- 번역원칙에 의한 용어영문표기 표준화 작업 · 대상용어 선별, 용어 선정 · 기존영문 용어와 비교, 목록 작성 · 선정된 용어 시트화	* 기존 영문이 없는 용어는 영문 새 번역 - 역사적인 내용과 언어적 내용 동시 검토
6. 5	- 대한민국역사박물관 전시 예정 자료 목록 입수 · 기선정 용어와 비교하며 영역 작업. · 선정 용어 목록 보완, 첨가	* 전시예정 자료명 목록 1,500여개와 비전시물 2,880여개의 용어 선정
6. 7	- 3차회의 개최 · 과업 수행 중간 점검 · 영역 대상 용어 확정, 이에 따른 영문화 작업 조정 · 기존 영문 용어 수정 시에는 수정이유 표기	* 영문용어 시트지 통일 작업

7. 26	- 중간보고회의 개최 · 연구 용역 과업 수행 중간보고	
8. 1 ~ 8. 10	- 용역과업 완수 · 용역 과업 시트지 완성 · 과업 내용 감수 시행 · 수정 및 통일화 작업	* 영역 용어의 내용적, 언어적 차원 감수
8. 12	- 과업 완수 보고회의	* 과업 완수
8. 13	- 제1차 검증회의	홍석민, 김명섭, 김마이클, 김동형, 이영관, 이정은 강규형, 이명화, 조윤정, 박현주, 강창국
8. 16	- 1차 검증회의 지적 사항 수정	
8. 17	- 제2차 검증회의	홍석민, 김명섭, 김마이클, 김동형, 이영관, 이정은 강규형, 이명화, 조윤정, 박현주, 강창국
8. 18 ~ 8. 19	- 2차 검증회의 지적 사항 수정 · 용역완료 보고서 작성	
8. 22	- 용역 과업 최종 완수	* 용역 완료 보고서 제출

4. 용어 선정 기준

4-1 한국근대사 부문
○ 현행 중·고등학교 한국사 및 근현대사 교과서 및 역사부도에서 공통으로 다루고 있는 용어 선정
○ 대한민국역사박물관 전시 주제 해설 기초자료연구용역 결과 보고서, 주요 저서 및 논문 등 참고
○ 대한민국역사박물관 전시 선정 관련 용어

4-2 한국현대사 부문
- ○ 한국현대사를 균형감 있게 다루고 일정정도 이상 구체적인 사실 설명에 필요한 용어 선정
- ○ 현행 중·고등학교 한국사 및 근현대사 교과서, 역사부도 참고
- ○ 김진국·정창현 공저, www.한국현대사.com 참조 : 사실관계를 균형 있게 다루면서 내용을 잘 정리하고, 북한에 대해서도 충실하게 다루고 있음.
- ○ 대한민국역사박물관 전시 주제 해설 기초자료연구용역 결과 보고서, 주요 저서 및 논문 등 참고
- ○ 인터넷 영문 사전 사이트 www.wikipedia 참고 : 구체적인 분류사적 용어 보완
- ○ 대한민국역사박물관 전시 선정 관련 용어

5. 근현대사 주요용어 영문번역 표준원칙

5-1 목적
- ○ 본 과업은 현 영문표준화가 각기 상이하게 또는 부적절한 표현으로 사용됨으로써 혼돈을 주는 일을 극복하고자 일관된 원칙과 기준에 따른 영문화 표기를 제시하는데 목적을 둔다.
- ○ 한국과 교류하는 외국인 및 한국을 찾는 외국인들의 이해를 높이고 원활한 의사소통을 위해 영어다운 표현을 사용하여 외국인의 이해를 쉽게 하고자 한다.
- ○ 현재 사용하고 있는 표현을 존중하되, 영어답지 못한 표현이거나 국제적인 통용에 문제가 있는 것을 영어다운 표현으로 제시한다.

5-2 대상시기 : 본 영문 표준화 대상 용어는 1876년 개항 이후 현재까지 시기를 한정하여 선정한다.

5-3 정리양식 : 본 영문표준화과업은 1) 용어, 2) 한문, 3) 영문, 4)로마자발음표기, 5) M/C발음표기, 6) 시대 및 연도, 7) 출전 순으로 기재한다.

5-4 배열순서 : 영문표준화 용어 순서는 우리말 가나다 순으로 배열한다.

5-5 한글표기 : 한글 용어 표기의 기본 원칙은 구어 표준 발음법에 따라 적는 것을 원칙으로 한다.

5-6 로마자표기(Romanization) : 기본적으로 정부 표기법(문화관광부 고시 '국어로마자표기법'(제 2000-8호, 20000. 7. 7)을 따른다. 그러나 이미 유명인사의 이름이나 사건 등이 기존에 이미 잘 알려진 영문 명칭이 있을 경우는 고유표기를 따른다. 외국인이 인터넷 혹은 다른 인쇄자료 검색 시, 쉽게 찾을 수 있도록 하기 위함.
- 조선일보 → Chosun Ilbo
- 이승만 → Syngman Rhee

5-7 외래어 표기 : 외래어 표기법은 1991년 외래어심의공동위원회에서 결정한 표기법을 따른다.

5-8 여러 가지 표현의 역사용어 : 여러 가지로 표현되는 역사용어는 교과서 표준 용어를 기준으로 선택한다.
- 5.16군사혁명 (×), 5.16군사정변 (○)
- 동학농민혁명 (×), 동학농민운동 (○)

5-9 날짜 등 숫자가 들어가는 역사용어
○ 날짜가 들어간 역사용어는 아라비아숫자로 표시하고 한문표기에서도 그대로 숫자로 표시한다.
- 4·19혁명 → 4·19革命(○), 四·一九革命(×)

○ 사건의 표기는 유명한 경우 숫자를 앞으로 내어 표시한다. 단, 공식적인 영문용어가 있는 경우에는 공식용어를 따른다. 기타는 영어로 월, 숫자로 쓴다.
- 6.29민주화선언 → June 29 Declaration (in favor of a new democratic constitution)
- April 3, February 28

5-10 문장 표기 원칙
○ 관사는 문장 안에서는 넣고 명사 표기 시에는 생략한다.
○ 일반 명사는 소문자로 표시한다.
○ 고유명사이나 간단하게 명사화 되지 않은 경우엔 설명식으로 기술한다.
○ 용어의 설명이 필요할 경우는 별도의 칸에서 설명한다.
○ 국가입장 관련의 용어는 한국측 입장을 우선 표현한다.
- 남북회담 → South-North Talks
○ 사건, 단체 등에서 신뢰할 만한 출처가 없고 여기저기서 각기 다르게 표현하고 있는 경우 제일 빈번하게 사용되며 영어가 어색하지 않은 이름을 선택한다. 외국인 입장에서 한국에 대해 더 찾아보고 싶으면 일단 인터넷 검색부터 하게 되는데, 자료를 쉽게 찾을 수 있는 이름으로 표기해야 검색 시 유리하기 때문임. 아예 참고 할만한 영문자료가 없을 경우엔 주로 설명함.

5-11 복합명사
○ 강, 산, 궁, 문, 도 등 고유명사와 일반명사가 복합명사를 이룰 경우는 국어의 로마자 표기법을 따른다.
예) • 한강 → Hangang River
- 남산 → Namsan Mountain (or Mt. Namsan)
- 경복궁 → Gyeongbokgung Palace

- 남대문 → Namdaemun Gate
- 경상남도 → Gyeongsangnam-do Province

○ 외국 지명 및 도시이름이 들어간 복합명사의 용어는 관용적인 한글 발음으로 한글 표제어를 표기하고 영문은 현지 발음으로 번역, 표기한다.
- 북경조약 → Beijing Treaty

5-12 고유명사

○ 사건, 사태 등 고유명사는 의미번역과 발음표기를 병기한다.
- Gapsin Coup of 1884 (Gapsin Jeongbyeon)
- Gabo Reforms of 1894 (Gabo Gaehyeok)

○ 사건의 구분 : 사건의 경우 필요할 경우 사건발생 연도를 병기한다.
- 임오군변 → Military Uprising of 1882 (Imo Gunbyeon)

○ 인명 : 인물이름에 대한 영문 표준화는 현 과업에서 제외한다.

○ 사건, 단체명 등의 고유명사는 일반적으로 잘 알려졌다해도 원칙적으로 공식 및 공문서상의 명칭을 용어로 채택한다.
- 노인동맹단 → 대한인노인동맹단
- 건국준비위원회 → 조선건국준비위원회
- 강성대국 : Strong and prosperous great power(×)
  strong and prosperous nation(○)

○ 정식명칭과 약칭명칭 모두를 가나다순 목록에서 제시하고 정식명칭을 찾을 수 있도록 한다.
- 광복군 → 한국광복군
- 한국광복군 → 광복군

5-13 공식 영문명

○ 미주 독립운동 등 : 미주지역 한인사회에서처럼 영문으로 공식 단체명과 사건에 관한 용어가 있을 경우는 당대의 표기를 그대로 따른다.

5-14 **출판물**
- 책의 제목은 영문(이탤릭체) 제목을 먼저 표기하고 한글 제목의 음차표기는 괄호 안에 표기한다.
- 신문은 한글이름 음차를 먼저표기하고 영문이름이 있을 경우에는 괄호 안에, 없을 경우는 daily newspaper 같은 설명을 붙인다.
- 잡지는 기본적으로 신문 표기와 같지만 경우에 따라 (잘알려진 잡지가 아니면 한글이름이 너무 길고 음차가 복잡한 경우) 영문 이름만 표기함.

5-15 **문화재** : 세계문화재로 지정된 경우에는 UNESCO site에서 사용하는 용어를 채택한다.
- 간결의 원칙 : 역사용어 번역이기 때문에 최대한 간결하게 의미 전달이 되는 방향을 취한다.

5-16 **올림픽 대회**
- 올림픽대회의 영문 표준화 표기는 올림픽 개최연도와 도시이름을 병기한다.
  - 서울올림픽 → 1988 Seoul Olympics
  - 런던올림픽 → 1948 London Olympics

5-17 **중국어·일본어 등 한문 외래어**
- 한글발음으로 용어화하고 현지화발음으로 번역, 표기한다.
  - 미쓰야 협정(三矢協定) → 삼시협정
  - 간토오대지진(關東大地震) → 관동대지진

5-18 **법률 용어** : Act는 주로 영미법에서 많이 쓰고 Law는 대륙법(한국, 일본 포함)에서 사용함. 한국과 일본의 경우는 Law를 쓰는 것이 법체계상 맞지만 번역문의 경우 영미법의 관습에 따라 Act를 사용하고 있음.

영미법의 경우 특별한 경우 따로 Act를 만들어 쓰고 나머지는 통상 관례를 통해 규율하게 되며 대륙법의 경우 세밀한 사항까지 전부 law를 만들어 규제하는 것이 일반적임. 현재 일본의 경우도 번역문의 경우 모두 Act로 표기하고 있으므로 Act로 가는 것이 좋다고 판단됨.

* Law의 경우 법률사전을 보면 : a statute, ordinance or regulation enacted by the legislative branch of a government and signed into law, or in some nations created by decree without any democratic process.로 정의됨. 당시 일본에 의회가 구성되어 있고, 해당 법이 의회에서 발의, 통과되어 법으로 제정된 경우가 아니라면 law라고 표기할 수 없다.

5-19 신뢰할만한 출처가 없고 영문화한 표현이 다수일 때, 어색하지 않은 영어를 표준화로 선정한다.

5-20 역사적 맥락의 고려 : 용어를 번역할 때 단어적 의미가 아닌, 역사적 맥락을 고려하여 번역 또는 영문 단어를 선택한다.
* 역사적 맥락 : 간도지역에 조선에서 두만강을 넘어 초기 월경농업을 하다 점차 이주정착하여 조선인 공동체를 형성해간 상황임
  * 간도개척 Gando develop → settlement of Gando
  * 거국가(去國歌) : 조국을 떠나면서 부른 노래
    a Nationwide Song → "Farewell to the Homeland"
    (sung by independence activist An Chang-ho)

6. 근현대사 주요용어 영문표기

NO	용어	한자	영문	RO	MC	시대 및 연도	출전
1	가격표시제	價格表示制	open price system	Gagyeok pyosije	Kagyŏk p'yosije	1975	번역 표준 원칙
2	가곡	歌曲	gagok (traditional long lyric songs)	Gagok	Kagok		번역 표준 원칙
3	가쓰라태프트 밀약	桂Taft 密約	Taft-Katsura Agreement	Gasseura-Taepeuteu miryak	Kassŭra-T'aep'ŭt'ŭ miryak	1905	번역 표준 원칙
4	가야산국립공원	伽倻山國立公園	Gayasan National Park	Gayasan gungnipgongwon	Kayasan kungnipkongwŏn	1972-?	번역 표준 원칙
5	가정교육	家庭敎育	family upbringing	Gajeong gyoyuk	Kajŏng kyoyuk		번역 표준 원칙
6	가정법률상담소	家庭法律相談所	Korea Legal Aid Center for Family Relations	Gajeong beomnyul sangdamso	Kajŏng pŏmnyul sangdamso	1956-?	번역 표준 원칙
7	가정의례준칙	家庭儀禮準則	The Simplified Family Ritual Standards (Gajeong uirye junchik)	Gajeong uirye junchik	Kachŏng ŭirye chunch'ik	1973-?	번역 표준 원칙
8	가정폭력방지법	家庭暴力防止法	Act on the Prevention of Domestic Violence and the Protection of Its Victims	Gajeong pongnyeok bangjibeop	Kajŏng p'ongnyŏk pangjipŏp	1997	번역 표준 원칙

NO	용어	한자	영문	RO	MC	시대 및 연도	출전
9	가정폭력상담소	家庭暴力相談所	domestic violence counselling center	Gajeong pongnyeok sangdamso	Kajŏng p'ongnyŏk sangdamso		번역 표준 원칙
10	가족계획	家族計劃	family planning	Gajok gyehoek	Kajok kyehoek	1960년대	번역 표준 원칙
11	가족계획실천운동	家族計劃實踐運動	Family Planning Movement	Gajok gyehoek silcheon undong	Kajok kyehoek silch'ŏn undong		번역 표준 원칙
12	가족법개정운동	家族法改定運動	Family Law Reform Movement	Gajokbeop gaejeong undong	Kajokpŏp kaejŏng undong	1989	번역 표준 원칙
13	가족복지	家族福祉	family welfare	Gajok bokji	Kajok pokchi		번역 표준 원칙
14	가칠봉 전투	加七峰 戰鬪	Battle of Gachil Peak	Gachilbong jeontu	Kach'ilbong chŏnt'u	1951	번역 표준 원칙
15	각개격파	各個擊破	defeat in detail	Gakgae gyeokpa	Kakkae gyŏkp'a		번역 표준 원칙
16	각개전투기술	各個戰鬪技術	individual combat skills and techniques	Gakgae jeontu gisul	Kakke chŏnt'u gisul		번역 표준 원칙

NO	용어	한자	영문	RO	MC	시대 및 연도	출전
17	간도	間島	Gando Province (Ch. Jiandao)	Gando	Kando	1909	번역 표준 원칙
18	간도 개척	間島 開拓	settlement of Gando (Ch. Jiando)	Gando gaecheok	Kando kaech'ŏk	1881	번역 표준 원칙
19	간도5·30사건	間島5·30事件	Gando (Ch. Jiando) Incident of May 30	Gando 5·30 sageon	Kando 5·30 sagŏn	1930	번역 표준 원칙
20	간도공산당사건	間島共産黨事件	Gando (Ch. Jiando) Communist Party Incident	Gando gongsandang sageon	Kando kongsandang sagŏn	1927-1930	번역 표준 원칙
21	간도사건(간도출병)	間島事件 (間島出兵)	dispatch of Japanese troops to Gando (Ch. Jiandao)	Gando sageon (Gando chulbyeong)	Kando sakŏn (Kando ch'ulbyŏng)	1920 간도출병사건	번역 표준 원칙
22	간도참변	間島慘變	Hunchun Incident of 1920 (massacre of Koreans in Gando by the Japanese)	Gando chambyeon	Kando ch'ambyŏn	1920	번역 표준 원칙
23	간도협약	間島協約	Gando (Ch. Jiando) Convention	Gando hyeobyak	Kando hyŏbyak	1909	번역 표준 원칙
24	간민교육회	墾民教育會	Ganmin Educational Association	Ganmin gyoyukhoe	Kanmin kyoyukhoe	1907-1911	번역 표준 원칙

NO	용어	한자	영문	RO	MC	시대 및 연도	출전
25	간민회	墾民會	Ganmin Association	Ganminhoe	Kanminhoe	1911	번역 표준 원칙
26	간부훈련학교	幹部訓練學校	Cadres Training School	Ganbu hulyeon hakgyo	Kanbu hullyŏn hakkyo		번역 표준 원칙
27	간척사업	干拓事業	land reclamation project	Gancheok saeop	Kanch'ŏk saŏp		번역 표준 원칙
28	간통쌍벌죄	姦通雙罰罪	punishment of both parties in adultery	Gantong ssangbeoljoe	Kant'ong ssangbŏljoe	1953	번역 표준 원칙
29	감사원	監査院	Board of Audit and Inspection	Gamsawon	Kamsawŏn	1963-?	번역 표준 원칙
30	갑산파	甲山派	Gapsan Faction	Gapsanpa	Kapsanp'a	1945-1968	한국학중앙연구원, 《영문한국백과》-한국
31	갑신정변	甲申政變	Gapsin Coup of 1884 (Gapsin Jeongbyeon)	Gapsinjeongbyeon	Kapsinjŏngbyŏn	1884	번역 표준 원칙
32	갑오개혁	甲午改革	Gabo Reforms of 1894 (Gabo Gaehyeok)	Gabogaehyeok	Kabogaehyŏk	1894-1896	번역 표준 원칙

NO	용어	한자	영문	RO	MC	시대 및 연도	출전
33	강강술래	강강술래	Ganggang-sullae (group circle dance)	Ganggang sullae	Kangkang sullae	기타	한국학중앙연구원, 《영문한국백과》-민요
34	강경대군치사사건	姜慶大君致死事件	death of college student Gang Gyeong-dae (due to suppression by riot police in 1991)	Ganggyeong daegun chisa sageon	Kang kyŏng-tae kun ch'isa sakŏn	1991	번역 표준 원칙
35	강남개발	江南開發	development of Gangnam	Gangnam gaebal	Kangnam kaebal		번역 표준 원칙
36	강릉 잠수함침투사건	江陵 潛水艦浸透事件	1996 Gangneung Submarine Infiltration Incident	Gangneung jamsuham chimtu sageon	Kangnŭng chamsuham ch'imt'u sakŏn	1996	번역 표준 원칙
37	강릉단오제	江陵端午祭	Gangneung Danoje (folk festival held in Gangneung, Gangwon-do, on Dano Day)	Gangneung danoje	Kangnŭng tanoje	기타	번역 표준 원칙
38	강서학살사건	江西虐殺事件	Gangseo Massacre	Gangseo haksal sageon	Kangsŏ haksal sagŏn	1919	번역 표준 원칙
39	강성대국	强盛大國	strong and prosperous nation	Gangseong daeguk	Kangsŏng taeguk	1998	번역 표준 원칙
40	강원도	江原道	Gangwon-do Province	Gangwondo	Kangwŏndo	1395-?	번역 표준 원칙

NO	용어	한자	영문	RO	MC	시대 및 연도	출전
41	강제공출	強制供出	forced requisition of goods	Gangje gongchul	Kangje kongch'ul	1946-1948	번역 표준 원칙
42	강제동원	強制動員	forced mobilization	Gangjae dongwon	Kangje tongwŏn		번역 표준 원칙
43	강제수용소	強制收容所	concentration camp	Gangje suyongso	Kangje suyongso		번역 표준 원칙
44	강제연행	強制連行	forced detainment	Gangjae yeonhaeng	Kangje yŏnhaeng		번역 표준 원칙
45	강제징병	強制徵兵	forced conscription	Gangje jingbyeong	Kangje chingbyŏng		번역 표준 원칙
46	강제징용	強制徵用	labor conscription (of Koreans by the Japanese)	Gangje jingyong	Kangje chingyong	1939-1945	번역 표준 원칙
47	강제퇴거제도	強制退去制度	compulsory eviction system	Gangje toegeo jedo	Kangje t'oegŏ chedo		번역 표준 원칙
48	강화도	江華島	Ganghwado Island	Ganghwado	Kanghwado		번역 표준 원칙

NO	용어	한자	영문	RO	MC	시대 및 연도	출전
49	강화도조약	江華島條約	Treaty of Ganghwa of 1876	Ganghwado joyak	Kanghwado choyak	1876	번역 표준 원칙
50	개국	開國	Gaeguk (reign name of King Gojong, 1894-1896)	Gaeguk	Kaeguk	1894-1896	번역 표준 원칙
51	개국정책	開國政策	open-door policy	Gaeguk jeongchaek	Kaeguk chŏngch'aek		번역 표준 원칙
52	개도국과학기술지원단	開途國科學技術支援團	Korea Techno Peace Corps Program (TPC)	Gaedoguk gwahakgisul jiwondan	Kaedoguk kwahak kisul chiwŏndan	2006-?	번역 표준 원칙
53	개량서당	改良書堂	modernized village school	Gaeryang seodang	Kaeryang sŏdang		번역 표준 원칙
54	개발도상국	開發途上國	developing country	Gaebal dosangguk	Kaebal tosangguk	1950-	번역 표준 원칙
55	개발이익환수제	開發利益還收制	restitution of development gains	Gaebal iik hwansuje	Kaebal iik hwansuje		번역 표준 원칙
56	개발제한구역	開發制限區域	greenbelt	Gaebal jehan guyeok	Kaebal chehan kuyŏk	1971-	번역 표준 원칙

NO	용어	한자	영문	RO	MC	시대 및 연도	출전
57	개방정책	開放政策	open-door policy	Gaebang jeongcheak	Kaebang cheongch'eak	조선	Robert E. Buswell Jr., Religions of Korea in Practice, Princeton, N.J.: Princeton University
58	개벽	開闢	Gaebyeok (Dawn of Civilization), magazine published by Cheongdogyo	Gaebyeok	Kaebyŏk	1930	번역 표준 원칙
59	개성공단	開城工團	Kaesong Industrial Complex	Gaeseong gongdan	Kaesŏng kongdan	2002	번역 표준 원칙
60	개성공단 화물열차	開城工團 貨物列車	freight train from Kaesong Industrial Complex	Gaeseong gongdan hwamul yeolcha	Kaesŏng kongdan hwamul yŏlch'a	2007	번역 표준 원칙
61	개성관광	開城觀光	tours to Kaesong, North Korea	Gaeseong gwangwang	Kaesong gwan'gwang	2007	번역 표준 원칙
62	개신교	改新敎	Protestantism	Gaesingyo	Kaesin'gyo	현대	한국학중앙연구원, 《영문한국백과》-기독교
63	개인숭배	個人崇拜	personality cult	Gaein sungbae	Kaein sungbae		번역 표준 원칙
64	개인정보보호법	個人情報保護法	Privacy Protection Act	Gaein jeongbo bohobeop	Kaein chŏngbo pohopŏp	2011	번역 표준 원칙

NO	용어	한자	영문	RO	MC	시대 및 연도	출전
65	개인택시	個人taxi	independent taxi	Gaein taeksi	Kaein t'aeksi		번역 표준 원칙
66	개정안 한글맞춤법 통일안	改正案 한글맞춤법 統一案	Revised Rules for Hangeul Orthography	Gaejeongan hangeul matchumbeop tongilan	Kaejŏngan han'gŭl match'umpŏp t'ongiran	1945	번역 표준 원칙
67	개조파	改造派	Reformist Faction (group advocating the reorganization of the Provisional Government of the Republic of Korea)	Gaejopa	Kaejop'a	1923	번역 표준 원칙
68	개항	開港	opening of ports	Gaehang	Kaehang	1876	번역 표준 원칙
69	개항불가론	開港不可論	arguments against the opening of ports	Gaehangbulgaron	Kaehangbulgaron		번역 표준 원칙
70	개항장	開港場	treaty port	Gaehangjang	Kaehangjang	1876-1910	번역 표준 원칙
71	개헌	改憲	constitutional amendment	Gaeheon	Kaehŏn		번역 표준 원칙
72	개헌문제에 관한 특별 담화문	改憲問題에 關한 特別 談話文	Special Statement on Constitutional Amendment	Gaeheon munjee gwanhan teukbyeol damhwamun	Kaehŏnmunjee kwanhan t'ŭkpyŏl tamhwamun		번역 표준 원칙

NO	용어	한자	영문	RO	MC	시대 및 연도	출전
73	개헌서명운동	改憲署名運動	signature collection drive for constitutional amendment	Gaeheon seomyeong undong	Kaehŏn sŏmyŏng undong	1986	번역 표준 원칙
74	개헌청원 100만인 서명운동	改憲請願 100萬人 署名運動	campaign to collect one million signatures for constitutional amendment	Gaeheon cheongwon 100manin seomyeong undong	Kaehŏn ch'ŏngwon 100manin sŏmyŏng undong	1973	번역 표준 원칙
75	개화	開化	enlightenment	Gaehwa	Kaehwa		Peter H. Lee, Sourcebook of Korean Civilization(Volume 2), Columbia University Press, 1993,
76	개화사상	開化思想	enlightenment thought	Gaehwasasang	Kaehwasasang	조선 1876전후	Ki-baik Lee, translated by Edward W. Wagner, A New History of Korea, Harvard University Press, 1984,
77	개화시대	開化時代	enlightenment period	Gaehwa sidae	Kaehwa sidae		번역 표준 원칙
78	개화정책	開化政策	enlightenment policy	Gaehwa jeongchaek	Kaehwa chŏngch'aek	1876-?	Ki-baik Lee, translated by Edward W. Wagner, A New History of Korea, Harvard University Press, 1984,
79	개화파	開化派	Enlightenment Faction (Gaehwapa)	Gaehwapa	Kaehwap'a	1876-1884	번역 표준 원칙
80	갤럭시S	Galaxy S	Samsung's Galaxy S smartphone	Gaelleoksi S	kaellŏksi S	2010	번역 표준 원칙

NO	용어	한자	영문	RO	MC	시대 및 연도	출전
81	거국가	去國歌	"Farewell to the Homeland" (sung by independence activist An Chang-ho)	Geogukga	Kŏgukka	1910	번역 표준 원칙
82	거문도사건	巨文島事件	British occupation of Geomundo Island	Geomundo sageon	Kŏmundo sagŏn	1885-1887	번역 표준 원칙
83	거문도점령	巨文島占領	Geomundo Island Incident	Geomundo jeomnyeong	Kŏmundo chŏmnyŏng	1885-1887	번역 표준 원칙
84	거점개발	據點開發	foothold development	Geojeom gaebal	Kŏchŏm kaebal		번역 표준 원칙
85	거점방어	據点防禦	strongpoint defense	Geojeom bangeo	Kŏchŏm bangŏ		번역 표준 원칙
86	거제도 포로수용소	巨濟島 捕虜收容所	Commandant of the Geojedo POW Camp	Geojedo poro suyongso	Kŏjedo p'oro suyongso	1950	번역 표준 원칙
87	거창 양민학살사건	居昌 良民虐殺事件	Geochang Massacre	Geochang yangmin haksal sageon	Kŏch'ang yangmin haksal sakŏn	1951	번역 표준 원칙
88	건국국채 일괄	建國國債 一括	National Foundation Bonds	Geonguk gukchae ilgwal	Kŏn'guk kukch'ae ilgwal	1950-1954	번역 표준 원칙

NO	용어	한자	영문	RO	MC	시대 및 연도	출전
89	건국대 농성사건	建國大 籠城事件	Konkuk University Incident	Geongukdae nongseong sageon	Kŏn'guktae nongsŏng sagŏn	1986	번역 표준 원칙
90	건국동맹	建國同盟	National Foundation Alliance	Geonguk dongmaeng	Kŏn'guk tongmaeng	1944-1945	번역 표준 원칙
91	건국부녀동맹	建國婦女同盟	Korean Women's League for National Foundation	Geonguk bunyeo dongmaeng	Kŏn'guk punyŏ tongmaeng	1945	번역 표준 원칙
92	건국준비위원회	建國準備委員會	Committee for the Establishment of the Korean State	Geonguk junbi wiwonhoe	Kŏnguk Chunbi Wiwonhoe	1945	번역 표준 원칙
93	건국치안대	建國治安隊	Peace-preservation Force	Geonguk chiandae	Kŏn'guk ch'iandae	1945	번역 표준 원칙
94	건국훈장	建國勳章	Order of Merit for National Foundation	Geonguk hunjang	Kŏnguk hunjang	1949	번역 표준 원칙
95	건설부	建設部	Ministry of Construction	Geonseolbu	Kŏnsŏlbu	1961-1994	송기중, 《한영우리문화용어집》, 지문당, 2001.
96	건양협회	建陽協會	Geonyang Association	Geonyang hyeophoe	Kŏnyang hyŏphoe	1896	번역 표준 원칙

NO	용어	한자	영문	RO	MC	시대 및 연도	출전
97	건전가요	健全歌謠	"wholesome songs" (added to the end of albums during the 4th and 5th Republics)	Geonjeon gayo	Kŏnjŏn kayo		번역 표준 원칙
98	건청궁	乾淸宮	Geoncheongjeon Hall in Gyeongbokgung Palace	Geoncheonggung	Kŏnch'ŏnggung	1873-1929	번역 표준 원칙
99	건축공학	建築工學	architecture	Geonchukhak	Kŏnch'uk'ak		번역 표준 원칙
100	검찰청	檢察廳	Supreme Prosecutors' Office (SPO)	Geomchalcheong	Kŏmch'alch'ŏng	1949-?	번역 표준 원칙
101	게릴라 전술	guerilla 戰術	guerrilla tactics	Gerilla jeonsul	Kerilla chŏnsul		번역 표준 원칙
102	겨울연가	겨울戀歌	"Winter Sonata" ("Gyeoul Yeonga," TV mini-series)	Gyeoul yeonga	Kyŏul yŏn'ga	2002	번역 표준 원칙
103	견마 로봇	犬馬 Robot	military quadruped robot	Gyeonma robot	Kyŏnma Robot	2008	번역 표준 원칙
104	견미사절단	遣美使節團	delegation to America	Gyeonmi sajeoldan	Kyŏnmi sajŏltan	1882	번역 표준 원칙

NO	용어	한자	영문	RO	MC	시대 및 연도	출전
105	견부진지	肩部陣地	shoulder critical point	Gyeonbujinji	Kyŏnbujinji		번역 표준 원칙
106	견인곡사포	牽引曲射砲	Towed Howizer	Gyeoningoksapo	Kyŏnin'goksap'o		번역 표준 원칙
107	경공업	輕工業	light industry	Gyeonggongeop	Kyŏnggongŏp		번역 표준 원칙
108	경기도	京畿道	Gyeonggi-do Province	Gyeonggido	Kyŏnggido	1414-?	번역 표준 원칙
109	경기영어마을	京畿英語마을	Gyeonggi English Village	Gyeonggi yeongeo maeul	Kyŏnggi yŏngŏ maŭl	2004	번역 표준 원칙
110	경무국장	警務局長	Director of Police Affairs	Gyeongmugukjang	Kyŏngmugukchang	1905	번역 표준 원칙
111	경무대	景武臺	Gyeongmudae (former name of Cheong Wa Dae)	Gyeongmudae	Kyŏngmudae	1948-1960	번역 표준 원칙
112	경무부	警務部	Police Administration Division	Gyeongmubu	Kyŏngmubu	1945-?	번역 표준 원칙

NO	용어	한자	영문	RO	MC	시대 및 연도	출전
113	경보병여단	輕步兵旅團	Light Infantry Brigade	Gyeongbobyeong yeodan	Kyŏngbobyŏng yŏdan		번역 표준 원칙
114	경복궁	景福宮	Gyeongbokgung Palace	Gyeongbokgung	Kyŏngbokkung	1395	번역 표준 원칙
115	경복궁 중건	景福宮 重建	reconstruction of Gyeongbokgung Palace	Gyeongbokgung junggeon	Kyŏngbokkung chunggŏn	1865~1868	번역 표준 원칙
116	경부고속도로	京釜高速道路	Seoul-Busan Expressway	Gyeongbu gosokdoro	Kyŏngbu kosoktoro	1970	번역 표준 원칙
117	경부고속도로 준공	京釜高速道路 竣工	completion of Seoul-Busan Expressway	Gyeongbu gosokdoro jungong	Kyŏngbu kosoktoro chungong	1970	번역 표준 원칙
118	경부철도	京釜鐵道	Seoul-Busan Railroad	Gyeongbu cheoldo	Kyŏngbu ch'ŏlto		번역 표준 원칙
119	경상남도	慶尙南道	Gyeongsangnam-do Province	Gyeongsangnamdo	Kyŏngsangnamdo	1896-?	번역 표준 원칙
120	경상북도	慶尙北道	Gyeongsangbuk-do Province	Gyeongsangbukdo	Kyŏngsangbukto	1896-?	번역 표준 원칙

NO	용어	한자	영문	RO	MC	시대 및 연도	출전
121	경성 트로이카	京城 Troika	Gyeongseong Troika	Gyeongseong teuroika	Kyŏngsŏng t'ŭroik'a	1933	번역 표준 원칙
122	경성감옥	京城監獄	Gyeongseong Prison (now Seodaemun Prison)	Gyeongseong gamok	Kyŏngsŏng kamok	1908	번역 표준 원칙
123	경성방송국	京城放送局	Kyongsong Broadcast Corporation	Gyeongseong bangsongguk	Kyŏngsŏng pangsongguk	1926	국사편찬위원회
124	경성방직주식회사	京城紡織株式會社	Gyeongseong Spinning and Weaving Company	Gyeongseong bangjik jusikhoesa	Kyŏngsŏng pangjik chusikhoesa	1919	번역 표준 원칙
125	경성의학교	京城醫學校	Gyeongseong Medical School	Gyeongseong uihakgyo	Kyŏngsŏng ŭihakkyo	1899-1916	한국학중앙연구원, 《영문한국백과》-대학
126	경성전기주식회사	京城電氣株式會社	Gyeongseong Electric Company	Gyeongseong jeongi jusikhoesa	Kyŏngsŏng chŏn'gi chusikhoesa	1898-1961	번역 표준 원칙
127	경성제국대학	京城帝國大學	Keijo Imperial University	Gyeongseong jeguk daehak	Kyŏngsŏng cheguk taehak	1924-1945	Ki-baik Lee, translated by Edward W. Wagner, A New History of Korea, Harvard University Press, 1984,
128	경성콤그룹	京城Com. Group	Gyeongseong Communist Group	Gyeongseong kom geurup	Kyŏngsŏng k'om kŭrup	1939-1941	번역 표준 원칙

NO	용어	한자	영문	RO	MC	시대 및 연도	출전
129	경수로 원자력 발전소	輕水爐 原子力 發電所	light-water nuclear reactor	Gyeongsuro wonjaryeok baljeonso	Kyŏngsuro wŏnjaryŏk palchŏnso		번역 표준 원칙
130	경신학교	儆新學校	Gyeongsin School	Gyeongsin hakgyo	Kyŏngsin hakkyo	1886	번역 표준 원칙
131	경운궁	慶運宮	Gyeongungung Palace	Gyeongungung	Kyŏngun'gung	?-1907	한국학중앙연구원, 《영문한국백과》-대한제국
132	경운궁 현판	慶運宮 懸板	plaque of Gyeongungung Palace	Gyeongungung hyeonpan	Kyŏngun'gung hyŏnp'an	1905	번역 표준 원칙
133	경원선	京元線	Seoul-Wonsan Railway	Gyeongwonseon	Kyŏngwŏnsŏn	1914	번역 표준 원칙
134	경의선	京義線	Seoul-Sinuiju Railway	Gyeonguiseon	Kyŏngŭisŏn	1905-1945	번역 표준 원칙
135	경인고속도로	京仁高速道路	Seoul-Incheon Expressway	Gyeongin gosokdoro	Kyŏngin kosoktoro	1967	번역 표준 원칙
136	경인선	京仁線	Seoul-Incheon Railway	Gyeonginseon	Kyŏnginsŏn	1899-?	번역 표준 원칙

NO	용어	한자	영문	RO	MC	시대 및 연도	출전
137	경인지역 산업부흥계획	京仁地域 産業復興計劃	Industrial Revival Plan for the Seoul-Incheon Area	Gyeongin jiyeok saneop buheung gyehoek	Kyŏngin chiyŏk sanŏp puhŭng kyehoek		번역 표준 원칙
138	경인철도	京仁鐵道	Seoul-Incheon Railroad	Gyeongin cheoldo	Kyŏngin ch'ŏlto	1897-?	번역 표준 원칙
139	경인철도 부설권	京仁鐵道 敷設權	Seoul-Incheon railway concession	Gyeongin cheoldo buseolgwon	Kyŏngin ch'ŏlto pusŏlkwŏn	1896	번역 표준 원칙
140	경제개발 3개년계획	經濟開發 3個年計劃	Three-Year Economic Development Plan	Gyeongje gaebal 3gaenyeon gyehoek	kyŏngje gaebal 3gaenyŏn gyehoek	1953	번역 표준 원칙
141	경제개발 5개년 계획	經濟開發 5個年 計劃	Five-Year Economic Development Plan	Gyeongje gaebal 5gaenyeon gyehoek	Kyŏngje kaebal 5kaenyŏn kyehoek	1962-1981	번역 표준 원칙
142	경제개발위원회	經濟開發檢討委員會	Economic Development Committee	Gyeongje gaebal wiwonhoe	Kyŏngje kaebal wiwonhoe		번역 표준 원칙
143	경제기획원	經濟企劃院	Economic Planning Board	Gyeongje gihoegwon	Kyŏngje kihoegwŏn	1961-1994	송기중, 《한영우리문화용어집》, 지문당, 2001.
144	경제동향보고회의	經濟動向報告會議	monthly briefing on economic trends	Gyeongje donghyang bogo hoeui	Kyŏngje tonghang pogo hoeŭi		번역 표준 원칙

NO	용어	한자	영문	RO	MC	시대 및 연도	출전
145	경제부총리	經濟副總理	deputy prime minister for economic affairs	Gyeongje buchongni	Kyŏngje puch'ongni		번역 표준 원칙
146	경제자유구역	經濟自由區域	Free Economic Zone	Gyeongje jayu guyeok	Kyŏngje chayu kuyŏk	2003	번역 표준 원칙
147	경제정의실천 시민연합	經濟正義實踐 市民聯合	Citizens' Coalition for Economic Justice	Gyeongje jeongui silcheon simin yeonhap	Kyŏngje chŏngŭi silch'ŏn simin yŏnhap	1989-?	번역 표준 원칙
148	경제지도부	經濟指導部	Economic Guidance Division	Gyeongje jidobu	Kyŏngje jidobu		번역 표준 원칙
149	경제학	經濟學	economics	Gyeongjehak	Kyŏngjehak		번역 표준 원칙
150	경제협력개발기구	經濟協力開發機構	Organization for Economic Cooperation and Development (OECD)	Gyeongje hyeomnyeok gaebal gigu	Kyŏngje hyŏmnyŏk kaebal kigu	1960-?	번역 표준 원칙
151	경제활동 인구	經濟活動 人口	economically active population	Gyeongje hwaldong ingu	Kyŏngje hwaltong ingu		번역 표준 원칙
152	경주 세계문화 엑스포	慶州 世界文化 Expo	Gyeongju World Culture Expo	Gyeongju segye munhwa ekseupo	Kyŏngju segye munhwa eksŭpo	1998	번역 표준 원칙

NO	용어	한자	영문	RO	MC	시대 및 연도	출전
153	경주 양동마을	慶州 良洞마을	Yangdong Village, Gyeongju	Gyeongju yangdong maeul	Kyŏngju yangdong maŭl		번역 표준 원칙
154	경주 역사유적지구	慶州 歷史遺蹟地區	Gyeongju Historic Areas	Gyeongju yeoksa yujeokjigu	Kyŏngju yŏksa yujŏkchigu		번역 표준 원칙
155	경주국립공원	慶州國立公園	Gyeongju National Park	Gyeongju gungnipgongwon	Kyŏngju kungnipkongwŏn	1968-?	번역 표준 원칙
156	경지정리사업	耕地整理事業	arable land readjustment project	Gyeongji jeongni saeop	Kyŏngji chŏngni saŏp	1964-?	번역 표준 원칙
157	경찰대학교	警察大學校	Korea National Police University	Gyeongchal daehakgyo	Kyŏngch'al taehakkyo	1980	번역 표준 원칙
158	경찰범처벌규칙	警察犯處罰規則	Police Offense Punishment Rules	Gyeongchalbeom cheobeol gyuchik	Kyŏngch'albŏm ch'ŏbŏl kyuch'ik	1912-?	번역 표준 원칙
159	경찰의 전투활동	警察의 戰鬪活動	combat activities by the Korea National Police	gyeongcharui jeontu hwaldong	Kyŏngch'arŭi chŏnt'u hwaldong	1948-1953	번역 표준 원칙
160	경찰청	警察廳	Korean National Police Agency (KNPA)	Gyeongchalcheong	Kyŏngch'alch'ŏng	1991	번역 표준 원칙

NO	용어	한자	영문	RO	MC	시대 및 연도	출전
161	경학사	耕學社	Society of Plowing and Studying (Gyeonghaksa)	Gyeonghaksa	Kyŏnghaksa	1911-1914	번역 표준 원칙
162	경향신문	京鄕新聞	*Kyunghyang Shinmun* (daily newspaper)	Gyeonghyang sinmun	Kyŏnghyang sinmun	1946-?	번역 표준 원칙
163	경향신문 폐간사건	京鄕新聞 廢刊事件	closure of the *Kyunghyang Shinmun*	Gyeonghyang sinmun pyegan sageon	Kyŏnghyang sinmun p'yegan sakŏn	1959	번역 표준 원칙
164	계급투쟁	階級鬪爭	class struggle	Gyegeup tujaeng	Kyegŭp t'ujaeng		번역 표준 원칙
165	계룡산국립공원	鷄龍山國立公園	Gyeryongsan National Park	Gyeryongsan gungnipgongwon	Kyeryongsan kungnipkongwŏn	1968-?	번역 표준 원칙
166	계엄령	戒嚴令	martial law	Gyeeomnyeong	Kyeŏmnyŏng		번역 표준 원칙
167	계엄사 합동수사본부장	戒嚴司 合同搜査本部長	head of the Joint Investigation Headquarters under Martial Law	Gyeeomsa hapdong susa bonbujang	Kyeŏmsa haptong susa ponbujang		번역 표준 원칙
168	계엄사령부	戒嚴司令部	Martial Law Command	Gyeeom saryeongbu	Kyeŏm saryŏngbu		번역 표준 원칙

NO	용어	한자	영문	RO	MC	시대 및 연도	출전
169	계획조선	計劃造船	state-led shipbuilding	Gyehoek joseon	Kyehoek chosŏn	1976	번역 표준 원칙
170	고고학	考古學	archaeology	Gogohak	Kogohak		번역 표준 원칙
171	고공강하	高空降下	high altitute low opening (HALO)	Gogong gangha	Kogong kangha		번역 표준 원칙
172	고교 평준화정책	高校 平準化政策	high school equalization policy	Gogyo pyeongjunhwa jeongchaek	Kogyo p'yŏngjunhwa chŏngch'aek	1974-?	번역 표준 원칙
173	고교야구	高校野球	high school baseball	Gogyo yagu	Kogyo yagu	1905-?	번역 표준 원칙
174	고난의 행군	苦難의 行軍	Arduous March	Gonan-ui haenggun	Konan-ŭi haenggun	1938-1939	번역 표준 원칙
175	고도성장기	高度成長期	period of rapid economic growth	Godo seongjanggi	Kodo sŏngjanggi		번역 표준 원칙
176	고등경찰	高等警察	Secret Police	Godeung gyeongchal	Kodŭng kyŏngch'al	1911-1945	번역 표준 원칙

NO	용어	한자	영문	RO	MC	시대 및 연도	출전
177	고랑포 땅굴	高浪浦 땅窟	1st Underground Tunnel at Gorangpo	Gorangpo ddanggul	Korangp'o ttangkul		번역 표준 원칙
178	고려경제회	高麗經濟會	Korea Economic Society	Goryeo gyeongjehoe	Koryŏ kyŏngjehoe		번역 표준 원칙
179	고려공산당	高麗共産黨	Goryeo Communist Party	Goryeo gongsandang	Koryŏ kongsandang	1921	한국학중앙연구원, 《영문한국백과》-고려공산당
180	고려공산당 선언	高麗共産黨 宣言	Goryeo Communist Party Declaration	Goryeo gongsandang seoneon	Koryŏ kongsandang sŏnŏn	1921	번역 표준 원칙
181	고려공산청년동맹	高麗共産靑年同盟	Goryeo Communist Youth Alliance	Goryeo gongsan cheongnyeon dongmaeng	Koryŏ kongsan ch'ŏngnyŏn tongmaeng	1921	번역 표준 원칙
182	고려대학생 데모사건	高麗大學生 示威事件	Korea Unversity Student Demonstration Incident	Goryeodae haksaeng demo sageon	Koryŏ taehaksaeng temo sakŏn	1960	번역 표준 원칙
183	고려민주당	高麗民主黨	Goryeo Democratic Party	Goryeo minjudang	Koryŏ minjudang	1945	번역 표준 원칙
184	고려연방제	高麗聯邦制	Koryo Confederal System	Goryeo yeonbangje	Koryŏ yŏnbangje	1960	번역 표준 원칙

NO	용어	한자	영문	RO	MC	시대 및 연도	출전
185	고려인	高麗人	ethnic Koreans living in former Soviet Union countries	Goryeoin	Koryŏin		번역 표준 원칙
186	고령화 사회	高齡化 社會	aging society	Goryeonghwa sahoe	Koryŏnghwa sahoe		번역 표준 원칙
187	고리 원자력발전소	古里 原子力發電所	Gori Nuclear Power Plant	Gori wonjaryeok baljeonso	Kori wŏnjaryŏk palchŏnso	1968-?	번역 표준 원칙
188	고립정책	孤立政策	isolation policy	Gorip jeongchaek	Korip chŏngch'aek	조선	Ki-baik Lee, translated by Edward W. Wagner, A New History of Korea, Harvard University Press, 1984,
189	고문정치	顧問政治	rule by Japanese advisors	Gomun jeongchi	Komun chŏngch'i	1904	번역 표준 원칙
190	고부봉기	古阜蜂起	Gobu County Rebellion	Gobu bonggi	Kobu ponggi	1894	번역 표준 원칙
191	고성능 병렬처리 컴퓨터	高性能 竝列處理 Computer	high-capacity computer capable of parallel processing	Goseongneung byeongnyeol cheori keompyuteo	Kosŏngnŭng pyŏngnyŏlch'ŏri k'ŏmp'yut'ŏ	1993	번역 표준 원칙
192	고속유탄기관총	高速榴彈機關銃	high-speed grenade launcher	Gosok yutan gigwanchong	Kosok yut'an kigwanch'ong		번역 표준 원칙

NO	용어	한자	영문	RO	MC	시대 및 연도	출전
193	고속철도	高速鐵道	Korea Train Express (KTX)	Gosok cheoldo	Kosok ch'ŏlto		번역 표준 원칙
194	고양대·임진강 부근 전투	高陽垈·臨津江 附近 戰鬪	Battle of Goyangdae and the Imjingang River	Goyangdae-imjingang bugeun jeontu	Koyangdae-imjingang pugŭn chŏnt'u		번역 표준 원칙
195	고엽제	枯葉劑	defoliant	Goyeopje	Koyŏpche		번역 표준 원칙
196	고용노동부	雇用勞動部	Ministry of Employment and Labor	Goyong nodongbu	Koyong nodongbu	1981	번역 표준 원칙
197	고용보험제도	雇用保險制度	employment insurance system	Goyong boheom jedo	Koyong pohŏm chedo	1995	번역 표준 원칙
198	고유모델 승용차	固有model 乘用車	Korean-made car	Goyu model seungyongcha	Koyu model sŭngyongcha		번역 표준 원칙
199	고유영토	固有領土	indigenous land	Goyu yeongto	Koyu yŏngt'o		번역 표준 원칙
200	고인돌	支石墓	dolmen	Goindol	Koindol	상고	번역 표준 원칙

NO	용어	한자	영문	RO	MC	시대 및 연도	출전
201	고종	高宗	King Gojong	Gojong	Kojong	1852-1919	번역 표준 원칙
202	고종 친정	高宗 親政	King Gojong's direct royal rule	Gojong chinjeong	Kojong ch'injŏng	1873	번역 표준 원칙
203	고종 환궁	高宗 還宮	King Gojong's return to the royal palace	Gojong hwangung	Kojong hwan'gung	1897	번역 표준 원칙
204	고지쟁탈전	高地爭奪戰	battle of recapturing the heights	Goji jaengtaljeon	Koji chaengt'aljŏn	1950	번역 표준 원칙
205	고지전	高地戰	Battle of the Highlands	Gojijeon	Kojijŏn		번역 표준 원칙
206	고창담양고속도로	高敞潭陽高速道路	Gochang-Damyang Expressway	Gochang damyang gosokdoro	Koch'ang tamyang kosoktoro	2001	번역 표준 원칙
207	곡가 조절미	穀價 調節米	strategic grain reserve	Gokga jojeolmi	Kokka chojŏlmi		번역 표준 원칙
208	곡창지대	穀倉地帶	rice-producing regions	Gokchang jidae	Kokch'ang chidae		번역 표준 원칙

NO	용어	한자	영문	RO	MC	시대 및 연도	출전
209	골리앗 크레인 농성	Goliath crane 籠城	labor struggle atop a Goliath Crane (by Hyundai Heavy Industries workers in 1990)	Goliat keurein nongseong	Kolliat k'ŭrein nongsŏng	1990	번역 표준 원칙
210	공개방송	公開放送	open broadcasting	Gonggae bangsong	Konggae pangsong		번역 표준 원칙
211	공개투표	公開投票	open vote	Gonggae tupyo	Konggae t'up'yo		번역 표준 원칙
212	공격개시선	攻擊開始線	Line of Departure (LD)	Gonggyeok gaesiseon	Konggyŏk kesisŏn		번역 표준 원칙
213	공공부분	公共部分	public sector	Gonggong bubun	Konggong pubun		번역 표준 원칙
214	공공요금	公共料金	public utility rates	Gonggong yogeum	Konggong yogŭm		번역 표준 원칙
215	공교육	公敎育	public education	Gonggyoyuk	Konggyoyuk		번역 표준 원칙
216	공군비행대대	空軍飛行大隊	Squadron, Air Force	Gonggun bihaeng daedae	Konggun pihaeng daedae		번역 표준 원칙

NO	용어	한자	영문	RO	MC	시대 및 연도	출전
217	공군사관학교	空軍士官學校	Korea Air Force Academy	Gonggun sagwanhakgyo	Konggun sagwanhakkyo	1949-?	번역 표준 원칙
218	공군수송단	空軍輸送團	Air Force Transport Group	Gonggun susongdan	Konggun susongdan	1990	번역 표준 원칙
219	공군작전	空軍作戰	Air Force Operations	Gonggun jakjeon	Konggun chakchŏn	1950	번역 표준 원칙
220	공군전투비행단	空軍戰鬪飛行團	Fighter Wing, Air Force	Gonggun jeontu bihaengdan	Konggun chŏntu bihaengdan		번역 표준 원칙
221	공기부양상륙정	空氣浮揚上陸艇	Landing Craft Air Cushion (LCAC)	Gonggibuyang sangnyukjeong	Konggibuyang sangnyukchŏng		번역 표준 원칙
222	공단근로자	工團勤勞者	workers at industrial complexes	Gongdan geulloja	Kongdan kŭlloja		번역 표준 원칙
223	공동경비구역	共同警備區域	Joint Security Area (JSA)	Gongdong gyeongbi guyeok	Kongdong kyŏngbi kuyŏk	1953-?	번역 표준 원칙
224	공동체의식	共同體意識	community spirit	Gongdongche uisik	Kongdongch'e ŭisik		번역 표준 원칙

NO	용어	한자	영문	RO	MC	시대 및 연도	출전
225	공립신보	共立新報	Gongnip Sinbo (The United Korean)	Gongnipsinbo	Kongnipsinbo	1905	번역 표준 원칙
226	공립협회	共立協會	United Korean Association	Gongnip hyeophoe	Kongnip hyŏphoe	1905	Robert E. Buswell & Timothy S. Lee. Christianity in Korea, Honolulu: University of Hawaii Press,
227	공명선거추진전국위원회	公明選擧推進全國委員會	National Committee for the Promotion of Fair Elections	Gongmyeong seongeo chujin junguk wiwonhoe	Kongmyŏng sŏn'gŏ ch'ujin chŏn'guk wiwŏnhoe		번역 표준 원칙
228	공무원 행동강령	公務員 行動綱領	Code of Conduct for Public Servants	Gongmuwon haengdong gangnyeong	Kongmuwŏn haengdong gangnyŏng	2003	번역 표준 원칙
229	공무원의 정치적 중립	公務員의 政治的 中立	political neutrality of civil servants	Gongmuwonui jeongchijeok jungnip	Kongmuwŏnŭi chŏngch'ijŏk chungnip		번역 표준 원칙
230	공보부	公報部	Ministry of Public Information	Gongbobu	Kongbobu	1946-1948	번역 표준 원칙
231	공산대학	共産大學	Communist College	Gongsan daehak	Kongsan taehak	1960-?	번역 표준 원칙
232	공산주의	共産主義	Communism	Gongsanjuui	Kongsanjuŭi		번역 표준 원칙

NO	용어	한자	영문	RO	MC	시대 및 연도	출전
233	공산주의운동	共産主義運動	Communist movement	Gongsanjuui undong	Kongsanjuǔi undong		번역 표준 원칙
234	공수부대	空輸部隊	paratroopers	Gongsu budae	Kongsu pudae		번역 표준 원칙
235	공습경보	空襲警報	air-raid siren	Gongseup gyeongbo	Kongsǔp kyǒngbo		번역 표준 원칙
236	공식발표	公式發表	official announcement	Gongsik balpyo	Kongsik palp'yo		번역 표준 원칙
237	공식사과	公式謝過	official apology	Gongsik sagwa	Kongsik sagwa		번역 표준 원칙
238	공안정국	公安政局	national security state	Gongan jeongguk	Kongan chǒngguk	1989-?	번역 표준 원칙
239	공약삼장	公約三章	Pledge of the Three Principles	Gongyak samjang	Kongyak samjang		번역 표준 원칙
240	공업단지 개발	工業團地 開發	development of industrial complexes	Gongeop danji gaebal	Kongǒp tanji kaebal		번역 표준 원칙

NO	용어	한자	영문	RO	MC	시대 및 연도	출전
241	공업단지 배후도시	工業團地 背後都市	satellite city of an industrial complex	Gongeop danji baehudosi	Kongŏp tanji paehu tosi		번역 표준 원칙
242	공업연구소	工業硏究所	industrial research institute	Gongeop yeonguso	Kongŏp yŏnguso		번역 표준 원칙
243	공업화	工業化	industrialization	Gongeophwa	Kongŏphwa		번역 표준 원칙
244	공용화기	共用火器	crew served weapon	Gongyonghwagi	Kongyonghwagi		번역 표준 원칙
245	공적 개발원조	公的 開發援助	official development assistance (ODA)	Gongjeok gaebal wonjo	Kongjŏk kaebal wŏnjo		번역 표준 원칙
246	공적연금	公的年金	public pension	Gongjeok yeongeum	Kongjŏk yŏn'gŭm		번역 표준 원칙
247	공적자금	公的資金	public funds	Gongjeok jageum	Kongjŏk chagŭm		번역 표준 원칙
248	공정거래위원회	公正去來委員會	Fair Trade Commission	Gongjeong georae wiwonhoe	Kongjŏng kŏrae wiwŏnhoe	1981	번역 표준 원칙

NO	용어	한자	영문	RO	MC	시대 및 연도	출전
249	공중기동작전	空中機動作戰	air mobile operations	Gongjung gidong jakjeon	Kongjung gidong chakchŏn		번역 표준 원칙
250	공중전투초계	空中戰鬪哨戒	combat air control (CAP)	Gongjung jeontu chogye	Kongjung chŏnt'u ch'ogye		번역 표준 원칙
251	공중조기경보	空中早期警報	airborne early warning (AEW)	Gongjeung jogi gyeongbo	Kongjung jogi gyŏngbo		번역 표준 원칙
252	공지합동	空地合同	air-ground cooperation	Gongji hapdong	Kongji haptong		번역 표준 원칙
253	공직부패	公職腐敗	bureaucratic corruption	Gongjik bupae	Kongjik pup'ae		번역 표준 원칙
254	공직자 재산공개	公職者 財産公開	asset declaration by public officials	Gongjikja jaesan gonggae	Kongjikcha chaesan konggae	1993	번역 표준 원칙
255	공직자 재산등록의무화	公職者 財産登錄義務化	compulsory declaration of assets and liabilities by public officials	Gongjikja jaesan deungnok uimuhwa	Kongjikcha chaesan tŭngnok ŭimuhwa	1981-	번역 표준 원칙
256	공직자윤리법	公職者倫理法	Public Service Ethics Act	Gongjikja yullibeop	Kongjikcha yullipŏp	1981	번역 표준 원칙

NO	용어	한자	영문	RO	MC	시대 및 연도	출전
257	공진회	共進會	Forward Together Society (Gongjinhoe)	Gongjinhoe	Kongjinhoe	1904	번역 표준 원칙
258	공출제도	供出制度	war-time quota delivery system	Gongchul jedo	Kongch'ul chedo	1939-1945	번역 표준 원칙
259	공해방지법	公害防止法	Pollution Prevention Act	Gonghae bangjibeop	Konghae pangjipŏp	1971	번역 표준 원칙
260	공화국연방제	共和國聯邦制	confederal republic	Gonghwaguk yeonbangje	Konghwaguk yŏnbangje		번역 표준 원칙
261	공화당	共和黨	Republican Party	Gonghwadang	Konghwadang	1956-?	번역 표준 원칙
262	공화주의	共和主義	republicanism	Gonghwajuui	Konghwajuŭi		번역 표준 원칙
263	과거사문제	過去事問題	historical issues between Korea and Japan	Gwageosa munje	Kwagŏsa munje		번역 표준 원칙
264	과거사진상규명위원회	過去史眞相糾明委員會	Commission for Historical Clarification	Gwageosa jinsang gyumyeong wiwonhoe	Kwagŏsa chinsang kyumyŏng wiwŏnhoe	2004	번역 표준 원칙

NO	용어	한자	영문	RO	MC	시대 및 연도	출전
265	과도입법의원	過渡立法議院	Interim Legislative Assembly	Gwado ipbeop uiwon	Kwado ippŏp ŭiwŏn	1946-1948	번역 표준 원칙
266	과도정부	過渡政府	South Korean Interim Government	Gwado jeongbu	Kwado chŏngbu	1947-1948	Ki-baik Lee, translated by Edward W. Wagner, A New History of Korea, Harvard University Press, 1984,
267	과수재배	果樹栽培	fruit growing	Gwasu jaebae	Kwasu chaebae		번역 표준 원칙
268	과외금지	課外禁止	ban on private tutoring	Gwaoe geumji	Kwaoe kŭmji	1980	번역 표준 원칙
269	과학기술개발장기 종합계획	科學技術開發長期 綜合計劃	Master Plan for the Long-term Development of Science and Technology	Gwahak gisul gaebal janggi jonghap gyehoek	Kwahak kisul kaebal changgi chonghap kyehoek	1967-1986	번역 표준 원칙
270	과학기술정책	科學技術政策	national science and technology policy	Gwahak gisul jeongchaek	Kwahak kisul chŏngch'aek		번역 표준 원칙
271	과학기술진흥 5개년계획	科學技術振興 5個年計劃	Five-year Plan for the Advancement of Science and Technology	Gwahak gisul jinheung 5gaenyeon gyehoek	Kwahak kisul chinhŭng 5kaenyŏn kyehoek		번역 표준 원칙
272	과학기술처	科學技術處	Ministry of Science and Technology	Gwahak gisulcheo	Kwahak kisulch'ŏ	현대	송기중, 《한영우리문화용어집》, 지문당, 2001

NO	용어	한자	영문	RO	MC	시대 및 연도	출전
273	과학기술훈장	科學技術勳章	Order of Science and Technology Merit	Gwahak gisul hunjang	Kwahak kisul hunjang	2001	번역 표준 원칙
274	관동군	關東軍	Kwanto Army	Gwandonggun	Kwandonggun	1906-1945	Wi Jo Kang, Christ and Caesar in Modern Korea: A History of Christianity and Politics, State University of
275	관동대지진	關東大地震	Great Kanto Earthquake	Gwandong daejijin	Kwandong taejijin	1923	번역 표준 원칙
276	관동학회	關東學會	Kangwon Educational Association	Gwandong hakhoe	Kwandong hakhoe	1908	Ki-baik Lee, translated by Edward W. Wagner, A New History of Korea, Harvard University Press, 1984,
277	관료정치	官僚政治	bureaucratic rule	Gwallyo jeongchi	Kwallyo chŏngch'i		번역 표준 원칙
278	관민공동회	官民共同會	mass meeting of officials and the citizenry	Gwanmin gongdonghoe	Kwanmin kongdonghoe	1898	Ki-baik Lee, translated by Edward W. Wagner, A New History of Korea, Harvard University Press, 1984,
279	관세 감면	關稅 減免	duty exemption	Gwanse gammyeon	Kwanse kammyŏn		번역 표준 원칙
280	관세 및 무역에 관한 일반협정	關稅 및 貿易에 關한 一般協定	General Agreement on Tariffs and Trade (GATT)	Gwanse mit muyeok-e gwanhan ilban hyeopjeong	Kwanse mit muyŏk-e kwanhan ilban hyŏpchŏng	1947-?	번역 표준 원칙

NO	용어	한자	영문	RO	MC	시대 및 연도	출전
281	관세장벽	關稅障壁	tariff barrier	Gwanse jangbyeok	Kwanse changbyŏk		번역 표준 원칙
282	관세철폐 계획	關稅撤廢 計劃	tariff elimination schedule	Gwanse cheolpye gyehoek	Kwanse ch'ŏlp'ye kyehoek		번역 표준 원칙
283	관재처	管財處	Office of Property Custody	Gwanjaecheo	Kwanjaech'ŏ	1946-?	번역 표준 원칙
284	관치금융	官治金融	government controlled finance	Gwanchi geumnyung	Kwanch'i kŭmyung	1961	번역 표준 원칙
285	관혼상제	冠婚喪祭	ceremonies for the coming of age, marriage, funerals, and ancestral rites	Gwanhonsangje	Kwanhonsangje		번역 표준 원칙
286	광동 호법정부	廣東 護法政府	Guangdong Militarist Government	Gwangdong hobeop jeongbu	Kwangdong hobŏp chŏngbu		번역 표준 원칙
287	광무개혁	光武改革	Gwangmu Reform	Gwangmu gaehyeok	Kwangmu kaehyŏk	1897-1904	번역 표준 원칙
288	광무정권	光武政權	Gwangmu Administration	Gwangmu jeonggwon	Kwangmu chŏnggwŏn		번역 표준 원칙

NO	용어	한자	영문	RO	MC	시대 및 연도	출전
289	광무황제	光武皇帝	Emperor Gwangmu (Gojong)	Gwangmu hwangjae	Kwangmu hwangje	1852-1919	번역 표준 원칙
290	광무황제 강제퇴위	光武皇帝 強制退位	Emperor Gwangmu's (Gojong) forced abdication	Gwangmu hwangjae gangjae toewi	Kwangmu hwangje kangje t'oewi	1907	번역 표준 원칙
291	광복	光復	liberation of Korea from Japanese rule (1945)	Gwangbok	Kwangbok	1945	번역 표준 원칙
292	광복군사령부	光復軍司令部	Restoration Army Headquarters	Gwangbokgun saryeongbu	Kwangbokkun saryŏngbu	1920	번역 표준 원칙
293	광복군총영	光復軍總營	Headquarters of the Korean Liberation Army Command	Gwangbokgun chongyeong	Kwangbokkun ch'ongyŏng	1920	번역 표준 원칙
294	광복단	光復團	Korea Restoration Corps	Gwangbokdan	Kwangboktan	1913	번역 표준 원칙
295	광성보	廣城堡	Gwangseongbo Fortress	Gwangseongbo	Kwangsŏngbo	1658-?	번역 표준 원칙
296	광양제철소	光陽製鐵所	Gwangyang Steelworks	Gwangyang jecheolso	Kwangyang chech'ŏlso	1982	번역 표준 원칙

NO	용어	한자	영문	RO	MC	시대 및 연도	출전
297	광역시	廣域市	metropolitan city	Gwangyeoksi	Kwangyŏksi	1995-?	번역 표준 원칙
298	광우병 파동	狂牛病 波動	mad cow controversy	Gwangubyeong padong	Kwangupyŏng p'adong	2008	번역 표준 원칙
299	광제원	廣濟院	Gwangje Hospital	Gwangjewon	Kwangjewŏn	1900-1907	번역 표준 원칙
300	광주 대단지사건	廣州 大團地事件	riots by forcibly relocated residents of Seoul in Gwangju, Gyeonggi-do Province	Gwangju daedanji sageon	Kwangju taedanji sagŏn	1971	번역 표준 원칙
301	광주 미문화원 방화사건	光州 美文化院 放火事件	arson attack on Gwangju U.S. Cultural Center (1980)	Gwangju mimunhwawon banghwa sageon	Kwangju mimunhwawŏn panghwa sakŏn	1980	번역 표준 원칙
302	광주광역시	光州廣域市	Gwangju Metropolitan City	Gwangju gwangyeoksi	Kwangju kwangyŏksi	1995-?	번역 표준 원칙
303	광주민주화운동	光州民主化運動	Gwangju Democratization Movement	Gwangju minjuhwa undong	Kwangju minjuhwa undong	1980	번역 표준 원칙
304	광주학생항일운동	光州學生抗日運動	Gwangju student demonstration against Japanese colonial rule	Gwangju haksaeng hangil undong	Kwangju haksaeng hangil undong	1929	번역 표준 원칙

NO	용어	한자	영문	RO	MC	시대 및 연도	출전
305	광한단	光韓團	Gwanghan Corps	Gwanghandan	Kwanghandan	1920-1923	번역 표준 원칙
306	광혜원	廣惠院	Gwanghyewon	Gwanghyewon	Kwanghyewŏn	1885	번역 표준 원칙
307	광화문	光化門	Gwanghwamun Gate	Gwanghwamun	Kwanghwamun	1395	번역 표준 원칙
308	광화문 광장	光化門 廣場	Gwanghwamun Square	Gwanghwamun gwangjang	Kwanghwamun kwangjang	2009	번역 표준 원칙
309	광화문 복원	光化門 復元	restoration of Gwanghwamun Gate	Gwanghwamun bogwon	Kwanghwamun pogwŏn	2010	번역 표준 원칙
310	교과서포럼	敎科書forum	Textbook Forum	Gyogwaseo poreom	Kyogwasŏ p'orŏm	2005	번역 표준 원칙
311	교남교육회	嶠南敎育會	Southeastern Educational Association	Gyonam gyoyukhoe	Kyonam kyoyukhoe	1908	Peter H. Lee, Sourcebook of Korean Civilization(Volume 2), Columbia University Press, 1993,
312	교대작전	交代作戰	relief operations	Gyodae jakjeon	Kyodae chakchŏn		번역 표준 원칙

NO	용어	한자	영문	RO	MC	시대 및 연도	출전
313	교련	敎鍊	military drill in schools	Gyoryeon	Kyoryŏn	현대	번역 표준 원칙
314	교련반대운동	敎鍊反對運動	anti-drill movement	Gyoryeon bandae undong	Kyoryŏn pandae undong	1970	번역 표준 원칙
315	교련철폐투쟁	敎鍊撤廢鬪爭	fight for abolition of military drill in high schools	Gyoryeon cheolpye tujaeng	Kyoryŏn ch'ŏlp'ye t'ujaeng	1971	번역 표준 원칙
316	교린관계	交隣關係	friendly relations with neighboring countries	Gyorin gwan-gye	Kyorin kwan'gye		번역 표준 원칙
317	교복자율화	校服自律化	liberalization of student dress codes in 1983	Gyobok jayulhwa	Kyobok chayurhwa	1983	번역 표준 원칙
318	교원노동조합	敎員勞動組合	Korean Union of Teaching and Education Workers	Gyowon nodong johap	kyowŏn nodong chohap	1960	번역 표준 원칙
319	교원노조운동	敎員勞組運動	movement to organize a teachers' union	Gyowon nojo undong	Kyowŏn nojo undong	1960	번역 표준 원칙
320	교육 칙어	敎育 勅語	1890 Imperial Rescript on Education (by Emperor Meiji of Japan)	Gyoyuk chigeo	Kyoyuk ch'igŏ	1890-1948	번역 표준 원칙

NO	용어	한자	영문	RO	MC	시대 및 연도	출전
321	교육개혁위원회	敎育改革委員會	Education Reform Commission	Gyoyuk gaehyeok wiwonhoe	Koyuk kaehyŏk wiwŏnhoe	1994-1998	번역 표준 원칙
322	교육과학기술부	敎育科學技術部	Ministry of Education, Science and Technology	Gyoyuk gwahak gisulbu	Kyoyuk kwahak kisulbu	2008-	번역 표준 원칙
323	교육민주화선언	敎育民主化宣言	Declaration of the Democratization of Education	Gyoyuk minjuhwa seoneon	Kyoyuk minjuhwa sŏnŏn	1986	번역 표준 원칙
324	교육방송	敎育放送	Educational Broadcasting System (EBS)	Gyoyuk bangsong	Kyoyuk pangsong	1951-	번역 표준 원칙
325	교육세법	敎育稅法	Educational Tax Act	Gyoyuk sebeop	Kyoyuk sepŏp	1981-	번역 표준 원칙
326	교육에 관한 임시특례법	敎育에 關한 臨時特例法	Special Provisional Act on Education	Gyoyuge gwanhan imsi teungnyebeop	Kyoug-e kwanhan imsi t'ŭngnyepŏp	1961	번역 표준 원칙
327	교육열	敎育熱	zeal for education	Gyoyugyeol	Kyoyugyŏl		번역 표준 원칙
328	교육운동	敎育運動	Education Movement	Gyoyuk undong	Kyoyuk undong		번역 표준 원칙

NO	용어	한자	영문	RO	MC	시대 및 연도	출전
329	교육입국 조서	教育立國 詔書	Decree on Nation Building through Education	Gyoyuk ipguk joseo	Kyoyuk ipkuk chosŏ	1895	번역 표준 원칙
330	교육자치제	教育自治制	educational autonomy system	Gyoyuk jachije	Kyoyuk chach'ije	1988-?	번역 표준 원칙
331	교조신원운동	敎祖伸寃運動	campaign to clear the name of the founder of Donghak of false charges	Gyojo sinwon undong	Kyojo sinwŏn undong	1864	번역 표준 원칙
332	교토의정서	京都議定書	Kyoto Protocol	Gyoto uijeongseo	Kyot'o ŭichŏngsŏ	2005발효	번역 표준 원칙
333	교통대란	交通大亂	traffic chaos	Gyotong daeran	Kyot'ong taeran		번역 표준 원칙
334	교통체신위원회	交通遞信委員會	Transportation and Communications Committee	Gyotong chesin wiwonhoe	Kyot'ong ch'esin wiwŏnhoe	1972-?	송기중,《한영우리문화용어집》, 지문당, 2001.
335	교통호	交通壕	connecting trenches	Gyotongho	Kyot'ongho		번역 표준 원칙
336	교형	絞刑	death by hanging	Gyohyeong	Kyohyŏng		번역 표준 원칙

NO	용어	한자	영문	RO	MC	시대 및 연도	출전
337	구국교육운동	救國教育運動	New Education Movement to Save the Nation	Guguk gyoyuk undong	Kuguk kyoyuk undong	1905-?	번역 표준 원칙
338	구국모험단	救國冒險團	National Salvation at Any Risk Party	Guguk moheomdan	Kuguk mohŏmdan	1919-?	구미위원부 생산 공문
339	구국의 소리방송	救國의 소리放送	(North Korea's) Voice of National Salvation broadcasts to South Korea	Gugugui sori bangsong	Kuguk-ŭi sori pangsong	1970	번역 표준 원칙
340	구로구청 사건	九老區廳 事件	Vote-rigging Incident at Guro District Office	Guro gucheong sageon	Kuro kuch'ŏng sakŏn	1987	번역 표준 원칙
341	구로동맹파업	九老同盟罷業	Guro District Strike of 1985	Guro dongmaeng paeop	Kuro tongmaeng p'aŏp	1985	번역 표준 원칙
342	구로수출공단	九老輸出工團	Guro Export Industrial Complex	Guro suchul gongdan	Kuro such'ul kongdan		번역 표준 원칙
343	구마고속도로	邱馬高速道路	Guma Expressway	Guma gosokdoro	Kuma kosoktoro	1977	번역 표준 원칙
344	구매사절단	購買使節團	export-seeking business delegation	Gumae sajeoldan	Kumae sajŏltan		번역 표준 원칙

NO	용어	한자	영문	RO	MC	시대 및 연도	출전
345	구미위원부	歐美委員部	Korean Commission to America and Europe	Gumi wiwonbu	Kumi wiwŏnbu	1919 ~ 1928	번역 표준 원칙
346	구미전자공업단지	龜尾電子工業團地	Gumi Electronic Industrial Complex	Gumi jeonja gongeop danji	Kumi chŏnja kongŏp tanji		번역 표준 원칙
347	구본신참	舊本新參	"accepting the new while preserving the old"	Gubon sincham	Kubon sinch'am	1896-1904	번역 표준 원칙
348	구식군인	舊式軍人	old military	Gusik gunin	Kusik kunin		번역 표준 원칙
349	구월산대	九月山隊	Guwolsan Korean Independence Corps	Guwolsandae	Kuwŏlsandae	1920	번역 표준 원칙
350	구포역 열차사고	龜浦驛 列車事故	train derailment at Gupo Station, Busan in 1993	Gupoyeok yeolcha sago	Kupoyŏk yŏlch'a sago	1993	번역 표준 원칙
351	구호소	救護所	aid station	Guhoso	Kuhoso		번역 표준 원칙
352	구호제품	救護製品	relief	Guho jepum	Kuho chep'um		번역 표준 원칙

NO	용어	한자	영문	RO	MC	시대 및 연도	출전
353	국가경쟁력	國家競爭力	national competitiveness	Gukga gyeongjaengnyeok	Kukka kyŏngjaengnyŏk		번역 표준 원칙
354	국가과학기술위원회	國家科學技術委員會	National Science and Technology Commission	Gukga gwahak gisul wiwonhoe	Kukka kwahak kisul wiwŏnhoe	1973-	번역 표준 원칙
355	국가관	國家觀	view of the nation	Gukgagwan	Kukkagwan		번역 표준 원칙
356	국가권력	國家權力	national power	Gukga gwollyeok	Kukka kwŏllyŏk		번역 표준 원칙
357	국가보안법	國家保安法	National Security Law	Gukga boanbeop	Kukka poanpŏp	1948-?	번역 표준 원칙
358	국가보위비상대책위원회	國家保衛非常對策委員會	Legislative Council for National Security	Gukga bowi bisang daechaek wiwonhoe	Kukka powi pisang taech'aek wiwŏnhoe	1980	번역 표준 원칙
359	국가보위에 관한 특별조치법	國家保衛에 關한 特別措置法	Special National Security Act	Gukga bowi-e gwanhan teukbyeol jochibeop	Kukka powi-e kwanhan t'ŭkpyŏl choch'ipŏp	1971	번역 표준 원칙
360	국가비상사태	國家非常事態	state of national emergency	Gukga bisang satae	Kukka pisang sat'ae		번역 표준 원칙

NO	용어	한자	영문	RO	MC	시대 및 연도	출전
361	국가성평등지도	國家性平等指導	national gender equality guidelines	gukga seong pyeongdeung jido	Kukka sŏng p'yŏngdŭng chido		번역 표준 원칙
362	국가안전기획부	國家安全企劃部	Agency for National Security Planning	Gukga anjeon gihoekbu	Kukka anjŏn kihoekpu	1980-1997	송기중, 《한영우리문화용어집》, 지문당, 2001.
363	국가안전보장회의	國家安全保障會議	National Security Council (NSC)	Gukga anjeon bojang hoeui	Kukka anjŏn pojang hoeŭi	1962	번역 표준 원칙
364	국가원수 모독죄	國家元首 冒瀆罪	lese-majesty	Gukga wonsu modokjoe	Kukka wŏnsu modokchoe	1975-1988	번역 표준 원칙
365	국가인권위원회	國家人權委員會	National Human Rights Commission	Gukga ingwon wiwonhoe	Kukka inkwŏn wiwŏnhoe	2001	번역 표준 원칙
366	국가재건비상조치법	國家再建非常措置法	Extraordinary Step Law for National Reconstruction	Gukga jaegeon bisang jochibeop	Kukka chaegŏn pisang choch'ipŏp	1961-1963	번역 표준 원칙
367	국가재건최고회의	國家再建最高會議	Supreme Council of National Reconstruction	Gukga jaegeon choego hoeui	Kukka chaegŏn ch'oego hoeŭi	1961-1963	한국학중앙연구원, 《영문한국백과》-박정희
368	국가재건최고회의법	國家再建最高會議法	Supreme Council Law for National Reconstruction	Gukga jaegeon choego hoeuibeop	Kukka chaegŏn ch'oego hoeŭipŏp	1961	번역 표준 원칙

NO	용어	한자	영문	RO	MC	시대 및 연도	출전
369	국가정보원	國家情報院	National Intelligence Service (NIS)	Gukga jeongbowon	Kukka chŏngbowŏn	1961	번역 표준 원칙
370	국가지수	國家指數	national index	Gukga jisu	Kukka chisu		번역 표준 원칙
371	국가총동원법	國家總動員法	National Mobilization Law	Gukga chongdongwonbeop	Kukka ch'ongdongwŏnpŏp	1938-1945	한국학중앙연구원, 《영문한국백과》-농민운동
372	국가통수 및 군사지휘기구	國家統帥 및 軍事指揮機構	National Command and Military Authority (NCMA)	Gukgatongsu mit gunsajihwigigu	Kukkat'ongsu mit kunsajihwigigu		번역 표준 원칙
373	국경검문소	國境檢問所	border checkpoint	Gukgyeong geommunso	Kukkyŏng kŏmmunso		번역 표준 원칙
374	국경일에 관한 법률	國慶日에 關한 法律	Law on Public Holidays	Gukgyeongire gwanhan beomnyul	Kukkyŏng'ire kwanhan pŏmnyul	2005	번역 표준 원칙
375	국공합작	國共合作	Kuomintang-Communist cooperation (in China)	Gukgong hapjak	Kukkong hapchak	1924-1927, 1937-1945	번역 표준 원칙
376	국교 수립	國交 樹立	establishment of diplomatic relations	Gukgyo surip	Kukkyo surip		번역 표준 원칙

NO	용어	한자	영문	RO	MC	시대 및 연도	출전
377	국군	國軍	ROK Army	Gukgun	Kukkun	1948-?	번역 표준 원칙
378	국군 총사령관	國軍 總司令官	Chief of Staff, ROK Armed Forces	Gukgun chongsaryeonggwan	Kukkun ch'ongsaryŏnggwan	1950-1953	번역 표준 원칙
379	국군 현대화	國軍 現代化	modernization of the ROK Military	Gukgun hyeondaehwa	Kukkun hyŏndaehwa		번역 표준 원칙
380	국군·유엔군 서울수복	國軍·UN軍 Seoul 收復	ROK and UN Forces Recovery of Seoul	Gukgun, yuengun seoul subok	Kukkun, yuengun sŏul subok	1950	번역 표준 원칙
381	국군방송	國軍放送	Korean Forces Network (KFN)	Gukgun bangsong	Kukkun pangsong	1954-	번역 표준 원칙
382	국군의 38선 돌파	國軍의 38線 突破	ROK Army's northward march across the 38th Parallel	Gukgunui 38seon dolpa	Kukkunŭi 38sŏn Tolp'a	1950	번역 표준 원칙
383	국군조직법	國軍組織法	National Army Organization Act	Gukgun jojikbeop	Kukkun chojikpŏp	1948	번역 표준 원칙
384	국군준비대	國軍準備隊	National Prepatory Army	Gukgun junbidae	Kukkun chunbidae	1945-1946	번역 표준 원칙

NO	용어	한자	영문	RO	MC	시대 및 연도	출전
385	국군창설	國軍創設	establishment of the ROK Armed Forces	Gukgun changseol	Kukkun ch'angsŏl	1946?	번역 표준 원칙
386	국군통수권이양협정	國軍統帥權移讓協定	Taejon Agreement of 1950	Gukgun tongsugwon iyang hyeopjeong	Kukkun t'ongsugwŏn iyang hyŏpchŏng	1950	번역 표준 원칙
387	국권회복운동	國權回復運動	Movement for the Restoration of Korean National Sovereignty	Gukgwon hoebok undong	Kukkwŏn hoebok undong	일제강점기	번역 표준 원칙
388	국기에 대한 맹세	國旗에 對한 盟誓	Pledge of Allegiance	Gukgie daehan maengse	Kukkie taehan maengse	1968-	번역 표준 원칙
389	국기하강식	國旗下降式	lowering of the national flag	Gukgi hagangsik	Kukki hagangsik		번역 표준 원칙
390	국내정진대	國內挺進隊	Korean Restoration Army Special Forces Unit for advance into Korea	Guknae jeongjindae	Kungnae chŏngjindae		번역 표준 원칙
391	국내파	國內派	internal faction	Gungnaepa	Kungnaep'a	1945?	번역 표준 원칙
392	국대안반대운동	國大案反對運動	campaign against the establishment of Seoul National University	Gukdaean bandae undong	Kuktaean pandae undong	1946	번역 표준 원칙

NO	용어	한자	영문	RO	MC	시대 및 연도	출전
393	국력의 조직화	國力의 組織化	systematization of national power	Gungnyeokui jojikhwa	Kungnyŏgŭi chojikhwa		번역 표준 원칙
394	국립 4·19묘지	國立 4·19墓地	April 19th National Cemetery	Gungnip 4.19 myoji	Kungnip 4.19 myoji	1963	국립4.19민주묘지 사이트 www.419.mpva.go.kr/
395	국립 고궁박물관	國立 故宮博物館	National Palace Museum of Korea	Gungnip gogung bangmulgwan	Kungnip kogung pangmulgwan		번역 표준 원칙
396	국립 과학박물관	國立 科學博物館	National Museum of Science	Gungnip gwahak bangmulgwan	Kungnip kwahak pangmunlgwan	1946-?	번역 표준 원칙
397	국립 민속박물관	國立 民俗博物館	National Folk Museum of Korea	Gungnip minsok bangmulgwan	Kungnip minsok pangmulgwan	1993	번역 표준 원칙
398	국립 중앙극장	國立 中央劇場	National Theater of Korea	Gungnip jungang geukjang	Kungnip chungang kŭkchang	1950	번역 표준 원칙
399	국립 중앙도서관	國立 中央圖書館	National Library of Korea	Gungnip jungang doseogwan	Kungnip chungang tosŏgwan	1945	번역 표준 원칙
400	국립 현대미술관	國立 現代美術館	National Museum of Contemporary Art	Gungnip hyeondae misulgwan	Kungnip hyŏndae misulgwan	1969	번역 표준 원칙

NO	용어	한자	영문	RO	MC	시대 및 연도	출전
401	국립 화학연구소	國立 化學硏究所	National Institute for Chemical Research	Gungnip hwahak yeonguso	Kungnip hwahak yŏn'guso	1945-?	번역 표준 원칙
402	국립공원	國立公園	national parks	Gungnipgongwon	Kungnipkongwŏn	1967-?	국사편찬위원회
403	국립국악원	國立國樂院	National Gugak Center	Gungnip gugagwon	Kungnip kugagwŏn	1951	번역 표준 원칙
404	국립국어원	國立國語院	National Institute of the Korean Language	Gungnip gugeowon	Kungnip kugŏwŏn	1984	번역 표준 원칙
405	국립도서관	國立圖書館	National Library of Korea	Gungnip doseogwan	Kungnip tosŏgwan		번역 표준 원칙
406	국립묘지	國立墓地	National Cemetery	Gungnim myoji	Kungnip myoji	1955	번역 표준 원칙
407	국립무용단	國立舞踊團	National Dance Company of Korea	Gungnim muyongdan	Kungnip muyongdan	1962	번역 표준 원칙
408	국립박물관	國立博物館	National Museum of Korea	Gungnip bangmulgwan	Kungnip pangmulgwan		번역 표준 원칙

NO	용어	한자	영문	RO	MC	시대 및 연도	출전
409	국립보건원	國立保健院	Korea National Institutes of Health	Gungnip bogeonwon	Kungnip pogŏnwŏn	1963	번역 표준 원칙
410	국립중앙박물관	國立中央博物館	National Museum of Korea	Gungnip jungang bangmulgwan	Kungnip chungang pangmulgwan	1945	번역 표준 원칙
411	국립천문대	國立天文臺	National Astronomical Observatory	Gungnip cheonmundae	Kungnip ch'ŏnmundae	1974	번역 표준 원칙
412	국립학교	國立學校	public school	Gungnip hakgyo	Kungnip hakkyo		번역 표준 원칙
413	국무성	國務省	Department of State	Gungmuseong	Kungmusŏng		번역 표준 원칙
414	국무총리	國務總理	prime minister	Gungmuchongni	Kungmuch'ongni		번역 표준 원칙
415	국무총리실	國務總理室	Prime Minister's Office	Gungmuchongnisil	Kungmuch'ongnisil	2008	번역 표준 원칙
416	국문연구소	國文硏究所	Korean Language Research Institute	Gungmun yeonguso	Kungmun yŏn'guso	1907	한국학중앙연구원, 〈영문한국백과〉-한글

NO	용어	한자	영문	RO	MC	시대 및 연도	출전
417	국문정리	國文正理	Gunngmun Jeongni (Korean grammar book by Lee Bong-un, 1897)	Gungmunjeongni	Kungmunjŏngni	1987	번역 표준 원칙
418	국민개납설	國民皆納說	argument for universal taxation	Gungmin gaenapseol	Kungmin kaenapsŏl		번역 표준 원칙
419	국민개병설	國民皆兵說	argument for universal conscription	Gungmin gaebyeongseol	Kungmin kaebyŏngsŏl		번역 표준 원칙
420	국민개업설	國民皆業說	argument for the People's employment	Gungmin gaeeopseol	Kungmin kaeŏpsŏl		번역 표준 원칙
421	국민건강보험법	國民健康保險法	National Health Insurance Act	Gungmin geongang boheombeop	Kungmin gŏn'gang bohŏmpŏp	1999	번역 표준 원칙
422	국민계몽운동	國民啓蒙運動	campaign for enlightenment of the people	Gungmin gyemong undong	Kungmin kyemong undong	1960	번역 표준 원칙
423	국민교육헌장	國民敎育憲章	National Charter of Education	Gungmin gyoyuk heonjang	Kungmin kyoyuk hŏnjang	1968	한국학중앙연구원, 《영문한국백과》·교육
424	국민교육회	國民敎育會	National Educational Association	Gungmin gyoyukhoe	Kungmin kyoyukhoe	1904-1907	번역 표준 원칙

NO	용어	한자	영문	RO	MC	시대 및 연도	출전
425	국민국가	國民國家	nation state	Gungmin gukga	Kungmin kukka		번역 표준 원칙
426	국민권익위원회	國民權益委員會	Anti-Corruption and Civil Rights Commission (ACRC)	Gungmin gwonik wiwonhoe	Kungmin kwŏnik wiwŏnhoe	2008	번역 표준 원칙
427	국민기본권의 보장	國民基本權의 保障	guarantee of the people's basic human rights	Gungmin gibongwonui bojang	Kungmin kibonkwŏnŭi pojang		번역 표준 원칙
428	국민대표	國民代表	national representatives	Gungmin daepyo	Kungmin taep'yo		번역 표준 원칙
429	국민대회준비회	國民大會準備會	Institutive Meeting for National Convention	Gungmin daehoe junbihoe	Kungmin taehoe chunbihoe	1945	번역 표준 원칙
430	국민반공대회	國民反共大會	National Anti-Communist Rally	Gungmin bangong daehoe	Kungmin ban'gong daehoe		번역 표준 원칙
431	국민방위군사건	國民防衛軍事件	National Defense Forces Incident	Gungmin bangwigun sageon	Kungmin pangwigun sakŏn	1951	번역 표준 원칙
432	국민보	國民報	*Gungminbo (The Korean National Herald)*	Gungminbo	Kungminbo	1913-1945	번역 표준 원칙

NO	용어	한자	영문	RO	MC	시대 및 연도	출전
433	국민복지연구회사건	國民福祉研究會事件	Research Society of National Welfare Incident of 1968	Gungmin bokji yeonguhoe sageon	Kungmin pokchi yŏn'guhoe sakŏn	1968	번역 표준 원칙
434	국민부	國民府	National People's Government	Gungminbu	Kungminbu	1929	한국학중앙연구원, 《영문한국백과》-신민부
435	국민소득	國民所得	national income	Gungmin sodeuk	Kungmin sodŭk		번역 표준 원칙
436	국민소득 2만 달러	國民所得 2萬 弗	$20,000 per capita GDP	Gungmin sodeuk 2man dalleo	Kungmin sodŭk 2man tallŏ		번역 표준 원칙
437	국민소환제	國民召還制	election recall system	Gungmin sohwanje	Kungmin sohwanje		번역 표준 원칙
438	국민신당	國民新黨	People's New Party	Gungmin sindang	Kungmin sindang	1997	번역 표준 원칙
439	국민연금제	國民年金制	national pension system	Gungmin yeongeumje	Kungmin yŏn'gŭmje	1988-?	번역 표준 원칙
440	국민윤리	國民倫理	national ethics	Gungmin yulli	Kungmin yulli		번역 표준 원칙

NO	용어	한자	영문	RO	MC	시대 및 연도	출전
441	국민윤리 강령	國民倫理 綱領	National Code of Ethics	Gungmin yulli gangnyeong	Kungmin yulli kangnŏng		번역 표준 원칙
442	국민의회	國民議會	National Assembly	Gungmin uihoe	Kungmin ŭihoe		한국학중앙연구원, 《영문한국백과》-대한민국임시정부
443	국민일보	國民日報	*Kukmin Ilbo (daily newspaper)*	Gungmin ilbo	Kungmin ilbo	1988	번역 표준 원칙
444	국민정신총동원운동	國民精神總動員運動	Movement for the General Mobilization of the National Spirit	Gungmin jeongsin chongdongwon undong	Kungmin chŏngsin ch'ongdongwon undong	1938-1940	번역 표준 원칙
445	국민정신총동원조선연맹	國民精神總動員朝鮮聯盟	Joseon National Spirit Mobilization League	Gungmin jeongsin chongdongwon joseon yeonmaeng	Kungmin chŏngsin ch'ongdongwŏn chosŏn yŏnmaeng	1938-1940	한국학중앙연구원, 《영문한국백과》-윤치호
446	국민주택건설기금	國民住宅建設基金	National Housing Fund	Gungmin jutaekgeonseol gigeum	Kungmin jut'aekkŏnsŏl gigŭm		번역 표준 원칙
447	국민직선제	國民直選制	direct elections	Gungmin jikseonje	Kungmin chiksŏnje		번역 표준 원칙
448	국민징용령	國民徵用令	National Conscription Ordinance	Gungmin jingyongnyeong	Kungmin chingyongnyŏng	1939-1945	번역 표준 원칙

NO	용어	한자	영문	RO	MC	시대 및 연도	출전
449	국민투자기금	國民投資基金	National Investment Fund	Gungmin tuja gigeum	Kungmin t'uja kigŭm		번역 표준 원칙
450	국민투자기금법	國民投資基金法	National Investment Fund Act	Gungmin tuja gigeumbeop	Kungmin t'uja kigŭmpŏp	1973-2002	번역 표준 원칙
451	국민투자채권	國民投資債券	national investment bonds	Gungmin tuja chaegwon	Kungmin t'uja ch'aegwŏn		번역 표준 원칙
452	국민투표	國民投票	referendum	Gungmin tupyo	Kungmin t'up'yo		번역 표준 원칙
453	국민평화 대행진	國民平和 大行進	Great National March of Peace (June 26, 1987)	Gungmin pyeonghwa daehaengjin	Kungmin p'yŏnghwa taehaengjin	1987	번역 표준 원칙
454	국민학교	國民學校	elementary school	Gungmin hakgyo	Kungmin hakkyo	1941-1995	번역 표준 원칙
455	국민회	國民會	Korean National Association	Gungminhoe	Kungminhoe	1909-?	한국학중앙연구원, 《영문한국백과》-청산리대첩
456	국민회군	國民會軍	Korean National Association Army	Gungminhoegun	Kungminhoegun	1914-?	번역 표준 원칙

NO	용어	한자	영문	RO	MC	시대 및 연도	출전
457	국민훈장	國民勳章	Order of Civil Merit	Gungmin hunjang	Kungmin hunjang	1951	번역 표준 원칙
458	국방경비대	國防警備隊	Preparatory Unit for the National Defense Forces	Gukbang gyeongbidae	Kukpang kyŏngbidae	1946-1948	번역 표준 원칙
459	국방경비대 14연대	國防警備隊 14聯隊	14th Regiment, the National Defense Guard	Gukbang gyeongbidae 14 yeondae	Kukpang gyŏngbidae 14 yŏndae	1948	번역 표준 원칙
460	국방경비대 창설	國防警備隊 創設	foundation of the National Defense Forces	gukbang gyeongbidae changseol	Kukpang kyŏngbidae ch'angsŏl	1946	번역 표준 원칙
461	국방경비사관학교	國防警備士官學校	National Constabulary Academy	Gukbang gyeongbi sagwanhakgyo	Kukpang kyŏngbi sagwan hakkyo	1946	번역 표준 원칙
462	국방과학연구소	國防科學硏究所	Agency for Defense Development	Gukbang gwahak yeonguso	Kukpang kwahak yŏn'guso	1970	번역 표준 원칙
463	국방백서	國防白書	defense white paper	Gukbang baekseo	Kukpang paeksŏ	1967-	번역 표준 원칙
464	국방부	國防部	Ministry of National Defense	Gukbangbu	Kukpangbu	1948	번역 표준 원칙

NO	용어	한자	영문	RO	MC	시대 및 연도	출전
465	국방위원회	國防委員會	National Defense Committee	Gukbang wiwonhoe	Kukpang wiwŏnhoe	1963	국방위원회 사이트 http://defense.assembly.go.kr
466	국방정보 판단서	國防情報 判斷書	Defense Intelligence Estimate	Gukbang jeongbo pandanseo	Kukpang chŏngbo p'andansŏ		번역 표준 원칙
467	국방체제 정립기	國防體制 定立期	building the national defense system	Gukbangcheje jeongnipgi	Kukpang ch'eje jŏngnipki	1945-1971	번역 표준 원칙
468	국방태세 발전기	國防態勢 發展期	enhancing the defensive posture	Gukbangtaese baljeongi	Kukpangt'aese paljŏngi	1991-	번역 표준 원칙
469	국세청	國稅廳	National Tax Service (NTS)	Guksecheong	Kuksech'ŏng	1966	번역 표준 원칙
470	국악의 해	國樂의 해	Year of Traditional Korean Music, 1994	Gugakui hae	Kugagŭi hae	1994	번역 표준 원칙
471	국어문법	國語文法	Korean grammar	Gugeo munbeop	Kugŏ munbŏp	?-?	번역 표준 원칙
472	국외중립	局外中立	neutrality	Gugoe jungnip	Kugoe chungnip		번역 표준 원칙

NO	용어	한자	영문	RO	MC	시대 및 연도	출전
473	국위선양활동	國威宣揚活動	enhancing national prestigie	Gugwi seonyang hwaldong	Kugwi sŏnyang hwaldong	2010	번역 표준 원칙
474	국유재산	國有財産	national property	Gugyu jaesan	Kugyu chaesn		번역 표준 원칙
475	국정감사	國政監査	parliamentary inspection of government ministries	Gukjeong gamsa	Kukchŏng kamsa	현대	번역 표준 원칙
476	국정조사권	國政調査權	parliamentary right to investigate state affairs	Gukjeong josagwon	Kukchŏng chosakwŏn	현대	번역 표준 원칙
477	국제 연합국 총사령부	國際 聯合國 總司令部	Supreme Command of Allied Powers (SCAP)	Gukje yeonhapguk chongsaryeongbu	Kukche yŏnhapkuk ch'ongsaryŏngbu	1945-1952	번역 표준 원칙
478	국제 유가	國際 油價	international oil prices	Gukje yuga	Kukche yuka		번역 표준 원칙
479	국제기능올림픽대회	國際技能Olympic 大會	WorldSkills	Gukje gineung ollimpik daehoe	Kukche kinŭng ollimp'ik taehoe	1950-?	번역 표준 원칙
480	국제노동기구(ILO)	國際勞動機構(ILO)	International Labor Organization (ILO)	Gukje nodong gigu	Kukche nodong kigu	1919-?	번역 표준 원칙

NO	용어	한자	영문	RO	MC	시대 및 연도	출전
481	국제도서전	國際圖書展	international book fair	Gukje doseojeon	Kukche dosŏjŏn		번역 표준 원칙
482	국제사면위원회	國際赦免委員會	Amnesty International	Gukje samyeon wiwonhoe	Kukche samyŏn wiwŏnhoe	1961	번역 표준 원칙
483	국제사회당 대회	國際社會黨 大會	Congress of the Labour and Socialist International	Gukje sahoedang daehoe	Kukche sahoedang taehoe		번역 표준 원칙
484	국제선교연맹	國際宣敎聯盟	International Missionary Conference	Gukje seongyo yeonmaeng	Kukche sŏngyo yŏnmaeng		번역 표준 원칙
485	국제수지 적자	國際收支 赤字	balance of payments deficit	Gukjesuji jeokja	Kukchesuji chŏkcha		번역 표준 원칙
486	국제신문편집인협회 (IPI) 한국위원회	國際新聞編輯人協會 (IPI) 韓國委員會	Korean National Committee of the International Press Institute (IPI)	Gukje sinmun pyeonjibin hyeophoe (IPI) Hanguk wiwonhoe	Kukche sinmun p'yŏnjibin hyŏphoe (IPI) Han'gug wiwŏnhoe	1961	번역 표준 원칙
487	국제신보	國際新報	Gukje Sinbo (The Kookje Daily News)	Gukjesinbo	Kukchesinbo	1950-1977	번역 표준 원칙
488	국제신탁통치	國際信託統治	international trusteeship	Gukje sintak tongchi	Kukche sint'ak t'ongch'i	1945-?	번역 표준 원칙

NO	용어	한자	영문	RO	MC	시대 및 연도	출전
489	국제에너지기구	國際energy機構	International Energy Agency (IEA)	Gukje eneoji gigu	Kukche enŏji kigu	1976	번역 표준 원칙
490	국제여성의 해	國際女性의 해	International Women's Year, 1975	Gukje yeoseongui hae	Kukche yŏsŏng-ŭi hae	1975	번역 표준 원칙
491	국제연맹	國際聯盟	League of Nations	Gukje yeonmaeng	Kukche yŏnmaeng	1920-1946	번역 표준 원칙
492	국제연맹 조사단, 리튼조사단	國際聯盟 調査團, Lytton 調査團	League of Nations Commission, the Lytton Commission	Gukje yeonmaeng josadan, riteun josadan	Kukche yŏnmaeng chosadan, rit'ŭn chosadan	1932?	번역 표준 원칙
493	국제연합	國際聯合	United Nations	Gukje yeonhap	Kukche yŏnhap	1945-?	번역 표준 원칙
494	국제연합 아동기금	國際聯合 兒童基金	United Nations Children's Fund (UNICEF)	Gukje yeonhap adong gigeum	Kukche yŏnhap adong kigŭm	1946-	번역 표준 원칙
495	국제연합 한국민사원조 사령부	國際聯合 韓國民事援助 司令部	United Nations Civil Assistance Command in Korea	Gukje yeonhap hanguk minsa wonjo saryeongbu	Kukche yŏnhap han'guk minsa wŏnjo saryŏngbu		번역 표준 원칙
496	국제연합군	國際聯合軍	United Nations Forces	Gukje yeonhapgun	Kukche yŏnhapkun		번역 표준 원칙

NO	용어	한자	영문	RO	MC	시대 및 연도	출전
497	국제연합안전보장이사회	國際聯合安全保障理事會	United Nations Security Council	Gukje yeonhap anjeon bojang isahoe	Kukche yŏnhap anjŏn pojang isahoe	1945-?	번역 표준 원칙
498	국제올림픽위원회	國際Olympic委員會	International Olympic Committee	Gukje ollimpik wiwonhoe	Kukche ollimp'ik wiwŏnhoe	1894-	번역 표준 원칙
499	국제원자력기구	國際原子力機構	International Atomic Energy Agency (IAEA)	Gukje wonjaryeok gigu	Kukche wŏnjaryŏk kigu	1957-?	번역 표준 원칙
500	국제자동전화 개통	國際自動電話 開通	launch of international direct distance dialing (IDDD) service	Gukje jadong jeonhwa gaetong	Kukche jadong jŏnhwa kaet'ong	1983	번역 표준 원칙
501	국제적십자사	國際赤十字社	International Federation of Red Cross and Red Crescent Societies	Gukje jeoksipjasa	Kukche chŏksipchasa	1919-	번역 표준 원칙
502	국제통신위성기구 가입	國際通信衛星機構 加入	accession to the International Telecommunications Satellite Organization (INTELSAT)	Gukje tongsin wiseonggigu gaip	Kukche t'ongsinwiŏnggigu kaip	1967	번역 표준 원칙
503	국제통화기금	國際通貨基金	International Monetary Fund (IMF)	Gukje tonghwa gigeum	Kukche t'onghwa kigŭm	1945	번역 표준 원칙
504	국제통화기금(IMF)	國際通貨基金 (IMF)	International Monetary Fund (IMF)	Gukje tonghwa gigeum (IMF)	Kukche t'onghwa kigŭm (IMF)	1946	번역 표준 원칙

NO	용어	한자	영문	RO	MC	시대 및 연도	출전
505	국제협조처(ICA)	國際協助處	International Cooperation Administration (ICA)	Gukje hyeopjocheo	Kukche hyŏpchoch'ŏ		번역 표준 원칙
506	국지도발	局地挑發	local provocation	Gukji dobal	Kukchi dobal		번역 표준 원칙
507	국채보상기성회	國債報償期成會	Association for Redemption of the National Debt	Gukchae bosang giseonghoe	Kukch'ae posang kisŏnghoe	1907	Ki-baik Lee, translated by Edward W. Wagner, A New History of Korea, Harvard University Press, 1984,
508	국채보상운동	國債報償運動	nationwide movement to redeem the national debt	Gukchae bosang undong	Kukch'ae posang undong	1907	번역 표준 원칙
509	국채보상취지서	國債報償趣旨書	Statement of the Association for Redemption of the National Debt	Gukchae bosang chwijiseo	Kukch'ae posang ch'wijisŏ	1907	번역 표준 원칙
510	국채상환	國債償還	redemption of national bonds	Gukchae sanghwan	Kukch'ae sanghwan		번역 표준 원칙
511	국책사업	國策事業	national project	Gukchaek saeop	Kukch'aek saŏp		번역 표준 원칙
512	국토개발종합계획	國土開發綜合計劃	national land development plan	Gukto gaebal jonghap gyehoek	Kukt'o kaebal chonghap kyehoek		번역 표준 원칙

NO	용어	한자	영문	RO	MC	시대 및 연도	출전
513	국토건설단	國土建設團	Nationwide Construction Corps	Gukto geonseoldan	Kukt'o kŏnsŏltan	1961	번역 표준 원칙
514	국토건설사업	國土建設事業	nationwide public works project	Gukto geonseol saeop	Kukt'o gŏnsŏl saŏp		번역 표준 원칙
515	국토균형개발	國土均衡開發	balanced land development	Gukto gyunhyeong gaebal	Kukt'o kyunhyŏng kaebal		번역 표준 원칙
516	국토보전시설	國土保全施設	facilities to conserve land	Gukto bojeon siseol	Kukt'o pojŏn sisŏl		번역 표준 원칙
517	국토통일원	國土統一院	Board of National Unification (1968-1990)	Gukto tongilwon	Kukt'o t'ongirwŏn	1968-?	번역 표준 원칙
518	국토해양부	國土海洋部	Ministry of Land,Transport and Maritime Affairs (MLTM)	Gukto haeyangbu	Kukt'o haeyangbu	2008	번역 표준 원칙
519	국풍 81	國風 81	Gukpung 81	Gukpung 81	Kukp'ung 81	1981	번역 표준 원칙
520	국학운동	國學運動	National Studies Movement	Gukhak undong	Kukhak undong		번역 표준 원칙

NO	용어	한자	영문	RO	MC	시대 및 연도	출전
521	국회내각책임제개헌기초위원회	國會內閣責任制改憲基礎委員會	Committee for Constitutional Amendment towards Establishment of the Parliamentary System	Gukhoe naegak chaegimje gaeheon gicho wiwonhoe	Kukhoe naegak ch'aegimje gaehŏn gich'o wiwŏnhoe		번역 표준 원칙
522	국회도서관	國會圖書館	National Assembly Library	Gukhoe doseogwan	Kuk'oe tosŏgwan	1955-?	번역 표준 원칙
523	국회법	國會法	National Assembly Act	Gukhoebeop	Kukhoepŏp	1948	번역 표준 원칙
524	국회의사당	國會議事堂	National Assembly of the Republic of Korea	Gukhoe uisadang	Kukhoe ŭisadang	1975-?	번역 표준 원칙
525	국회의원면책특권	國會議員免責特權	parliamentary privilege of speech	Gukhoeuiwon myeonchaek teukgwon	Kukhoeŭiwŏn myŏnch'aek t'ŭkkwŏn		번역 표준 원칙
526	국회의원선거법	國會議員選擧法	Act on the Election of National Assembly Members	Gukhoe uiwon seongeobeop	Kukhoe ŭiwŏn sŏn'gŏpŏp	1948	번역 표준 원칙
527	국회의원선거위원회	國會議員選擧委員會	appointment letter from the Board of Elections for members of the National Assembly	Gukhoe uiwon seongeo wiwonhoe	Kukhoe ŭiwŏn sŏn'gŏ wiwŏnhoe	1948	번역 표준 원칙
528	국회프락치사건	國會Fraktsiya事件	National Assembly Communist Spy Incident of 1949	Gukhoe peurakchi sageon	Kukhoe p'ŭrakch'i sakŏn	1949	번역 표준 원칙

NO	용어	한자	영문	RO	MC	시대 및 연도	출전
529	국회해산	國會解散	dissolution of the National Assembly	Gukhoe haesan	Kukhoe haesan		번역 표준 원칙
530	국회해산권	國會解散權	authority to dissolve the National Assembly	Gukhoe haesangwon	Kukhoe haesankwŏn	1948-1987	번역 표준 원칙
531	군	軍	Army	Gun	Gun	1950	번역 표준 원칙
532	군 소장파 정군운동	軍 少壯派 整軍運動	anti-corruption campaign by younger officers of the ROK Army	Gun sojangpa jeonggun undong	Kun sojangp'a chŏnggun undong		번역 표준 원칙
533	군국기무처	軍國機務處	Deliberative Council	Gunguk gimucheo	Kun'guk kimuch'ŏ	1894	Ki-baik Lee, translated by Edward W. Wagner, A New History of Korea, Harvard University Press, 1984,
534	군국주의	軍國主義	militarism	Gungukjuui	Kun'gukjuŭi	?-?	번역 표준 원칙
535	군단	軍團	Corps	Gundan	Gundan	1950	번역 표준 원칙
536	군당학교	郡黨學校	County's Party School	Gundang hakgyo	Kundang hakkyo		번역 표준 원칙

NO	용어	한자	영문	RO	MC	시대 및 연도	출전
537	군대사열	軍隊査閱	military inspection	Gundae sayeol	kundae sayŏl		국립중앙박물관 역사관 중형패널
538	군대해산	軍隊解散	dissolution of the Army	Gundae haesan	Kundae haesan	1907	번역 표준 원칙
539	군대해산령	軍隊解散令	decree to dissolve the Korean army	Gundae haesannyeong	Kundae haesannyŏng	1907	국사편찬위원회
540	군무도독부	軍務都督府	Military Directorate	Gunmu dodokbu	Kunmu todokpu	1919-?	번역 표준 원칙
541	군법	軍法	military law	Gunbeop	Kunbŏp		Shin Myung-ho, Translated by Timothy V. Atkinson, Joseon Royal Court Culture, Dolbegae Publishers,
542	군부	軍部	military authorities	Gunbu	Kunbu	1895-1897	번역 표준 원칙
543	군부통치	軍部統治	military rule	Gunbu tongchi	Kunbut'ongch'i		번역 표준 원칙
544	군사간부회의	軍事幹部會議	Military Executive Council	Gunsa ganbu hoeui	Kunsa kanbu hoeŭi		번역 표준 원칙

NO	용어	한자	영문	RO	MC	시대 및 연도	출전
545	군사권	軍事權	right to have a military	Gunsagwon	Kunsakwŏn		번역 표준 원칙
546	군사기만	軍事欺瞞	military deception	Gunsa giman	Kunsa giman		번역 표준 원칙
547	군사분계선	軍事分界線	Military Demarcation Line	Gunsa bungyeseon	Kunsa pun'gyesŏn	1953-?	번역 표준 원칙
548	군사재판	軍事裁判	court martial	Gunsa jaepan	Kunsa chaep'an		번역 표준 원칙
549	군사정전위원회	軍事停戰委員會	Military Armistice Commission	Gunsa jeongjeon wiwonhoe	Kunsa chŏngjŏn wiwŏnhoe	1953-?	번역 표준 원칙
550	군사조직	軍事組織	military organization	Gunsa jojik	Kunsa chojik		Ki-baik Lee, translated by Edward W. Wagner, A New History of Korea, Harvard University Press, 1984,
551	군사지도	軍事地圖	military maps	Gunsa jido	Kunsa chido		번역 표준 원칙
552	군사혁명위원회	軍事革命委員會	Millitary Revolutionary Committee	Gunsa hyeongmyeong wiwonhoe	Kunsa hyŏngmyŏng wiwŏnhoe	1961	번역 표준 원칙

NO	용어	한자	영문	RO	MC	시대 및 연도	출전
553	군사훈련	軍事訓練	military training	Gunsa hullyeon	Kunsa hullyŏn		번역 표준 원칙
554	군수공업화	軍需工業化	military industrialization	Gunsu gongeophwa	Kunsu kongŏp'wa		번역 표준 원칙
555	군수기지사령부	軍需基地司令部	Command of the Logistic Bases	Gunsu giji saryeongbu	Kunsu kiji saryŏngbu	1960	번역 표준 원칙
556	군수물자 해상수송	軍需物資 海上輸送	marine transportation of military supplies	Gunsu mulja haesang susong	Kunsu mulcha haesang susong		번역 표준 원칙
557	군수지원단	軍需支援團	Logistics Support Group (LSG)	Gunsu jiwondan	Kunsu chiwŏndan		번역 표준 원칙
558	군인복무규율	軍人服務規律	Decree on Military Service	Gunin bongmu gyuyul	Kunin pongmu kyuyul		번역 표준 원칙
559	군인수지	軍人須知	*Gunin Suji* (the soldiers manual)	Gunin suji	Kunin suji		번역 표준 원칙
560	군인의 길	軍人의 길	Code of Miltary Conduct	Guninui gil	Kuninŭi kil		번역 표준 원칙

NO	용어	한자	영문	RO	MC	시대 및 연도	출전
561	군정	軍政	military administration	Gunjeong	Kunjŏng		번역 표준 원칙
562	군정청 장관	軍政廳 長官	Military Governor	Je2dae gunjeongcheong janggwan	Che2tae kunjŏngch'ŏng changgwan		번역 표준 원칙
563	군정청 포고령 제1호	軍政廳 布告令 第1號	Military Government Decree No. 1	Gunjeongcheong pogoryeong je1ho	Kunjŏngch'ŏng p'ogoryŏng che1ho	1945-1948	번역 표준 원칙
564	궁성요배	宮城遙拜	bowing in the direction of Japan's Imperial Palace	Gungseong yobae	Kungsŏng yobae	1910-1945	번역 표준 원칙
565	권력세습	勸力世襲	hereditary succession of power	Gwollyeok seseup	Kwŏllyŏk sesŭp		번역 표준 원칙
566	권업신문	勸業新聞	*Gwoneop Sinmun*, newspaper of the Korean Independence Group in Russia	Gwoneop sinmun	Kwŏnŏp sinmun	1912	번역 표준 원칙
567	권업회	勸業會	Korean Independence Group in Russia (Gwoneophoe)	Gwoneophoe	Kwŏnŏphoe	1911-1914	번역 표준 원칙
568	권위주의	權威主義	authoritarianism	Gwonwijuui	Kwŏnwijuŭi		번역 표준 원칙

NO	용어	한자	영문	RO	MC	시대 및 연도	출전
569	귀속농지	歸屬農地	government-vested land / seized Japanses plan	Gwisok nongji	Kwisok nongji	1945	번역 표준 원칙
570	귀속농지불하	歸屬農地拂下	disposition of seized Japanese land holdings (after liberation from Japanese colonial rule)	Gwisok nongji bulha	Kwisok nongji pulha		번역 표준 원칙
571	귀속농지특별조치법	歸屬農地特別措置法	Special Act on Government-vested Land	Gwisok nongji teukbyeol jochibeop	Kwisok nongji t'ŭkpyŏl choch'ipŏp		번역 표준 원칙
572	귀속재산	歸屬財産	siezed Japanese property	Gwisok jaesan	Kwisok chaesan	1948	번역 표준 원칙
573	귀속재산불하	歸屬財産拂下	disposition of seized Japanese property (vested to the U.S. military government)	Gwisok jaesan bulha	Kwisok chaesan purha	1945-1948	번역 표준 원칙
574	귀순자	歸順者	North Korean defector	Gwisunja	Kwisunja	현대	번역 표준 원칙
575	그네뛰기	그네뛰기	swinging	Geune ttwigi	Kŭne ttwigi		번역 표준 원칙
576	그린벨트	Greenbelt	greenbelt	Geurin belteu	Kŭrin pelt'ŭ		번역 표준 원칙

NO	용어	한자	영문	RO	MC	시대 및 연도	출전
577	극동인민대표대회	極東人民大表大會	Congress of the Oppressed People of the Far East	Geukdong inmin daepyo daehoe	Kŭktong inmin taep'yo hoeŭi	1922	번역 표준 원칙
578	극동전략방면군	極東戰略方面軍	Far Eastern Front (Soviet Union)	Geukdong jeollyak bangmyeongun	Kŭktong chŏllyak pangmyŏn'gun		번역 표준 원칙
579	극동해군	極東海軍	Naval Forces, Far East	Geukdong haegun	Kŭktong haegun	1950	번역 표준 원칙
580	극예술연구회	劇藝術研究會	Theater Arts Research Society	Geugyesul yeonguhoe	Kŭgyesul yŏn'guhoe	1931	번역 표준 원칙
581	근대국가	近代國家	modern nation	Geundae gukga	Kŭndae kukka		번역 표준 원칙
582	근로기준법	勤勞基準法	Labor Standards Act	Geullo gijunbeop	Kŭllo kijunpŏp	1997-?	번역 표준 원칙
583	근로보국대	勤勞報國隊	National Labor Corps	Geullo bogukdae	Kŭllo poguktae	1941-1945	번역 표준 원칙
584	근로인민당	勤勞人民黨	Working People's Party	Geunno inmindang	Kŭllo inmindang	1947	번역 표준 원칙

NO	용어	한자	영문	RO	MC	시대 및 연도	출전
585	근로자의 날	勤勞者의 날	May Day / Labor Day	Geulloja-ui nal	Kŭlloja-ŭi nal	1884-?	번역 표준 원칙
586	근면,자조,협동	勤勉,自助,協同	diligence, self-help and cooperation	Geunmyeon, jajo, hyeopdong	Kŭnmyŏn, chajo, hyŏptong		번역 표준 원칙
587	근우회	槿友會	Geunuhoe (women's organization)	Geunuhoe	Kŭnuhoe	1927-1931	번역 표준 원칙
588	근접 항공지원	近接 航空支援	Close Air Support (CAS)	Geunjeop hanggong jiwon	kŭnjŏp hanggong jiwŏn		번역 표준 원칙
589	근정훈장	勤政勳章	Order of Service Merit	Geunjeong hunjang	Kŭnjŏng hunjang	1952	번역 표준 원칙
590	금강산 관광	金剛山 觀光	Mt. Kumgangsan tours	Geumgangsan gwangwang	Kŭmgangsan kwan'gwang	1988-	번역 표준 원칙
591	금강산 관광개발	金剛山 觀光開發	Mt. Kumgangsan Development Project	Geumgangsan gwangwang gaebal	Kŭmgangsan kwangwang kaebal		번역 표준 원칙
592	금강산 관광지구법	金剛山 觀光地區法	Mt. Kumgangsan Tourism Area Act	Geumgangsan gwangwang jigubeop	Kŭmgangsan kwan'gwang chigupŏp		번역 표준 원칙

NO	용어	한자	영문	RO	MC	시대 및 연도	출전
593	금강산 댐	金剛山 Dam	Mt. Kumgangsan Dam	Geumgangsan daem	Kŭmgangsan taem	2003	번역 표준 원칙
594	금강산 유람선	金剛山 遊覽船	Mt. Kumgangsan Ferry	Geumgangsan yuramseon	Kŭmgangsan yuramsŏn	1998	번역 표준 원칙
595	금강산 육로관광	金剛山 陸路觀光	land route to Mt. Kumgangsan	Geumgangsan yungno gwangwang	Kŭmgangsan yungno kwangwang	2003	번역 표준 원칙
596	금강산 총격사건	金剛山 銃擊事件	Shooting Incident at Mt. Kumgangsan (2008)	Geumgangsan chonggyeok sageon	Kŭmgangsan ch'onggyŏk sakŏn	2008	번역 표준 원칙
597	금남로	錦南路	Geumnam-ro (in Gwangju)	Geumnamno	Kŭmnamro		번역 표준 원칙
598	금리인하	金利引下	interest rate cut	Geumni inha	Kŭmni inha		번역 표준 원칙
599	금모으기운동	金모으기運動	gold collection drive during the Asian financial crisis of 1997	Geummoeugi undong	Kŭmmoŭgi undong	1997	번역 표준 원칙
600	금성돌출부 선단전투	金城突出部 先端戰鬪	Battle of the Edge of Geumseong Sailent	Geumseong dolchulbu seondan jeontu	Kŭmsŏng dolch'ulbu sŏndan chŏnt'u		번역 표준 원칙

NO	용어	한자	영문	RO	MC	시대 및 연도	출전
601	금성사	金星社	Goldstar	Geumseongsa	Kŭmsŏngsa	1958-?	번역 표준 원칙
602	금성전투	錦城戰鬪	Battle of Geumseong	Geumseong jeontu	Kŭmsŏng chŏnt'u		번역 표준 원칙
603	금수강산	錦繡江山	"land of majestic rivers and mountains"	Geumsu gangsan	Kŭmsu kangsan		번역 표준 원칙
604	금연구역	禁煙區域	non-smoking area	Geumnyeon guyeok	Kŭmyŏn kuyŏk		번역 표준 원칙
605	금융감독원	金融監督院	Financial Supervisory Service	Geumnyung gamdogwon	Kŭmyung kamdogwŏn	1999-?	번역 표준 원칙
606	금융규제개혁	金融規制改革	financial regulatory reform	Geumnyung gyuje gaehyeok	Kŭmyung Kyuje Kaehyŏk		번역 표준 원칙
607	금융노조운동	金融勞組運動	movement to organize a finance workers' union	Geumnyung nojo undong	Kŭmnyung nojo undong	1960-?	번역 표준 원칙
608	금융실명제	金融實名制	real-name financial transaction system	Geumnyung silmyeongje	Kŭmyung silmyŏngje	1993-?	Wi Jo Kang, Christ and Caesar in Modern Korea: A History of Christianity and Politics, State University of

NO	용어	한자	영문	RO	MC	시대 및 연도	출전
609	금융조합	金融組合	financial society	Geumyung johap	Kŭmyung chohap	1907-1956	번역 표준 원칙
610	금주단연동맹	禁酒斷煙同盟	League for Giving up Drinking and Smoking	Geumju danyeon dongmaeng	Kŭmju tanyŏn tongmaeng		번역 표준 원칙
611	금지곡	禁止曲	banned songs	Geumjigok	Kŭmjigok		번역 표준 원칙
612	급진개화파	急進開化派	progressive group within the Enlightenment Faction	Geupjin gaehwapa	Kŭpchin kaehwap'a	1876-1884	번역 표준 원칙
613	기간산업	基幹産業	key industries	Gignan saneop	Kigan saŏp	현대	번역 표준 원칙
614	기간산업의 수입대체 공업화정책	基幹産業의 輸入代替 工業化政策	import substitution industrialization policy for basic industries	Gigansaneopui suip daeche gongeophwa jeongchaek	Kigan sanŏp-ŭi suip taech'e kongŏphwa chŏngch'aek		번역 표준 원칙
615	기간수송망	基幹輸送網	key transportation network	Gigan susongmang	Kigan susongmang		번역 표준 원칙
616	기계공업 근대화 방안	機械工業 近代化 方案	measures for modernization of the machine industry	Gigye gongeop geundaehwa bangan	Kigye kongŏp kŭndaehwa pangan		번역 표준 원칙

NO	용어	한자	영문	RO	MC	시대 및 연도	출전
617	기계전투	杞溪戰鬪	Battle of Gigye	Gigye jeontu	Kigye chŏnt'u		번역 표준 원칙
618	기계화 보병부대	機械化 步兵部隊	Mechanized Infantry Unit	Gigyehwa bobyeong budae	Kigyehwa bobyŏngbudae		번역 표준 원칙
619	기기창	機器廠	machinery plant	Gigichang	Kigich'ang	1883-1894	번역 표준 원칙
620	기능공	技能工	technicians	Gineunggong	Kinŭnggong		번역 표준 원칙
621	기능올림픽	技能Olympic	WorldSkills	Gineung ollimpik	Kinŭng ollimp'ik	1950-?	번역 표준 원칙
622	기능장려법	技能獎勵法	Act on the Encouragement of Technical Skills	Gineung jangnyeobeop	Kinŭng changnyŏpŏp		번역 표준 원칙
623	기대수명	期待壽命	life expectancy	Gidae sumyeong	Kidae sumyŏng		번역 표준 원칙
624	기독교	基督敎	Christianity	Gidokgyo	Kidokkyo		번역 표준 원칙

NO	용어	한자	영문	RO	MC	시대 및 연도	출전
625	기독교농촌연구회	基督敎農村硏究會	Christian Rural Communities Research Society	Gidokgyo nongchon yeonguhoe	Kidokkyo nongch'on yŏnguhoe		번역 표준 원칙
626	기독교여민회	基督敎女民會	Korea Association of Christian Women for Women Minjung	Gidokgyo yeominhoe	Kidokkyo yŏminhoe		번역 표준 원칙
627	기독교연구회	基督敎硏究會	Christian Research Association	Gidokgyo yeonguhoe	Kidokkyo yŏnguhoe		번역 표준 원칙
628	기독교조선감리회	基督敎朝鮮監理會	Joseon Methodist Church	Gidokgyo joseon gamnihoe	Kidokkyo chosŏn gamnihoe	일제	번역 표준 원칙
629	기독신우회	基督信友會	Association of Christian Believers	Gidok sinuhoe	Kidok sinuhoe		번역 표준 원칙
630	기독청년면려회	基督靑年勉勵會	Young Christian Endeavour	Gidok cheongnyeon myeollyeohoe	Kidok ch'ŏngnyŏn myŏllyŏhoe		번역 표준 원칙
631	기러기 가족	기러기 家族	"goose family" (families living apart to enable children to attend school in English-speaking countries)	Gireogi gajok	Kirŏgi kajok		번역 표준 원칙
632	기무사령부	機務司令部	Defense Security Command	Gimu saryeongbu	Kimu saryŏngbu	1991	번역 표준 원칙

NO	용어	한자	영문	RO	MC	시대 및 연도	출전
633	기병사단	騎兵師團	Cavalry Division	Gibyeongsadan	Kibyŏngsadan		번역 표준 원칙
634	기상위성	氣象衛星	meteorological satellite	Gisang wiseong	Kisang wisŏng		번역 표준 원칙
635	기상청	氣象廳	Korea Meteorological Administraion (KMA)	Gisangcheong	Kisangch'ŏng	1949	번역 표준 원칙
636	기술교범	技術敎範	technical manual	Gisul gyobeom	Kisul gyobŏm		번역 표준 원칙
637	기유각서	己酉覺書	takeover of domestic laws	Giyugakseo	Kiyugaksŏ	1909	번역 표준 원칙
638	기지촌	基地村	military camp town	Gijichon	Kijich'on		번역 표준 원칙
639	기초노령연금	基礎老齡年金	basic old-age pension	Gicho noryeong yeongeum	Kich'o noryŏng yŏngŭm	2007제정 2008시행	번역 표준 원칙
640	기초생활보장	基礎生活保障	basic livelihood security benefits	Gicho saenghwal bojang	Kich'o saenghwal pojang		번역 표준 원칙

NO	용어	한자	영문	RO	MC	시대 및 연도	출전
641	기초생활보장대상자	基礎生活保障代償者	recipients of basic livelihood security benefits	Gicho saenghwal bojang daesangja	Kich'o saenghwal pojang taesangja		번역 표준 원칙
642	기호흥학회	畿湖興學會	Seoul and Central Region Association for Education	Giho heunghakhoe	Kiho hŭnghakhoe	1908-1910	Peter H. Lee, Sourcebook of Korean Civilization(Volume 2), Columbia University Press, 1993,
643	기획재정부	企劃財政部	Ministry of Strategy and Finance	Gihoek Jaejeongbu	Kihoek chaejŏngbu	2008	번역 표준 원칙
644	기후변화협약	氣候變化協約	United Nations Framework Convention on Climate Change (UNFCCC)	Gihu byeonhwa hyeobyak	Kihu pyŏnhwa hyŏbyak	1992	번역 표준 원칙
645	긴급조치	緊急措置	emergency measures	Gingeup jochi	Kin'gŭp choch'i	1974~1975	번역 표준 원칙
646	긴급조치 9호	緊急措置 9號	Emergency Measure No. 9	Gingeup jochi 9ho	Kin'gŭp choch'i 9ho		번역 표준 원칙
647	긴급조치 9호 철폐운동	緊急措置 9號 撤廢運動	campaign for abolition of Emergency Measure No. 9	Gingeup jochi 9ho cheolpye undong	Kin'gŭp choch'i 9ho ch'ŏlp'ye undong	1975-1979	번역 표준 원칙
648	긴급조치 제1호	緊急措置 第1號	Emergency Measure No. 1	Gingeupjochi je 1ho	Kingŭpjoch'i che 1ho	1974	번역 표준 원칙

NO	용어	한자	영문	RO	MC	시대 및 연도	출전
649	긴급조치 제4호	緊急措置 第4號	Emergency Measure No. 4	Gingeupjochi je 4ho	Kingŭpjoch'i che 4ho	1974	번역 표준 원칙
650	길림성	吉林省	Jilin Province, China	Gillimseong	Killimsŏng		번역 표준 원칙
651	김대중 납치사건	金大中 拉致事件	attempted kidnapping of Kim Dae-jung	Kim Dae-jung napchi sageon	Kim Tae-chung napch'i sakŏn	1973	번역 표준 원칙
652	김대중 내란음모사건	金大中 內亂陰謀事件	case of Kim Dae-jung's alleged conspiracy to incite rebellion	Kim Dae-jung naeran eummo sageon	Kim Tae-chung naeran ŭmmo sakŏn	1980	번역 표준 원칙
653	김대중 노벨평화상	金大中 Nobel平和賞	President Kim Dae-jung's winning of the Nobel Peace Prize in 2000	Kim Dae-jung nobel pyeonghwasang	Kim Tae-chung nobel p'yŏnhwasang	2000	번역 표준 원칙
654	김대중-김정일 정상회담	金大中-金正日 頂上會談	June 15 Inter-Korea Summit: Kim Dae-jung and Kim Jong-il Summit	Kim Dae-jung - Kim Jeong-il jeongsang hoedam	Kim Tae-chung - Kim Chŏng-il chŏngsang hoedam	2000	번역 표준 원칙
655	김수영 문학상	金洙暎 文學賞	Kim Su-young Literary Award	Kim suyeong munhaksang	Kimsuyŏng munhaksang	1981	번역 표준 원칙
656	김영삼 총재 의원직 제명파동	金泳三 總裁 議員職 除名波動	expulsion of Kim Young-sam from the National Assembly	Kim Yeong-sam chongjae uiwonjik jemyeong padong	Kim Yŏng-sam ch'ongjae ŭiwŏnjik chemyŏng p'adong	1979	번역 표준 원칙

NO	용어	한자	영문	RO	MC	시대 및 연도	출전
657	김일성 1인 독재체제	金日成 1人 獨裁體制	Kim Il-sung's absolute dictatorship	Kim Il-seong 1in dokje cheje	Kim Il-sŏng 1in tokchae ch'eje		번역 표준 원칙
658	김일성 헌법	金日成 憲法	Kim Il Sung Constitution: DPRK Socialist Constitution	Kim Il-seong heonbeop	Kim Il-sŏng hŏnpŏp	1992	번역 표준 원칙
659	김일성고지 전투	金日成高地 戰鬪	Battle of Kim Il-sung Hill	Kim Il-seong goji jeontu	Kim Il-sŏng koji chŏnt'u	1951	번역 표준 원칙
660	김일성우상화	金日成偶像化	idolization of Kim Il-sung	Kim Il-seong usanghwa	Kim Il-sŏng usanghwa		번역 표준 원칙
661	김일성의 5대 강령	金日成의 5大 綱領	Kim Il-sung's Five Doctrines	Kim Il-seong 5dae gangnyeong	Kim Il-sŏng-ŭi 5tae kangnyŏng		번역 표준 원칙
662	김종필, 오히라 마사요시 메모	金鍾泌, 大平 正芳 Memo	Kim Jong-pil and Masayoshi Ohira memos	Kim Jong-pil, Ohira Masayosi memo	Kim Chong-p'il, Ohira Masayosi memo	1962	번역 표준 원칙
663	김치		Kimchi	kimchi	Gimchi	Kimch'i	번역 표준 원칙
664	김풍익 소령	金豊益 少領	Major Kim Pung-ik	Kim Pung-ik soryeong	Kimp'ungik soryŏng	1950	번역 표준 원칙

NO	용어	한자	영문	RO	MC	시대 및 연도	출전
665	나가사키	長崎	Nagasaki	Nagasaki	Nagasaki	1945	번역 표준 원칙
666	나로호	羅老號	Korean space rocket Naro	Naroho	Naroho		번역 표준 원칙
667	나진선봉 자유무역지대	羅津先鋒 自由貿易地帶	Rajin-Sonbong Special Economic Zone	Najin seonbong jayu muyeok jidae	Najin sŏnbong chayu muyŏk jidae		번역 표준 원칙
668	낙동강 방어선	洛東江 防禦線	Nakdonggang River Defense Line	Nakdonggang bangeoseon	Naktonggang pangŏsŏn	1950	번역 표준 원칙
669	낙동강 방어전투	洛東江 防禦戰鬪	Battle of the Nakdonggang River Defense Line	Nakdonggang bangeo jeontu	Naktonggang pangŏ chŏnt'u	1950	번역 표준 원칙
670	낙동강 페놀유출 사고	洛東江 phenol流出 事故	phenol spill in the Nakdonggang River	Nakdonggang penoryuchul sago	Naktonggang p'enol yuch'ul sago	1991	번역 표준 원칙
671	낙동강전선 돌파작전	洛東江戰線 突破作戰	Penetration Operations at the Nakdonggang River Front	Nakdonggang jeonseon dolpajakjeon	Nakonggang jŏnsŏn tolp'ajakchŏn		번역 표준 원칙
672	낙양군관학교	洛陽軍官學校	Loyang Military Academy	Nagyang gungwanhakgyo	Nagyang kun'gwanhakkyo	1933	번역 표준 원칙

NO	용어	한자	영문	RO	MC	시대 및 연도	출전
673	난민송환위원회	難民送還委員會	Refugee Repatriation Commission	Nanmin songhwan wiwonhoe	Nanmin songhwan wiwŏnhoe		번역 표준 원칙
674	난장이가 쏘아올린 작은 공	난장이가 쏘아올린 작은 공	The Ball Shot by a Midget (Nanjangi-ga ssoaollin gong), novel by Jo Se-hui, 1970; movie directed by Lee Won-se, 1981	Nanjangiga ssoaollin jageun gong	Nanjangiga ssoaollin chagŭn kong	1976	번역 표준 원칙
675	난징대학살	南京大虐殺	Nanjing Massacre	Nanjing daehaksal	Nanjing taehaksal	1937	번역 표준 원칙
676	남경조약	南京條約	Treaty of Nanking	Namgyeong joyak	Namgyŏng choyak	1842	번역 표준 원칙
677	남녀고용평등법	男女雇傭平等法	Act on Gender Equality in Employment	Namnyeo goyong pyeongdeungbeop	Namnyŏ koyong p'yŏngdŭngbŏp	1987-?	번역 표준 원칙
678	남대문	南大門	Sungnyemun Gate (aka Namdaemun Gate)	Namdaemun	Namdaemun		번역 표준 원칙
679	남로당파	南勞黨派	South Korean Workers' Party (Namnodong) Faction	Namnodangpa	Namnodangp'a		번역 표준 원칙
680	남만주철도주식회사 (만철)	南滿洲鐵道株式會社 (滿鐵)	South Manchuria Railway Co.	Nammanju cheoldo jusik hoesa (mancheol)	Namman ch'ŏldo chusik hoesa (manch'ŏl)	1906-1945	번역 표준 원칙

NO	용어	한자	영문	RO	MC	시대 및 연도	출전
681	남면북양정책	南棉北羊政策	Japanese colonial policy to increase production of cotton in the south and wool in the north	Nammyeon bugyang jeongchaek	Nammyŏn bugyang chŏngch'aek		번역 표준 원칙
682	남민전사건	南民戰事件	South Korean People's Liberation Front Incident of 1979	Namminjeon sageon	Namminjŏn sakŏn	1979	번역 표준 원칙
683	남방한계선	南方限界線	Southern Boundary of DMZ	Nambang hangyeseon	Nambang han'gyesŏn	1953	번역 표준 원칙
684	남베트남 민족해방전선	南Vietnam 民族解放戰線	South Vietnamese National Liberation Front	Nambeteunam minjok haebang jeonseon	Nambet'ŭnam minjok haebang chŏnsŏn		번역 표준 원칙
685	남베트남 임시혁명정부	南Vietnam 臨時革命政府	Provisional Revolutionary Government of the Republic of South Vietnam	Nambeteunam imsi hyeongmyeong jeongbu	Nambet'ŭnam imsi hyŏngmyŏng chŏngbu		번역 표준 원칙
686	남북 고위급 회담	南北 高位級 會談	South-North high-level talks	Nambuk gowigeup hoedam	Nambuk kowigŭp hoedam	1990-?	번역 표준 원칙
687	남북 고향방문단	南北 故鄕訪問團	visits by separated families in South and North Korea	Nambuk gohyang bangmundan	Nambuk kohyang pangmundan	1985	번역 표준 원칙
688	남북 국회회담	南北 國會會談	South-North National Assembly Conference	Nambuk gukhoe hoedam	Nambuk kukhoe hoedam	1985-?	번역 표준 원칙

NO	용어	한자	영문	RO	MC	시대 및 연도	출전
689	남북 사이의 화해와 불가침 및 교류협력에 관한 합의서	南北 사이의 和解와 不可侵 및 交流協力에 關한 合意書	Basic Agreement on Reconciliation, Nonaggression, and Exchange and Cooperation between South and North Korea	Nambuk sai-ui hwahae-wa bulgachim mit gyoryu hyeomnyeok-e gwanhan habuiseo	Nambuk sai-ŭi hwahaewa pulgach'im mit kyoryu hyŏmnyŏge kwanhan habŭisŏ	1991	번역 표준 원칙
690	남북 실무자 간 비밀 접촉	南北 實務者 間 秘密接觸	secret working-level talks between South and North Korea	Nambuk silmuja gan bimil jeopchok	Nambuk silmuja kan pimil chŏpch'ok		번역 표준 원칙
691	남북 이산가족 고향방문	南北 離散家族 故鄕訪問	hometown visits by separated families of South and North Korea	Nambuk isangajok gohyang bangmun	Nambuk isangajok kohyang pangmun	1985	번역 표준 원칙
692	남북 이산가족 상봉	南北 離散家族 相逢	reunion of separated families of South and North Korea	Nambuk isan gajok sangbong	Nambuk isan kajok sangbong		번역 표준 원칙
693	남북 조선의 제정당 사회단체 연석회의	南北 朝鮮의 諸政黨 社會團體 連席會議	Joint Meeting of Political Parties and Social Organizations of the Two Koreas	Nambuk joseonui jejeongdang sahoedanche yeonseokhoeui	Nambuk josŏnŭi chejŏngdang sahoedanche yŏnsŏkhoeŭi	1948	번역 표준 원칙
694	남북 직통전화	南北 直通電話	South-North Hotline	Nambuk jiktong jeonhwa	Nambuk chikt'ong chŏnhwa	1971-?	번역 표준 원칙
695	남북 체제경쟁	南北 體制競爭	two Koreas' competition for supremacy of their political systems in the early 1970s	Nambuk cheje gyeongjaeng	Nambuk ch'eje kyŏngjaeng		번역 표준 원칙
696	남북경제협력 실무회담	南北經濟協力 實務會談	working-level talks for inter-Korean economic cooperation	Nambuk gyeongje hyeomnyeok silmuhoedam	Nambuk kyŏngje hyŏmnyŏk silmuhoedam		번역 표준 원칙

NO	용어	한자	영문	RO	MC	시대 및 연도	출전
697	남북경제회담	南北經濟會談	South-North Economic Conference	Nambuk gyeongje hoedam	Nambuk kyŏngje hoedam	1984-?	번역 표준 원칙
698	남북교류·협력공동위원회	南北交流·協力共同委員會	North-South Joint Exchange and Cooperation Commission	Nambuk gyoryu·hyeomnyeok gongdong wiwonhoe	Nambuk kyoryu·hyŏmnyŏk kongdong wiwŏnhoe		번역 표준 원칙
699	남북교류협력에 관한 법률	南北交流協力에 關한 法律	Inter-Korea Exchange and Cooperation Act	Nambuk gyoryu hyeomnyeoge gwanhan beomnyul	Nambuk kyoryu hyŏmnyŏk-e kwanhan pŏmnyul	공포일 2009.1 2.29 시행일 2010.1 2.30	번역 표준 원칙
700	남북군사공동위원회	南北軍事共同委員會	South-North Joint Military Commission	Nambuk gunsa gongdong wiwonhoe	Nambuk kunsa kongdong wiwŏnhoe		번역 표준 원칙
701	남북군사공동위원회 구성·운영에 관한 합의서	南北軍事共同委員會 構成·運營에 關한 合意書	Agreement on the Formation and Operation of the North-South Joint Military Commission	Nambuk gunsa gongdong wiwonhoe guseong-unyeonge gwanhan habuiseo	Nambuk kunsagongdong wiwonhoe kusŏng·unyŏng-e kwanhan habŭisŏ	1992	번역 표준 원칙
702	남북기본합의서와 비핵화공동선언	南北基本合意書와 非核化共同宣言	Joint Declaration on the Denuclearization of the Korean Peninsula	Nambuk gibon habuiseo-wa bihaekhwa gongdong seoneon	Nambuk kibon habŭisŏ-wa pihaekhwa kongdong sŏnŏn	1992	번역 표준 원칙
703	남북노동당 중앙위원회 연석회의	南北勞動黨 中央委員會 連席會議	South-North Worker's Party Central Committee Joint Conference	Nambung nodongdang jungang wiwonhoe yeonseokhoeui	Nambuk nodongdang chungang wiwŏnhoe yŏnsŏk hoeŭi	1949	번역 표준 원칙
704	남북단일팀	南北單一Team	single inter-Korean team	Nambuk daniltim	Nambuk tanilt'im		번역 표준 원칙

NO	용어	한자	영문	RO	MC	시대 및 연도	출전
705	남북대화	南北對話	inter-Korean dialogue	Nambuk daehwa	Nambuk taehwa	1971-?	번역 표준 원칙
706	남북연락사무소	南北連絡事務所	inter-Korean liaison office (at the truce village of Panmunjeom)	Nambuk yeollak samuso	Nambuk yŏllak samuso	1992	번역 표준 원칙
707	남북연락사무소 설치·운영에 관한 합의서	南北連絡事務所 設置·運營에 關한 合意書	Agreeement on the Installation and Operation of the Inter-Korean Liaison Office	Nambuk yeollak samuseo seolchi-unyeonge gwanhan habuiseo	Nambuk yŏllak samuso sŏlch'i-unyŏng-e kwanhan habŭisŏ	1992	번역 표준 원칙
708	남북연방제통일방안	南北聯邦制統一方案	proposal for federation system for South-North unification	Nambuk yeonbangje tongil bangan	Nambuk yŏnbangje t'ongil pangan	1960-?	번역 표준 원칙
709	남북연석회의	南北連席會議	South-North Joint Meeting	Nambuk yeonseok hoeui	Nambuk yŏnsŏk hoeŭi	1988-?	번역 표준 원칙
710	남북이산가족	南北離散家族	separated families of South and North Korea	Nambuk isan gajok	Nambuk isan kajok	1985	번역 표준 원칙
711	남북적십자회담	南北赤十字會談	South-North Red Cross talks	Nambuk jeoksipja hoedam	Nambuk chŏksipcha hoedam	1971	번역 표준 원칙
712	남북정상회담	南北頂上會談	inter-Korean summit	Nambuk jeongsang hoedam	Nambuk chŏngsang hoedam	2000-?	번역 표준 원칙

NO	용어	한자	영문	RO	MC	시대 및 연도	출전
713	남북정치협상	南北政治協商	political negotiations between South and North Korea	Nambuk jeongchi hyeopsang	Nambuk chŏngch'I hyŏpsang		번역 표준 원칙
714	남북조절위원회	南北調節委員會	South-North Coordinating Committee	Nambuk jojeol wiwonhoe	Nambuk chojŏl wiwŏnhoe	1972-1973	번역 표준 원칙
715	남북청년학생 공동선언문	南北靑年學生 共同宣言文	Joint Statement on the Nation's Independent, Peaceful Reunification by students of the two Koreas on July 7,	Nambuk cheongnyeon haksaeng gongdong seoneonmun	Nambuk ch'ŏngnyŏn haksaeng kongdong sŏnŏnmun	1989	번역 표준 원칙
716	남북총리회담	南北總理會談	First Working Level Representatives Meeting for South-North Prime Ministers Talks	Nambuk chongni hoedam	Nambuk ch'ŏngni hoedam		번역 표준 원칙
717	남북총리회담을 위한 제1차 실무대표접촉	南北總理會談을 爲한 第1次 實務代表接觸	First Working-Level Representatives Meeting for South-North Prime Ministers' Talks	Nambuk chongni hoedameul wihan je1cha silmudaepyo jeopchok	Nambuk ch'ongni hoedamŭl wihan che1ch'a silmudaep'yo chŏpch'ok		번역 표준 원칙
718	남북통일축구대회	南北統一蹴球大會	Inter-Korean Unification Soccer Match	Nambuk tongil chukgu daehoe	Nambuk t'ongil ch'ukku taehoe	1990	번역 표준 원칙
719	남북학생회담	南北學生會談	South-North Student Talks	Nambuk haksaeng hoedam	Nambuk haksaeng hoedam		번역 표준 원칙
720	남북학생회담 환영 민족통일촉진 권리대회	南北學生會談 歡迎 民族統一促進 權利大會	National Unification Acceleration Rights Meeting for Welcoming the South-North Student Talks	Nambuk haksaenghoedam hwannyeong minjoktongil chokjin gwollidaehoe	Nambuk haksaenghoedam hwanyŏng minjokt'ongil ch'okchin kwollidaehoe		번역 표준 원칙

NO	용어	한자	영문	RO	MC	시대 및 연도	출전
721	남북한 동시 초청안	南北韓 同時 招請案	proposal to invite the two Koreas to simultaneously attend the UN General Assembly meetings	Nambukhan dongsi chocheongan	Nambukhan tongsi ch'och'ŏngan		번역 표준 원칙
722	남북한 무조건 동시 초청안	南北韓 無條件 同時招請案	proposal to unconditionally invite the two Koreas to simultaneously attend the UN General Assembly	Nambukhan mujogeon dongsi chocheongan	nambukhan mujokŏn tongsich'och'ŏngan		번역 표준 원칙
723	남북한 올림픽 동시입장	南北韓 Olympics 同時立場	joint entry of the two Koreas in the Sydney Olympic Games Opening Cermony	Nambukhan ollimpik dongsi ipjang	Nambukhan ollimp'ik tongsi ipchang		번역 표준 원칙
724	남북한 유엔 동시 가입	南北韓 UN 同時 加入	two Koreas' simultaneous admission to the UN	Nambukhan yuen dongsi gaip	Nambukhan yuen tongsi kaip	1991	번역 표준 원칙
725	남북한교역	南北韓交易	trade between South and North Korea	Nambukhan gyoyeok	Nambuk'an kyoyŏk	1945-1949	번역 표준 원칙
726	남북합의서	南北合意書	Basic Agreement between South and North Korea	Nambuk habuiseo	Nambuk habŭisŏ		번역 표준 원칙
727	남북협상	南北協商	South-North negotiations	Nambuk hyeopsang	Nambuk hyŏpsang	1948	번역 표준 원칙
728	남사당놀이	男사당놀이	*namsadang nori* (performances by itinerant male entertainers)	Namsadangnori	Namsadangnori		번역 표준 원칙

NO	용어	한자	영문	RO	MC	시대 및 연도	출전
729	남여고용평등법	男女雇傭平等法	Equal Employment Act	Namnyeo goyong pyeongdeungbeop	Namnyŏ koyong p'yŏngdŭngpŏp	1987	번역 표준 원칙
730	남여평등권 법령	男女平等權 法令	(North Korean) Law on Gender Equality	Namnyeo pyeongdeunggwon beomnyeong	Namyŏ p'yŏngdŭngkwŏn bŏmnyŏng		번역 표준 원칙
731	남연군묘 도굴사건	南延君墓 盜掘事件	robbery of Prince Namyeon's tomb	Namyeongun myo dogul sageon	Namyŏn'gun myo togul sakŏn	1868	번역 표준 원칙
732	남원 학살사건	南原 虐殺事件	Namwon Massacre of 1919	Namwon haksal sageon	Namwŏn haksal sagŏn	1919	번역 표준 원칙
733	남조선과도입법의원	南朝鮮過渡立法議院	South Korean Interim Legislative Assembly	Namjoseon gwado ipbeop uiwon	Namjosŏn kwado ippŏp	1946-1948	번역 표준 원칙
734	남조선과도정부	南朝鮮過渡政府	South Korean Interim Government	Namjoseon gwado jeongbu	Namjosŏn kwado chŏngbu	1947-1948	번역 표준 원칙
735	남조선국민대표 민주의원	南朝鮮國民代表 民主議院	Representative Democractic Council of South Korea	Namjoseon gungmin daepyo minjuuiwon	Namjosŏn kungmin taep'yo minjuŭiwŏn	1946	번역 표준 원칙
736	남조선국방경비대	南朝鮮國防警備隊	South Korea National Defense Forces	Namjoseon gukbang gyeongbidae	Namjosŏn kukpang kyŏngbidae	1946-1948	번역 표준 원칙

NO	용어	한자	영문	RO	MC	시대 및 연도	출전
737	남조선노동당	南朝鮮勞動黨	Worker's Party of South Korea	Namjoseon nodongdang	Namjosŏn nodongdang	1946-1949	번역 표준 원칙
738	남조선인민대표자대회	南朝鮮人民代表者大會	South Korean Congress of the People's Representatives	Namjoseon inmin daepyoja daehoe	Namjosŏn inmin taep'yoja taehoe	1948	번역 표준 원칙
739	남조선해방과 통일전략 계획	南朝鮮解放과 統一戰略 計劃	Liberation of South Korea and Unification Strategy Plans	Namjoseon haebanggwa tongil jeonryak gyehoek	Namjosŏn haebang-kwa t'ongil chŏllyak kyehoek		번역 표준 원칙
740	남조선혁명	南朝鮮革命	revolution against South Korea	Namjoseon hyeongmyeong	Namjosŏn hyŏngmyŏng		번역 표준 원칙
741	남침땅굴사건	南侵땅窟事件	discovery of North Korea's underground tunnel for invasion of South Korea	Namchim ddanggul sageon	Namch'im ttanggul sakŏn		번역 표준 원칙
742	남한 단독 초청안	南韓 單獨 招請案	proposal to invite only South Korea to the UN General Assembly meetings	Namhan dandok chocheongan	Namhan tandok ch'och'ŏngan		번역 표준 원칙
743	남한 단독선거	南韓 單獨選擧	separate elections in South Korea only	Namhan dandok seongeo	Namhan tandok sŏn'gŏ	1948	번역 표준 원칙
744	남한단독정부론	南韓單獨政府論	argument for establishment of the South Korean government first	Namhan dandok jeongburon	Namhan tandok chŏngburon	1945-1948	번역 표준 원칙

NO	용어	한자	영문	RO	MC	시대 및 연도	출전
745	남한대토벌작전	南韓大討伐作戰	operation for the subjugation of South Korea	Namhan daetobeol jakjeon	Namhan taet'obŏl chakchŏn	1909	번역 표준 원칙
746	남한수해물자	南韓水害物資	(North Korea's) flood relief for South Korea	Namhan suhaemulja jeondal	Namhan suhae mulcha chŏndal		번역 표준 원칙
747	남한수해물자 전달	南韓水害物資 傳達	delivery of flood relief to South Korea	Namhan suhaemulja jeondal	Namhan suhaemulja chŏndal		번역 표준 원칙
748	남한의 공산화	南韓의 共産化	Communization of South Korea	Namhanui gongsanhwa	Namhanŭi kongsanhwa		번역 표준 원칙
749	남한조선노동당 중부지역당 사건	南韓朝鮮勞動黨 中部地域黨 事件	espionage case involving members of the South Korean Central Region Branch of the North Korean Workers' Party in the early	Namhan joseon nodongdang jungbu jiyeokdang sageon	Namhan chosŏn notongdan jungbu chiyŏktang sakŏn		번역 표준 원칙
750	남해	南海	South Sea	Namhae	Namhae		번역 표준 원칙
751	남해고속도로	南海高速道路	Namhae (South Coast) Expressway	Namhae gosokdoro	Namhae kosoktoro	1973	번역 표준 원칙
752	남화한인청년연맹	南華韓人靑年聯盟	League of Korean Young Anarchists in South China	Namhwa hanin cheongnyeon yeonmaeng	Namhwa hanin ch'ŏngnyŏn yŏnmaeng	1930	번역 표준 원칙

NO	용어	한자	영문	RO	MC	시대 및 연도	출전
753	납북 월북 미술작가 규제해제	拉北 越北 美術作家 規制解除	removal of restrictions on works of artists abducted by North Korea or who went to the North voluntarily	Napbuk wolbuk misuljakga gyujehaeje	Nappuk wŏlbuk misuljakka kyujehaeje		번역 표준 원칙
754	납북자 송환교섭	拉北者 送還交涉	negotiations for repatriation of those kidnapped to North Korea	Napbukja songhwan gyoseop	Nappukcha songhwan kyosŏp		번역 표준 원칙
755	낮은 단계의 연방제안	낮은 段階의 聯邦制案	proposal for low-level South-North federation system	Najeun dangyeui yeonbangjean	Najŭn tan'gye-ŭi yŏnbangjean		번역 표준 원칙
756	내각	內閣	cabinet	Naegak	Naegak		번역 표준 원칙
757	내각책임제	內閣責任制	parliamentary system	Naegak chaegimje	Naegak ch'aegimje		번역 표준 원칙
758	내각책임제 개헌안	內閣責任制 改憲案	Bill for Constitutional Amendment to the Parliamentary System	Naegak Chaegimje Gaeheonan	Naegak ch'aegimje kaehŏnan		번역 표준 원칙
759	내각총리	內閣總理	prime minister	Naegak chongni	Naegak ch'ongni		번역 표준 원칙
760	내각최고인민회의	內閣最高人民會議	Supreme People's Assembly	Negak choego inmin hoeui	Naegak ch'oego inmin hoeŭi		번역 표준 원칙

NO	용어	한자	영문	RO	MC	시대 및 연도	출전
761	내무위원회	內務委員會	Home Affairs Committee	Naemu wiwonhoe	Naemu wiwonhoe	현대	송기중, 《한영우리문화용어집》, 지문당, 2001.
762	내선일체	內鮮一體	"Japan Proper and Korea form One Body"	Naeseon ilche	Naesŏn ilch'e	1937-1945	번역 표준 원칙
763	내외경제신문	內外經濟新聞	Naewoe Gyeongje (Naeway Economic Daily)	Naeoe gyeongje sinmun	Naeoe kyŏngje sinmun	1989-?	번역 표준 원칙
764	내장산국립공원	內藏山國立公園	Naejangsan National Park	Naejangsan gungnipgongwon	Naejangsan kungnipkongwŏn	?-?	번역 표준 원칙
765	내재적 발전론	內在的 發展論	internal development theory	Naejaejeok baljeonnon	Naejaejŏk paljŏnnon	1960-?	번역 표준 원칙
766	냅코 작전		NAPKO Project	NAPKO project	Naepko jakjeon	Naepk'o chakchŏn	국가보훈처, 「NAPKO Project OF OSS」 2001
767	냉전	冷戰	Cold War	Naengjeon	Naengjŏn	1945-1990	번역 표준 원칙
768	네거티브 리스트 시스템		negative list system	negative list system	Negeotibeu riseuteu siseutem	Negŏt'ibŭ risŭt'ŭ sisŭt'em	현대	번역 표준 원칙

- 116 -

NO	용어	한자	영문	RO	MC	시대 및 연도	출전
769	네이산 보고	Nathan 報告	"The Nathan Report: Reconstruction Plan for the Korean Economy"	Neisan bogo	Neisan pogo	1956	번역 표준 원칙
770	네이산 조사단	Nathan 調査團	Nathan Associates investigation team	Neisan josadan	Neisan chosadan		번역 표준 원칙
771	넥타이부대	necktie部隊	white collar demonstrators	Nektai budae	Nekt'ai pudae		번역 표준 원칙
772	노구교사건	蘆溝橋事件	Marco Polo Bridge Incident	Nogugyo sageon	Nogugyo sakŏn	1937	번역 표준 원칙
773	노근리 양민학살사건	老斤里 良民虐殺事件	Nogeunri Massacre	Nogeulli yangmin haksal sageon	Nogŭn-ri yangmin haksal sakŏn	1950	번역 표준 원칙
774	노농적위대	勞農赤衛隊	Worker-Peasant Red Guards	Nonong jeogwidae	Nonong chŏgwidae	1959-?	번역 표준 원칙
775	노동당 규약	勞動黨 規約	Regulations of the Workers' Party of Korea	Nodongdang gyuyak	Nodongdang kyuyak		번역 표준 원칙
776	노동당출판사	勞動黨出版社	Workers' Party of Korea Publishing Company	Nodongdang chulpansa	Nodongdang ch'ulp'ansa	1945-?	번역 표준 원칙

NO	용어	한자	영문	RO	MC	시대 및 연도	출전
777	노동법	勞動法	Labor Act	Nodongbeop	Nodongbŏp	1953-?	번역 표준 원칙
778	노동법 개악반대투쟁	勞動法 改惡反對鬪爭	protests against retrogressive revision of the Labor Act	Nodongbeop geak bandae tujaeng	Nodongpŏp kaeak pandae t'ujaeng		번역 표준 원칙
779	노동법 개정	勞動法 改定	Revision of the Labor Act	Nodongbeop gaejeong	Nodongpŏp kaejŏng	1980	번역 표준 원칙
780	노동부	勞動部	Ministry of Labor	Nodongbu	Nodongbu	1981-?	번역 표준 원칙
781	노동시장의 유연화	勞動市場의 柔軟化	flexible labor market	Nodong sijangui yuyeonhwa	Nodong sijang-ŭi yuyŏnhwa		번역 표준 원칙
782	노동신문	勞動新聞	*Rodong Sinmun (Workers' Daily)*	Nodong sinmun	Nodong sinmun	1949-현대	번역 표준 원칙
783	노동운동	勞動運動	labor movement	Nodong undong	Nodong undong	일제	번역 표준 원칙
784	노동위원회법	勞動委員會法	Labor Relations Commission Act	Nodong wiwonhoebeop	Nodong wiwŏnhoepŏp	1963	번역 표준 원칙

NO	용어	한자	영문	RO	MC	시대 및 연도	출전
785	노동쟁의	勞動爭議	labor disputes	Nodong jaengui	Nodong chaengŭi	일제	Ki-baik Lee, translated by Edward W. Wagner, A New History of Korea, Harvard University Press, 1984,
786	노동쟁의조정법	勞動爭議調整法	Labor Conflict Conciliation Act	Nodong jaengui jojeongbeop	Nodong chaengŭi chojŏngpŏp	1963-?	번역 표준 원칙
787	노동조합법	勞動組合法	Labor Union Act	Nodong johapbeop	Nodong chohappŏp	1963-?	번역 표준 원칙
788	노동조합설립운동	勞動組合設立運動	drive for the establishment of labor unions	Nodong johap seolip undong	Nodong johap sŏllip undong		번역 표준 원칙
789	노동집약적 산업화정책	勞動集約的 産業化政策	policy focusing on labor-intensive industries	Nodong jibyakjeok saneophwa jeongchaek	Nodong chibyakchŏk sanŏphwa chŏngch'aek		번역 표준 원칙
790	노령임시정부	露領臨時政府	Provisional Government of Korea in Vladivostok	Noryeong imsi jeongbu	Noryŏng imsi chŏngbu	1919	번역 표준 원칙
791	노무현 탄핵기각	盧武鉉 彈劾棄却	rejection of the impeachment motion against Roh Moo-hyun	Roh Moo-hyun tanhaekgigak	Nomuhyŏn tanaek kigak	2004	번역 표준 원칙
792	노무현 탄핵안	盧武鉉 彈劾案	impeachment motion against Roh Moo-hyun	Roh Moo-hyun tanhaekan	Nomuhyŏn tanaegan		번역 표준 원칙

NO	용어	한자	영문	RO	MC	시대 및 연도	출전
793	노무현-김정일 정상회담	盧武鉉-金正日 頂上會談	Inter-Korea Summit 2007: Roh Moo-hyun and Kim Jung-il Summit	Roh Moo-hyun - Kim Jeong-il jeongsang hoedam	Nomuhyŏn - Kim Chŏng-il chŏngsang hoedam		번역 표준 원칙
794	노사관계	勞使關係	labor-management relations	Nosa gwangye	Nosa kwangye		번역 표준 원칙
795	노사정위원회	勞使政委員會	Labor-Management-Government Tripartite Commission	Nosajeong wiwonhoe	Nosajŏng wiwŏnhoe	1998	번역 표준 원칙
796	노숙자	露宿者	homeless person	Nosukja	Nosukcha		번역 표준 원칙
797	노인공경	老人恭敬	respect for the elderly	Noin gonggyeong	Noin konggyŏng		번역 표준 원칙
798	노인문제	老人問題	elderly health and social issues	Noin munje	Noin munje		번역 표준 원칙
799	노조파업	勞組罷業	labor unrest	Nojo paeop	Nojo p'aŏp		번역 표준 원칙
800	노학연대	勞學連帶	student-labor solidarity	Nohak yeondae	Nohak yŏndae		번역 표준 원칙

NO	용어	한자	영문	RO	MC	시대 및 연도	출전
801	녹색성장 정책	綠色成長 政策	green growth policy	Noksaek seongjang jeongchaek	Noksaeng sŏngjang chŏngchaek		번역 표준 원칙
802	녹색신고제	綠色申告制	reporting system for agrichemicals used on agricultural imports	Noksaek singoje	Noksaek sin'goche		번역 표준 원칙
803	녹색연합	綠色聯合	Green Korea United	Noksaek yeonhap	Noksaek yŏnhap	1994	번역 표준 원칙
804	녹색혁명	綠色革命	Green Revolution	Noksaek hyeongmyeong	Noksaek hyŏngmyŏng		번역 표준 원칙
805	녹화사업	綠化事業	Nokhwa Project (conscription of student activists by the Chun Doo-hwan regime)	Nokhwa saeop	Nokhwa saŏp		번역 표준 원칙
806	농경지확충 5개년 계획	農耕地擴充 5個年 計劃	Five-year Plan for the Expansion of Farmland	Nonggyeongji hwakchung 5gaenyeon gyehoek	Nonggyŏngji hwakch'ung 5kaenyŏn kyehoek		번역 표준 원칙
807	농공병진정책	農工竝進政策	agriculture and industry parallel growth policy	Nonggong byeongjin jeongchaek	Nonggong pyŏngjin chŏngch'aek		번역 표준 원칙
808	농림수산식품부	農林水山食品部	Ministry of Food, Agriculture, Forestry and Fisheries	Nongnim susan sikpumbu	Nongnim susan sikp'umbu	2008	번역 표준 원칙

NO	용어	한자	영문	RO	MC	시대 및 연도	출전
809	농무부	農務部	Department of Agriculture	Nongmubu	Nongmubu	1946-1947	번역 표준 원칙
810	농민운동	農民運動	peasant movement	Nongmin undong	Nongmin undong	일제	번역 표준 원칙
811	농민전쟁	農民戰爭	peasant uprising	Nongmin jeonjaeng	Nongmin chŏnjaeng		번역 표준 원칙
812	농민조합	農民組合	Peasants Association	Nongmin johap	Nongmin chohap		번역 표준 원칙
813	농민조합운동	農民組合運動	Peasants Association Movement	Nongmin johap undong	Nongmin chohap undong	1926-1935	번역 표준 원칙
814	농민조합총연맹	農民組合總聯盟	Federation of Peasant Associations	Nongmin johap chongyeonmaeng	Nongmin chohap ch'ongyŏnmaeng	1945-	번역 표준 원칙
815	농어촌 고리대 정리사업	農漁村 高利貸 整理事業	freeze of interest payments on high-interest private loans to farmers	Nongeochon goridae jeongni saeop	Nongŏch'on koridae chŏngni saŏp		번역 표준 원칙
816	농어촌 소득증대	農漁村 所得增大	income growth in farming and fishing villages	Nongeuchon sodeuk jeungdae	Nongŏch'on sodŭk chŭngdae		번역 표준 원칙

NO	용어	한자	영문	RO	MC	시대 및 연도	출전
817	농어촌 전화사업	農漁村 電化事業	project to connect farming and fishing villages to electricity	Nongeochon jeonhwa saeop	Nongŏch'on chŏnhwa saŏp		번역 표준 원칙
818	농어촌근대화촉진법	農漁村近代化促進法	Act on Promoting the Modernization of Farming and Fishing Communities	Nongeochon geundaehwa chokjinbeop	Nongŏch'on kŭndaehwa ch'okchinpŏp		번역 표준 원칙
819	농어촌발전특별조치법	農漁村發展特別措置法	Act on Special Measures for Development of Agricultural and Fishing Villages	Nongeochon baljeon teukbyeol jochibeop	Nongŏch'on paljŏn t'ŭkpyŏl choch'ibŏp	1990-?	번역 표준 원칙
820	농어촌정비법	農漁村整備法	Act on the Advancement of Farming and Fishing Villages	Nongeochon jeongbibeop	Nongŏch'on chŏngbipŏp	1994	번역 표준 원칙
821	농업진흥청	農業振興廳	Agricultural Promotion Administration	Nongeop jinheungcheong	Nongŏp jinŭngch'ŏng		번역 표준 원칙
822	농업협동조합	農業協同組合	National Agricultural Cooperative Federation	Nongeop hyeopdong johap	Nongŏp hyŏptong johap	1961	번역 표준 원칙
823	농업협동화	農業協同化	agricultural cooperatives	Nongeop hyeopdonghwa	Nongŏp hyŏptonghwa	1953-1958	번역 표준 원칙
824	농지개간	農地開墾	farmland cultivation	Nongji gaegan	Nongji kaegan		번역 표준 원칙

NO	용어	한자	영문	RO	MC	시대 및 연도	출전
825	농지개혁	農地改革	farmland reform	Nongji gaehyeok	Nongji kaehyŏk	1949-1951	번역 표준 원칙
826	농지개혁법 시행령	農地改革法 施行令	Enforcement Order of the Farmland Reform Act	Nongji gaehyeokbeop sihaengnyeong	Nongji kaehyŏkpŏp sihaengnyŏng	1950	번역 표준 원칙
827	농지분배	農地分配	farmland distribution	Nongji bunbae	Nongji punbae	1950	번역 표준 원칙
828	농지상환	農地償還	farmland redemption	Nongji sanghwan	Nongji sanghwan	1953	번역 표준 원칙
829	농지위원회	農地委員會	Farmland Committee	Nongji wiwonhoe	Nongji wiwŏnhoe	1950	번역 표준 원칙
830	농촌계몽운동	農村啓蒙運動	Rural Enlightenment Movement	Nongchon gyemong undong	Nongch'on kyemong undong	일제	한국학중앙연구원, 《영문한국백과》-농촌계몽운동
831	농촌공동화	農村空洞化	hollowing-out of rural communities	Nongchon gongdonghwa	Nongch'on kongdonghwa		번역 표준 원칙
832	농촌근대화촉진법	農村近代化促進法	Act on Promoting the Modernization of Rural Areas	Nongchon geundaehwa chokjinbeop	Nongch'on kŭndaehwa ch'okchinpŏp	1970-1995	번역 표준 원칙

NO	용어	한자	영문	RO	MC	시대 및 연도	출전
833	농촌진흥운동	農村振興運動	Rural Revival Movement	Nongchon jinheung undong	Nongch'on chinhŭng undong	1932-1940	Ki-baik Lee, translated by Edward W. Wagner, A New History of Korea, Harvard University Press, 1984,
834	농촌진흥청	農村振興廳	Rural Development Administration (RDA)	Nongchon jinheungcheong	Nongch'on chinhŭngch'ŏng	1962-?	번역 표준 원칙
835	농촌활동	農村活動	activism in farming villages	Nongchon hwaldong	Nongch'on hwaldong	1970-?	번역 표준 원칙
836	뉴델리 밀담설	New Delhi 密談說	New Delhi Secret Conversation controversy	Nyudelli mildamseol	Nyudelli miltamsŏl		번역 표준 원칙
837	뉴욕 남북한영화제 개최	New York 南北韓映畵祭 開催	South-North Korean Film Festival in New York	Nyuyok nambukhan yeonghwaje gaechoe	Nyuyok nambukhanyŏnghwaje kaech'oe		번역 표준 원칙
838	능률의 극대화	能率의 極大化	maximization of efficiency	Neungnyului geukdaehwa	Nŭngnyurŭi Kŭktaehwa		번역 표준 원칙
839	니항 사건	泥港 事件	Nikolayevsk Incident of 1920	Nihang sageon	Nihang Sakŏn	1920	번역 표준 원칙
840	닉슨 독트린		Nixon Doctrine	Nixon Doctrine	Nikseun dokteurin	Niksŭn tokt'ŭrin	1969	번역 표준 원칙

NO	용어	한자	영문	RO	MC	시대 및 연도	출전
841	님비현상	NIMBY現象	not in my backyard (NIMBY) syndrome	Nimbi hyeonsang	Nimbi hyŏnsang		번역 표준 원칙
842	님의 침묵	님의 沈默	"Silence of the Beloved" (Nimui chimmuk), poem by Han Yong-un	Nim-ui chimmuk	Nim-ŭi ch'immuk	1926	번역 표준 원칙
843	다국적군	多國籍軍	Coalition Force, Muitinational Force	Dagukjeokgun	Tagukchŏkkun		번역 표준 원칙
844	다도해 해상국립공원	多島海 海上國立公園	Dadohaehaesang National Park	Dadohae haesang gungnip gongwon	Tadohae haesang kungnip kongwon	1981-?	번역 표준 원칙
845	다목적댐	多目的Dam	multipurpose dam	Damokjeok daem	Tamokchŏk taem		번역 표준 원칙
846	다문화 가정	多文化 家庭	multicultural family	Damunhwa gajeong	Tamunhwa kajŏng		번역 표준 원칙
847	다부동 전투	多富洞 戰鬪	Battle of Dabudong	Dabudong jeontu	Tabudong chŏnt'u	1950	번역 표준 원칙
848	다연장 로켓	多聯裝 Rocket	multiple rocket launcher	Dayeonjang roket	Tayŏnjang rok'et		번역 표준 원칙

NO	용어	한자	영문	RO	MC	시대 및 연도	출전
849	다자간 투자협정	多者間 投資協定	multilateral agreement on investment	Dajagan tuja hyeopjeong	Tajagan t'uja hyŏpchŏng	1960-	번역 표준 원칙
850	단계적 철수	段階的 撤收	phased withdrawal	Dangyejeok cheolsu	Tangyejŏk ch'ŏlsu		번역 표준 원칙
851	단군교	檀君敎	Dangungyo (worship of Dangun)	Dangungyo	Tan'gun'gyo	1910-?	번역 표준 원칙
852	단기수출금융	短期輸出金融	short-term export financing	Dangi suchul geumyung	Tan'gi such'ul kŭmyung		번역 표준 원칙
853	단기적인 투기적 자본	短期的인 投機的 資本	short-term investment capital	Dangijeokin tugijeok jabon	Tan'gijŏgin t'ugijŏk chabon		번역 표준 원칙
854	단기차관	短期借款	short-term loans	Dangi chagwan	Tan'gi ch'agwan		번역 표준 원칙
855	단발령	斷髮令	prohibition of topknots	Danballyeong	Tanballyŏng	1895	번역 표준 원칙
856	단선단정	單選單政	separate election and separate government	Danseon danjeong	Tansŏn tanjŏng		번역 표준 원칙

NO	용어	한자	영문	RO	MC	시대 및 연도	출전
857	단성사	團成社	Dansungsa Theater	Danseongsa	Tansŏngsa	1907-?	번역 표준 원칙
858	단원제	單院制	unicameral parliament system	Danwonje	Tanwŏnje		번역 표준 원칙
859	단일민족국가	單一民族國家	ethnically homogeneous nation	Danil minjok gukga	Tanil minjok kukka		번역 표준 원칙
860	단일변동환율제	單一變動換率制	single floating exchange rate system	Danil byeondong hwanyulje	Tanil byŏndong hwanyulje	1964-1980	번역 표준 원칙
861	단자회사	短資會社	short-term investment finance company	Danja hoesa	Tanja hoesa		번역 표준 원칙
862	단장의 능선 전투	斷腸의 稜線 戰鬪	Battle of Heartbreak Ridge	Danjang-ui neungseon jeontu	Tanjang-ŭi nŭngsŏn chŏnt'u	1951	번역 표준 원칙
863	단장의 미아리고개	斷腸의 彌阿里고개	"Miari Pass of Pain" ("Danjang-ui Miari Gogae"), sung by Lee Hae-yeon, 1956	Danjangui miari gogae	Tanchang-ŭi miari kogae	1956	번역 표준 원칙
864	단종애사	端宗哀史	"The Tragedy of King Danjong" ("Danjong aesa"), movie directed by Jeon Chang-geun, 1956	Danjongaesa	Tanjongaesa	1956	번역 표준 원칙

NO	용어	한자	영문	RO	MC	시대 및 연도	출전
865	단지동맹(단지회)	斷指同盟(斷指會)	Society of the Cut Finger (group of patriots)	Danji dongmaeng	Tanji tongmaeng	1909	번역 표준 원칙
866	단파방송 밀청사건	短波放送 密聽事件	arrests for secretly listening to shortwave broadcasts (Voice of America)	Danpa bangsong milcheong sageon	Tanp'a pangsong milch'ŏng sakŏn	1942-1943	번역 표준 원칙
867	달동네	달동네	poor hillside village	Daldongne	Taltongne		번역 표준 원칙
868	달러위기	dollar危機	U.S. dollar crisis	Dalleo wigi	Tallŏ wigi		번역 표준 원칙
869	당 대표자대회	黨 代表者大會	Korean Workers' Party Representatives Convention	Dangdaepyoja daehoe	Tangdaep'yoja taehoe		번역 표준 원칙
870	당 정치위원회	黨 政治委員會	Political Committee of the Korean Workers' Party	Dang jeongchi wiwonhoe	Tang chŏngch'i wiwŏnhoe		번역 표준 원칙
871	당 중앙검사위원회	黨 中央檢査委員會	Korean Workers' Party Central Auditing Committee	Dang jungang geomsa wiwonhoe	Tang chungang kŏmsa wiwŏnhoe		번역 표준 원칙
872	당 중앙군사위원회	黨 中央軍事委員會	Military Committee of the Party Center	Dang jungang gunsa wiwonhoe	Tang chungang kunsa wiwŏnhoe	1962-?	번역 표준 원칙

NO	용어	한자	영문	RO	MC	시대 및 연도	출전
873	당 중앙위원회	黨 中央委員會	Central Committee of the Korean Workers' Party	Dang jungang wiwonhoe	Tang chungang wiwŏnhoe	1946-?	번역 표준 원칙
874	당대회	黨大會	Party Congress	Dangdaehoe	Tangdaehoe	1946	Ki-baik Lee, translated by Edward W. Wagner, A New History of Korea, Harvard University Press, 1984,
875	당백전	當百錢	Dangbaekjeon (100-*jeon* coin)	Dangbaekjeon	Tangbaekchŏn	1866	번역 표준 원칙
876	당세포	黨細胞	Party Cell	Dangsepo	Tangsep'o	1945-?	번역 표준 원칙
877	당오전	當五錢	Dangojeon (5-*jeon* coin)	Dangojeon	Tangojŏn	1883-1894	번역 표준 원칙
878	당인리발전소	唐人里發電所	Danginri Power Station	Dangilli baljeonso	Tangilli paljŏnso	1930-?	번역 표준 원칙
879	당포함 피격사건	唐浦艦 被擊事件	Shooting of the PCE-56 Patrol Craft	Dangpoham pigyeok sageon	Tangp'oham p'igyŏk sakŏn	1967	번역 표준 원칙
880	대가족	大家族	extended family	Daegajok	Taegajok		번역 표준 원칙

NO	용어	한자	영문	RO	MC	시대 및 연도	출전
881	대공 육안감시소	對空 肉眼監視所	Air Observation Post (AOP)	Daegong yugan gamsiso	Taegong yugan gamsiso		번역 표준 원칙
882	대공산권 봉쇄정책	對共産圈 封鎖政策	Communism containment policy	Daegongsan-gwon bongswae Jeongchaek	Taegongsankwŏn pongswae chŏngch'aek		번역 표준 원칙
883	대공포	對空砲	anti-aircraft gun	Daegongpo	Taegongp'o		번역 표준 원칙
884	대구 10·1 폭동사건	大邱 10·1 暴動事件	Daegu October 1 Incident	Daegu 10·1 pokdong sageon	Taegu 10·1 p'oktong sakŏn	1946	번역 표준 원칙
885	대구 10월사건	大邱 10月事件	Daegu October 1 riots (1946)	Daegu 10wol sageon	Taegu 10wŏl sakŏn	1946	번역 표준 원칙
886	대구 대한방직쟁의	大邱 大韓紡織爭議	labor struggle by Taihan Textile workers in Daegu	Degu dehan bangjik jaengui	Taegu taehan pangjik chaengŭi		번역 표준 원칙
887	대구 세계육상선수권대회	大邱 世界陸上選手權大會	2011 Athletics World Championships in Daegu	Daegu segye yuksang seonsugwon daehoe	Taegu segye yuksang sŏnsukwŏn taehoe	2011	번역 표준 원칙
888	대구 유니버시아드	大邱 Universiade	2003 Summer Universiade in Daegu	Daegu yunibeosiadeu	Taegu yunibŏsiadŭ	2003	번역 표준 원칙

NO	용어	한자	영문	RO	MC	시대 및 연도	출전
889	대구 지하철 가스폭발	大邱 地下鐵 Gas爆發	gas explosion at a subway construction site in Daegu, 1995	Daegu jihacheol gaseu pokbal	taegu chihachŏl kasŭ p'okp'al	1995	번역 표준 원칙
890	대구광역시	大邱廣域市	Daegu Metropolitan City	Daegu gwangyeoksi	Taegu kwangyŏksi	1995-?	번역 표준 원칙
891	대구매일신문 습격사건	大邱每日新聞 襲擊事件	attack on *Maeil Shinmun* office in Daegu	Daegu maeilsinmun seupgyeok sageon	Taegu maeilsinmun sŭ pkyŏk sagŏn	1955	번역 표준 원칙
892	대구부산고속도로	大邱釜山高速道路	Daegu-Busan Expressway	Daegu busan gosokdoro	Taegu pusan kosoktoro		번역 표준 원칙
893	대기성차관자금	待期性借款資金	stand-by loans	Daegiseong chagwan jageum	Taegisŏng ch'agwan chagŭm		번역 표준 원칙
894	대기업집단	大企業集團	business group	Daegieop jipdan	Taegiŏp chiptan		번역 표준 원칙
895	대기환경보전법	大氣環境保全法	Clean Air Conservation Act	Daegi hwangyeong bojeonbeop	Taegi hwangyŏng pojŏ npŏp	공포일 2011 시행일 2012	번역 표준 원칙
896	대남사업총정치국	對南事業總政治局	actions against the South by the General Political Bureau	Daenam saeop chong jeongchiguk	Taenam saŏp ch'ongjŏ ngch'iguk		번역 표준 원칙

NO	용어	한자	영문	RO	MC	시대 및 연도	출전
897	대대	大隊	Battalion	Daedae	Daedae	1950	번역 표준 원칙
898	대덕벨리	大德valley	Daedeok Valley	Daeduk belli	Taedŏk pelli		번역 표준 원칙
899	대덕연구단지	大德硏究團地	Daedeok Research Complex	Daedeok yeongu danji	Taedŏk yŏn'gu tanji	1978	번역 표준 원칙
900	대독일선전포고	對獨逸宣戰布告	declaration of war against Germany	Daedogil seonjeon pogo	Taedogil sŏnjŏn p'ogo		번역 표준 원칙
901	대동공보	大同公報	The New Korean Worldwide (Daedong Gongbo)	Daedonggongbo	Taedongkongbo	1907-1909	번역 표준 원칙
902	대동단결선언	大同團結宣言	Declaration of the Solidarity of the Korean People	Daedong dangyeol seoneon	Taedong tan'gyŏl sŏnŏn	1917	번역 표준 원칙
903	대동보국회	大同保國會	United Korean Reform Association (Daedong Bogukhoe)	Daedong bogukhoe	Taedong pogukhoe	1907	번역 표준 원칙
904	대동상회	大同商會	Daedong Trading Company	Daedong sanghoe	Taedong sanghoe	1905	번역 표준 원칙

NO	용어	한자	영문	RO	MC	시대 및 연도	출전
905	대동아공영권	大東亞共榮圈	Greater East Asia Co-Prosperity Sphere	Daedonga gongyeonggwon	Taedonga kongyŏngkwŏn	1940-1945	Han Woo-Keun, translated by Kyung-Shik Lee, The History of Korea, Eul-Yoo Pub, 1970, p.493.
906	대동아전쟁	大東亞戰爭	Greater East Asia War	Daedonga jeonjaeng	Taedonga chŏnjaeng	1941-1945	번역 표준 원칙
907	대동청년단	大同靑年團	Daedong Youth Corps	Daedong cheongnyeondan	Taedong ch'ŏngnyŏndan	1947-1948	번역 표준 원칙
908	대동합방론	大同合邦論	Union of the Great East (Daito Gappo-ron)	Daedong hapbangnon	Taedong happangnon		번역 표준 원칙
909	대량기습 선제공격	大量奇襲 先制攻擊	large-scale preemptive and surprise attack	Daeryang giseup seonjegonggyeok	Taeryang kisŭp sŏnje konggyŏk		번역 표준 원칙
910	대량보복전략	大量報復戰略	Massive Retaliation Strategy	Daeryang bobok jeollyak	Taeryang bobok chŏllyak		번역 표준 원칙
911	대량살상무기	大量殺傷武器	weapons of mass destruction (WMD)	Daeryang salsang mugi	Taeryang salsang mugi		번역 표준 원칙
912	대례의궤	大禮儀軌	State Record of Emperor Gojong's Coronation (Daerye Uigwe)	Daerye uigwe	Taerye ŭigwe	1897	번역 표준 원칙

NO	용어	한자	영문	RO	MC	시대 및 연도	출전
913	대륙간탄도탄	大陸間彈導彈	Intercontinental Ballistic Missile (ICBM)	Daeryuk gan tandotan	Taeryuk kan t'andotan		번역 표준 원칙
914	대륙낭인	大陸浪人	prewar Japanese adventurers (political activists) in mainland China	Daeryuk nangin	Taeryuk nangin		번역 표준 원칙
915	대륙병참기지화	大陸兵站基地化	imperial Japan's policy to turn Korea into a military base	Daeryuk byeongcham gijihwa	Taeryuk pyŏngch'am kijihwa	1931-1945	번역 표준 원칙
916	대륙식산회사	大陸殖産會社	Continent Industrial Co.	Daeryuk siksan hoesa	Taeryuk siksa hoesa		번역 표준 원칙
917	대리투표	代理投票	proxy vote	Daeri tupyo	Taeri t'up'yo		번역 표준 원칙
918	대마도	對馬島	Tsushima Island	Daemado	Taemado		번역 표준 원칙
919	대마도 해전	對馬島 海戰	Battle of Tsushima	Daemado haejeon	Taemado haejŏn		번역 표준 원칙
920	대마초	大麻草	marijuana / cannabis	Daemacho	Taemach'o		번역 표준 원칙

NO	용어	한자	영문	RO	MC	시대 및 연도	출전
921	대만 단교선언	臺灣 斷交宣言	Taiwan's announcement of severance of diplomatic relations with South Korea in 1992	Daeman dangyo seoneon	taeman tan'gyo sŏnŏn		번역 표준 원칙
922	대목장	大木匠	*daemokjang* (builder of traditional wooden architecture)	Daemokjang	Taemokchang		번역 표준 원칙
923	대민지원	對民支援	Military Support to Civil Authority (MSCA)	Daemin jiwon	Taemin chiwŏn		번역 표준 원칙
924	대법원	大法院	Supreme Court of Korea	Daebeopwon	Taebŏbwŏn	1948-?	번역 표준 원칙
925	대보름	大보름	Daeboreum (fifteenth day of the first lunar month)	Daeboreum	Taeborŭm		번역 표준 원칙
926	대북 비밀송금	對北 秘密送金	secret fund remittance to North Korea	Daebuk bimil songgeum	Taebuk pimil songgŭm		번역 표준 원칙
927	대북 식량차관	對北 食糧借款	food loan to North Korea (providing food grain in the form of a long-term loan)	Daebuk singnyang chagwan	Taebuk singnyang ch'agwan	2000-	번역 표준 원칙
928	대북한 경제우위	對北韓 經濟優位	(Seoul's) economic supremacy over Pyongyang	Daebukhan gyeongje uwi	Taebukhan kyŏngje uwi		번역 표준 원칙

NO	용어	한자	영문	RO	MC	시대 및 연도	출전
929	대비정규전	對非正規戰	counter unconventional warfare	Daebi jeonggyujeon	Taebi jŏnggyujŏn		번역 표준 원칙
930	대성학교	大成學校	Daeseong School	Daeseong hakgyo	Taesŏng hakkyo	1908-1912	번역 표준 원칙
931	대양보	大洋報	*Daeyangbo (The Ocean News)*	Daeyangbo	Taeyangbo		번역 표준 원칙
932	대외군사판매	對外軍事販賣	Foreign Military Sale (FMS)	Daeoe gunsa panmae	Taewoe gunsa p'anmae		번역 표준 원칙
933	대외신뢰도	對外信賴度	market confidence	Daeoe silloedo	Taeoe silloedo		번역 표준 원칙
934	대외채무지급불능 사태	對外債務支給不能 事態	foreign debt default	Daeoe chaemu jigeup bulneung satae	Taeoe ch'aemu chigŭp pullŭng sat'ae		번역 표준 원칙
935	대우그룹 베트남공장	大宇Group Vietnam工場	Daewoo Group plant in Vietnam	Daeu geurup beteunam gongjang	Taeu gŭrup petŭnam gongjang		번역 표준 원칙
936	대우자동차 파업투쟁	大宇自動車 罷業鬪爭	Daewoo Motors workers' strike	Daeu jadongcha paeop tujaeng	Taeu chadongch'a p'aŏp t'ujaeng	1985	번역 표준 원칙

NO	용어	한자	영문	RO	MC	시대 및 연도	출전
937	대운하사업	大運河事業	Grand Canal Project	Daeunha saeop	Daeunha saŏp		번역 표준 원칙
938	대원군	大院君	Daewongun (Prince regent, father of King Gojong)	Daewongun	Taewŏn'gun	1820 ~ 1898	번역 표준 원칙
939	대원군 하야	大院君 下野	Daewongun's removal from power	Daewongun haya	Taewŏn'gun haya	1873	번역 표준 원칙
940	대일선전포고	對日宣傳布告	official proclamation of war against Japan	Daeil seonjeon pogo	Taeil sŏnjŏn p'ogo	1941	번역 표준 원칙
941	대일청구권 문제	對日請求權 問題	issue of Japan's compensation for itscolonial rule of Korea	Daeil cheonggugwon munje	Taeil ch'ŏnggukwŏn munje	1945-?	번역 표준 원칙
942	대일청구권 자금	對日請求權 資金	Japan's compensation for its colonial rule of Korea	Daeil cheonggugwon jageum	Taeil ch'ŏnggukwŏn chagŭm		번역 표준 원칙
943	대일청구권 관리위원회	對日請求權 管理委員會	Commission for the Management of Compensation from Japan for Its Colonial Rule of Korea	Daeil cheonggugwon gwalli wiwonhoe	Taeil ch'ŏnggukwŏn kwalli wiwŏnhoe		번역 표준 원칙
944	대장금	大長今	"Jewel in the Palace" ("Daejanggeum"), TV drama series from 2003	Daejanggeum	Taejanggŭm	2003	번역 표준 원칙

NO	용어	한자	영문	RO	MC	시대 및 연도	출전
945	대전광역시	大田廣城市	Daejeon Metropolitan City	Daejeon gwangyeoksi	Taejŏn kwangyŏksi	1995-?	번역 표준 원칙
946	대전남부 순환고속도로	大田南部 循環高速道路	Daejeon Southern Beltway	Daejeon nambu sunhwan gosokdoro	Taejŏn nambu sunhwan kosoktoro	2001	번역 표준 원칙
947	대전자령전투	大甸子嶺戰鬪	Battle of Daidianziling	Daejeon jaryeong jeontu	Taejŏn jaryŏng chŏnt'u	1933	번역 표준 원칙
948	대전전투	大田戰鬪	Battle of Daejeon	Daejeon jeontu	Taechŏn chŏnt'u	1950	번역 표준 원칙
949	대전차방어	對戰車防禦	anti-tank defense	Daejeoncha bangeo	Taejŏnch'a bangŏ		번역 표준 원칙
950	대전회통	大典會通	Comprehensive Collection of National Codes (Daejeon Hoetong)	Daejeon hoetong	Taejŏn hoet'ong	1865	한국학중앙연구원, 《영문한국백과》-법제
951	대조선공화국	大朝鮮共和國	Korean National Independence League	Daejoseon gonghwaguk	Taejosŏn konghwaguk	1919	번역 표준 원칙
952	대조선국민군	大朝鮮國民軍	Korean Military Corporation	Daejoseon gungmingun	Taejosŏn kungmingun		번역 표준 원칙

NO	용어	한자	영문	RO	MC	시대 및 연도	출전
953	대조선국민군단	大朝鮮國民軍團	Korean National Brigade	Daejoseon gungmin gundan	Taejosŏn kungmin gundan	1914-?	번역 표준 원칙
954	대조선국민군단사관학교	大朝鮮國民軍團士官學校	Korean Millitary Academy (in Hawaii)	Daejoseon gungmin gundan sagwan hakgyo	Taejosŏn kungmin gundan sagwan hakkyo		번역 표준 원칙
955	대조선독립단	大朝鮮獨立團	Korean National Independence League	Daejoseon dongnipdan	Taejosŏn tongniptan	1919-1933	번역 표준 원칙
956	대종교	大倧敎	Daejonggyo (indigenous South Korean religion worshipping Dangun)	Daejonggyo	taejonggyo	1909-?	번역 표준 원칙
957	대종교총본사	大倧敎總本司	Headquarters of Daejonggyo (indigenous religion worshipping Dangun)	Daejonggyo chongbonsa	Taejonggyo ch'ongbonsa	근대	번역 표준 원칙
958	대종상	大鐘賞	Daejong Film Award	Daejongsang	Taejongsang	1961-?	번역 표준 원칙
959	대중가요	大衆歌謠	Korean pop song (music)	Daejung gayo	Taejung kayo	1950~80년대	번역 표준 원칙
960	대중경제론	大衆經濟論	President Kim Dae-jung's theory of mass participatory economy	Daejung gyeongjeron	Taejung kyŏngjeron		번역 표준 원칙

NO	용어	한자	영문	RO	MC	시대 및 연도	출전
961	대중문화	大衆文化	popular culture	Daejung munhwa	Taejung munhwa		번역 표준 원칙
962	대중음악	大衆音樂	popular music	Daejung eumak	Taejung ŭmak		한국학중앙연구원,《영문한국백과》·음악
963	대청다목적댐	大淸多目的Dam	Daecheong multi-purpose dam	Daecheong damokjeokdaem	Taech'ŏng damokchŏk taem	1980.12.	번역 표준 원칙
964	대체에너지	代替Energy	alternative energy	Daeche eneoji	Taech'e enŏji		번역 표준 원칙
965	대충자금	對充資金	counterpart fund	Daechungjageum	Taech'ungjagŭm	1953-1968	번역 표준 원칙
966	대통령 7년 단임제	大統領 7年 單任制	single seven-year presidential term	Daetongnyeong 7nyeon danimje	Taet'ongnyŏng 7nyŏn tanimje		번역 표준 원칙
967	대통령 간선제	大統領 間選制	indirect presidential election	Daetongnyeong ganseonje	Taet'ongnyŏng kansŏnje		번역 표준 원칙
968	대통령 권한대행	大統領 權限代行	acting president	Daetongnyeong gwonhan daehaeng	Taet'ongnyŏng kwŏnhan taehaeng		번역 표준 원칙

NO	용어	한자	영문	RO	MC	시대 및 연도	출전
969	대통령 선거	大統領 選擧	presidential election	Daetongnyeong seongeo	Taet'ongnyŏng sŏn'gŏ		번역 표준 원칙
970	대통령 선거인단	大統領 選擧人團	electoral college for presidential elections	Daetongnyeong seongeo indan	Taet'ongnyŏng sŏn'gŏ indan		번역 표준 원칙
971	대통령 직선제	大統領 直選制	direct presidential election	Daetongnyeong jikseonje	Taet'ongnyŏng chiksŏnje	1987-?	번역 표준 원칙
972	대통령 직선제 개헌 1000만명 서명운동	大統領 直選制 改憲 1000萬名 署名運動	1986 campaign to collect 10 million signatures for constitutional amendment to allow direct presidential elections	Daetongnyeong jikseonje gaeheon 1000man seomyeong undong	Taet'ongnyŏng chiksŏnje kaehŏn 1000man myŏng sŏmyŏng undong	1986	번역 표준 원칙
973	대통령실	大統領室	Presidential Office	Daetongnyeongsil	Taet'ongnyŏngsang		번역 표준 원칙
974	대통령직 인수위원회	大統領職 引受委員會	Presidential Transition Committee	Daetongnyeongjik insu wiwonhoe	Taet'ongnyŏngjik insu wiwonhoe		번역 표준 원칙
975	대학가요제	大學歌謠祭	University Song Festival	Daehak gayoje	Taehak kayoje	1978	번역 표준 원칙
976	대학교수단 데모	大學敎授團 示威	demonstration by university professors in 1960	Daehak gyosudan demo	Taehak kyosudan temo	1960	번역 표준 원칙

NO	용어	한자	영문	RO	MC	시대 및 연도	출전
977	대학박물관	大學博物館	university museum	Daehak bangmulgwan	Taehak pangmulgwan		번역 표준 원칙
978	대학본고사 폐지	大學本考查 廢止	abolition of university-administered admission examination	Daehak bongosa pyeji	Taehak pon'gosa p'yeji		번역 표준 원칙
979	대학수학능력시험	大學修學能力試驗	College Scholastic Ability Test (CSAT)	Daehak suhak neungnyeok siheom	Taehak suhak nŭngnyŏk sihŏm	1994	번역 표준 원칙
980	대학입학예비고사	大學入學豫備考查	Preliminary Exam for College Admission	Daehak iphak yebigosa	Taehak ip'ak yebigosa	1969-1981	번역 표준 원칙
981	대학입학학력고사	大學入學學力考查	national college entrance examination	Daehak iphak hangnyeokgosa	Taehak ip'ak hangnyŏkkosa	1982-1993	번역 표준 원칙
982	대학평가인정제	大學評價認定制	university accreditation system	Daehak pyeongga injeongje	Taehak p'yŏngga anjŏngje		번역 표준 원칙
983	대한경제원조	對韓經濟援助	economic assistance to the ROK	Daehan gyeongje wonjo	Taehan kyŏngje wŏnjo		번역 표준 원칙
984	대한광복군정부	大韓光復軍政府	Government of the Korean Restoration Army	Daehan gwangbokgun jeongbu	Taehan kwangbokkun chŏngbu	1914	번역 표준 원칙

NO	용어	한자	영문	RO	MC	시대 및 연도	출전
985	대한광복회	大韓光復會	Korea Liberation Corps	Daehan gwangbokhoe	Taehan kwangbokhoe	1915-1918	번역 표준 원칙
986	대한국국제	大韓國國制	Constitution of the Great Han Empire	Daehangukgukje	Taehan'gukkukche	1899-1910	번역 표준 원칙
987	대한국민군	大韓國民軍	Korean National Army (independence army)	Daehan gungmingun	Taehan kungmingun	1920-?	번역 표준 원칙
988	대한국민대표 민주의원	大韓國民代表民主議院	Korean Peoples Representative Democracy Parliament	Daehan gungmin daepyo minju uiwon	Taehan kungmin taep'yo minju ŭiwŏn	1946	번역 표준 원칙
989	대한국민의회	大韓國民議會	National Council of Korea (in Vladivostok)	daehanin gungminhoe	Taehan kungmin ŭihoe	1919	번역 표준 원칙
990	대한국민회	大韓國民會	Korean National Association	Daehan gungminhoe	Taehan kungminhoe	1910-?	Robert E. Buswell & Timothy S. Lee. Christianity in Korea, Honolulu: University of Hawaii Press,
991	대한국제	大韓國制	Charter of the Great Han Empire	Daehangukje	Taehangukche		번역 표준 원칙
992	대한국제경제협의체	對韓國際經濟協議體	International Economic Consultative Organization for Korea	Daehan gukje gyeongje hyeobuiche	Taehan kukche kyŏngje hyŏbŭich'e	1966	번역 표준 원칙

NO	용어	한자	영문	RO	MC	시대 및 연도	출전
993	대한국제법학회	大韓國際法學會	Korean International Law Society	Daehan gukje beophakhoe	Taehan kukche pŏphakhoe	1956-?	번역 표준 원칙
994	대한국제제철차관단	大韓製鐵國際借款團	Korean International Steel Association (KISA)	Daehan gukje jecheol chagwandan	Taehan kukche chech'ŏl ch'agwandan	1966	번역 표준 원칙
995	대한군정서	大韓軍政署	Korean Army Command	Daehan gunjeongseo	Taehan kunjŏngsŏ	1919	번역 표준 원칙
996	대한노동조합총연합	大韓勞動組合總聯合	Federation of Korean Trade Unions	Daehan nodong johap chongnyeonhap	Taehan nodong chohap ch'ongnyŏnhap	1946-1960	번역 표준 원칙
997	대한독립군	大韓獨立軍	Korean Independence Army	Daehan dongnipgun	Taehan tongnipkun	1919-1920	Peter H. Lee, Sourcebook of Korean Civilization(Volume 2), Columbia University Press, 1993,
998	대한독립단	大韓獨立團	Korean Independence Corps	Daehan dongnipdan	Taehan tongniptan	1919-1920	한국학중앙연구원, 《영문한국백과》-간도
999	대한독립선언서	大韓獨立宣言書	Korean Declaration of Independence in Manchuria	Daehan dongnip seoneonseo	Taehan tongnip sŏnŏnsŏ	1919	번역 표준 원칙
1000	대한독립의군부	大韓獨立義軍府	Righteous Army for Korean Independence	Daehan dongnip uigunbu	Taehan tongnip ŭigunbu	1912-1914	번역 표준 원칙

NO	용어	한자	영문	RO	MC	시대 및 연도	출전
1001	대한독립촉성국민회	大韓獨立促成國民會	Great Korean Independence Acceleration Council	Daehan dongnip chokseong gungminhoe	Taehan tongnip ch'oksŏng kungminhoe	1946	번역 표준 원칙
1002	대한독립촉성노동총동맹	大韓獨立促成勞動總同盟	General Federation of Korean Labor Unions	Daehan dongnip chokseong nodong chongdongmaeng	Taehan tongnip ch'oksŏng nodong ch'ongdongmaeng	1946-1960	번역 표준 원칙
1003	대한매일신보	大韓每日申報	*Daehan Maeil Sinbo (The Korea Daily News)*	Daehanmaeil-sinbo	Taehanmaeil-sinbo	1904-1910	번역 표준 원칙
1004	대한무역진흥공사	大韓貿易振興公社	Korea Trade-Investment Promotion Agency (KOTRA)	Daehan muyeok jinheung gongsa	Taehan muyŏk chinhŭng kongsa	1962-?	번역 표준 원칙
1005	대한민국 IT 봉사단	大韓民國 IT 奉仕團	Korea IT Volunteer Program (KIV)	Daehanminguk IT bongsadan	Taehanmin'guk IT pongsadan		번역 표준 원칙
1006	대한민국 거류민단	大韓民國 居留民團	Association of Korean Residents in Japan (who support the Republic of Korea)	Daehanminguk georyu mindan	Taehanmin'guk kŏryumindan	1948-?	번역 표준 원칙
1007	대한민국 건국 강령	大韓民國 建國 綱領	basic principles and policies for the establishment of the Republic of Korea	Daehanminguk geonguk gangnyeong	Taehanmin'guk kŏn'guk kangnyŏng	1941	번역 표준 원칙
1008	대한민국 관보 제1호	大韓民國 官報 第1號	*ROK Official Gazette*, No. 1.	Daehanminguk gwanbo je1ho	Taehanmin'guk kwanbo che1ho	1948	번역 표준 원칙

NO	용어	한자	영문	RO	MC	시대 및 연도	출전
1009	대한민국 국악제	大韓民國 國樂祭	Korean Traditional Performing Arts Festival	Daehanminguk gugakje	Taehanmin'guk kugakche	1981-?	번역 표준 원칙
1010	대한민국 국회	大韓民國 國會	National Assembly of the Republic of Korea	Daehanminguk gukhoe	Taehanminguk kukhoe	1948-	대한민국 국회 공식 사이트 http://www.assembly.go.kr
1011	대한민국 산업교통 지도	大韓民國 産業交通 地圖	map of Korea's major industrial facilities and transportation networks	Daehanminguk saneop gyotong jido	Taehanmin'guk sanŏp kyot'ong chido	1952	번역 표준 원칙
1012	대한민국 애국부인회	大韓民國 愛國婦人會	Korean Women's Patriotic Association	Daehanminguk aeguk buinhoe	Taehanmin'guk aeguk puinhoe	1919	번역 표준 원칙
1013	대한민국 역사박물관	大韓民國 歷史博物館	National Museum of Korean Contemporary History	Daehanminguk yeoksa bangmulgwan	Taehanminguk yŏksa pangmulgwan	2012예정	번역 표준 원칙
1014	대한민국 임시약헌	大韓民國 臨時約憲	Provisional Constitution of Korea	Daehanminguk imsi yakheon	Taehanmin'guk imsi yakhŏn	1927(제3차 개헌), 1940(제4차 개헌)	번역 표준 원칙
1015	대한민국 임시의정원	大韓民國 臨時議政院	Provisional Legislative Assembly	Daehanminguk imsi uijeongwon	Taehanmin'guk imsi ŭijŏngwŏn	1919	번역 표준 원칙
1016	대한민국 임시정부 연통제	大韓民國 臨時政府 聯通制	special liaison system of the Provisional Government of the Republic of Korea	Daehanminguk imsijeongbu yeontongje	Taehanmin'guk imsi chŏngbu yŏnt'ongje	1919-1921	번역 표준 원칙

NO	용어	한자	영문	RO	MC	시대 및 연도	출전
1017	대한민국 임시헌법	大韓民國 臨時憲法	Provisional Constitution of the Republic of Korea	Daehanminguk imsi heonbeop	Taehanmin'guk imsi hŏnpŏp	1919(제1차 개헌), 1925(제2차 개헌)	번역 표준 원칙
1018	대한민국 임시헌장	大韓民國 臨時憲章	Tentative Constitution of the Provisional Government of the Republic of Korea	Daehanminguk imsi heonjang	Taehanmin'guk imsi hŏnjang	1919	번역 표준 원칙
1019	대한민국 초대 내각	大韓民國 初代 內閣	first cabinet of the ROK Government	Daehanminguk chodae naegak	Taehanmin'guk ch'odae naegak	1948	번역 표준 원칙
1020	대한민국 파리위원부	大韓民國 Paris委員部	Provisional Government of the Republic of Korea's Commission for Paris	Daehanminguk pari wiwonbu	Taehanmin'guk p'ari wiwŏnbu	1919-1923	번역 표준 원칙
1021	대한민국 헌법	大韓民國 憲法	the Constitution of the Republic of Korea	Daehanminguk heonbeop	Taehanmin'guk hŏnpŏp	1948	번역 표준 원칙
1022	대한민국 헌법 공포	大韓民國 憲法 公布	promulgation of the Constitution of the Republic of Korea	Daehanminguk heonbeop gongpo	Taehanmin'guk hŏnpŏp kongp'o	1948	번역 표준 원칙
1023	대한민국과 일본국 간의 기본 관계에 관한 조약	大韓民國과 日本國 間의 基本 關係에 關한 條約	Treaty on Basic Relations between the Republic of Korea and Japan	Daehanmingukgwa ilbonguk ganui gibon gwangye-e gwanhan joyak	Taehanmin'guk-kwa ilbon'gukkan-ŭi kibon kwankye-e kwanhan choyak	1965	번역 표준 원칙
1024	대한민국수립	大韓民國樹立	establishment of the Republic of Korea	Daehanminguk surip	Taehanminguk surip	1948	번역 표준 원칙

NO	용어	한자	영문	RO	MC	시대 및 연도	출전
1025	대한민국임시정부	大韓民國臨時政府	Korean Provisional Government / Provisional Government of the Republic of Korea	Daehanminguk imsi jeongbu	Taehanmin'guk imsi chŏngbu	1919 ~ 1945	번역 표준 원칙
1026	대한민국임시정부 교통국	大韓民國臨時政府 交通局	Transportation Bureau, Provisional Government of the Republic of Korea	Daehanminguk imsi jeongbu gyotongguk	Taehanmin'guk imsi chŏngbu kyot'ongguk	1919-1921	번역 표준 원칙
1027	대한민국임시정부 국내공작위원회	大韓民國臨時政府 國內工作委員會	Covert Operations Committee, Provisional Government of the Republic of Korea	Daehanminguk imsi jeongbu guknae gongjak wiwonhoe	Taehanmin'guk imsi chŏngbu kungnae kongjak wiwŏnhoe		번역 표준 원칙
1028	대한민국임시정부 군사위원회	大韓民國臨時政府 軍事委員會	Military Committee, Provisional Government of the Republic of Korea	Daehanminguk imsi jeongbu gunsa wiwonhoe	Taehanmin'guk imsi chŏngbu kunsa wiwŏnhoe		번역 표준 원칙
1029	대한민국임시정부 군사특파단	大韓民國臨時政府 軍事特派團	Military Dispatch Unit, Provisional Government of the Republic of Korea	Daehanminguk imsi jeongbu gunsa teukpadan	Taehanmin'guk imsi chŏngbu kunsa t'ŭkp'adan	1938-1940	번역 표준 원칙
1030	대한민국임시정부 사료조사편찬회	大韓民國臨時政府 史料調査編纂會	Historical Research and Compilation Committee, Provisional Government of the Republic of Korea	Daehanminguk imsi jeongbu saryo josa pyeonchanhoe	Taehanmin'guk imsi chŏngbu saryo chosa p'yŏnch'anhoe	1919	번역 표준 원칙
1031	대한민국임시정부 육군 무관학교	大韓民國臨時政府 陸軍 武官學校	Military School, established by the Provisional Government of the Republic of Korea	Daehanminguk imsi jeongbu yukgun mugwan hakgyo	Taehanmin'guk imsi chŏngbu yukkun mugwan hakkyo	1919-?	번역 표준 원칙
1032	대한민국임시정부 인성학교	大韓民國臨時政府 仁成學校	Inseong School, established by the Provisional Government of the Republic of Korea	Daehanminguk imsi jeongbu inseong hakgyo	Taehanmin'guk imsi chŏngbu insŏng hakkyo	1917-1975	번역 표준 원칙

NO	용어	한자	영문	RO	MC	시대 및 연도	출전
1033	대한민국임시정부의 대일 선전 성명서	大韓民國臨時政府의 對日 宣戰 聲明書	document of declaration of war on Japan by the Provisional Government of the Republic of Korea	Daehanminguk imsi jeongbuui daeil seonjeon seongmyeongseo	Taehanmin'guk imsi chŏngbu-ŭi taeil sŏnjŏn sŏngmyŏngsŏ		번역 표준 원칙
1034	대한민국정부 수립 기념식	大韓民國政府 樹立 記念式	ceremony marking establishment of the ROK Government	Daehanminguk jeongbu surip ginyeomsik	Taehanmin'guk chŏngbu surip kinyŏmsik	1948	번역 표준 원칙
1035	대한민국-필리핀 무역협정	大韓民國-Philippines 貿易協定	Trade Agreement between Korea and the Philippines	Daehanminguk-Pillipin muyeok hyeopjeong	Taehanmin'guk-p'illip'in muyŏk hyŏpchŏng		번역 표준 원칙
1036	대한민보	大韓民報	*Daehan Minbo (Korea People's Daily)*	Daehan minbo	Taehanminbo	1909-1910	번역 표준 원칙
1037	대한민주청년총동맹	大韓民主靑年總同盟	General Federation of Democratic Korean Youth	Daehan minju cheongnyeon chongdongmaeng	Teahan minju ch'ŏngnyŏn tongmaeng	1946	번역 표준 원칙
1038	대한반공청년단	大韓反共靑年團	Anti-Communist Youth Corps	Daehan bangong cheongnyeondan	Taehan pan'gong ch'ŏngnyŏndan	1960	번역 표준 원칙
1039	대한방침	對韓方針	Japan's policies for the colonization of Korea	Daehan bangchim	Taehan bangch'im		번역 표준 원칙
1040	대한부인회	大韓婦人會	Daehan Women's Association	Daehan buinhoe	Taehan puinhoe	1946	번역 표준 원칙

NO	용어	한자	영문	RO	MC	시대 및 연도	출전
1041	대한상공회의소	大韓商工會議所	Korea Chamber of Commerce and Industry	Daehan sanggong hoeuiso	Taehan sanggong hoeŭiso	1948-?	번역 표준 원칙
1042	대한상이용사회	大韓傷痍勇士會	Wounded Veterans' Association of Korea	Daehan sangiyong sahoe	Taehan sangiyong sahoe	1951	번역 표준 원칙
1043	대한시설강령	對韓施設綱領	Japan's policies and action plans for the colonization of Korea	Daehan siseol gangnyeong	Taehan sisŏl kangnyŏng	1904	번역 표준 원칙
1044	대한여성교육동지회	大韓女性敎育同志會	Korean Women Educators' Association	Daehan yeoseong gyoyuk dongjihoe	Taehan yŏsŏng kyoyuk dongchihoe		번역 표준 원칙
1045	대한여자국민당	大韓女子國民黨	Korea Women's National Party (Daehan Yeoja Gungmindang)	Daehan yeoja gungmindang	Taehan yŏja kungmindang	1945-1961	번역 표준 원칙
1046	대한여자애국단	大韓女子愛國團	Korean Women's Patriotic Corps	Daehan yeoja aegukdan	Taehan yŏja aeguktan	1919	번역 표준 원칙
1047	대한의원	大韓醫院	Daehan Hospital	Daehan uiwon	Taehan ŭiwŏn	1907-1910	번역 표준 원칙
1048	대한인거류민단(KRA)	大韓人居留民團	Korean Residents Association	Daehanin georyumindan	Taehanin kŏryumindan		번역 표준 원칙

NO	용어	한자	영문	RO	MC	시대 및 연도	출전
1049	대한인교민단	大韓人僑民團	Association of Korean Nationals in Hawaii	Daehan ingyo mindan	Taehanin kyomindan	1922-1933	번역 표준 원칙
1050	대한인국민회	大韓人國民會	Korean National Association	Daehanin gungminhoe	Taehanin kungminhoe	1910-1945	번역 표준 원칙
1051	대한인국민회 만주지방총회	大韓人國民會 滿洲地方總會	Korean National Association, Manchuria Branch	Daehanin gungminhoe manju jibang chonghoe	Taehanin kungminhoe manju chibang ch'onghoe	1910-?	도산안창호선생 기념사업회 . 도산학회, 「미주 국민회자료집」, 경인문화사, 2005
1052	대한인국민회 북미지방총회	大韓人國民會 北美地方總會	Korean National Association, America Branch	Daehanin gungminhoe bukmi jibang chonghoe	Taehanin kungminhoe pungmi chibang ch'onghoe		도산안창호선생 기념사업회 . 도산학회, 「미주 국민회자료집」, 경인문화사, 2005
1053	대한인국민회 시베리아지방총회	大韓人國民會 Siberia地方總會	Korean National Association, Siberia Branch	Daehanin gungminhoe siberia jibang chonghoe	Taehanin kungminhoe siberia chibang ch'onghoe	1910년대 전반기	도산안창호선생 기념사업회 . 도산학회, 「미주 국민회자료집」, 경인문화사, 2005
1054	대한인국민회 중앙총회	大韓人國民會 中央總會	Central Council of the Korean National Association	Daehanin gungminhoe jungang chonghoe	Taehanin kungminhoe chibang ch'onghoe		도산안창호선생 기념사업회 . 도산학회, 「미주 국민회자료집」, 경인문화사, 2005
1055	대한인국민회 하와이 지방총회	大韓人國民會 Hawaii地方會	Korean National Association, Hawaii Branch	Daehanin gungminhoe hawai jibang chonghoe	Taehanin kungminhoe hawai chibang ch'onghoe	1909-?	도산안창호선생 기념사업회 . 도산학회, 「미주 국민회자료집」, 경인문화사, 2005
1056	대한인동지회 북미총회	大韓人同志會 北美總會	North America General Meeting of Dong Ji Hoi Society	Daehanin dongjihoe bukmichonghoe	Taehanin tongjihoe pungmi ch'onghoe		번역 표준 원칙

NO	용어	한자	영문	RO	MC	시대 및 연도	출전
1057	대한자강회	大韓自强會	Korea Self-Strengthening Society	Daehan jaganghoe	Taehan chaganghoe	1906-1907	
1058	대한적십자사	大韓赤十字社	Korean National Red Cross	Daehan jeoksipjasa	Taehan chŏksipchasa	1905-?	번역 표준 원칙
1059	대한정책	對韓政策	foreign countries' policy toward Korea	Daehan jeongchaek	Taehan chŏngch'aek		번역 표준 원칙
1060	대한제국	大韓帝國	Great Han Empire	Daehanjeguk	Taehanjeguk	1897-1910	번역 표준 원칙
1061	대한제국 애국가	大韓帝國 愛國歌	National Anthem of the Great Han Empire	Daehanjeguk aegukga	Taehanjeguk aegukka		번역 표준 원칙
1062	대한제국 해외여행장	大韓帝國 海外旅行狀	passport from the Great Han Empire	Daehanjeguk haeoe yeohaengjang	Taehancheguk haeoe yŏhaengchang	1902	번역 표준 원칙
1063	대한제국기	大韓帝國期	Great Han Empire period	Daehan jegukgi	Taehan jegukki		번역 표준 원칙
1064	대한조선공사	大韓造船工社	Korea Shipbuilding & Eng. Corp.	Daehan joseon gongsa	Taehan chosŏn kongsa	1962.12.29	번역 표준 원칙

NO	용어	한자	영문	RO	MC	시대 및 연도	출전
1065	대한주택공사	大韓住宅公社	Korea Housing Corporation	Daehan jutaek gongsa	Taehan chut'aek kongsa	1962-?	번역 표준 원칙
1066	대한증권거래소	大韓證券去來所	Korea Stock Exchange	Daehan jeunggwon georaeso	Taehan chŭnggwŏn kŏ raeso	1956-?	번역 표준 원칙
1067	대한지지	大韓地誌	Geography of Korea (Daehan Jiji)	Daehan jiji	Taehan chiji	1906	번역 표준 원칙
1068	대한철도회사	大韓鐵道會社	Korea Railway Company	Daehan cheoldo hoesa	Taehan ch'ŏlto hoesa	1899-?	Ki-baik Lee, translated by Edward W. Wagner, A New History of Korea, Harvard University Press, 1984,
1069	대한청년단	大韓靑年團	Korea Youth Corps	Daehan cheongnyeondan	Taehan ch'ŏngnyŏndan	1949-1953	번역 표준 원칙
1070	대한청년단연합회	大韓靑年團聯合會	Federation for Korean Youth Corps	Daehan cheongnyeondan yeonhaphoe	Taehan ch'ŏngnyŏndan yŏnhaphoe	1919-1920	번역 표준 원칙
1071	대한통의부	大韓統義府	Korea Independence Association (Daehan Tonguibu)	Daehan tonguibu	Taehan t'ongŭibu	1922	번역 표준 원칙
1072	대한협회	大韓協會	Korea Association	Daehan hyeophoe	Taehan hyŏphoe	1907-1910	한국학중앙연구원,《영문한국백과》-남궁억

NO	용어	한자	영문	RO	MC	시대 및 연도	출전
1073	대화력전	對火力戰	counterfire operations	Daehwaryeokjeon	Taehwaryŏkchŏn		번역 표준 원칙
1074	덕수궁	德壽宮	Deoksugung Palace	Deoksugung	Tŏksugung	?-?	번역 표준 원칙
1075	덕수궁 석조전	德壽宮 石造殿	Seokjojeon Hall at Deoksugung Palace	Deoksugung seokjojeon	Tŏksugung sŏkchojŏn	1900-1910	번역 표준 원칙
1076	덕유산국립공원	德裕山國立公園	Deogyusan National Park	Deogyusan gungnipgongwon	Tŏgyusan kungnipkongwŏn	1975-?	번역 표준 원칙
1077	덕진진	德津鎭	Deokjinjin Fortress	Deokjinjin	Tŏkchinjin	고대/남북국	번역 표준 원칙
1078	데니 태극기	Denny 太極旗	Owen Denny Taegeukgi	Deni taegeukgi	Teni t'aegŭkki	1882-1910	번역 표준 원칙
1079	데라우치 총독 암살미수사건	寺內正毅 總督 暗殺未遂 事件	plot to assassinate Governor-General Terauchi	Derauchi chongdok amsal misu sageon	Terauch'i ch'ongdok amsal misu sakŏn	1910	번역 표준 원칙
1080	데모규제법	示威規制法	Act on Assembly and Demonstration	Demo gyujebeop	Temo kyujepŏp		번역 표준 원칙

NO	용어	한자	영문	RO	MC	시대 및 연도	출전
1081	도(직할시)재판소	道(直轄市)裁判所	Provincial (Direct Control City) Court	Do (jikhalsi) jaepanso	To (chikhalsi) chaep'anso		번역 표준 원칙
1082	도로명주소	道路名住所	street-name address system	Doromyeong juso	Toromyŏng chuso	2011-	번역 표준 원칙
1083	도미노 이론	Domino 理論	domino theory	Domino iron	Tomino iron		번역 표준 원칙
1084	도보지도부	圖報指導部	News Guidance Division	Dobojidobu	Tobochidobu		번역 표준 원칙
1085	도상위치(지리좌표)	圖上位置(地理座標)	geographic coordinates	Dosang wichi (jirijwapyo)	Tosang wich'I (chirijwap'yo)		번역 표준 원칙
1086	도섭능력	渡涉能力	ability to ford a river	Doseop neungnyeok	Tosŏp nŭngnyŏk		번역 표준 원칙
1087	도솔산 전투	兜率山 戰鬪	Battle of Dosolsan Mountain	Dosolsan jeontu	Tosolsan chŏnt'u	1951	번역 표준 원칙
1088	도시 새마을운동	都市 새마을運動	Saemaeul (New Village) Movement in urban areas	Dosi saemaeul undong	Tosi saemaŭl undong		번역 표준 원칙

NO	용어	한자	영문	RO	MC	시대 및 연도	출전
1089	도시빈민	都市貧民	urban poor	Dosi binmin	Tosi binmin		번역 표준 원칙
1090	도시산업선교회	都市産業宣敎會	Protestant-Sponsored Urban Industrial Mission	Dosi saneop seongyohoe	Tosi sanŏp sŏn'gyohoe	1957-	번역 표준 원칙
1091	도시인구의 과밀화	都市人口의 過密化	overpopulation in cities	Dosi inguui gwamilhwa	Tosi in'gu-ŭi kwamirhwa		번역 표준 원칙
1092	도시인구집중	都市人口集中	concentration of population in urban areas	Dosi ingu jipjung	Tosi in'gu chipchung		번역 표준 원칙
1093	도시지역 의료보험	都市地域 醫療保險	medical insurance for the urban self-employed	Dosijiyeok uiryoboheom	Tosijiyŏk ŭiryobohŏm	1989	번역 표준 원칙
1094	도시화	都市化	urbanization	Dosihwa	Tosihwa		번역 표준 원칙
1095	도시화 가속	都市化 加速	accelerating urbanization	Dosihwa gasok	Tosihwa kasok		번역 표준 원칙
1096	도청 접수	道廳 接受	citizens' occupation of the provincial government building in Gwangju during the democratic uprising against the military regime in	Docheong jeopsu	Toch'ŏng chŏpsu		번역 표준 원칙

NO	용어	한자	영문	RO	MC	시대 및 연도	출전
1097	독도	獨島	Dokdo Islands	Dokdo	Tokto		번역 표준 원칙
1098	독도 공중전화	獨島 公衆電話	public telephones on Dokdo Islands	Dokdo gongjung jeonhwa	Tokto kongjung jŏnhwa		번역 표준 원칙
1099	독도 침탈	獨島 侵奪	dispossession of Dokdo Islands	Dokdo chimtal	Tokto ch'imt'al		번역 표준 원칙
1100	독도문제	獨島問題	Japanese claims over Dokdo Islands	Dokdo munje	Tokto munje		번역 표준 원칙
1101	독립 유공자	獨立 有功者	Man of Merit (for contribution to the Independence Movement)	Dongnip yugongja	Tongnip yugongja		번역 표준 원칙
1102	독립공고서	獨立公告書	appeal for Korean independence	Dongnip gonggoseo	Tongnip konggosŏ		번역 표준 원칙
1103	독립공원	獨立公園	Independence Park	Dongnip gongwon	Tongnip kongwŏn	1896	번역 표준 원칙
1104	독립공채	獨立公債	Independence Bond	Dongnip gongchae	Tongnip kongch'ae	1919	번역 표준 원칙

NO	용어	한자	영문	RO	MC	시대 및 연도	출전
1105	독립관	獨立館	Independence Hall	Dongnipgwan	Tongnipkwan	1896	번역 표준 원칙
1106	독립국가	獨立國家	independent state	Dongnip gukga	Tongnip kukka		번역 표준 원칙
1107	독립군	獨立軍	Independence Army	Dongnipgun	Tongnipkun	1910-1945	번역 표준 원칙
1108	독립군기지 개척	獨立軍基地 開拓	development of Korean Independence Army base	Dongnipgun giji gaecheok	Tongnipkun kiji kaech'ŏk		번역 표준 원칙
1109	독립군기지 창건운동	獨立軍基地 創建運動	movement to establish Korean Independence Army base	Dongnipgun giji changgeon undong	Tongnipkun kiji ch'anggŏn undong	1910-?	번역 표준 원칙
1110	독립기념관	獨立紀念館	Independence Hall of Korea	Dongnip ginyeomgwan	Tongnip kinyŏmgwan	1987-?	번역 표준 원칙
1111	독립당	獨立黨	Independence Party	Dongnipdang	Tongniptang		번역 표준 원칙
1112	독립문	獨立門	Independence Gate	Dongnimmun	Tongnimmun	1897	번역 표준 원칙

NO	용어	한자	영문	RO	MC	시대 및 연도	출전
1113	독립선언서	獨立宣言書	Declaration of Independence	Dongnip seoneonseo	Tongnip sŏnŏnsŏ	1919	번역 표준 원칙
1114	독립신문	獨立新聞	*Dongnip Shinmun (The Independent)*	Dongnip sinmun	Tongnip sinmun	1896	번역 표준 원칙
1115	독립운동가	獨立運動家	independence activist	Dongnip undongga	Tongnip undongga		번역 표준 원칙
1116	독립운동방략	獨立運動方略	Independence Movement Plan	Dongnip undong bangnyak	Tongnip undong pangnyak		번역 표준 원칙
1117	독립의군부	獨立義軍府	Korean Independence and Justice Corps	Dongnip uigunbu	Tongnip ŭigunbu	1912-1914	번역 표준 원칙
1118	독립임시사무소	獨立臨時事務所	Office for the Establishment of the Provisional Government of the Republic of Korea	Dongnip imsi samuso	Tongnip imsi samuso	1919	번역 표준 원칙
1119	독립전쟁론	獨立戰爭論	theory of war of independence	Dongnip jeonjaengnon	Tongnip chŏnjaengnon	1910-1945	번역 표준 원칙
1120	독립촉성중앙협의회	獨立促成中央協議會	Central Council for the Rapid Realization of Korean Independence	Dongnip chokseong jungang hyeobuihoe	Tongnip ch'oksŏng chungang hyŏbŭihoe	1945-1946	번역 표준 원칙

NO	용어	한자	영문	RO	MC	시대 및 연도	출전
1121	독립협회	獨立協會	Independence Club	Dongnip hyeophoe	Tongnip hyŏphoe	1896	한국학중앙연구원, 《영문한국백과》-민족독립운동
1122	독립협회 규칙	獨立協會 規則	Regulations of the Independence Club	Dongnip hyeophoe gyuchik	Tongnip hyŏphoe kyuch'ik	1898	번역 표준 원칙
1123	독립협회 마크	獨立協會 mark	Independence Club badge	Dongnip gyeophoe makeu	Tongnip hyŏphoe mak'ŭ		번역 표준 원칙
1124	독립협회 회보	獨立協會 會報	Independence Club Bulletin	Dongnip hyeophoe hoebo	Tongnip hyŏphoe hoebo	1896-1897	번역 표준 원칙
1125	독립협회운동	獨立協會運動	Independence Club Movement	Dongnip hyeophoe undong	Tongnip hyŏphoe undong		번역 표준 원칙
1126	독사신론	讀史新論	A New Reading of History (Doksa Sinnon)	Doksasillon	Toksasillon	1908	번역 표준 원칙
1127	독수리작전	독수리作戰	Eagle Project	Doksuri jakjeon	Toksuri chakchŏn		국가보훈처, 「NAPKO Project OF OSS」 2001
1128	독자 모델 승용차	獨自 model 乘用車	independently developed car	Dokja model seungyongcha	Tokcha model sŭngyongch'a		번역 표준 원칙

NO	용어	한자	영문	RO	MC	시대 및 연도	출전
1129	독재자	獨裁者	dictator	Dokjaeja	Tokchaeja		번역 표준 원칙
1130	돌격작전	突擊作戰	assault operations	Dolgyeok jakjeon	Tolgyŏk chakchŏn		번역 표준 원칙
1131	돗드 준장	Dodd 准將	BG Dodd	Dotdeu junjang	Tottŭ chunjang	1952	번역 표준 원칙
1132	동경성 전투	東京城 戰鬪	Battle of Dongjingcheng	Donggyeongseong jeontu	Tonggyŏngsŏng chŏnt'u	1933	번역 표준 원칙
1133	동낙리 전투	同樂里 戰鬪	Battle of Dongnak-ri Village	Dongnakri jeontu	Tongnakri chŏnt'u	1950	번역 표준 원칙
1134	동남아 집단방위체제	東南亞 集團防衛體制	Southeast Asia Treaty Organization (SEATO)	Dongnama jipdan bangwi cheje	Tongnama chiptan pangwi ch'eje		번역 표준 원칙
1135	동대문	東大門	Dongdaemun Gate (East Gate)	Dongdaemun	Tongdaemun	1398	번역 표준 원칙
1136	동대문 발전소	東大門 發電所	Dongdaemun Power Plant	Dongdaemun baljeonseo	Tongdaemun palchŏnso	1899? 1900?	번역 표준 원칙

NO	용어	한자	영문	RO	MC	시대 및 연도	출전
1137	동대문 종합상가	東大門 綜合商街	Dongdaemun Shopping Complex	Dongdaemun jonghap sangga	Tongdaemun jonghap sangga	1905-?	번역 표준 원칙
1138	동대문운동장 철거	東大門運動場 撤去	demolition of Dongdaemun Stadium	Dongdaemun undongjang cheolgeo	Tongdaemun undongjang ch'ŏlgŏ	2007	번역 표준 원칙
1139	동도서기론	東道西器論	theory of Eastern ways, Western technology	Dongdo seogiron	Tongdo sŏgiron	1880년대 초	번역 표준 원칙
1140	동력자원부	動力資源部	Ministry of Energy and Resources	Dongnyeok jawonbu	Tongnyŏk chawŏnbu	1991	송기중, 《한영우리문화용어집》, 지문당, 2001.
1141	동맹파업	同盟罷業	solidarity strike	Dongmaeng paeop	Tongmaeng p'aŏp		번역 표준 원칙
1142	동맹휴학	同盟休學	students' solidarity boycott of classes	Dongmaeng hyuhak	Tongmaeng hyuhak	근대	번역 표준 원칙
1143	동문학	同文學	Dongmunhak (first foreign language school in Korea)	Dongmunhak	Tongmunhak	1883-1886	번역 표준 원칙
1144	동방노력자공산대학	東方勞力者共産大學	Communist University of the Toilers of the East	Dongbang noryeokja gongsan daehak	Tongbang noryŏkcha kongsan taehak	1921-1938	번역 표준 원칙

NO	용어	한자	영문	RO	MC	시대 및 연도	출전
1145	동방아나키스트대회	東方Anarchists大會	General Meeting of Anarchists in the Orient	Dongbang anakiseuteu daehoe	Tongbang anak'isŭtŭ taehoe		번역 표준 원칙
1146	동방예의지국	東方禮儀之國	"country of courteous people in the East" (Korea)	dongbang yeui jiguk	Tongbang yeŭi chiguk	조선	번역 표준 원칙
1147	동백림사건	東伯林事件	East Berlin Incident of 1967	Dongbaengnim sageon	Tongbaengnim sakŏn	1967	번역 표준 원칙
1148	동북공정	東北工程	China's Northeast Project	Dongbuk gongjeong	Tongbuk kongjŏng		번역 표준 원칙
1149	동북삼성	東北三省	China's three northeastern provinces of Liaoning, Jilin and Heilongjiang	Dongbuksamseong	Tongbuksamsŏng		번역 표준 원칙
1150	동북의용군	東北義勇軍	Korean Volunteer Army of the Northeast Anti-Japanese Allies	Dongbuk uiyonggun	Tongbuk ŭiyonggun		번역 표준 원칙
1151	동북인민혁명군	東北人民革命軍	Northeast People's Revolutionary Army	Dongbuk inmin hyeongmyeonggun	Tongbuk inmin hyŏngmyŏnggun	1933-1936	번역 표준 원칙
1152	동북항일연군	東北抗日聯軍	Northeast Anti-Japanese United Army	Dongbuk hangil yeongun	Tongbuk hangil yŏn'gun	1936-?	번역 표준 원칙

NO	용어	한자	영문	RO	MC	시대 및 연도	출전
1153	동북항일연군 교도려	東北抗日聯軍 編導旅	Northeast Anti-Japanese United Army Organization	Dongbuk hangil yeongun gyodoryeo	Tongbuk hangil yŏn'gun kyodoryŏ	1942-1945	번역 표준 원칙
1154	동서냉전 해소	東西冷戰 解消	end of the Cold War	Dongseo naengjeon haeso	Tongsŏ naengjŏn haeso		번역 표준 원칙
1155	동시통합성	同時統合性	synchronization	Dongsi tonghapseong	Tongsi t'onghapsŏng		번역 표준 원칙
1156	동아마라톤	東亞Marathon	Dong-A Marathon	Donga maraton	Tonga marat'on	1931-?	번역 표준 원칙
1157	동아방송	東亞放送	Dong-A Broadcasting System	Donga bangsong	Tonga pangsong	1963-1980	번역 표준 원칙
1158	동아일보	東亞日報	The Dong-A Ilbo (daily newspaper)	Dongailbo	Tongailbo	1920-?	번역 표준 원칙
1159	동아일보 광고탄압사건	東亞日報 廣告彈壓事件	Dong-A Ilbo advertising coercion and forced layoff case	Dongailbo gwanggo tanap sageon	Tongailbo kwanggo t'anap sakŏn	1974	번역 표준 원칙
1160	동양척식주식회사	東洋拓殖株式會社	Oriental Development Company	Dongyang cheoksik jusikhoesa	Tongyang ch'ŏksik chusikhoesa	1908-1945	Ki-baik Lee, translated by Edward W. Wagner, A New History of Korea, Harvard University Press, 1984,

NO	용어	한자	영문	RO	MC	시대 및 연도	출전
1161	동양척식회사 폭파사건	東洋拓殖會社 爆破事件	bombing of the Oriental Development Company Building	Dongyang cheoksik hoesa pokpa sageon	Tongyang ch'ŏksik hoesa p'okp'a sakŏn	1926	번역 표준 원칙
1162	동양텔레비전방송	東洋Television放送	Tongyang Broadcasting Company (TBC)	Dongyang tellebijeon bangsong	Tongyang t'ellebijyŏn pangsong	1964-1980	번역 표준 원칙
1163	동양평화론	東洋平和論	"On Peace in East Asia" (essay by An Jung-geun)	Dongyang pyeonghwaron	Tongyang p'yŏnghwaron	1910	번역 표준 원칙
1164	동우회사건	同友會事件	Suyang Donguhoe Incident of 1937	Donguhoe sageon	Tonguhoe sagŏn	1937	번역 표준 원칙
1165	동원예비군	動員豫備軍	Mobilized Reserve Forces	Dongwon yebigun	Tongwŏn yebigun		번역 표준 원칙
1166	동의대사태	東義大事態	Dong-eui University Incident of 1989	Donguidae satae	Tongŭidae sat'ae	1989	번역 표준 원칙
1167	동의보감	東醫寶鑑	Exemplar of Korean Medicine (Donguibogam)	Donguibogam	Tong'ŭipogam	조선	Ki-baik Lee, translated by Edward W. Wagner, A New History of Korea, Harvard University Press, 1984,
1168	동일방직사건	東一紡織事件	Dongil Textile Labor Conflict of 1978	Dongil bangjik sageon	Tongil pangjik sakŏn	1978	번역 표준 원칙

NO	용어	한자	영문	RO	MC	시대 및 연도	출전
1169	동지미포대표회	同志美布代表會	Congress of Dong Ji Hoi Society's North America Representatives (Honolulu, 1930)	Dongjimipo daepyohoe	Tongjimip'o taep'yohoe		번역 표준 원칙
1170	동지회	同志會	Dong Ji Hoi Society (Comrades Society)	Dongjihoe	Tongjihoe	1921-?	번역 표준 원칙
1171	동지회 식산회사	同志會 殖産會社	Dong Ji Hoi Society Investment Company	Dongjihoe siksanhoesa	Tongjihoe siksanhoesa		번역 표준 원칙
1172	동지회 중앙부	同志會 中央部	Headquarters of Dong Ji Hoi Society	Dongjihoe jungangbu	Tongchihoe chungangbu		번역 표준 원칙
1173	동청철도	東淸鐵道	Chinese Eastern Railway	Dongcheong cheoldo	Tongch'ŏng ch'ŏlto	1896-?	번역 표준 원칙
1174	동티모르 파병	東Timor 派兵	dispatch of troops to East Timor	Dongtimoreu pabyeong	Tongt'imorŭ p'abyŏng		번역 표준 원칙
1175	동학	東學	Donghak (lit. Eastern Learning)	Donghak	Tonghak	1860	Peter H. Lee, Sourcebook of Korean Civilization(Volume 2), Columbia University Press, 1993,
1176	동학농민군	東學農民軍	Donghak Peasant Army	Donghak nongmingun	Tonghak nongmin'gun	1894	번역 표준 원칙

NO	용어	한자	영문	RO	MC	시대 및 연도	출전
1177	동학농민운동	東學農民運動	Donghak Peasant Movement	Donghak nongmin undong	Tonghak nongmin undong	1894-1895	한국학중앙연구원, 《영문한국백과》-김홍집
1178	동학사상	東學思想	Donghak (Eastern Learning) thought	Donghak sasang	Tonghak sasang		번역 표준 원칙
1179	동학혁명기념탑	東學革命記念塔	Donghak Peasant Movement Commemorative Tower	Donghak hyeongmyeong ginyeomtap	Tonghak hyŏngmyŏng ginyŏmt'ap	1963	번역 표준 원칙
1180	동해	東海	East Sea	Donghae	Tonghae		번역 표준 원칙
1181	동해고속도로	東海高速道路	Donghae (East Coast) Expressway	Donghae gosokdoro	Tonghae kosoktoro	1975	번역 표준 원칙
1182	동해항	東海港	Donghae Port	Donghaehang	Tonghaehang		번역 표준 원칙
1183	두뇌유출	頭腦流出	brain drain	Dunoe yuchul	Tunoe yuch'ul		번역 표준 원칙
1184	두뇌한국 21사업	頭腦韓國 21事業	Brain Korea 21	Dunoe hanguk 21 saeop	Tunoe han'guk 21 saŏp		번역 표준 원칙

NO	용어	한자	영문	RO	MC	시대 및 연도	출전
1185	두만강	豆滿江	Tumen River	Dumangang	Tuman'gang		번역 표준 원칙
1186	둑코전투	Duc Co 戰鬪	Battle of Duc Co	Dukko jeontu	Tukk'o chŏnt'u	1966	번역 표준 원칙
1187	디스코	Disco	disco	Diseuko	Disŭk'o		번역 표준 원칙
1188	땅굴	땅窟	North Korean infiltration tunnel	Ttanggul	Ttanggul	1971	번역 표준 원칙
1189	땡전뉴스	땡全news	"ttaengjeon news," literally "ring Chun news" (excessive coverage of Chun Doo-hwan at the head of every news broadcast)	Ttaengjeon nyuseu	Ttangjŏn nyusŭ	1981-1987	번역 표준 원칙
1190	라오스 내전	Laos 內戰	Laos Civil War	Raoseu naejeon	Raosŭ naejŏn		번역 표준 원칙
1191	람사르 협약	람사르 協約	Ramsar Convention	Ramsareu hyeobyak	Ramsarŭ hyŏbyak	1971	번역 표준 원칙
1192	랴오둥 반도	遼東 半島	Liaodong Peninsula	Ryaottung bando	Ryaottung pando		번역 표준 원칙

NO	용어	한자	영문	RO	MC	시대 및 연도	출전
1193	러시아 10월혁명	Russia 10月革命	Bolshevik Revolution (October 1917 Revolution in Russia)	Reosia 10wol hyeongmyeong	Rŏsia 10wol hyŏngmyŏng	1917	번역 표준 원칙
1194	러시아 2월혁명	Russia 2月革命	February Revolution of 1917 in Russia	Reosia 2wol hyeongmyeong	Rŏsia 2wol hyŏngmyŏng	1917	번역 표준 원칙
1195	러시아 남하	Russia 南下	Russia's southward expansion	Reosia namhwa	Rŏsia namhwa		번역 표준 원칙
1196	러시아 노농정부	Russia 勞農政府	Soviet government	Reosia nonong jeongbu	Rŏsia nonong chŏngbu		번역 표준 원칙
1197	러시아공사관	Russia公使館	Russian Legation	Reosia gongsagwan	Rŏsia kongsagwan	1890	번역 표준 원칙
1198	러시아공산당	Russia共産黨	Russian Communist Party	Reosia gongsandang	Rŏsia kongsandang		번역 표준 원칙
1199	러시아공산당 극동국	Russia共産黨 極東局	Far East Bureau of the Central Committee of the Russian Communist Party	Reosia gongsandang geukdongguk	Rŏsia kongsandang kŭktongguk	1920	번역 표준 원칙
1200	러시아혁명	Russia革命	Russian Revolution	Reosia hyeongmyeong	Rŏsia hyŏngmyŏng		번역 표준 원칙

NO	용어	한자	영문	RO	MC	시대 및 연도	출전
1201	러일 협상	露日 協商	Russia-Japan negotiations	Reoil hyeopsang	Rŏil hyŏpsang		번역 표준 원칙
1202	러일강화회의	露日講和會議	Russo-Japanese Peace Conference of 1905	Reoil ganghwa hoeui	Rŏil kanghwa hoeŭi	1905	번역 표준 원칙
1203	러일전쟁	露日戰爭	Russo-Japanese War	Reoil jeonjaeng	Rŏil chŏnjaeng	1904-1905	Wi Jo Kang, Christ and Caesar in Modern Korea: A History of Christianity and Politics, State University of
1204	레닌주의 정치학교	Lein主義 政治學校	Leninism School of Political Studies	Reninjuui jeongchi hakgyo	Reninjuŭi chŏngch'i hakkyo	1929?1930	번역 표준 원칙
1205	로동신문	勞動新聞	*Rodong Sinmun* (Workers' Daily)	Rodong sinmun	Nodong sinmun	1949-	번역 표준 원칙
1206	로드암허스트 호	Lord Amherst 號	the *Lord Amherst*	Rodeuamheosteu ho	Rodŭamhŏsŭt'ŭ ho		번역 표준 원칙
1207	로스쿨		Law school	law school	Roseukul	Rosŭk'ul	2009	번역 표준 원칙
1208	로젠-니시협정	Rojen-Nishi協定	Nishi-Rosen Agreement	Rojen-nisi hyeopjeong	Rojen-nisi hyŏpchŏng		번역 표준 원칙

NO	용어	한자	영문	RO	MC	시대 및 연도	출전
1209	리마비동맹외상회의	Lima非同盟外相會議	Ministerial Conference of Non-Aligned Countries in Lima, Peru in 1975	Rima bidongmaeng oesang hoeui	Rima pidongmaeng oesang hoeŭi	1975	번역 표준 원칙
1210	리베이트근절법	리베이트根絶法	Anti-Kickback Act	Ribeiteu geunjeolbeop	Ribeitŭ gŭnjŏlbŏp		번역 표준 원칙
1211	리비아 대수로공사	Libya 大水路工事	Great Man-made River Project in Libya	Ribia daesuro gongsa	Ribia taesuro kongsa	1984-?	번역 표준 원칙
1212	리콜제도	recall制度	recall system	Rikol jedo	Rikol chedo		번역 표준 원칙
1213	리튼보고서	Lytton報告書	Lytton Report	Riteun bogoseo	Rit'ŭn pogosŏ		번역 표준 원칙
1214	마닐라정상회의	Manila頂上會議	Manila Summit Conference (October 1966)	Manilla jeongsang hoeui	Manilla chŏngsang hoeŭi		번역 표준 원칙
1215	마르크스주의	Marx主義	Marxism	Mareukeuseujuui	Marŭk'ŭsŭjuŭi		번역 표준 원칙
1216	마산사건조사단	馬山事件調査團	group of lawmakers sent to investigate the Masan March 15 Democratic Movement of 1960	Masan sageon josadan	Masan sakŏn josadan		번역 표준 원칙

NO	용어	한자	영문	RO	MC	시대 및 연도	출전
1217	마산수출자유지역	馬山輸出自由地域	Masan Free Export Zone	Masan suchul jayu jiyeok	Masan such'ul chayu chiyŏk	1970-?	번역 표준 원칙
1218	마산수출자유지역 관리청	馬山輸出自由地域 管理廳	Masan Free Export Zone Administration Office	Masan suchul jayu jiyeok gwallicheong	Masan such'ul chayu chiyŏk kwallich'ŏng		번역 표준 원칙
1219	마산전투	馬山戰鬪	Battle of Masan	Masan jeontu	Masan chŏnt'u		번역 표준 원칙
1220	마샬 플랜	Marshall plan	European Recovery Program (aka Marshall Plan)	Masyal peullaen	Masyal p'ŭllaen	1947	번역 표준 원칙
1221	마이어협정 (한미경제조정협정)	Meyer協定 (韓美經濟調整協定)	Agreement on Economic Coordination between the Republic of Korea and the Unified Command	Maieo hyeopjeong (hanmi gyeongje jojeong hyeopjeong)	Maiŏ hyŏpchŏng (hanmi kyŏngje chojŏng hyŏpchŏng)	1952	번역 표준 원칙
1222	마포형무소	麻浦刑務所	Mapo Prison	Mapo hyeongmuso	Map'o hyŏngmuso	1908	번역 표준 원칙
1223	막걸리	막걸리	*makgeolli* (cloudy rice wine)	Makgeolli	Makkŏlli		번역 표준 원칙
1224	막걸리선거	막걸리選擧	vote buying with *makgeolli*	Makgeolli seongeo	Makkŏlli sŏngŏ	1960?	번역 표준 원칙

NO	용어	한자	영문	RO	MC	시대 및 연도	출전
1225	막사이사이상	Magsaysay賞	Magsaysay Award	Maksaisai sang	Maksaisai sang	1958	번역 표준 원칙
1226	만경봉호	萬景峰號	Mangyongbong Ferry	Mangyeongbongho	Man'gyŏngbongho	1971-?	번역 표준 원칙
1227	만국공법	萬國公法	international law	Manguk gongbeop	Man'guk kongpŏp		번역 표준 원칙
1228	만국사회당대회	萬國社會黨大會	International Socialist Congress	Manguk sahoedang daehoe	Man'guk sahoedang taehoe	1920	번역 표준 원칙
1229	만국우편조약	萬國郵便條約	Universal Postal Convention	Manguk upyeon joyak	Man'guk up'yŏn choyak	1951	번역 표준 원칙
1230	만국평화회의	萬國平和會議	Hague Peace Conferences (1889-1907)	Manguk pyeonghwa hoeui	Man'guk p'yŏnghwa hoeŭi	1899-1907	번역 표준 원칙
1231	만민공동회	萬民共同會	mass protest meeting	Manmin gongdonghoe	Manmin kongdonghoe	1898	Ki-baik Lee, translated by Edward W. Wagner, A New History of Korea, Harvard University Press, 1984,
1232	만보산사건	萬寶山事件	Wanpaoshan Incident of 1931	Manbosan sageon	Manbosan sakŏn	1931	번역 표준 원칙

NO	용어	한자	영문	RO	MC	시대 및 연도	출전
1233	만선사관	滿鮮史觀	the view of Japanese scholars integrating the histories of Korea and Manchuria	Manseon sagwan	Mansŏn sagwan	20세기 초	번역 표준 원칙
1234	만세보	萬歲報	*Mansebo (The Independence News)*	Mansebo	Mansebo	1906-1907	번역 표준 원칙
1235	만인소	萬人疏	memorial used as a form of protest by Confucian scholars during the Joseon dynasty	Maninso	Maninso	조선	한국학중앙연구원, 《영문한국백과》-만인소
1236	만장일치	滿場一致	unanimous vote	Manjangilchi	Manjangilch'i		번역 표준 원칙
1237	만주	滿洲	Manchuria	Manju	Manju	근대	Ki-baik Lee, translated by Edward W. Wagner, A New History of Korea, Harvard University Press, 1984,
1238	만주 이주	滿洲 移住	relocation to Manchuria	Manju iju	Manju iju	?-1945	번역 표준 원칙
1239	만주국	滿洲國	Manchukuo (Manchurian State 1932-1945)	Manjuguk	Manjuguk	1932-1945	번역 표준 원칙
1240	만주사변	滿洲事變	Manchurian Incident of 1931 (Mukden Incident)	Manju sabyeon	Manju sabyŏn	1931	번역 표준 원칙

NO	용어	한자	영문	RO	MC	시대 및 연도	출전
1241	만주제국	滿洲帝國	Manzhouguo (Manchurian Empire)	Manju jeguk	Manju cheguk	일제	번역 표준 원칙
1242	만한교환론	滿韓交換論	idea of Korea in exchange for Manchuria	Manhan gyohwallon	Manhan kyohwallon	1898	번역 표준 원칙
1243	맘보바지	맘보바지	drainpipe trousers	Mambo baji	Mambo paji	50년대 말	번역 표준 원칙
1244	매니페스토운동	Manifesto運動	Manifesto Movement	Maenipeseuto undong	Maenip'esŭto undong		번역 표준 원칙
1245	매독스호	Maddox號	Destroyer USS Maddox DD-731	Maedokseuho	Maedoksŭho		번역 표준 원칙
1246	매사냥	매사냥	falconry	Maesanyang	Maesanyang		UNESCO 공식 사이트 http://www.unesco.org/culture/ich/en/RL/00442
1247	매일신문	每日新聞	Maeil Sinmun (daily newspaper)	Maeil sinmun	Maeil sinmun	1960-?	번역 표준 원칙
1248	매천야록	梅泉野錄	Collected Works of Hwang Hyeon (Macheon Yarok)	Maecheonnyarok	Maech'ŏnnyarok	근대	번역 표준 원칙

NO	용어	한자	영문	RO	MC	시대 및 연도	출전
1249	매천집	梅泉集	Collection of Patriot Hwang Hyeon's works (Maecheon-jip)	Maecheonjip	Maech'ŏnjip	근대	번역 표준 원칙
1250	매판자본	買辦資本	comprador capital	Maepan jabon	Maep'an chabon	?-?	번역 표준 원칙
1251	맹호군	猛虎軍	Tiger Brigade	Maenghogun	Maenghogun	1942-?	번역 표준 원칙
1252	맹호부대	猛虎部隊	Capital Garrison Command	Maengho budae	Maengho pudae	1948-?	번역 표준 원칙
1253	메모리 반도체	Memory 半導體	memory chips	Memori bandoche	Memori pandoch'e		번역 표준 원칙
1254	메이지유신	明治維新	Meiji Restoration	Meiji yusin	Meiji yusin	1867	Ki-baik Lee, translated by Edward W. Wagner, A New History of Korea, Harvard University Press, 1984,
1255	멕시코 이민	Maxico 移民	emigration to Mexico	Meksiko imin	Meksik'o imin	1905-	번역 표준 원칙
1256	멕시코 한인사회	Maxico 韓人社會	Korean community in Mexico	Meksiko hanin sahoe	Meksik'o hanin sahoe		번역 표준 원칙

NO	용어	한자	영문	RO	MC	시대 및 연도	출전
1257	멜로 드라마	Melo drama	melodrama	Mello deurama	Mello tŭrama		번역 표준 원칙
1258	면방직공업	綿紡織工業	spinning industry	Myeonbangjik gongeop	Myŏnbangjik kongŏp		번역 표준 원칙
1259	면세	免稅	tax exemption	Myeonse	Myŏnse		Ki-baik Lee, translated by Edward W. Wagner, A New History of Korea, Harvard University Press, 1984,
1260	면암집	勉庵集	Collection of the Patriotic Scholar Choi Ik-hyeon's works (Myeonan-jip)	Myeonamjip	Myŏnamjip	1908	번역 표준 원칙
1261	멸공훈련	滅共訓鍊	anti-Communist drills	Myeolgong hullyeon	Myŏlgong hullyŏn		번역 표준 원칙
1262	명동사건	明洞事件	Myeongdong Incident of 1976	Myeongdong sageon	Myŏngdong sakŏn	1976	번역 표준 원칙
1263	명동성당	明洞聖堂	Myeongdong Cathedral	Myeongdong seongdang	Myŏngdong sŏngdang	1898-?	한국학중앙연구원,《영문한국백과》-명동성당
1264	명동예술극장	明洞藝術劇場	Myeongdong Theater	Myeongdong yesul geukjang	Myŏngdong yesul gŭkchang	2009	번역 표준 원칙

NO	용어	한자	영문	RO	MC	시대 및 연도	출전
1265	명동촌	明東村	Myeongdong Village (ethnic Korean community in northern Gando)	Myeongdongchon	Myŏngdongch'on		번역 표준 원칙
1266	명동학교	明東學校	Myeongdong School (for the education of ethnic Koreans in northern Gando)	Myeongdong hakgyo	Myŏngdong hakkyo	1909-1925	번역 표준 원칙
1267	명성그룹사건	明星group事件	Myungsung Group scandal (illegal channeling of funds into speculation)	Myeongseong geurup sageon	Myŏngsŏng kŭrup sagŏn	1983	번역 표준 원칙
1268	명성황후	明成皇后	Empress Myeongseong	Myeongseong hwanghu	Myŏngsŏng hwanghu	1851-1895	번역 표준 원칙
1269	모범택시 도입	模範taxi 導入	introduction of deluxe taxis	Mobeom taeksi doip	Mopŏm t'aeksi toip		번역 표준 원칙
1270	모스전신기	Morse電信機	Morse's telegraph system	Moseu jeonsingi	Mosŭ chŏnsin'gi		번역 표준 원칙
1271	모스크바3상회의	Moscow3相會議	Moscow Conference of the Three Foreign Ministers	Moseukeuba 3sang hoeui	Mosŭk'ŭba 3sang hoeŭi	1945	번역 표준 원칙
1272	모스크바3상회의 지지결의대회	Moscow3相會議 支持決意大會	Rally in Support of the Moscow Conference of the Three Foreign Ministers	Moseukeuba 3sanghoeui jiji gyeorui daehoe	Mosŭk'ŭba 3sang hoeŭi chiji kyŏrŭi taehoe		번역 표준 원칙

NO	용어	한자	영문	RO	MC	시대 및 연도	출전
1273	모스크바삼상회의	Moscow三相會議	Moscow Conference of the Three Foreign Ministers	Moseukeuba 3sang hoeui	Mosŭkŭba 3sang hoeŭi	1945	번역 표준 원칙
1274	모자보건법	母子保健法	Mother and Child Health Act	Moja bogeonbeop	Moja bogŏnpŏp	1973-?	번역 표준 원칙
1275	모택동고지전투	毛澤東高地戰鬪	Battle of Mao's Hill	Motaekdong goji jeontu	Mot'aektong koji chŏnt'u	1951	번역 표준 원칙
1276	모화관	慕華館	Mohwagwan (guesthouse for Chinese envoys during the Joseon period)	Mohwagwan	Mohwagwan	1429-1894	번역 표준 원칙
1277	무공해연료	無公害燃料	eco-friendly fuel	Mugonghae yeonryo	Mugonghae yŏllyo		번역 표준 원칙
1278	무공훈장	武功勳章	Order of Military Merit	Mugong hunjang	Mugong hunjang	1950	번역 표준 원칙
1279	무궁화	無窮花	Rose of Sharon (Korean national flower)	Mugunghwa	Mugunghwa		번역 표준 원칙
1280	무궁화 대훈장	無窮花 大勳章	Grand Order of Mugunghwa	Mugunghwa daehunjang	Mugunghwa taehunjang	1949	번역 표준 원칙

NO	용어	한자	영문	RO	MC	시대 및 연도	출전
1281	무궁화 위성	無窮花 衛星	Mugunghwa satellite, Korea's first telecommunications and broadcasting satellite (aka KOREASAT)	Mugunghwa wiseong	Mugunghwa wisŏng	1995-	번역 표준 원칙
1282	무극리 전투	無極里 戰鬪	Battle of Mugeuk-ri Village	Mugeungni jeontu	Mugŭkri chŏnt'u	1950	번역 표준 원칙
1283	무기도입 사업	武器導入 事業	arms purchase projects	Mugi doip saeop	Mugi toip saŏp		번역 표준 원칙
1284	무단통치	武斷統治	militaristic rule (by the Japanese colonial government in the 1910s)	Mudan tongchi	Mudan t'ongch'i	1910-1919	번역 표준 원칙
1285	무당주의	無黨主義	non-partisanism	Mudangjuui	Mudangjuŭi		번역 표준 원칙
1286	무력충돌	武力衝突	armed conflict	Muryeok chungdol	Muryŏk ch'ungdol		번역 표준 원칙
1287	무명잡세	無名雜稅	miscellaneous taxes	Mumyeong japsae	Mumyŏng chapse		번역 표준 원칙
1288	무산자동맹회	無産者同盟會	Proletarian Alliance (Musanja Dongmaenghoe)	Musanja dongmaenghoe	Musanja tongmaenghoe	1922-?	번역 표준 원칙

NO	용어	한자	영문	RO	MC	시대 및 연도	출전
1289	무상공여	無償供與	grant assistance	Musang gongyeo	Musang kongyŏ		번역 표준 원칙
1290	무상교육	無償教育	free education	Musang gyoyuk	Musang kyoyuk		번역 표준 원칙
1291	무상원조	無償援助	grant-type aid	Musang wonjo	Musang wŏncho		번역 표준 원칙
1292	무상의무교육	無償義務教育	free, compulsory education	Musang uimu gyoyuk	Musang ŭimu kyouk		번역 표준 원칙
1293	무선호출기	無線呼出機	pager / beeper	Museon hochulgi	Musŏn hoch'ulgi	1980년대	번역 표준 원칙
1294	무선호출기 한글서비스	無線呼出機 한글Service	Korean-language service on pagers	Museon hochulgi hangeul seobiseu	Musŏn hoch'ulgi han'gul sŏpisŭ		번역 표준 원칙
1295	무소속	無所屬	independent (politician)	Musosok	Musosok		번역 표준 원칙
1296	무역금융	貿易金融	trade finance	Muyeok geumnyung	Muyŏk kŭmyung		번역 표준 원칙

NO	용어	한자	영문	RO	MC	시대 및 연도	출전
1297	무역장벽	貿易障壁	trade barrier	Muyeok jangbyeok	Muyŏk changbyŏk		번역 표준 원칙
1298	무역협상위원회	貿易協商委員會	Trade Negotiations Committee (TNC)	Muyeok hyeopsang wiwonhoe	Muyŏk hyŏpsang wiwŏnhoe		번역 표준 원칙
1299	무연탄	無煙炭	anthracite	Muyeontan	Muyŏnt'an		번역 표준 원칙
1300	무인항공기	無人航空機	Unmanned Aerial Vehicle (UAV)	Muin hanggonggi	Muin hanggonggi		번역 표준 원칙
1301	무임승차문제	無賃乘車問題	problems regarding free riding on public transportation	Muim seungcha munje	Muim sŭngch'a munje		번역 표준 원칙
1302	무작정 상경	無酌定 上京	"My Seoul" ("Mujakjeong sanggyeong"), movie directed by Kim Ki-duk, 1970	Mujakjeong sanggyeong	Mujakchŏng sanggyŏng	1970	번역 표준 원칙
1303	무장간첩	武裝間諜	armed spy	Mujang gancheop	Mujang kanchŏp		번역 표준 원칙
1304	무장대 군사총책	武裝隊 軍事總責	Military Secretary of the Armed Forces	Mujangdae gunsa chongchaek	Mujangdae kunsa ch'ongch'aek		번역 표준 원칙

NO	용어	한자	영문	RO	MC	시대 및 연도	출전
1305	무장독립전쟁	武裝獨立戰爭	armed struggle for independence	Mujang dongnip jeonjaeng	Mujang tongnip chŏnjaeng	근대/일제강점기	번역 표준 원칙
1306	무장해제	武裝解除	disarmament	Mujang haeje	Mujang haeje		번역 표준 원칙
1307	무정	無情	The Heartless (Mujeong), novel by Lee Gwang-su, 1917	Mujeong	Mujŏng	1917	번역 표준 원칙
1308	무정부주의	無政府主義	anarchism	Mujeongbujuui	Mujŏngbujuŭi		번역 표준 원칙
1309	무정부주의운동	無政府主義運動	anarchist movement	Mujeongbujuui undong	Mujŏngbujuŭi undong		번역 표준 원칙
1310	무허가 비닐하우스	無許可 vinyl house	unauthorized plastic greenhouses	Muheoga binil hauseu	Muhŏga pinil hausŭ		번역 표준 원칙
1311	무허가 판자촌	無許可 板子村	unauthorized shantytown	Muheoga panjachon	Muhŏga p'anjach'on		번역 표준 원칙
1312	무형문화유산보호협약	無形文化遺産保護協約	Convention for the Safeguarding of the Intangible Cultural Heritage	Muhyeong munhwa yusan boho hyeobyak	Muhyŏng munhwa yusan poho hyŏbyak		번역 표준 원칙

NO	용어	한자	영문	RO	MC	시대 및 연도	출전
1313	문경 양민학살사건	聞慶 良民虐殺事件	Mungyeong Massacre	Mungyeong yangmin haksal sageon	Mun'gyŏng yangmin haksal sakŏn	1949	번역 표준 원칙
1314	문교부	文敎部	Ministry of Education	Mungyobu	Mun'gyobu	1945-?	번역 표준 원칙
1315	문교사회위원회	文敎社會委員會	Education and Society Committee	Mungyo sahoe wiwonhoe	Mun'gyo sahoe wiwŏnhoe		번역 표준 원칙
1316	문맹퇴치운동	文盲退治運動	Illiteracy Eradication Campaign (after national liberation in 1945)	Munmaeng toechi undong	Munmaeng t'oech'i undong	1930년대	번역 표준 원칙
1317	문명개화론	文明開化論	Theory of Civilization (advocating Westernization as modernization)	Munmyeong gaehwaron	Munmyŏng kaehwaron	19세기 후반	번역 표준 원칙
1318	문산전투	汶山戰鬪	Battle of Munsan	Munsan jeontu	Munsan chŏnt'u	1950	번역 표준 원칙
1319	문수산성	文殊山城	Munsu-sanseong Mountain Fortress	Munsu sanseong	Munsu sansŏng	1694	번역 표준 원칙
1320	문익환 목사 방북사건	文益煥 牧師 訪北事件	Rev. Moon Ik-hwan's visit to North Korea in March 1989	Mun Ik-hwan moksa bangbuk sageon	Mun Ik-hwan moksa pangbuk sakŏn	1989	번역 표준 원칙

NO	용어	한자	영문	RO	MC	시대 및 연도	출전
1321	문자보급운동	文字普及運動	Illiteracy Eradication Campaign (during Japanese colonial period)	Munja bogeup undong	Munja pogŭp undong	1929	번역 표준 원칙
1322	문학단체	文學團體	literary organization	Munhak danche	Munhak tanch'e		번역 표준 원칙
1323	문학인 101인선언	文學人 101人宣言	Declaration of 101 Writers	Munhagin 101in seoneon	Munhagin 101in sŏnŏn	1974	번역 표준 원칙
1324	문호개방	門戶開放	opening the nation's doors	Munho gaebang	Munho kaebang		번역 표준 원칙
1325	문화방송	文化放送	Munhwa Broadcasting Corporation (MBC)	Munhwa bangsong	Munhwa pangsong	1961-?	MBC 공식 사이트 http://www.imbc.com
1326	문화운동	文化運動	cultural movement	Munhwa undong	Munhwa undong		번역 표준 원칙
1327	문화일보	文化日報	*Munhwa Ilbo* (daily newspaper)	Munhwa ilbo	Munhwa ilbo	1991	번역 표준 원칙
1328	문화재	文化財	cultural heritage	Munhwajae	Munhwajae		번역 표준 원칙

NO	용어	한자	영문	RO	MC	시대 및 연도	출전
1329	문화재 반환 (해외문화재)	文化財 反還 (海外文化財)	repatriation of Korean cultural heritage overseas	Munhwajae banhwan (Haeoe munhwajae)	Munhwajae panhwan (Haeoe munhwajae)		번역 표준 원칙
1330	문화재보호법	文化財保護法	Cultural Heritage Protection Act	Munhwajae bohobeop	Munhwajae bohobŏp	1962	번역 표준 원칙
1331	문화재복원	文化財復元	restoration of cultural heritage	Munhwajae bogwon	Munhwajae pogwŏn		번역 표준 원칙
1332	문화적 충돌	文化的 衝突	cultural conflict	Munhwajeok chungdol	Munhwajŏk ch'ungdol		번역 표준 원칙
1333	문화정치	文化政治	cultural rule	Munhwa jeongchi	Munhwa chŏngch'i		번역 표준 원칙
1334	문화주의	文化主義	culturism	Munhwajuui	Munhwajuŭi		번역 표준 원칙
1335	문화지도부	文化指導部	Cultural Guidance Division	Munhwa jidobu	Munhwa chidobu		번역 표준 원칙
1336	문화체육관광부	文化體育觀光部	Ministry of Culture, Sports and Tourism	Munhwa cheyuk gwangwangbu	Munhwa ch'eyuk kwangwangbu	2008	번역 표준 원칙

NO	용어	한자	영문	RO	MC	시대 및 연도	출전
1337	문화콘텐츠	文化contents	culture contents	Munhwa kontencheu	Munhwa k'ont'ench'ŭ		번역 표준 원칙
1338	문화통치	文化統治	cultural administration	Munhwa tongchi	Munhwa t'ongch'i	1919-1930	번역 표준 원칙
1339	문화훈장	文化勳章	Order of Culture Merit	Munhwa hunjang	Munhwa hunjang	1973	번역 표준 원칙
1340	물가안정대책	物價安定對策	price-stabilization measures	Mulga anjeong daechaek	Mulka anjŏng daechaek		번역 표준 원칙
1341	물가행정처	物價行政處	Office of Price Administration	Mulga haengjeongcheo	Mulka haengjŏngch'ŏ		번역 표준 원칙
1342	물물교환	物物交換	barter	Mulmul gyohwan	Mulmul Kyohwan		번역 표준 원칙
1343	물산장려운동	物産獎勵運動	campaign to promote Korean-made products	Mulsan jangnyeo undong	Mulsan changnyŏ undong	1923-?	번역 표준 원칙
1344	물자수탈	物資收奪	exploitation of goods	Mulja sutal	Mulja sutal		번역 표준 원칙

NO	용어	한자	영문	RO	MC	시대 및 연도	출전
1345	미 10군단 상륙기동	美 10軍團 上陸機動	Amphibious Movement of X Corps	Mi 10gundan sangnyuk gidong	Mi 10kundan sangnyuk kidong		번역 표준 원칙
1346	미 10군단 압록강 진격	美 10軍團 鴨綠江 進擊	Advance of X Corps to the Yalu River	Mi 10gundan amnokgang jingyeok	Mi 10kundan amnokkang chingyŏk		번역 표준 원칙
1347	미 군정 헌법안	美 軍政 憲法案	Draft of the Constitution by the U.S. Military Government in Korea	Mi gunjeong heonbeoban	Mi kunjŏng hŏnpŏban		번역 표준 원칙
1348	미 극동공군사령부	美 極東空軍司領部	Far East Air Force Command, U.S.	Mi geukdong donggun saryeongbu	Mi kŭktong gonggun saryŏngbu		번역 표준 원칙
1349	미 극동군사령관	美 極東軍司令官	Commander of the Far East Command, U.S.	Mi geukdonggun saryeonggwan	Mi gŭktonggun saryŏnggwan	1950	번역 표준 원칙
1350	미 극동군총사령부	美 極東軍總司令部	General Headquarters of the Far East Command, U.S.	Mi geukdonggun chongsaryeongbu	Mi kŭktonggun ch'ongsaryŏngbu		번역 표준 원칙
1351	미 극동해군사령부	美 極東海軍司領部	Far East Navy Command, U.S.	Mi geukdong haegunsaryeongbu	Mi kŭktong haegunsaryŏngbu		번역 표준 원칙
1352	미 잉여농산물 원조	美 剩餘農産物 援助	U.S. food aid using agricultural surplus	Mi ingyeo nongsanmul wonjo	Mi ingyŏ nongsanmul wŏnjo	1955	번역 표준 원칙

NO	용어	한자	영문	RO	MC	시대 및 연도	출전
1353	미 전략첩보국	美 戰略諜報局	Office of Strategic Services (OSS)	Mi jeollyak cheopboguk	Mi chŏllyak ch'ŏppoguk		국가보훈처, 「NAPKO Project OF OSS」 2001
1354	미 정보조정국	美 情報調整局	Coordinator of Information (COI)	Mi jeongbo jojeongguk	Mi chŏngbo chojŏngguk		국가보훈처, 「NAPKO Project OF OSS」 2001
1355	미 제24군단장	美 第24軍團長	24th Corps of the U.S. Tenth Army	Mi je24 gundanjang	Mi che24 kundanjang		번역 표준 원칙
1356	미국 공법 480호	美國 公法 480號	Public Law, PL 480 - Agricultural Trade Development and Assistance Act of 1954	Miguk gongbeop 480ho	Miguk kongpŏp 480ho	1955	번역 표준 원칙
1357	미국 무비자 방문	美國 無visa 訪問	sa-free travel to the U	Miguk mubija bangmun	Miguk mubija pangmun	2008	번역 표준 원칙
1358	미국 아시아함대	美國 Asia艦隊	Asian Fleet of the U.S. Navy	Miguk asia hamdae	Miguk asia hamdae		번역 표준 원칙
1359	미국 원조	美國 援助	American aid poster	Miguk wonjo	Miguk wŏnjo	1940-50	번역 표준 원칙
1360	미국 원조품	美國 援助品	aid from the U.S.	Miguk wonjopum	miguk wŏnjop'um		번역 표준 원칙

NO	용어	한자	영문	RO	MC	시대 및 연도	출전
1361	미국 육군부 작전국	美國 陸軍部 作戰局	U.S. Army Operations Division	Miguk yukgunbu jakjeonguk	Miguk yukkunbu chakchŏn'guk		번역 표준 원칙
1362	미국 육군부(현재의 미국 국방부) 작전국 (OPD)	美國 陸軍部(現在의 美國 國防部) 作戰局 (OPD)	U.S. Army Operations Division	Miguk yukgunbu (hyeonjaeui miguk gukbangbu) jakjeonguk (OPD)	Miguk yukkunbu (hyŏnjae-ŭi miguk kukpangbu) chakchŏnbu (OPD)	1945	번역 표준 원칙
1363	미국 육군사령부 군정청	美國 陸軍司令部 軍政廳	U.S. Army Military Government in Korea	Migun yukgun saryeongbu gunjeongcheong	Miguk yukkun saryŏngbu kunjŏngch'ŏng		번역 표준 원칙
1364	미국 지상군	美國 地上軍	U.S. Ground Forces	Miguk jisanggun	Miguk chisanggun	1950	번역 표준 원칙
1365	미국 합동전쟁기획 위원회	美國 合同戰爭企劃 委員會	U.S. Joint War Plans Committee	Miguk hapdong jeonjaeng gihoek wiwonhoe	Miguk haptong chŏnjaeng kihoek wiwŏnhoe		번역 표준 원칙
1366	미국경제사절단	美國經濟使節團	U.S. economic delegation	Miguk gyeongje sajeoldan	Miguk kyŏngje sajŏltan		번역 표준 원칙
1367	미국상원외교위원회	美國上院外交委員會	Foreign Relations Committee (FRC)	Miguk sangwon oegyo wiwonhoe	Miguk sangwŏn oegyo wiwŏnhoe		번역 표준 원칙
1368	미국선교본부	美國宣敎本部	American Board of Commissioners for Foreign Missions	Miguk seongyo bonbu	Miguk sŏngyo ponbu		번역 표준 원칙

NO	용어	한자	영문	RO	MC	시대 및 연도	출전
1369	미국의 청와대 도청	美國의 靑瓦臺 盜聽	U.S. eavesdropping on the Korean presidential office	Migugui cheongwadae docheong	Miguk-ŭi ch'ŏngwadae toch'ŏng	1970년대	번역 표준 원칙
1370	미군 PX	美軍 PX	post exchanges (retail stores on U.S. Army bases)	Migun PX	Migun PX		번역 표준 원칙
1371	미군 공병단	美軍 工兵團	U.S. Engineer Corps	Migun gongbyeongdan	Migun kongbyŏngdan		번역 표준 원칙
1372	미군 유해공동발굴	美軍 遺骸共同發掘	U.S.-North Korea Joint Recovery Operation	Migun yuhae gongdong balgul	Migun yuhae kongdong palgul	1996-2005	번역 표준 원칙
1373	미군 유해송환	美軍 遺骸送還	repatriation of remains of American soldiers	Migun yuhae songhwan	Migun yuhae songhwan		번역 표준 원칙
1374	미군사 고문단	美軍事 顧問團	U.S. Military Advisory Group to the ROK	Mi gunsa gomundan	Mi kunsa gomundan		번역 표준 원칙
1375	미군정	美軍政	U.S. Military Government in Korea	Migunjeong	Migunjŏng	1945-1948	번역 표준 원칙
1376	미군정 미6사단기	美軍政 美6師團旗	6th Division Flag, U.S. Military Governemnt in Korea	Migunjeong Mi 6sadangi	Migunjŏng mi 6sadan'gi	1945	번역 표준 원칙

NO	용어	한자	영문	RO	MC	시대 및 연도	출전
1377	미군정 법령집	美軍政 法令集	Statute book of the U.S. Military Government in Korea	Migunjeong beomnyeongjip	Migunjŏng pŏmnyŏngjip	1946	번역 표준 원칙
1378	미군정 장관	美軍政 長官	American Military Governor	Migunjeong janggwan	Migunjŏng changgwan		번역 표준 원칙
1379	미군정기 법령	美軍政期 法令	Laws and Regulations of the U.S. Military Government in Korea	Migunjeonggi beomnyeong	Migunjŏnggi pŏmnyŏng	1945-1948	번역 표준 원칙
1380	미군정청 포고	美軍政廳 布告	decree of the U.S. Military Government in Korea	Mi gunjeongcheong pogo	Mi gunjŏngch'ŏng p'ogo		번역 표준 원칙
1381	미군진주	美軍進駐	stationing of U.S. Forces in Korea	Migunjinju	Migunjinju		번역 표준 원칙
1382	미니스커트		Miniskirt	miniskirt	Miniseukeoteu	Minisŭk'ŏt'ŭ		번역 표준 원칙
1383	미드웨이 해전	MIDWAY 海戰	Battle of Midway	Mideuwaei haejeon	Midŭwei haejŏn	1942	번역 표준 원칙
1384	미라이 학살사건	My Lai 虐殺事件	My Lai Massacre	Mirai haksal sageon	Mirai haksal sakŏn	1968	번역 표준 원칙

NO	용어	한자	영문	RO	MC	시대 및 연도	출전
1385	미래 병사	未來 兵士	Future Warrior	Mirae byeongsa	Mirae pyŏngsa	2000	번역 표준 원칙
1386	미-북 기본합의문	美-北 基本合意文	U.S.-DPRK Agreed Framework (signed on October 21, 1994)	Mi-buk gibon habuimun	Mi-buk kibon habŭimun		번역 표준 원칙
1387	미소공동위원회	美蘇共同委員會	Russo-American Joint Commission	Miso gongdong wiwonhoe	Miso kongdong wiwŏnhoe	1945-1947	번역 표준 원칙
1388	미술단체	美術團體	art organization	Misul danche	Misul tanche		번역 표준 원칙
1389	미아리 방어선	彌阿里 防禦線	Miari Defense Line	Miari bangeoseon	Miari pangŏsŏn		번역 표준 원칙
1390	미일안보조약	美日安保條約	Japan-U.S. Security Treaty of 1951 (officially, the "Treaty of Mutual Cooperation and Security between the United States and	Miil anbo joyak	Miil anbo choyak	1951	번역 표준 원칙
1391	미주리함	Missouri艦	the USS Missouri	Mijuriham	Mijuriham		번역 표준 원칙
1392	미주한인연합회	美洲韓人聯合會	United Korean Association of America	Miju hanin yeonhaphoe	Miju hanin yŏnhaphoe	1931-1933	번역 표준 원칙

NO	용어	한자	영문	RO	MC	시대 및 연도	출전
1393	미태평양지역 연합군 최고 사령관	美太平洋地域 聯合軍 最高 司令官	Supreme Commander for the Allied Powers (SCAP)	Mi taepyeongyang jiyeok yeonhapgun choego saryeonggwan	Mi t'aep'yŏngyang chiyŏk yŏnhapkun ch'oego saryŏnggwan		번역 표준 원칙
1394	미통상법 301조	美通商法 301條	Section 301 of U.S. Omnibus Trade and Competitiveness Act of 1974	Mitongsangbeop 301jo	Mit'ongsangpŏp 301jo	1974	번역 표준 원칙
1395	미풍양속	美風良俗	beautiful traditions and customs	Mipungyangsok	Mip'ungyangsok		번역 표준 원칙
1396	미합동참모본부	美合同參謀本部	American Joint Chiefs of Staff	Mi hapdong chammo bonbu	Mi haptong ch'ammo ponbu		번역 표준 원칙
1397	민간경제백서	民間經濟白書	Private Sector Economic White Paper	Mingan gyeongje baekseo	Mingan gyŏngje baeksŏ	현대	번역 표준 원칙
1398	민간상업차관	民間商業借款	private (commercial) loans	Mingan sangeop chagwan	Mingan sangŏp ch'agwan		번역 표준 원칙
1399	민간요법	民間療法	folk remedies	Mingan nyobeop	Mingan yopŏp		번역 표준 원칙
1400	민간인 통제선	民間人 統制線	Civilian Control Line (CCL)	Minganin tongjeseon	Minganin t'ongjesŏn		번역 표준 원칙

NO	용어	한자	영문	RO	MC	시대 및 연도	출전
1401	민군작전	民軍作戰	Civil Military Operations (CMO)	Mingun jakjeon	Min'gun chakchŏn		번역 표준 원칙
1402	민권사상	民權思想	idea of civil rights	Mingwon sasang	Minkwŏn sasang		번역 표준 원칙
1403	민립대학기성회	民立大學期成會	Support Association for the Foundation of Private Korean Universities	Millip daehak giseonghoe	Millip taehak kisŏnghoe	1923-?	번역 표준 원칙
1404	민립대학설립운동	民立大學設立運動	campaign for the foundation of private Korean universities	Millip daehak seollip undong	Millip taehak sŏllip undong	1922-?	번역 표준 원칙
1405	민방위	民防衛	Civil Defense Corps	Minbangwi	Minbangwi	1951	번역 표준 원칙
1406	민방위기본법	民防衛基本法	Framework Act on Civil Defense	Minbangwi gibonbeop	Minbangwi kibonpŏp	1975-?	번역 표준 원칙
1407	민방위대원	民防衛隊員	Civil Defense Corps member	Minbangwi daewon	Minbangwi daewŏn	1976.10.1	번역 표준 원칙
1408	민사심리전	民事心理戰	Civil Affairs and Psychological Warfare	Minsa simnijeon	Minsa simnijŏn		번역 표준 원칙

NO	용어	한자	영문	RO	MC	시대 및 연도	출전
1409	민생단사건	民生團事件	Minsaengdan Incident	Minsaengdan sageon	Minsaengdan sakŏn	1930년대	번역 표준 원칙
1410	민생안정정책	民生安定政策	policies on stabilizing living standards	Minsaeng anjeong jeongchaek	Minsaeng anjŏng chŏngch'aek		번역 표준 원칙
1411	민속놀이	民俗놀이	folk entertainment	Minsongnori	Minsongnori		국사편찬위원회
1412	민속문화	民俗文化	folk culture	Minsok munhwa	Minsok munhwa		번역 표준 원칙
1413	민영탄광	民營炭鑛	private coal mines	Minyeong tangwang	Minyŏng t'an'gwang		번역 표준 원칙
1414	민영환 간찰	閔泳煥 簡札	letter written by Min Yeong-hwan	Min Yeong-hwan ganchal	Min Yŏng-hwan kanch'al		번역 표준 원칙
1415	민영환 유서	閔泳煥 遺書	suicide note of Min Yeong-hwan	Min Yeong-hwan yuseo	Min Yŏng-hwan yusŏ	1905	번역 표준 원칙
1416	민의원	民議院	House of Representatives	Minuiwon	Minŭiwŏn	1960-1961	번역 표준 원칙

NO	용어	한자	영문	RO	MC	시대 및 연도	출전
1417	민정관리총국	民政管理總局	General Bureau of Civil Administration Management	Minjeong gwalli chongguk	Minjŏng kwalli ch'ongguk		번역 표준 원칙
1418	민정당사 점거농성 사건	民正黨舍 占據籠城 事件	students' sit-in protest at the Democratic Justice Party headquarters (1984)	Minjeongdang jeomgeo nongseong sageon	Minjŏngdangsa chŏmgŏ nongsŏng sakŏn	1984	번역 표준 원칙
1419	민정복귀에 관한 특별성명	民政復歸에 關한 特別聲明	Special Statement on a Return to Civil Government	Minjeong bokgwie gwanhan teukbyeol seongmyeong	Minjŏng bokkwie kwanan tŭkpyŏl sŏngmyŏng		번역 표준 원칙
1420	민정이양	民政移讓	transfer of power to civil government	Minjeong iyang	Minjŏng iyang	1948	번역 표준 원칙
1421	민정장관	民政長官	civil administrator	Minjeong janggwan	Minjŏng changgwan	1947-1948	번역 표준 원칙
1422	민족 지도자	民族 指導者	national leader	Minjok jidoja	Minjok chidoja		번역 표준 원칙
1423	민족개량주의	民族改良主義	idea of improving the nation's competence	Minjok gaeryangjuui	Minjok kaeryangjuŭi		번역 표준 원칙
1424	민족개조론	民族改造論	"On National Reconstruction" (article by novelist Yi Gwang-su)	Minjok gaejoron	Minjok kaejoron	1922	번역 표준 원칙

NO	용어	한자	영문	RO	MC	시대 및 연도	출전
1425	민족교육	民族敎育	nationalistic education	Minjok gyoyuk	Minjok kyoyuk		번역 표준 원칙
1426	민족기지 건설작업	民族基地 建設作業	National Base Construction Project	Minjok giji geonseol jageop	Minjok kiji kŏnsŏl chagŏp		번역 표준 원칙
1427	민족대표 33인	民族代表 33人	33 National Independence Leaders	Minjok daepyo 33in	Minjok taep'yo 33in	1919	번역 표준 원칙
1428	민족말살정책	民族抹殺政策	Japanese campaign to eradiate Korean national identity	Minjok malsal jeongchaek	Minjok malsal chŏngch'aek	근대/일제강점기	Ki-baik Lee, translated by Edward W. Wagner, A New History of Korea, Harvard University Press, 1984,
1429	민족문학	民族文學	national literature	Minjok munhak	Minjok munhak	현대	번역 표준 원칙
1430	민족문화수호운동	民族文化守護運動	movement for the safeguarding of Korean culture	Minjok munhwa suho undong	Minjok munhwa suho undong		번역 표준 원칙
1431	민족보위국	民族保衛局	National Security Bureau	Minjok bowiguk	Minjok powiguk		번역 표준 원칙
1432	민족분열정책	民族分裂政策	"divide and rule" policy	Minjok bunyeol jeongchaek	Minjok punyŏl chŏngch'aek		번역 표준 원칙

NO	용어	한자	영문	RO	MC	시대 및 연도	출전
1433	민족사학	民族史學	national historical studies	Minjok sahak	Minjok sahak	일제	번역 표준 원칙
1434	민족산업육성운동	民族産業育成運動	movement for the promotion of national industries	Minjok saneop yukseong undong	Minjok sanŏp yuksŏng undong		번역 표준 원칙
1435	민족실력양성운동	民族實力養成運動	Capacity-enhancing Movement (as a way to gain Korea's independence)	Minjok sillyeok yangseong undong	Minjok sillyŏk yangsŏng undong	일제	번역 표준 원칙
1436	민족예술	民族藝術	national art	Minjok yesul	Minjok yesul		번역 표준 원칙
1437	민족유일당운동	民族唯一黨運動	United National Front Movement	Minjok yuildang undong	Minjok yuiltang undong	1920년대 후반	번역 표준 원칙
1438	민족일보	民族日報	Minjok Ilbo (People's Daily)	Minjogilbo	Minjogilbo	1961	번역 표준 원칙
1439	민족자결권선포대회	民族自決權宣布大會	National Self-determination Rights Proclamation Meeting	Minjok jagyeolgwon seonpodaehoe	Minjok chagyŏlkwŏn sŏnp'o taehoe		번역 표준 원칙
1440	민족자결주의	民族自決主義	principle of self-determination	Minjok jagyeoljuui	Minjok chagyŏljuŭi	1918	번역 표준 원칙

NO	용어	한자	영문	RO	MC	시대 및 연도	출전
1441	민족자본	民族資本	national capital	Minjok jabon	Minjok chabon	?-?	번역 표준 원칙
1442	민족자존과 번영을 위한 대통령특별선언	民族自存과 繁榮을 爲한 大統領特別宣言	Special Declaration for National Self-Esteem, Unification and Prosperity of 1988	Minjok jajon-gwa beonyeong-eul wihan daetongnyeong teukbyeol seoneon	Minjok chajon-kwa pŏnyŏng-ŭl wihan taet'ongnyŏng t'ŭkpyŏl sŏnŏn	1988	번역 표준 원칙
1443	민족자주연맹	民族自主聯盟	People's Autonomy League	Minjok jaju yeonmaeng	Minjok chaju yŏnmaeng	1947-1948	번역 표준 원칙
1444	민족자주통일중앙협의회	民族自主統一中央協議會	Central Association for Autonomous National Reunification	Minjok jaju tongil jungang hyeobuihoe	Minjok chaju t'ongil chungang hyŏbŭihoe	1960	번역 표준 원칙
1445	민족적 민주주의	民族的 民主主義	national democracy	Minjokjeok minjujuui	Minjokchŏk minjujuŭi		번역 표준 원칙
1446	민족전선연맹	民族戰線聯盟	Korean National Front Federation	Minjok jeonseon yeonmaeng	Minjok chŏnsŏn yŏnmaeng		번역 표준 원칙
1447	민족전선통일운동	民族戰線統一運動	National Front Unification Movement	Minjok jeonseon tongil undong	Minjok chŏnsŏn t'ongil undong		번역 표준 원칙
1448	민족주의	民族主義	nationalism	Minjokjuui	Minjokjuŭi		번역 표준 원칙

NO	용어	한자	영문	RO	MC	시대 및 연도	출전
1449	민족주의사학	民族主義史學	nationalist historiography	Minjokjuui sahak	Minjokjuŭi sahak	일제	번역 표준 원칙
1450	민족주의운동	民族主義運動	nationalist movement	Minjokjuui undong	Minjokjuŭi undong	근대/일제강점기	번역 표준 원칙
1451	민족중흥	民族中興	national regeneration	Minjok jungheung	Minjok chunghŭng		번역 표준 원칙
1452	민족차별	民族差別	discrimination against ethnic groups	Minjok chabyeol	Minjok ch'abyŏl		번역 표준 원칙
1453	민족청년단	韓國民主黨	National Youth Corps	Minjok cheongnyeondan	Minjok ch'ŏngnyŏndan	1946-1954	번역 표준 원칙
1454	민족통일대축전	民族統一大祝典	June 15 National Unification Grand Festival	Minjok tongil daechukjeon	Minjok t'ongil daech'ukchŏn		번역 표준 원칙
1455	민족통일 전국학생연맹 준비위원회	民族統一 全國學生聯盟 準備委員會	National Student's League for National Unification Preparation Committee	Minjok tongil jeonguk haksaeng yeonmaeng junbi wiwonhoe	Minjok t'ongil chŏn'guk haksaeng yŏnmaeng chunbi wiwŏnhoe	1960-1961	번역 표준 원칙
1456	민족통일전선	民族統一戰線	Anti-Japanese National United Front	Minjok tongil jeonseon	Minjok t'ongil chŏnsŏn		번역 표준 원칙

NO	용어	한자	영문	RO	MC	시대 및 연도	출전
1457	민족해방운동	民族解放運動	National Liberation Movement	Minjok haebang undong	Minjok haebang undong		번역 표준 원칙
1458	민족해방운동기지건설	民族解放運動基地建設	establishment of the base for the campaign for liberation of the Korean people	Minjok haebang undong giji geonseol	Minjok haebang undong kiji kŏnsŏl		번역 표준 원칙
1459	민족해방 인민민주주의혁명	民族解放 人民民主義革命	National Liberation and People's Democratic Revolution (NLPDR)	Minjok haebang inmin minjujuui hyeongmyeong	Minjok haebang inmin minjujuŭi hyŏngmyŏng	1970	번역 표준 원칙
1460	민족협동전선	民族協同戰線	National United Front	Minjok hyeopdong jeonseon	Minjok hyŏptong chŏnsŏn		번역 표준 원칙
1461	민족협동전선운동	民族協同戰線運動	National United Front Movement	Minjok hyeopdong jeonseon undong	Minjok hyŏptong chŏnsŏn undong		번역 표준 원칙
1462	민족화합민주통일방안	民族和合民主統一方案	National Reconciliation and Democratic Unification Measures	Minjok hwahap minju tongil bangan	Minjok hwahap minju t'ongil pangan	1982	번역 표준 원칙
1463	민족화해협의회	民族和解協議會	National Reconciliation Council	Minjok hwahae hyeobuihoe	Minjok hwahae hyŏbŭihoe		번역 표준 원칙
1464	민주개혁정치모임	民主改革政治모임	Group for Democratic Political Reform	Minju gaehyeok jeongchi moim	Minju gaehyŏk jŏngch'imoim		번역 표준 원칙

NO	용어	한자	영문	RO	MC	시대 및 연도	출전
1465	민주공화당	民主共和黨	Democratic Republican Party	Minju gonghwadang	Minju konghwadang	1963-1980	번역 표준 원칙
1466	민주공화정체	民主共和政體	democratic-republican government	Minju gonghwajeongche	Minju konghwajŏngch'e		번역 표준 원칙
1467	민주국민당	民主國民黨	Democratic National Party	Minju gungmindang	Minju kungmindang	1949-1955	번역 표준 원칙
1468	민주기지노선	民主基地路線	Democratic Base Line	Minju giji noseon	Minju kiji nosŏn	1946-?	번역 표준 원칙
1469	민주노조운동	民主勞組運動	movement to establish a democratic labor union	Minju nojo undong	Minju nojo undong	1970-1980	번역 표준 원칙
1470	민주당	民主黨	Democratic Party	Minjudang	Minjudang	1955-1965	한국학중앙연구원, 《영문한국백과》-한국
1471	민주당구파	民主黨舊派	Old Faction, Democratic Party	Minjudang gupa	Minjudang kup'a		번역 표준 원칙
1472	민주당신파	民主黨新派	New Faction, Democratic Party	Minjudang sinpa	Minjudang sinp'a		번역 표준 원칙

NO	용어	한자	영문	RO	MC	시대 및 연도	출전
1473	민주대동파	民主大同派	Democratic Union Faction	Minju daedongpa	Minju taedongp'a		번역 표준 원칙
1474	민주독립당	民主獨立黨	Democratic Independence Party	Minju dongnipdang	Minju tongniptang	1947-1948	번역 표준 원칙
1475	민주반역자에 대한 형사사건 임시처리법	民主反逆者에 對한 刑事事件 臨時處理法	Act on Tentative Handling of Criminal Cases Regarding Anti-democratic Activities	Minju banyeokjae daehan hyeongsasageon imsicheoribeop	Minju banyŏkchae taehan hyŏngsasakŏn imsich'ripŏp		번역 표준 원칙
1476	민주복지국가	民主福祉國家	democratic welfare state	Minju bokji gukga	Minju pokchi kukka		한국학중앙연구원, 《영문한국백과》-한국
1477	민주사회주의	民主社會主義	democratic socialism	Minju sahoejuui	Minju sahoejuǔi		번역 표준 원칙
1478	민주수호국민협의회	民主守護國民協議會	Civil Association for the Protection of Democracy	Minju suho gungmin hyeobuihoe	Minju suho kungmin hyŏbǔihoe	1971-1972	번역 표준 원칙
1479	민주자유당	民主自由黨	Democratic Liberal Party	Minju jayudang	Minju chayudang	1990-1995	한국학중앙연구원, 《영문한국백과》-한국
1480	민주정의당	民主正義黨	Democratic Justice Party (DJP)	Minju jeonguidang	Minju chŏngǔidang	1981-1990	번역 표준 원칙

NO	용어	한자	영문	RO	MC	시대 및 연도	출전
1481	민주주의민족전선	民主主義民族戰線	National Democratic Front	Minjujuui minjok jeonseon	Minjujuŭi minjok chŏnsŏn	1946-1949	번역 표준 원칙
1482	민주주의와 민족통일을 위한 국민연합	民主主義와 民族統一을 爲한 國民聯合	National Alliance for Democracy and Reunification	Minjujuui-wa minjok tongil-eul wihan gungmin yeonhap	Minjujuŭi-wa minjok t'ongil-ŭl wihan kungmin yŏnhap	1979-?	번역 표준 원칙
1483	민주주의의 토착화	民主主義의 土着化	naturalization of democracy	Minjujuuiui tochakhwa	Minjuju-ŭi t'och'akhwa		번역 표준 원칙
1484	민주진영	民主陣營	democratic camp	Minju jinnyeong	Minju chinyŏng		번역 표준 원칙
1485	민주통일민중운동 연합	民主統一民衆運動 聯合	People's Movement Coalition for Democracy and Reunification	Minju tongil minjung undong yeonhap	Minju t'ongil minjung undong yŏnhap	1985-1989	번역 표준 원칙
1486	민주투쟁위원회	民主鬪爭委員會	Committee for the Struggle for Democracy	Minju tujaeng wiwonhoe	Minju t'ujaeng wiwŏnhoe		번역 표준 원칙
1487	민주학생 투쟁 취지문	民主學生 鬪爭 趣旨文	Statement of the Pro-democracy Student Uprising of 1960	Minjuhaksaeng tujaeng chwijimun	Minju haksaeng t'ujaeng ch'wijimun	1960	번역 표준 원칙
1488	민주헌법 쟁취를 위한 범국민 서명운동 선언	民主憲法 爭取를 爲한 汎國民 署名運動 宣言	declaration of a nationwide signature-collecting campaign for a democratic constitution on March 5, 1986	Minju heonbeop jaengchwireul wihan beomgungmin seomyeongundong seoneon	Minju hŏnpŏp chaengch'wi-rŭl wihan pŏmgungmin sŏmyŏng undong sŏnŏn		번역 표준 원칙

- 206 -

NO	용어	한자	영문	RO	MC	시대 및 연도	출전
1489	민주헌법쟁취 국민운동본부	民主憲法爭取 國民運動本部	National Headquarters for Obtaining a Democratic Constitution	Minju heonbeop jaengchwi gungmin undong bonbu	Minju hŏnpŏp chaengch'wi kungmin undong ponbu	1987	번역 표준 원칙
1490	민주혁명	民主革命	democratic revolution	Minju hyeongmyeong	Minju hyŏngmyŏng		번역 표준 원칙
1491	민주화를 위한 전국교수협의회	民主化를 위한 全國敎授協議會	National Association of Professors for Democratic Society	Minjuhwareul wihan jeonguk gyosu hyeobuihoe	Minjuhwarŭl wihan chŏnguk kyosu hyŏbŭihoe	1987	번역 표준 원칙
1492	민주화세력	民主化勢力	forces for democratization	Minjuhwa seryeok	Minjuhwa seryŏk		번역 표준 원칙
1493	민주화실천가족운동협의회	民主化實踐家族運動協議會	Family Conference for Implementation of Democratization (Minkahyup)	Minjuhwa silcheon gajok undong hyeobuihoe	Minjuhwa silch'ŏn kajok undong hyŏbŭihoe	1985-?	번역 표준 원칙
1494	민주화운동청년연합	民主化運動靑年聯合	Korean Democratic Youth Federation	Minjuhwa undong cheongnyeon yeonhap	Minjuhwa undong ch'ŏngnyŏn yŏnhap	1983-1992	번역 표준 원칙
1495	민주화추진위원회 사건	民主化推進委員會 事件	Incident of the Committee for the Promotion of Democracy	Minjuhwa chujin wiwonhoe sageon	Minjuhwa ch'ujin wiwŏnhoe sagŏn	1985	번역 표준 원칙
1496	민주화추진협의회	民主化推進協議會	Council for the Promotion of Democracy (founded May 1984)	Minjuhwa chujin hyeobuihoe	Minjuhwa ch'ujin hyŏbŭihoe	1984	번역 표준 원칙

NO	용어	한자	영문	RO	MC	시대 및 연도	출전
1497	민주회복국민회의	民主回復國民會議	National Meeting for the Restoration of Democracy	Minju hoebok gungmin hoeui	Minju hoebok kungmin hoeŭi	1974	번역 표준 원칙
1498	민중대회	民衆大會	people's rally	Minjung daehoe	Minjung taehoe		번역 표준 원칙
1499	민중문학	民衆文學	Minjung ("people's") literature	Minjung munhak	Minjung munhak		번역 표준 원칙
1500	민중문화운동	民衆文化運動	Minjung ("people's") cultural movement	Minjung munhwa undong	Minjung munhwa undong	1970-1980	번역 표준 원칙
1501	민중신문	民衆新聞	*Minjung Shinmun (The People's Newspaper)*	Minjung sinmun	Minjung sinmun	1987.6.19, 1987.12.27	번역 표준 원칙
1502	민중의 소리	民衆의 소리	"Minjung-ui Sori" ("Voice of the People")	Minjungui sori	Minjung-ŭi sori	1987.3.31	번역 표준 원칙
1503	민중자결단	民衆自決團	People's Self-determination Group	Minjung jagyeoldan	Minjung chagyŏltan		번역 표준 원칙
1504	민청학련사건	民靑學聯事件	National Federation of Democratic Youth and Students Incident	Mincheong hangnyeon sageon	Minch'ŏng hangnyŏn sakŏn	1974	번역 표준 원칙

NO	용어	한자	영문	RO	MC	시대 및 연도	출전
1505	민흥회	民興會	People's Prosperity Society	Minheunghoe	Minhŭnghoe	1926-1927	번역 표준 원칙
1506	밀무역	密貿易	smuggling	Milmuyeok	Milmuyŏk		번역 표준 원칙
1507	밀산부	密山府	Mishan (in northern Manchuria, base for Korean independence activists)	Milsanbu	Milsanbu		번역 표준 원칙
1508	밀수방지요강	密輸防止要綱	Guidelines for the Prevention of Smuggling	Milsu bangji yogang	Milsu bangji yogang		번역 표준 원칙
1509	밀수품	密輸品	contraband	Milsupum	Milsup'um		번역 표준 원칙
1510	밀양학살사건	密陽虐殺事件	Miryang Massacre	Miryang haksal sageon	Miryang haksal sagŏn	1919	번역 표준 원칙
1511	바다이야기 사건	바다이야기 事件	"Sea Story" scandal (aracde game scandal)	Badaiyagi sageon	Padaiyagi sakŏn	2006	번역 표준 원칙
1512	바덴바덴 IOC 총회	Baden Baden IOC 總會	Congress of the International Olympic Committee in Baden-Baden, Germany in 1981	Badenbaden IOC chonghoe	Padenbaden IOC ch'onghoe	1981	번역 표준 원칙

NO	용어	한자	영문	RO	MC	시대 및 연도	출전
1513	바레인 조선소 건설공사	Bahrain 造船所 建設工事	project to build a shipyard in Bahrain	Barein joseonso geonseolgongsa	Parein chosŏnso kŏnsŏl kongsa		번역 표준 원칙
1514	바르셀로나 올림픽	Barcelona Olympic	1992 Barcelona Olympic Games	Bareusellona ollimpik	Parŭsellona ollimp'ik	1992	번역 표준 원칙
1515	바보회	바보會	Fools' Association (Babohoe, labor activist group formed by Jeon Tae-il)	Babohoe	Pabohoe	1968	번역 표준 원칙
1516	바지선 운반작업	Barge船 運搬作業	transportation of barges	Bajiseon unban jageop	Pajisŏn unban chagŏp		번역 표준 원칙
1517	박달학원	博達學院	Bakdal Institute	Bakdal hagwon	Paktal hagwŏn	1913	번역 표준 원칙
1518	박동선 로비사건	朴東宣 로비事件	Park Tong-sun lobby scandal (Koreagate)	Bak Dong-seon robi sageon	Pak Tong-sŏn robi sakŏn	1976	번역 표준 원칙
1519	박정희 대통령의 서독방문	朴正熙 大統領의 西獨訪問	President Park Chung-hee's visit to West Germany in 1964	Bak Jeong-hui daetongnyeongui seodok bangmun	Pak Chŏng-hŭi taet'ongnyŏng-ŭi sŏdok pangmun	1964	번역 표준 원칙
1520	박정희, 케네디 공동성명	朴正熙, Kennedy 共同聲明	Joint Statement by President Park Chung-hee and President John F. Kennedy, November 1961	Bak Jeong-hui, Kenedi gongdong seongmyeong	Pak Chŏng-hŭi, K'enedi kongdong sŏngmyŏng	1961	번역 표준 원칙

NO	용어	한자	영문	RO	MC	시대 및 연도	출전
1521	박종철 고문치사사건	朴鐘哲 拷問致死事件	torture of Park Jong-cheol	Bak Jong-cheol gomun chisa sageon	Pak Chong-ch'ŏl komun ch'isa sakŏn	1987	번역 표준 원칙
1522	반값등록금	半갑登錄金	half-price tuition	Bangap deungnokgeum	Pankap tŭngnokkŭm		번역 표준 원칙
1523	반공교육	反共敎育	anti-Communist education	Bangong gyoyuk	pan'gonggyoyuk		번역 표준 원칙
1524	반공독본	反共讀本	An Anti-Communist Reader	Bangong dokbon	Pan'gongdokpon	1954	번역 표준 원칙
1525	반공방첩	反共防諜	anti-Communist and counter intelligence	Bangong bangcheop	Pan'gong pangch'ŏp		번역 표준 원칙
1526	반공법	反共法	Anti-Communist Act	Bangongbeop	Pan'gongpŏp	1961-1980	번역 표준 원칙
1527	반공임시특별법안	反共臨時特別法案	Anti-Communist Special Tentative Bill	Bangong imsi teukbyeol beoban	Pangong imsi t'ŭkpyŏl pŏban		번역 표준 원칙
1528	반공주의	反共主義	anti-Communism	Bangongjuui	Pan'gongjuŭi		번역 표준 원칙

NO	용어	한자	영문	RO	MC	시대 및 연도	출전
1529	반공포로석방	反共捕虜釋放	release of anti-Communist prisoners of war	Bangong poro seokbang	Pan'gong p'oro sŏkpang	1953	번역 표준 원칙
1530	반공회관	反共會館	Anti-Communist Hall	Bangonghoegwan	Pan'gonghoegwan		번역 표준 원칙
1531	반군사독재 학생운동	反軍事獨裁 學生運動	Student Movement against Military Dictatorship	Bangunsa dokjae haksaeng undong	Pan'gunsa tokchae haksaeng undong		번역 표준 원칙
1532	반덤핑제소	反dumping提訴	filing an anti-dumping suit	Bandeomping jeso	Pandŏmp'ing cheso		번역 표준 원칙
1533	반도상사 노동자투쟁	半島商社 勞動者鬪爭	Bando Trading Company workers' strikes	Bando sangsa nodongja tujaeng	Pando sangsa nodongja t'ujaeng	1974-1981	번역 표준 원칙
1534	반도체산업	半導體産業	semiconductor industry	Bandoche saneop	Pandoch'e sanŏp		번역 표준 원칙
1535	반독재민주수호연맹	反獨裁民主守護聯盟	Anti-dictatorship and Pro-Democracy League	Bandokjae minjusuho yeonmaeng	Pandokche minjusuho yŏnmaeng	1960	번역 표준 원칙
1536	반독재호헌구국대회	反獨裁護憲救國大會	Anti-dictatorship Constitution-protection Save-the-Nation Meeting	Bandokjae hoheon guguk daehoe	Pandokchae hohŏn kuguk taehoe		번역 표준 원칙

NO	용어	한자	영문	RO	MC	시대 및 연도	출전
1537	반동계급	反動階級	reactionary class	Bandong gyegeup	Pandong kyegŭp		번역 표준 원칙
1538	반동분자	反動分子	reactionary elements	Bandong bunja	Pandong punja		번역 표준 원칙
1539	반미자주화운동	反美自主化運動	anti-American movement toward self-reliance	Banmi jajuhwa undong	Panmi chajuhwa undong	1980년대-?	번역 표준 원칙
1540	반민족행위처벌법	反民族行爲處罰法	Act on Punishment for Anti-National Activities	Banminjok haengwi cheobeolbeop	Panminjok haengwi ch'ŏbŏlpŏp	1948	번역 표준 원칙
1541	반민주국회의원규탄대회	反民主國會議員糾彈大會	Impeachment Meeting Against Anti-democratic Assembly Members	Banminju gukhoe uiwon gyutan daehoe	Panminju kukhoe ŭiwŏn kyut'an taehoe		번역 표준 원칙
1542	반민주행위자 공민권제한법	反民主行爲者公民權制限法	Act on Restriction of Civil Rights of Those Engaged in Anti-democratic Activities	Banminju haengwija gongmingwon jehanbeop	Panminju haengwija kongminkwŏn jehanpŏp	1960	번역 표준 원칙
1543	반봉건	反封建	anti-feudal	Banbonggeon	Panbonggŏn		번역 표준 원칙
1544	반봉건항쟁	反封建抗爭	anti-feudal movement	Banbonggeon hangjaeng	Panbonggŏn hangjaeng		번역 표준 원칙

NO	용어	한자	영문	RO	MC	시대 및 연도	출전
1545	반상회	班常會	neighborhood associations	Bansanghoe	Pansanghoe	현대	번역 표준 원칙
1546	반외세	反外勢	anti-foreign influence	Banoesae	Panoese		번역 표준 원칙
1547	반월 국가산업단지	半月 國家産業團地	Banwol Industrial Complex	Banwol gukga saneop danji	Panwŏl kukka sanŏp tanji	현대	번역 표준 원칙
1548	반유신운동	反維新運動	Anti-Yushin Movement	Banyusin undong	Panyusin undong		번역 표준 원칙
1549	반일민족통일전선	反日民族統一戰線	Anti-Japanese National United Front	Banil minjok tong-il jeonseon	Panil minjok t'ongil chŏnsŏn		번역 표준 원칙
1550	반일인민유격대	反日人民遊擊隊	Anti-Japanese Peoples' Guerrilla Unit	Banil inmin yugyeokdae	Panil inmin yugyŏktae		번역 표준 원칙
1551	반전여론	反戰輿論	anti-war sentiment	Banjeon yeoron	Panjŏn yŏron		번역 표준 원칙
1552	반전운동	反戰運動	anti-war movement	Banjeon undong	Panjŏn undong		번역 표준 원칙

NO	용어	한자	영문	RO	MC	시대 및 연도	출전
1553	반제동맹	反帝同盟	Anti-Imperialist League	Banje dongmaeng	Panje tongmaeng	일제	번역 표준 원칙
1554	반탁	反託	opposition to trusteeship	Bantak	Pant'ak		번역 표준 원칙
1555	발신번호표시	發信番號票示	identification of incoming calls	Balsin beonho pyosi	Palsin pŏnho p'yosi		번역 표준 원칙
1556	발전소 복구계획	發電所 復舊計劃	Power Plant Recovery Plan	Baljeonso bokgu gyehoek	Palchŏnso pokku kyehoek		번역 표준 원칙
1557	발췌개헌	拔萃改憲	Selected Constitutional Amendmnet	Balchwe gaeheon	Palch'we kaehŏn	1952	번역 표준 원칙
1558	발췌개헌안	拔萃改憲案	Selective Constitutional Revision Bill	Balchwe gaeheonan	Palch'we kaehŏnan	1952	Ki-baik Lee, translated by Edward W. Wagner, A New History of Korea, Harvard University Press, 1984,
1559	발포사건	發砲事件	shooting incident	Balpo sageon	Palp'o sakŏn		번역 표준 원칙
1560	방곡령	防穀令	Order of the Grain Export Bans	Banggongnyeong	Panggongnyŏng	1889-1894	번역 표준 원칙

NO	용어	한자	영문	RO	MC	시대 및 연도	출전
1561	방곡령사건	防穀令事件	Incident of the Grain Export Bans	Banggongnyeong sageon	Panggongnyŏng sakŏn	1889	번역 표준 원칙
1562	방공식별구역	防空識別區域	Air Defense Indentification Zone (ADIZ)	Banggong sikbyeol guyeok	Panggong sikpyŏl guyŏk		번역 표준 원칙
1563	방공포병대대	防空砲兵大隊	Anti-aircraft Artillery Battalion	Banggong pobyeongdaedae	Panggong p'obyŏngdaedae		번역 표준 원칙
1564	방사성폐기물	放射性廢棄物	radioactive waste	Bangsaseong pyegimul	Pangsasŏng p'yegimul		번역 표준 원칙
1565	방송통신심의위원회	放送審議委員會	Korea Communications Standards Commission	Bangsong tongsin simui wiwonhoe	Pangsong t'ongsin simŭi wiwŏnhoe	2008	번역 표준 원칙
1566	방송통신위원회	放送通信委員會	Korea Communications Commission (KCC)	Bangsong tongsin wiwonhoe	Pangsong t'ongsin wiwŏnhoe		번역 표준 원칙
1567	방송프로그램 등급제 시행	放送program 等級制 施行	implementation of TV Content Ratings System	Bangsong peurogeuraem deunggeupje sihaeng	Pangsong p'ŭrogŭraem tŭnggŭpche sihaeng	2001?	번역 표준 원칙
1568	방어전	防禦戰	defensive operations	Bangeojeon	Pangŏjŏn		번역 표준 원칙

NO	용어	한자	영문	RO	MC	시대 및 연도	출전
1569	방어준비태세	防禦準備態勢	Defense Readiness Condition (DEFCON)	Bangeo junbitaese	Pangŏ junbit'aese		번역 표준 원칙
1570	방어진	防禦陣	defense position	Bangeojin	Pangŏjin	?-1914	번역 표준 원칙
1571	방위사업청	防衛事業廳	Defense Acquisition Program Administration (DAPA)	Bangwi saeopcheong	Pangwi saŏpch'ŏng	2006	번역 표준 원칙
1572	방위산업 육성	防衛産業 育成	promotion of defense industries	Bangwi saneop yukseong	Pangwi sanŏp yuksŏng		번역 표준 원칙
1573	방위성금	防衛誠金	donation to the National Defense Fund	Bangwi seonggeum	Pangwi sŏnggŭm		번역 표준 원칙
1574	방위세	防衛稅	defense tax	Bangwise	Pangwise	1975	번역 표준 원칙
1575	방위세법	防衛稅法	defense tax law	Bangwisebeop	Pangwisebŏp	1975-1990	번역 표준 원칙
1576	방직협회	紡織協會	Spinners and Weavers Association of Korea	Bangjik hyeophoe	Pangjik hyŏphoe		번역 표준 원칙

NO	용어	한자	영문	RO	MC	시대 및 연도	출전
1577	방첩부대	防諜部隊	Counter Intelligence Corps	Bangcheop budae	Pangch'ŏp pudae		번역 표준 원칙
1578	방첩함	防諜函	postbox dedicated to the collection of propaganda leaflets	Bangcheobham	Pangch'ŏpham		번역 표준 원칙
1579	방파제	防波堤	seawall	Bangpaje	Pangp'aje		번역 표준 원칙
1580	방호철조망	防護鐵條網	protective wire entanglement	Bangho cheoljomang	Pangho ch'ŏlchomang		번역 표준 원칙
1581	배달민족	倍達民族	the Korean people	Baedal minjok	Paedal minjok		번역 표준 원칙
1582	배재학당	培材學堂	Paichai Hakdang (now Paichai School)	Baejae hakdang	Paejae haktang	1885	번역 표준 원칙
1583	배화여학교	培花女學校	Paiwha Girls' School (now Paiwha Girl's High School)	Baehwa yeohakgyo	Paehwa yŏhakkyo	1898-1910	번역 표준 원칙
1584	백골단	白骨團	Baekgoldan (White Skull Corps)	Baekgoldan	Paekkoltan		번역 표준 원칙

NO	용어	한자	영문	RO	MC	시대 및 연도	출전
1585	백구부대	白鷗部隊	White Gull Unit	Baekgu budae	Paekku pudae		번역 표준 원칙
1586	백두산 관광단 방북	白頭山 觀光團 訪北	visits of South Koreans to North Korea for tours of Mt. Baekdusan	Baekdusan gwangwangdan bangbuk	Paektusan kwangwangdan pangbuk	2000	번역 표준 원칙
1587	백두산정계비	白頭山定界碑	Mt. Baekdusan Demarcation Stone	Baekdusan jeonggyebi	Paektusan chŏnggyebi	1712-1931	번역 표준 원칙
1588	백마고지 전투	白馬高地 戰鬪	Battle of White Horse Hill	Baengmagoji jeontu	Paengmagoji chŏnt'u	1952	번역 표준 원칙
1589	백범일지	白凡逸志	Autobiography of Kim Gu	Baekbeomilji	Paekpŏmilchi	1947	번역 표준 원칙
1590	백산상회	白山商會	Paeksan Trading Company	Baeksan sanghoe	Paeksan sanghoe	1914-1927	Ki-baik Lee, translated by Edward W. Wagner, A New History of Korea, Harvard University Press, 1984,
1591	백색혁명	白色革命	White Revolution	Baeksaek hyeongmyeong	Paeksaek hyŏngmyŏng		번역 표준 원칙
1592	백서농장	白西農莊	Baekseonongjang Garrison	Baekseo nongjang	Paeksŏ nongjang	1914-1919	번역 표준 원칙

NO	용어	한자	영문	RO	MC	시대 및 연도	출전
1593	백악관 안보회의	白堊館 安保會議	White House National Security Council	Baegakgwan anbo hoeui	Paegakkwan anbo hoeŭi		번역 표준 원칙
1594	백의사	白衣社	Baeguisa (secret terrorist organization)	Baeguisa	Paegŭisa	1945-1949	번역 표준 원칙
1595	백조	白潮	*Baekjo* (literary magazine)	Baekjo	Paekcho	1922-1923	번역 표준 원칙
1596	백화론	白禍論	"White Peril" Belief	Baekhwaron	Paekhwaron		번역 표준 원칙
1597	밴플리트사절단	밴플리트使節團	Van Fleet Mission to the Far East	Baenpeulliteu sajeoldan	Paenp'ŭllitŭ sajŏltan		번역 표준 원칙
1598	버스안내양	Bus案內孃	female bus conductors	Beoseu annaeyang	Pŏsŭ annaeyang	현대	번역 표준 원칙
1599	버스전용차선	Bus專用車線	bus-only lanes	Beoseu jeonyong chaseon	Pŏsŭ jŏnyong ch'asŏn		번역 표준 원칙
1600	범국민조림운동	汎國民造林運動	nationwide afforestation campaign	Beomgungmin jorim undong	Pŏmgungmin chorim undong		번역 표준 원칙

NO	용어	한자	영문	RO	MC	시대 및 연도	출전
1601	범민족대회	汎民族大會	Pan-national Rally for Peace and Reunification of Korea	Beomminjok daehoe	Pŏmminjok taehoe	1989-	번역 표준 원칙
1602	범민족대회남측추진본부	凡民族大會南側推進本部	South Korean headquarters for the Pan-national Rally for Peace and Reunification of Korea	Beomminjok daehoe namcheuk chujin bonbu	Pŏmminjok taehoe namch'ŭk ch'ujin bonbu		번역 표준 원칙
1603	범죄와의 전쟁	犯罪와의 戰爭	war against crime	Beomjoewaui jeonjaeng	Pŏmjoewaŭi chŏnjaeng	1990	번역 표준 원칙
1604	범죄와의 전쟁 선포	犯罪와의 戰爭 宣布	declaration of War Against Crime	Beomjoewaui jeonjaeng seonpo	Pŏmjoewaŭi chŏnjaeng sŏnp'o	1990	번역 표준 원칙
1605	범태평양노동조합	汎太平洋勞動組合	Pan-Pacific Trade Union	Beomtaepyeongyang nodong johap	Pŏmt'aep'yŏngyang nodong chohap	1927-1929	번역 표준 원칙
1606	범태평양조선협회	汎太平洋朝鮮協會	Korean Branch of the Pan-Pacific Union	Beomtae pyeongyang joseon hyeophoe	Pŏmt'ae p'yŏngyang chosŏn hyŏphoe		번역 표준 원칙
1607	범태평양협회	汎太平洋協會	Pan-Pacific Union	Beomtaepyeongyang hyeophoe	Pŏmt'aep'yŏngyang hyŏphoe		번역 표준 원칙
1608	법무부	法務部	Department of Justice	Beommubu	Pŏpmubu	1948	번역 표준 원칙

NO	용어	한자	영문	RO	MC	시대 및 연도	출전
1609	법정관리	法定管理	court receivership	Beopjeong gwalli	Pŏpchŏng kwalli		번역 표준 원칙
1610	법정재산상속분의 균등화	法定財産相續分의 均等化	equal distribution of inheritance	Beopjeong jaesan sangsokbunui gyundeunghwa	Pŏpchŏng chaesan sangsokpun-ŭi kyundŭnghwa		번역 표준 원칙
1611	법제사법위원회	法制司法委員會	Legislation and Judiciary Committee	Beopje sabeop wiwonhoe	Pŏpche sabŏp wiwŏnhoe	현대	번역 표준 원칙
1612	법제처	法制處	Ministry of Government Legislation	Beopjecheo	Pŏpchech'ŏ	1948	번역 표준 원칙
1613	법치국가	法治國家	Rechtsstaat (constitutional state)	Beopchi gukga	Pŏpch'I kukka		번역 표준 원칙
1614	벙커고지 전투	Bunker高地 戰鬪	Battle of Bunker Hill	Beongkeogoji jeontu	Pŏngk'ŏgoji chŏnt'u	1951	번역 표준 원칙
1615	베르사이유조약	Versailles條約	Treaty of Versailles	Bereusaiyu joyak	Perŭsaiyu choyak	1919	Ki-baik Lee, translated by Edward W. Wagner, A New History of Korea, Harvard University Press, 1984,
1616	베를린 선언	Berlin 宣言	Berlin Declaration, (proposals for peace and unification on the Korean Peninsula made by President Kim Dae-jung in 2000)	Bereullin seoneon	Perŭllin sŏnŏn	2000	번역 표준 원칙

- 222 -

NO	용어	한자	영문	RO	MC	시대 및 연도	출전
1617	베를린 올림픽	Berlin Olympics	1936 Berlin Olympic Games	Bereullin olimpik	Perŭllin ollimp'ik	1936	번역 표준 원칙
1618	베타적 경제수역법	排他的 經濟水域法	Exclusive Economic Zone Act	Betajeok gyeongje suyeokbeop	Pet'ajŏk kyŏngje suyŏkpŏp	1996	번역 표준 원칙
1619	베트남 공화국	Vietnam 共和國	Republic of Vietnam (South Vietnam)	Beteunam gonghwaguk	Pet'ŭnam konghwaguk		번역 표준 원칙
1620	베트남 사회주의 공화국	Vietnam 社會主義 共和國	Socialist Republic of Vietnam	Beteunam sahoehjuui gonghwaguk	Pet'ŭnam sahoejuŭi konghwaguk		번역 표준 원칙
1621	베트남 전쟁	Vietnam 戰爭	Vietnam War	Beteunam jeonjaeng	Pet'ŭnam chŏnjaeng	1964-1973	번역 표준 원칙
1622	베트남 패망	Vietnam 敗亡	Collapse of South Vietnam	Beteunam paemang	Pet'ŭnam p'aemang		번역 표준 원칙
1623	베트콩		Viet Cong	Beteukong	Pet'ŭk'ong	1960	번역 표준 원칙
1624	베티고지 전투	Betty 高地 戰鬪	Battle of Betty Ridge	Betigoji jeontu	Pet'igoji chŏnt'u	1953	번역 표준 원칙

NO	용어	한자	영문	RO	MC	시대 및 연도	출전
1625	벤처기업	Venture企業	venture	Bencheo gieop	Pench'ŏ kiŏp	20세기 말	번역 표준 원칙
1626	벤처벨리	Venture Valley	startup cluster	Bencheo belli	Pench'ŏ pelli		번역 표준 원칙
1627	변법자강운동	變法自彊運動	Reform Movement of 1898 (China)	Byeonbeop jagang undong	Pyŏnpŏp chagang undong	1898	번역 표준 원칙
1628	변산반도국립공원	邊山半島國立公園	Byeonsanbando National Park	Byeonsan bando gungnip gongwon	Pyŏnsan pando kungnip konwŏn	1988-?	번역 표준 원칙
1629	별기군	別技軍	Byeolgigun, Special Skills Forces	Byeolgigun	Pyŏlgigun	1881-1882	번역 표준 원칙
1630	병무청	兵務廳	Military Manpower Administration	Byeongmucheong	Pyŏngmuch'ŏng	1970-	번역 표준 원칙
1631	병역의무	兵役義務	mandatory military service	Byeongyeog uimu	Pyŏngyŏk ŭimu		번역 표준 원칙
1632	병영집체훈련 반대	兵營集體訓鍊 反對	nationwide student movement of 1980 against the policy forcing freshmen to receive military training	Byeongyeong jipche hullyeon bandae	Pyŏngyŏng chipch'e hullyŏn pandae		번역 표준 원칙

NO	용어	한자	영문	RO	MC	시대 및 연도	출전
1633	병원윤리 강령	病院倫理 綱領	Hospital Code of Ethics	Byeongwon yulli gangnyeong	Pyŏngwŏn yulli gangnyŏng	1981 제정	번역 표준 원칙
1634	병인박해	丙寅迫害	Byeongin Persecution of 1886	Byeonginbakhae	Pyŏnginbakhae	1866-1871	번역 표준 원칙
1635	병인양요	丙寅洋擾	Foreign Disturbance of 1866 (Byeongin Yangyo)	Byeonginnyangyo	Pyŏnginyangyo	1866	한국학중앙연구원, 《영문한국백과》-이항로
1636	병자수호조약	丙子修好條約	Korea-Japan Treaty of Peace and Amity, 1876	Pyongja suho choyak	Pyŏngja suho choyak	1876	번역 표준 원칙
1637	병참선	兵站線	Line of Communcation (LOC)	Byeongchamseon	Pyŏngchamsŏn		번역 표준 원칙
1638	보건복지부	保健福祉部	Ministry of Health and Welfare	Bogeon bokjibu	Pogŏn pokchibu	1994, 2010	번역 표준 원칙
1639	보건위생지도부	保健衛生指導部	Health and Hygiene Guidance Division	Bogeon wisaeng jidobu	Pogŏn wisaeng chidobu		번역 표준 원칙
1640	보건후생부	保健厚生部	Department of Health and Human Services	Bogeon husaengbu	Pogŏn husaengbu	1946	번역 표준 원칙

NO	용어	한자	영문	RO	MC	시대 및 연도	출전
1641	보국안민	輔國安民	strengthening the nation and ensuring the livelihood of the people	Boguganmin	Poguganmin	1894	번역 표준 원칙
1642	보국훈장	保國勳章	Order of National Security Merit	Boguk hunjang	Poguk hunjang	1961	번역 표준 원칙
1643	보궐선거	補闕選擧	Protection and Guidance League	Bogwol seongeo	Pogwŏl sŏn'gŏ		번역 표준 원칙
1644	보도연맹	保導聯盟	Protection and Guidance League	Bodo yeonmaeng	Podo yŏnmaeng	1949-?	번역 표준 원칙
1645	보도연맹사건	保導聯盟事件	Bodo (Protection and Guidance) League Massacre	Bodo yeonmaeng sageon	Podo yŏnmaeng sakŏn	1950	번역 표준 원칙
1646	보도지도부	報道指導部	News Guidance Division	Bodojidobu	Podojidobu		번역 표준 원칙
1647	보도지침	報道指針	government's reporting guidelines for the news media (during the Chun Doo-hwan regime)	Bodo jichim	Podo chich'im	제5공화국 시절	번역 표준 원칙
1648	보릿고개	보릿고개	spring famine (literally "barley hump")	Boritgogae	Poritkogae		번역 표준 원칙

NO	용어	한자	영문	RO	MC	시대 및 연도	출전
1649	보부상	褓負商	peddler	Bobusang	Pobusang	조선	번역 표준 원칙
1650	보빙사	報聘使	Korean diplomatic mission to the U.S. in 1883 (Bobingsa)	Bobingsa	Pobingsa	1883-?	번역 표준 원칙
1651	보성전문학교	普成專門學校	Boseong College	Boseong jeonmun hakgyo	Posŏng chŏnmun hakkyo	1905-1946	번역 표준 원칙
1652	보세가공	保稅加工	bonded processing	Bose gagong	Pose kagong		번역 표준 원칙
1653	보신각	普信閣	Bosingak Belfry	Bosingak	Posingak	1398	번역 표준 원칙
1654	보안간부훈련소	保安幹部訓練所	Security Cadres Training Center	Boan ganbu hullyeonso	Poan kanbu hullyŏnso	1946-1947	번역 표준 원칙
1655	보안대	保安隊	National Security Force	Boandae	Poandae	1945	번역 표준 원칙
1656	보안법	保安法	Security Law	Boanbeop	Poanpŏp	1907-1945	번역 표준 원칙

NO	용어	한자	영문	RO	MC	시대 및 연도	출전
1657	보안법 파동	保安法 波動	Security Law constroversy	Boanbeop padong	Poanbŏp p'adong	1958	번역 표준 원칙
1658	보안사령부	保安司令部	Defense Security Command	Boan saryeongbu	Poan saryŏngbu		번역 표준 원칙
1659	보안회	保安會	Korean Preservation Council	Boanhoe	Poanhoe	1904	번역 표준 원칙
1660	보완준비금융	補完準備金融	Supplemental Reserve Facility	Bowan junbi geumyung	Powan chunbi kŭmyung		번역 표준 원칙
1661	보전협동공격	步戰協同攻擊	Combined Arms Operation	Bojeon hyeopdong gonggyeok	Pojŏn hyŏptong gonggyŏk		번역 표준 원칙
1662	보천보 전투	普天堡 戰鬪	Battle of Bocheonbo	Bocheonbo jeontu	Poch'ŏnbo chŏnt'u	1937	번역 표준 원칙
1663	보충수업	補充授業	supplementary lessons	Bochung sueop	Poch'ung suŏp		번역 표준 원칙
1664	보통경찰제도	普通警察制度	Demilitarizing Police Operation	Botong gyeongchal jedo	Pot'ong kyŏngch'al chedo	1919-1945	Ki-baik Lee, translated by Edward W. Wagner, A New History of Korea, Harvard University Press, 1984,

NO	용어	한자	영문	RO	MC	시대 및 연도	출전
1665	보통선거	普通選擧	general election	Botong seongeo	Pot'ong sŏn'gŏ		번역 표준 원칙
1666	보트 피플		boat people	Boteu pipeul	Pot'ŭ p'ip'ŭl	1975	번역 표준 원칙
1667	보합단	普合團	Bohapdan (independence activist group based in Pyeonganbuk-do Province)	Bohapdan	Pohaptan	1920-1923	번역 표준 원칙
1668	보현산 전투	普賢山 戰鬪	Battle of Mt. Bohyeonsan	Bohyeonsan jeontu	Pohyŏnsan chŏnt'u	1950	번역 표준 원칙
1669	보호국	保護國	protectorate	Bohoguk	Pohoguk	1905-1910	번역 표준 원칙
1670	보호무역주의	保護貿易主義	protectionism	Bohomuyeokjuui	Pohomuyŏkjuŭi		번역 표준 원칙
1671	보황주의	保皇主義	royalism	Bohwangjuui	Pohwangjuŭi		번역 표준 원칙
1672	보훈처	報勳處	Ministry of Patriots and Veterans Affairs	Bohuncheo	Pohunch'ŏ	1985-?	번역 표준 원칙

NO	용어	한자	영문	RO	MC	시대 및 연도	출전
1673	복벽주의	復辟主義	idea of reinstating the Joseon Dynasty	Bokbyeokjuui	Pokpyŏkjuŭi		번역 표준 원칙
1674	복수노조	複數勞組	multiple labor unions	Boksu nojo	Poksu nojo		번역 표준 원칙
1675	복수환율제	複數換率制	multiple exchange rate system	Boksu hwanyulje	Poksu hwanyulje		번역 표준 원칙
1676	복식돌파	複式突破	Multiple Penetration	Boksikdolpa	Poksikdolp'a		번역 표준 원칙
1677	본고사폐지	本考査廢止	abolition of university-administered entrance exams	Bongosa pyeji	Pongosa p'yeji		번역 표준 원칙
1678	봉금정책	封禁政策	Isolation Policy (prohibiting access to certain areas in China)	Bonggeum jeongchaek	Ponggŭm chŏngch'aek		번역 표준 원칙
1679	봉금지대	封禁地帶	no man's land	Bonggeumjidae	Ponggŭmjidae		번역 표준 원칙
1680	봉담동탄고속도로	峰潭東灘高速道路	Bongdam-Dongtan Expressway	Bongdam dongtan gosokdoro	Pongdam tongt'an kosoktoro		번역 표준 원칙

- 230 -

NO	용어	한자	영문	RO	MC	시대 및 연도	출전
1681	봉쇄정책	封鎖政策	Containment Policy	Bongswae jeongchaek	Pongswae chŏngch'aek		번역 표준 원칙
1682	봉오동 전투	鳳梧洞 戰鬪	Battle of Fengwudong	Bongodong jeontu	Pongodong chŏnt'u	1920	번역 표준 원칙
1683	봉직전쟁	奉直戰爭	Zhili-Fengtian War	Bongjik jeonjaeng	Pongjik chŏnjaeng		번역 표준 원칙
1684	부가가치세	附加價値稅	value added tax (VAT)	Buga gachise	Puga kach'ise	현대	번역 표준 원칙
1685	부국강병	富國强兵	rich nation with a strong military	Buguk gangbyeong	Puguk kangbyŏng	조선	한국학중앙연구원, 《영문한국백과》-조선경국전
1686	부국강병책	富國强兵策	measures for the enhancement of national prosperity and defense	Buguk gangbyeongchaek	Puguk kangbyŏngch'aek		번역 표준 원칙
1687	부녀 새마을운동	婦女 새마을運動	Women's Saemaeul (New Village) Movement	Bunyeo saemaeul undong	Punyŏ saemaŭl undong	현대	번역 표준 원칙
1688	부다페스트 한국영화주간	Budapest 韓國映畵週刊	Korean Film Week in Budapest	Budapeseuteu hanguk yeonghwa jugan	Pudapesŭtŭ han'guk yŏnghwa jugan		번역 표준 원칙

NO	용어	한자	영문	RO	MC	시대 및 연도	출전
1689	부대예규	部隊例規	Standard Operating Procedures (SOP)	Budaeyegyu	Pudaeyegyu		번역 표준 원칙
1690	부동산 거래실명제	不動産 去來實名制	real-name property ownership system	Budongsan georae silmyeongje	Pudongsan kŏrae silmyŏngje	1995-	번역 표준 원칙
1691	부동산 투기	不動産 投機	real estate speculation	Budongsan tugi	Pudongsan t'ugi		번역 표준 원칙
1692	부마항쟁	釜馬抗爭	Busan-Masan Uprising	Buma hangjaeng	Puma hangjaeng	1979	번역 표준 원칙
1693	부민관투탄의거	府民館投彈義擧	Hand Grenade Incident at the Civic Auditorium (1945)	Bumingwan tutan uigeo	Pumin'gwan t'ut'an ŭigŏ	1945	번역 표준 원칙
1694	부민단	扶民團	Korean People's Association (Bumindan)	Bumindan	Pumindan	1912-1919	번역 표준 원칙
1695	부산 APEC 정상회담	釜山 APEC 頂上會談	APEC 2005 Summit Korea	Busan APEC jeongsang hoedam	Pusan APEC chŏngsang hoedam	2005	번역 표준 원칙
1696	부산 국제고무공장	釜山 國際고무工場	Busan plant of International Rubber (now LS Networks)	Busan gukje gomu gongjang	Pusan kukche gomu gongjang		번역 표준 원칙

NO	용어	한자	영문	RO	MC	시대 및 연도	출전
1697	부산 조선방직 노동쟁의	釜山 朝鮮紡織 勞動爭議	Chosun Spinning and Weaving Company labor dispute	Busan joseon bangjik nodong jaengui	Pusan chosŏn pangjik nodong chaengŭi	1949	번역 표준 원칙
1698	부산광역시	釜山廣域市	Busan Metropolitan City	Busan gwangyeoksi	Pusan kwangyŏksi	1995-?	번역 표준 원칙
1699	부산국제영화제	釜山國際映畵祭	Busan International Film Festival (BIFF)	Busan gukje yeonghwaje	Pusan gukche yŏnghwaje	1996-	번역 표준 원칙
1700	부산미문화원 방화사건	釜山美文化院 放火事件	Arson Incident of the U.S. Information Agency in Busan (1982)	Busan mimunhwawon banghwa sageon	Pusan mimunhwawŏn panghwa sagŏn	1982	번역 표준 원칙
1701	부산울산고속도로	釜山蔚山高速道路	Busan-Ulsan Expressway	Busan ulsan gosokdoro	Pusan ulsan kosoktoro		번역 표준 원칙
1702	부산정치파동	釜山政治波動	Busan Political Disturbance of 1952	Busan jeongchi padong	Pusan chŏngch'i p'adong	1952	번역 표준 원칙
1703	부상자	負傷者	Wounded in Action (WIA)	Busangja	Pusangja		번역 표준 원칙
1704	부실기업	不實企業	insolvent enterprise	Busilgieop	Pusilkiŏp		번역 표준 원칙

NO	용어	한자	영문	RO	MC	시대 및 연도	출전
1705	부실기업정리	不實企業整理	liquidation of failing firms	Busil gieop jeongni	Pusil kiŏp chŏngni		번역 표준 원칙
1706	부역자	附逆者	collaborator	Buyeokja	Puyŏkcha		번역 표준 원칙
1707	부익부 빈익빈	富益富 貧益貧	the rich get richer and the poor get poorer	Buikbu binikbin	Puikpin pinikpin		번역 표준 원칙
1708	부재자 투표	不在者 投票	absentee ballot	Bujaeja tupyo	Pujaeja t'up'yo		번역 표준 원칙
1709	부정축재처리법	不正蓄財處理法	Illegally Amassed Wealth Disposition Act	Bujeong chukjae cheoribeop	Pujŏng ch'ukchae ch'ŏripŏp	1961	번역 표준 원칙
1710	부주석	副主席	vice president	Bujuseok	Pujusŏk	1944-1945	번역 표준 원칙
1711	부천 국제판타스틱 영화제	富川 國際Fantastic 映畵祭	Pucheon International Fantastic Film Festival (PiFan)	Bucheon gukje pantaseutik yeonghwaje	Puchŏn kukche p'ant'asŭt'ik yŏnghwaje	1997-	번역 표준 원칙
1712	부천서 성고문사건	富川署 性拷問事件	Bucheon Sexual Torture Incident of 1986 (sexual assault of a female student activist during police interrogation at a Bucheon police station)	Bucheonseo seonggomun sageon	Puch'ŏnsŏ sŏnggomun sakŏn	1986	번역 표준 원칙

NO	용어	한자	영문	RO	MC	시대 및 연도	출전
1713	부흥부	復興部	Ministry of Reconstruction	Buheungbu	Puhŭngbu	1955-1961	번역 표준 원칙
1714	북·중 경제기술협조협정	北·中 經濟技術協調協定	Agreement for Economic and Technical Cooperation between North Korea and China	Bukjung gyeongje gisul hyeopjo hyeopjeong	Pukchung kyŏngje kisul hyŏpcho hyŏpchŏng		번역 표준 원칙
1715	북간도	北間島	North Gando (North Jiandao)	Bukgando	Pukkando	1392-?	번역 표준 원칙
1716	북경군사통일촉성회	北京軍事統一促成會	Beijing Society for a Unified Independence Army	Bukgyeong gunsa tongil chokseonghoe	Pukkyŏng kunsa t'ongil ch'oksŏnghoe		번역 표준 원칙
1717	북경조약	北京條約	Beijing Agreement	Bukgyeong joyak	Pukkyŏng choyak	1860	번역 표준 원칙
1718	북로군정서	北路軍政署	Northern Route Army Command	Bungno gunjeongseo	Pungno kunjŏngsŏ	1919-1922	번역 표준 원칙
1719	북만철도(동지철도)	北滿鐵道(東支鐵道)	North Manchuria Railway Co.	Bungman cheoldo (Dongji cheoldo)	Pungman ch'ŏldo (Tongji ch'ŏldo)		번역 표준 원칙
1720	북미 고위급 회담	北美 高位級 會談	U.S. -North Korea High-level Talks	Bungmi gowigeup hoedam	Pungmi kowigŭp hoedam		번역 표준 원칙

NO	용어	한자	영문	RO	MC	시대 및 연도	출전
1721	북미 대한인국민회	北美 大韓人國民會	Korean National Association in North America	Bungmi daehanin gungminhoe	Pungmi taehanin kungminhoe	1922	번역 표준 원칙
1722	북미 대한인유학생 총회	北美 大韓人留學生 總會	Korean Students' Alliance of North America	Bukmi daehanin yuhaksaeng chonghoe	Pungmi taehanin yuhaksaeng ch'onghoe		번역 표준 원칙
1723	북미 참사관급회담	北美 參事官級會談	U.S.-North Korea Councilor-level Talks	Bungmi chamsagwangeup hoedam	Pungmi ch'amsagwan'gŭp hoedam		번역 표준 원칙
1724	북미간 기본합의서	北美間 基本合意書	Agreed Framework between the United States of America and the Democratic People's Republic of Korea	Bungmigan gibon habuiseo	Pungmigan kibon habŭisŏ		번역 표준 원칙
1725	북미간 연락사무소	北美間 連絡事務所	U.S.-North Korea Liaison Office	Bukmigan yeollak samuso	Pungmigan yŏllak samuso		번역 표준 원칙
1726	북미동지 미포대회	北美同志 美布大會	Congress of Dong Ji Hoi Society's North America Representatives (Honolulu, 1930)	Bukmi dongji mipo daehoe	Pungmi tongji mipo taehoe		번역 표준 원칙
1727	북미상항친목회	北美桑港親睦會	Friendship Society of San Francisco	Bukmi sanghang chinmokhoe	Pungmi sanghang ch'inmokhoe	1903	번역 표준 원칙
1728	북미실업주식회사	北美實業株式會社	North America Enterprises	Bukmi sileop jusikhoesa	Pungmi silŏp chusikhoesa		번역 표준 원칙

NO	용어	한자	영문	RO	MC	시대 및 연도	출전
1729	북방정책	北方政策	Northern policy (during the Park Chung-hee regime)	Bukbang jeongchaek	Pukpang chŏngch'aek	1973-?	번역 표준 원칙
1730	북방한계선	北方限界線	Northern Limit Line (NLL)	Bukbang hangyeseon	Pukpang han'gyesŏn	1953	번역 표준 원칙
1731	북방한계선 무효선언	北方限界線 無效宣言	declaration of the Northern Limit Line as invalid	Bukbang hangyeseon muhyoseoneon	Pukpang han'gyesŏn muhyosŏnŏn	1999	번역 표준 원칙
1732	북방한계선(NLL) 침범	北方限界線(NLL) 侵犯	violations of the Northern Limit Line (NLL)	Bukbang hangyeseon (NLL) chimbeom	Pukhan han'gyesŏn (NLL) ch'imbŏm		번역 표준 원칙
1733	북베트남	北Vietnam	North Vietnam	Bukbeteunam	Pukpet'ŭnam		번역 표준 원칙
1734	북성회	北星會	North Star Association (Bukseonghoe)	Bukseonghoe	Puksŏnghoe	1923-1925	번역 표준 원칙
1735	북소상호우호협력 및 원조조약	北蘇相互友好協力 및 援助條約	Mutual Friendship and Assistance Treaty between the Democratic People's Republic of Korea and the Soviet Union	Bukso sangho uho hyeomnyeok mit wonjo joyak	Pukso sangho uho hyŏmnyŏk mit wŏnjo choyak		번역 표준 원칙
1736	북조선 중앙 보안간부학교	北朝鮮 中央 保安幹部學校	Central Security Officers Training School	Bukjoseon jungang boan ganbu hakgyo	Pukchosŏn chungang poan kanbu hakkyo	1946-?	번역 표준 원칙

NO	용어	한자	영문	RO	MC	시대 및 연도	출전
1737	북조선5도행정국	北朝鮮5道行政局	Five Province Administrative Bureau	Bukjoseon 5do haengjeongguk	Pukchosŏn 5to haengjŏngguk	1945-1946	번역 표준 원칙
1738	북조선공산당	北朝鮮共産黨	North Korean Communist Party	Bukjoseon gongsandang	Pukchosŏn kongsandang	1946-?	번역 표준 원칙
1739	북조선노동당	北朝鮮勞動黨	Workers' Party of North Korea	Bukjoseon nodongdang	Pukchosŏn nodongdang	1946-1949	번역 표준 원칙
1740	북조선노동당창립대회	北朝鮮勞動黨創立大會	Founding Congress of the Workers' Party of North Korea	Bukjoseon nodongdang changnip daehoe	Pukchosŏn nodongdang ch'angnip taehoe	1946	번역 표준 원칙
1741	북조선인민위원회	北朝鮮人民委員會	People's Committee of North Korea	Bukjoseon inmin wiwonhoe	Pukchosŏn inmin wiwŏnhoe	1947-	Ki-baik Lee, translated by Edward W. Wagner, A New History of Korea, Harvard University Press, 1984,
1742	북조선인민집단군사령부	北朝鮮人民集團軍司令部	North Korean Army Group Command	Bukjoseon inmin jipdangun saryeongbu	Pukchosŏn inmin chiptan'gun saryŏngbu	1947-?	번역 표준 원칙
1743	북조선임시인민위원회	北朝鮮臨時人民委員會	North Korean Provisional People's Committee	Bukjoseon imsi inmin wiwonhoe	Pukchosŏn imsi inmin wiwŏnhoe	1946-1947	번역 표준 원칙
1744	북중국첩보작전	北中國諜報作戰	North China Intelligence Project	Bukjungguk cheopbo jakjeon	Pukchungguk ch'ŏppo chakchŏn		번역 표준 원칙

NO	용어	한자	영문	RO	MC	시대 및 연도	출전
1745	북중상호우호협력 및 원조조약	北中相互友好協力 및 援助條約	Treaty of Friendship, Cooperation and Mutual Assistance between the Democratic People's Republic of Korea and the People's	Bukjung sangho uho hyeomnyeok mit wonjo joyak	Pukchung sangho uho hyŏmnyŏk mit wŏnjo choyak	1961	번역 표준 원칙
1746	북진통일론	北進統一論	Argument for Unification by Marching North	Bukjin tongillon	Pukchin t'ongillon	이승만 정권	번역 표준 원칙
1747	북풍회	北風會	North Wind Association	Bukpunghoe	Pukp'unghoe	1924-1926	번역 표준 원칙
1748	북학파	北學派	Northern Learning Faction	Bukhakpa	Pukhakp'a	17-18 세기	번역 표준 원칙
1749	북한 NPT 탈퇴	北韓 NPT 脫退	North Korea's withdrawal from the Nuclear Non-Proliferation Treaty (NPT)	Bukhan NPT taltoe	Pukhan NPT t'alt'oe	1993	번역 표준 원칙
1750	북한 선전용 삐라	北韓 宣傳用 傳單	North Korean propaganda leaflet	Bukhan seonjeonyong ppira	Pukhan sŏnjŏnnyong ppira		번역 표준 원칙
1751	북한 유엔대표부	北韓 UN代表部	North Korean Mission to the United Nations	Bukhan yuen daepyobu	Pukhan yuen taep'yobu		번역 표준 원칙
1752	북한 이탈주민 보호 및 정착지원에 관한 법률	北韓 離脫住民 保護 및 定着支援에 關한 法律	Act on North Korean Defectors' Protection and Settlement Support	Bukhan ital jumin boho mit jeongchak jiwon-e gwanhan beomnyul	Pukhan it'al chumin poho mit chŏngch'ak chiwŏn-e kwanhan pŏmnyul	1997	번역 표준 원칙

NO	용어	한자	영문	RO	MC	시대 및 연도	출전
1753	북한 핵실험	北韓 核實驗	North Korean nuclear weapons test	Bukhan haek silheom	Pukhan haek silhŏm	1차:2006, 2차:2009,	번역 표준 원칙
1754	북한군	北韓軍	North Korean People's Army (NKPA)	Bukhangun	Pukhangun	1950	번역 표준 원칙
1755	북한군의 기습남침	北韓軍의 奇襲南侵	surprise attack by the North Korean People's Army (NKPA)	Bukhangunui giseup namchim	Pukhangunŭi kisŭp namch'im	1950	번역 표준 원칙
1756	북한민주화 네트워크	北韓民主化 network	Network for North Korean Democracy and Human Rights	Bukhan minjuhwa neteuwokeu	Pukhan minjuhwa net'ŭ wŏk'ŭ	1999	번역 표준 원칙
1757	북한붕괴론	北韓崩壞論	Argument on the Collapse of North Korea	Bukhan bunggoeron	Pukhan punggoeron		번역 표준 원칙
1758	북한산국립공원	北漢山國立公園	Bukhansan National Park	Bukhansan gungnipgongwon	Puk'ansan kungnipkongwŏn	1983-?	번역 표준 원칙
1759	북한의 도발	北韓의 挑發	provocations from North Korea	Buhanui dobal	Pukhanŭi tobal	1953-	번역 표준 원칙
1760	북한의 불법남침	北韓의 不法南侵	North Korean invasion against the ROK	Bukhanui bulbeop namchim	Pukhanŭi pulpŏp namch'im	1950	번역 표준 원칙

NO	용어	한자	영문	RO	MC	시대 및 연도	출전
1761	북한인권법	北韓人權法	North Korean Human Rights Act	Bukhan ingwonbeop	Pukhan ingwŏnpŏp	2004	번역 표준 원칙
1762	북한측 중립국 감독위원회 철수	北韓側 中立國 監督委員會 撤收	withdrawal of North Korean-sided nations from the Neutral Nations Supervisory Commission	Bukhan cheuk jungnipguk gamdogwiwonhoe cheolsu	Pukhan ch'ŭk chungnipkuk kamdogwiwŏnhoe ch'ŏlsu	1953-	번역 표준 원칙
1763	북한폭격 계획	北韓爆擊 計劃	plan for a pre-emptive strike over North Korea	Bukhan pokgyeok gyehoek	Pukhan p'okkyŏk kyehoek		번역 표준 원칙
1764	분단시대	分斷時代	Bundan Sidae (literary magazine)	Bundan sidae	Pundan sidae		번역 표준 원칙
1765	분단영구화	分斷永久化	perpetuation of national division	Bundan yeongguhwa	Pundan yŏngguhwa		번역 표준 원칙
1766	분신자살	焚身自殺	self-immolation	Bunsin jasal	Punsin chasal		번역 표준 원칙
1767	분쟁수역화	紛爭水域化	(turning into) disputed waters	Bunjaeng suyeokhwa	Punjaeng suyŏkhwa		번역 표준 원칙
1768	불교	佛教	Buddhism	Bulgyo	Pulgyo		번역 표준 원칙

NO	용어	한자	영문	RO	MC	시대 및 연도	출전
1769	불국사	佛國寺	Bulguksa Temple	Bulguksa	Pulkuksa	통일신라/발해	번역 표준 원칙
1770	불모고지 부근 전투	不毛高地 附近 戰鬪	Battle around Old Baldy	Bulmogoji bugeun jeontu	Pulmogoji pugŭn chŏnt'u		번역 표준 원칙
1771	불법어업	不法漁業	illegal fishing	Bulbeob eoeop	Pulbŏp ŏŏp		번역 표준 원칙
1772	불법체류자	不法滯留者	illegal alien	Bulbeop cheryuja	Pulbŏp ch'eryuja		번역 표준 원칙
1773	불시착	不時着	forced landing	Bulsichak	Pulsich'ak		번역 표준 원칙
1774	불평등조약	不平等條約	unequal treaty	Bulpyeongdeung joyak	Pulp'yŏngdŭng choyak	조선	Ki-baik Lee, translated by Edward W. Wagner, A New History of Korea, Harvard University Press, 1984,
1775	붉은기 사상	붉은旗 思想	Ideology of the Red Flag	Bulgeungi sasang	Pulgŭn'gi sasang	1997	번역 표준 원칙
1776	붉은기 철학	붉은旗 哲學	Philosophy of the Red Flag	Bulgeungi cheolhak	Pulgŭn'gi ch'ŏrhak	1996	번역 표준 원칙

NO	용어	한자	영문	RO	MC	시대 및 연도	출전
1777	붉은악마 응원단	붉은惡魔 應援團	Red Devils	Bulgeun angma eungwondan	Pulgŭn angma ŭngwŏndan		번역 표준 원칙
1778	붉은청년근위대	붉은靑年近衛隊	Red Young Guards	Bulgeun cheongnyeon geunwidae	Pulgŭn ch'ŏngnyŏn kŭnwidae	1970	번역 표준 원칙
1779	브·나로드운동	V Narod運動	V Narod Movement	Beunarodeu undong	Pŭnarodŭ undong	1931-1934	번역 표준 원칙
1780	브라운 각서	Brown 覺書	Brown Memorandum of 1966	Beuraun gakseo	Pŭraun kaksŏ	1966	번역 표준 원칙
1781	브레인풀제	Brain Pool制	"Brain Pool" Program	Beureinpulje	Pŭreinp'ulje	1992	번역 표준 원칙
1782	브리사	Brisa	Brisa (KIA sedan)	Beurisa	Pŭrisa		번역 표준 원칙
1783	비대칭작전	非對稱作戰	Asymmetric Operations	Bidaeching jakjeon	Pidaech'ing chakchŏn		번역 표준 원칙
1784	비동맹	非同盟	non-alignment	Bidongmaeng	Pidongmaeng		번역 표준 원칙

NO	용어	한자	영문	RO	MC	시대 및 연도	출전
1785	비동맹외교	非同盟外交	non-alignment diplomacy	Bidongmaeng oegyo	Pidongmaeng oegyo	현대	번역 표준 원칙
1786	비동맹정상회담	非同盟頂上會談	non-aligned summit	Bidongmaeng jeongsang hoedam	Pidongmaeng chŏngsang hoedam		번역 표준 원칙
1787	비동맹제국회의	非同盟諸國會議	Non-aligned Movement	Bidongmaeng jeguk hoeui	Pidongmaeng cheguk hoeŭi	1961-?	번역 표준 원칙
1788	비둘기부대	비둘기部隊	Pigeon/Dove Unit	Bidulgi budae	Pidulgi pudae		번역 표준 원칙
1789	비례대표제	比例代表制	proportional representation system	Birye daepyoje	Pirye taep'yoje	2002-	국사편찬위원회
1790	비료공장	肥料工場	fertilizer plant	Biryo gongjang	Piryo kongjang		번역 표준 원칙
1791	비무장지대	非武裝地帶	DMZ (demilitarized zone)	Bimujang jidae	Pimujang chidae	1951-?	번역 표준 원칙
1792	비무장지대의 평화적 이용	非武裝地帶의 平和的 利用	Peaceful Use of the Demilitarized Zone	Bimujang jidaeui pyeonghwajeok iyong	Pimujang chidae-ŭi p'yŏnghwajŏk iyong		번역 표준 원칙

NO	용어	한자	영문	RO	MC	시대 및 연도	출전
1793	비상계엄	非常戒嚴	emergency martial law	Bisang gyeeom	Pisang kyeŏm		번역 표준 원칙
1794	비상계엄 해제 요구	非常戒嚴 解除 要求	call for the lifting of martial law	Bisang gyeeom haeje yogu	Pisang kyeŏm haeje yogu		번역 표준 원칙
1795	비상계엄 확대 선포	非常戒嚴 擴大 宣布	expansion of martial law to the whole country on May 17, 1980	Bisang gyeeom hwakdae seonpo	Pisang kyeŏm hwaktae sŏnp'o	1980	번역 표준 원칙
1796	비상국무회의	非常國務會議	emergency cabinet meeting	Bisang gungmu hoeui	Pisang kungmu hoeŭi	1972-1973	번역 표준 원칙
1797	비상시국대책위원회	非常時局對策委員會	Emergency Measures Committee	Bisang siguk daechaek wiwonhoe	Pisang siguk taech'aek wiwŏnhoe		번역 표준 원칙
1798	비상조치	非常措置	emergency measures	Bisangjochi	Pisangchoch'i	1980-	번역 표준 원칙
1799	비상활주로	非常滑走路	emergency landing strip	Bisanghwaljuro	Pisanghwalchuro		번역 표준 원칙
1800	비자금	秘資金	slush funds	Bijageum	Pijagŭm		번역 표준 원칙

NO	용어	한자	영문	RO	MC	시대 및 연도	출전
1801	비전투 손실	非戰鬪 損失	non-battle casualty	Bijeontu sonsil	Pijŏnt'u sonsil		번역 표준 원칙
1802	비전향 장기수	非轉向 長期囚	unconverted long-term (North Korean) political prisoners	Bijeonhyang janggisu	Pijŏnhyang changgisu	1975-?	번역 표준 원칙
1803	비정규직	非正規職	non-regular work	Bijeonggyujik	Pijŏnggyujik		번역 표준 원칙
1804	비정규직법	非正規職法	Act on the Protection of Non-regular Workers	Bijeonggyujikbup	Pijŏnggyujikpŏp	2007-	번역 표준 원칙
1805	비정치적 분야 남북교류	非政治的 分野 南北交流	non-political exchange between South and North Korea	Bijeongchijeok bunya nambuk gyoryu	Pijŏngch'ijŏk punya nambuk kyoryu		번역 표준 원칙
1806	비철금속단지	經濟企劃院	nonferrous metal refining complex	Bicheolgeumsok danji	Pich'ŏlkŭmsok tanji		번역 표준 원칙
1807	비축유	備蓄油	oil reserves	Bichugyu	Pich'ugyu		번역 표준 원칙
1808	비판적 지지	批判的 支持	critical support	Bipanjeok jiji	Pip'anjŏk chiji		번역 표준 원칙

NO	용어	한자	영문	RO	MC	시대 및 연도	출전
1809	비핵전쟁	非核戰爭	conventional war (non-nuclear war)	Bihaek jeonjaeng	Pihaek chŏnjaeng	1945-	번역 표준 원칙
1810	비핵화공동선언	非核化共同宣言	Joint Declaration on the Denuclearization of the Korean Peninsula	Bihaekhwa gongdong seoneon	Pihaekhwa kongdong sŏnŏn	1992.1.23	번역 표준 원칙
1811	비행작전본부	飛行作戰本部	Flight Operation Center (FOC)	Bihaeng jakjeon bonbu	Pihaeng chakchŏn bonbu		번역 표준 원칙
1812	빈민운동	貧民運動	poor people's movement	Binmin undong	Pinmin undong		번역 표준 원칙
1813	빈부차별	貧富差別	discrimination based on wealth	Binbuchabyeol	Pinbuch'abyŏl	조선	번역 표준 원칙
1814	빨갱이	빨갱이	the Reds	Ppalgaengi	Ppalgaengi		번역 표준 원칙
1815	빨치산	partisan	partisan guerillas	Ppalchisan	Ppalch'isan	?-1953	번역 표준 원칙
1816	사교육	私敎育	private education	Sagyoyuk	Sagyoyuk		번역 표준 원칙

NO	용어	한자	영문	RO	MC	시대 및 연도	출전
1817	사단	師團	Division	Sadan	Sadan	1950	번역 표준 원칙
1818	사단법인 국제기능올림픽대회 한국위원회	社團法人 國際技能Olympic 大會 韓國委員會	WorldSkills Korea Committee	Sadanbeobin gukjegineung ollimpik daehoe hanguk wiwonhoe	Sadanpŏbin kukchekinŭng ollimp'ik taehoe han'guk wiwŏnhoe	1966	번역 표준 원칙
1819	사대주의	事大主義	flunkeyism	Sadaejuui	Sadaejuŭi	현대	한국학중앙연구원,《영문한국백과》-사회교육
1820	사립학교	私立學校	private school	Sarip hakgyo	Sarip hakkyo		M. Deuchler, The Confucian Transformation of Korea: A Study of Society and Ideology, Harvard
1821	사립학교령	私立學校令	private school regulations	Sarip hakgyoryeong	Sarip hakkyoryŏng	1908	번역 표준 원칙
1822	사면복권	赦免復權	restoration of civil rights	Samyeon bokgwon	Samyŏn pokkwŏn		번역 표준 원칙
1823	사민의 비무장지대 출입에 관한 협의	私民의 非武裝地帶 出入에 關한 協議	consultation regarding civilian access to the DMZ	Samineui bimujang jidae chulibe gwanhan hyeobui	Samin-ŭi pimujang chidae ch'urip-e kwanhan hyŏbŭi		번역 표준 원칙
1824	사발통문	沙鉢通文	secret circular	Sabaltongmun	Sabalt'ongmun	조선	번역 표준 원칙

NO	용어	한자	영문	RO	MC	시대 및 연도	출전
1825	사법부	司法部	Department of Judiciary	Sabeopbu	Sabŏppu	1946-1948	번역 표준 원칙
1826	사법지도부	司法指導部	Judicial Guidance Division	Sabeop jidobu	Sabŏp chidobu		번역 표준 원칙
1827	사법파동	司法波動	jurisdiction crisis	Sabeop padong	Sabŏp p'adong	1971	번역 표준 원칙
1828	사북탄광노동쟁의	舍北炭鑛勞動爭議	coal mine workers' struggle in Sabuk, Gangwon-do Province (April 1980)	Sabuk tangwang nodong jaengui	Sabuk t'an'gwang nodong chaengŭi	1980	번역 표준 원칙
1829	사북탄광사태	舍北炭鑛事態	Sabuk Mine Incident	Sabuk tangwang satae	Sabuk t'an'gwang sat'ae	1980	번역 표준 원칙
1830	사사오입개헌	四捨五入改憲	'"Rounding-up" Constitutional Amendment Incident	Sasaoip gaeheon	Sasaoip kaehŏn	1954	번역 표준 원칙
1831	사상계	思想界	*Sasanggye (World of Thought)*	Sasanggye	Sasanggye	1953-1970	번역 표준 원칙
1832	사상논쟁	思想論爭	ideological conflict	Sasang nonjaeng	Sasang nonjaeng		번역 표준 원칙

NO	용어	한자	영문	RO	MC	시대 및 연도	출전
1833	사스	SARS	severe acute respiratory syndrome (SARS)	Saseu	Sasŭ	2002?2003?	번역 표준 원칙
1834	사이밍턴 청문회	Symington 聽聞會	Stuart Symington Hearing	Saimingteon cheongmunhoe	Saimingt'ŏn ch'ŏngmunhoe	1970	번역 표준 원칙
1835	사적지	史跡地	historic site	Sajeokji	Sajŏkchi		번역 표준 원칙
1836	사전투표	事前投票	preliminary vote	Sajeon tupyo	Sajŏn t'up'yo		번역 표준 원칙
1837	사진 신부	寫眞 新婦	picture bride	Sajin sinbu	Sajin sinbu		번역 표준 원칙
1838	사찰령	寺刹令	Temple Act	Sachallyeong	Sach'allyŏng	1911-1945	Han Woo-Keun, translated by Kyung-Shik Lee, The History of Korea, Eul-Yoo Pub, 1970, p.471.
1839	사창리 전투	史倉里 戰鬪	Battle of Sachang-ri Village	Sachang-ri jeontu	Sach'ang-ri chŏnt'u	1951	번역 표준 원칙
1840	사창제	社倉制	village granary system	Sachangje	Sach'angje	조선	James B. Palais, Politics and Policy in Traditional Korea, Harvard University Press, 1991, p.136.

NO	용어	한자	영문	RO	MC	시대 및 연도	출전
1841	사채보증신용제도	私債保證信用制度	credit guarantee program for private loans	Sachae bojeung sinyong jedo	Sachae pojŭng sinyong chedo		번역 표준 원칙
1842	사천강 전투	泗川江 戰鬪	Battle of the Sacheongang River	Sacheongang jeontu	Sach'ŏngang chŏnt'u	1952	번역 표준 원칙
1843	사천학살사건	砂川虐殺事件	Sacheon Massacre	Sacheon haksal sageon	Sach'ŏn haksal sagŏn	1919	번역 표준 원칙
1844	사치추방운동	奢侈追放運動	campaign to root out extravagance	Sachi chubang undong	Sach'i ch'ubang undong		번역 표준 원칙
1845	사포대	射砲隊	Cannon Corps	Sapodae	Sap'odae		번역 표준 원칙
1846	사할린 교포 모국 방문	Sakhalin 僑胞 母國 訪問	Sakhalin Koreans' visit to the motherland	Sahallin gyopo moguk bangmun	Sahallin kyop'o moguk pangmun		번역 표준 원칙
1847	사할린섬	Sakhalin섬	Sakhalin	Sahallin seom	Sahallin sŏm		번역 표준 원칙
1848	사회간접자본	社會間接資本	social overhead capital	Sahoe ganjeop jabon	Sahoe kanjŏp chabon	현대	번역 표준 원칙

NO	용어	한자	영문	RO	MC	시대 및 연도	출전
1849	사회경제사학	社會經濟史學	socioeconomic historical studies	Sahoe gyeongje sahak	Sahoe kyŏngje sahak	근대	번역 표준 원칙
1850	사회계층	社會階層	social classes	Sahoe gyecheung	Sahoe kyech'ŭng		번역 표준 원칙
1851	사회교육	社會敎育	social education	Sahoe gyoyuk	Sahoe kyoyuk		한국학중앙연구원, 《영문한국백과》-사회교육
1852	사회당사건	社會黨事件	Socialist Party Incident	Sahoedang sageon	Sahoedang sakŏn		번역 표준 원칙
1853	사회대중당	社會大衆黨	Social Mass Party	Sahoe daejungdang	Sahoe daejungdang	1960-1961	번역 표준 원칙
1854	사회민주당	社會民主黨	Social Democratic Party	Sahoe minjudang	Sahoe minjudang	1946-?	번역 표준 원칙
1855	사회보장제도	社會保障制度	social security system	Sahoe bojang jedo	Sahoe pojang chedo		한국학중앙연구원, 《영문한국백과》-사회보장제도
1856	사회보호법	社會保護法	Social Protection Act	Sahoe bohobeop	Sahoe pohobŏp	1980	번역 표준 원칙

NO	용어	한자	영문	RO	MC	시대 및 연도	출전
1857	사회안전법	社會安全法	Social Security Law	Sahoe anjeonbeop	Sahoe anjŏnbŏp	1975-?	번역 표준 원칙
1858	사회운동	社會運動	social movement	Sahoe undong	Sahoe undong		번역 표준 원칙
1859	사회정화	社會淨化	social purification	Sahoe jeonghwa	Sahoe chŏnghwa		번역 표준 원칙
1860	사회정화위원회	社會淨化委員會	Social Purification Committee	Sahoe jeonghwa wiwonhoe	Sahoe chŏnghwa wiwŏnhoe	1980-1989	번역 표준 원칙
1861	사회주의	社會主義	socialism	Sahoejuui	Sahoejuŭi		번역 표준 원칙
1862	사회주의 강성대국	社會主義 强盛大國	Strong and Prosperous Socialist Nation	Sahoejuui gangseong daeguk	Sahoejuŭi kangsŏng taeguk		번역 표준 원칙
1863	사회주의 헌법	社會主義 憲法	Socialist Constitution	Sahoejuui heonbeop	Sahoejuŭi hŏnpŏp	1972	번역 표준 원칙
1864	사회주의 헌법 공포	社會主義 憲法 公布	promulgation of the Socialist Constitution	Sahoejuui heonbeop gongpo	Sahoejuŭi hŏnpŏp kongp'o		번역 표준 원칙

NO	용어	한자	영문	RO	MC	시대 및 연도	출전
1865	사회주의운동	社會主義運動	Socialist Revolutionary Movement	Sahoejuui undong	Sahoejuŭi undong		번역 표준 원칙
1866	사회진화론	社會進化論	Social Darwinism	Sahoe jinhwaron	Sahoe chinhwaron		번역 표준 원칙
1867	사회혁신당	社會革新黨	Social Progressive Party	Sahoe hyeoksindang	Sahoe hyŏksindang		번역 표준 원칙
1868	산남의 진	山南義陳	Righteous Army Camp in Gyeongsang-do Province	Sannam uijin	Sannam ŭijin	1905-1909	번역 표준 원칙
1869	산림녹화	山林綠化	afforestation	Sallim nokhwa	Sallim nokhwa		번역 표준 원칙
1870	산림청	山林廳	Korea Forest Service	Sallimcheong	Sallimch'ŏng	1948	번역 표준 원칙
1871	산미증식계획	産米增殖計畵	plan to increase rice production	Sanmi jeungsik gyehoek	Sanmi chŭngsik kyehoek	1920-1934	한국학중앙연구원, 《영문한국백과》-산미증식계획
1872	산업 훈장	産業 勳章	Order of Industrial Service Merit	Saneop hunjang	Sanŏp hunjang	1962	번역 표준 원칙

NO	용어	한자	영문	RO	MC	시대 및 연도	출전
1873	산업개발위원회	産業開發委員會	Committee for Industrial Development	Saneop gaebal wiwonhoe	Sanŏp kaebal wiwŏnhoe		번역 표준 원칙
1874	산업구조고도화	産業構造高度化	shift to high value-added industries	Saneop gujo godohwa	Sanŏp kujo kodohwa		번역 표준 원칙
1875	산업구조조정	産業構造調整	industrial restructuring	Saneop gujojojeong	Sanŏp kujojojŏng		번역 표준 원칙
1876	산업기반시설	産業基盤施設	industrial facilities	Saeop giban siseol	Sahoe kiban sisŏl		번역 표준 원칙
1877	산업은행, 한국산업은행	産業銀行, 韓國産業銀行	Korea Development Bank	Saneop eunhaeng, hanguk saneop eunhaeng	Sanŏp ŭnhaeng, han'guk sanŏp ŭnhaeng	1954-?	번역 표준 원칙
1878	산업정책	産業政策	industrial policy	Saneop jeongchaek	Sanŏp chŏngch'aek		번역 표준 원칙
1879	산업진흥운동	産業振興運動	promotion of industry	Saneop jinheung undong	Sanŏp chinhŭng undong		번역 표준 원칙
1880	산업체부설학교	産業體附設學校	schools in the workplace	Saneopche buseol hakgyo	Sanŏpch'e pusŏl hakkyo	1977-?	번역 표준 원칙

NO	용어	한자	영문	RO	MC	시대 및 연도	출전
1881	산업합리화	産業合理化	rationalization of industry	Saneop hamnihwa	Sanŏp hapnihwa		번역 표준 원칙
1882	산업화세력	産業化勢力	forces driving industrialization	Saneophwa seryeok	Sanŏphwa seryŏk		번역 표준 원칙
1883	산업훈장	産業勳章	Order of Industrial Service Merit	Saneop hunjang	Sanŏp hunjang	1962-	번역 표준 원칙
1884	산조전집	散調全集	"Complete Works of Traditional Instrumental Solo Music" (album)	Sanjo jeonjip	Sanjo jŏnjip		번역 표준 원칙
1885	살상지대	殺傷地帶	killing zone	Salsang jidae	Salsang jidae		번역 표준 원칙
1886	삼광작전	三光作戰	"Three Light" Operations (kill, burn and destroy operations)	Samgwang jakjeon	Samkwang chakjŏn	중일전쟁	번역 표준 원칙
1887	삼국간섭	三國干涉	Triple Intervention	Samguk ganseop	Samguk kansŏp	1895	번역 표준 원칙
1888	삼군부	三軍府	Three Armies Headquarters (Joseon Dynasty)	Samgunbu	Samgunbu	1865-1880, 1882	번역 표준 원칙

NO	용어	한자	영문	RO	MC	시대 및 연도	출전
1889	삼권분립	三權分立	separation of the three branches of government	Samgwon bullip	Samkwŏn pullip		번역 표준 원칙
1890	삼균주의	三均主義	Principle of Three Equalities	Samgyunjuui	Samgyunjuŭi	1931-1945	번역 표준 원칙
1891	삼남지방	三南地方	three southern provinces (Chungcheong-do, Jeolla-do and Gyeongsang-do)	Samnam jibang	Samnam chibang		번역 표준 원칙
1892	삼림령	森林令	Forestry Order	Samnimnyeong	Samnimnyŏng	1911	번역 표준 원칙
1893	삼민주의	三民主義	Three Principles of the People	Samminjuui	Samminjuŭi	1896-?	번역 표준 원칙
1894	삼백산업	三白産業	three pivotal industries in the 1950s (flour, sugar and spinning)	Sambaek saneop	Sambaek sanŏp	1950년대	번역 표준 원칙
1895	삼부	三府	three branches of government	Sambu	Sambu	조선	번역 표준 원칙
1896	삼선개헌 반대투쟁	三選改憲 反對鬪爭	Struggle Against Constitutional Amendment for a Third-term Presidency	3seon gaeheon bandae tujaeng	3sŏn kaehŏn pandae t'ujaeng	1969	번역 표준 원칙

NO	용어	한자	영문	RO	MC	시대 및 연도	출전
1897	삼성 갤럭시폰	三星 Galaxy phone	Samsung Galaxy phone	Samseong gaelleoksipon	Samsŏng kaellŏksip'on	2010-	번역 표준 원칙
1898	삼성전자	三星電子	Samsung Electronics	Samseong jeonja	Samsŏng chŏnja	1969	번역 표준 원칙
1899	삼시협정	三矢協定	Mitsuya Miyamatsu-Zhang Zuolin Pact	Samsi hyeopjeong	Samsi hyŏpchŏng	1925	번역 표준 원칙
1900	삼일고가도로	三一高架道路	Samil Overpass	Samil gogadoro	Samil kogadoro		번역 표준 원칙
1901	삼일운동	31運動	March First Independence Movement of 1919	Samil undong	Samil undong	1919	번역 표준 원칙
1902	삼청교육대	三淸敎育隊	Samcheong Correction Camp	Samcheong gyoyukdae	Samch'ŏng kyoyuktae	1980-1981	번역 표준 원칙
1903	삼청교육대사건	三淸敎育隊事件	Samcheong Training Camp Incident of 1980 (detainment of civilians in military "re-education" camps by the Chun Doo-hwan regime)	Samcheong gyoyukdae sageon	Samch'ŏng kyoyuktae sakŏn	1980	번역 표준 원칙
1904	삼풍백화점 붕괴	三豊百貨店 崩壞	collapse of Sampoong Department Store in 1995	Sampung baekhwajeom bunggoe	Samp'ung baekwajŏm punggoe	1995	번역 표준 원칙

NO	용어	한자	영문	RO	MC	시대 및 연도	출전
1905	삽탄장전식	挿彈裝塡式	magazine loading	Saptan jangjeonsik	Sapt'an jangjŏnsik		번역 표준 원칙
1906	상공부	商工部	Department of Commerce and Industry	Sanggongbu	Sanggongbu	1948-1998	번역 표준 원칙
1907	상권수호운동	商權守護運動	movement to protect commercial rights	Sanggwon suho undong	Sangkwŏn suho undong	1898-?	번역 표준 원칙
1908	상근예비군	常勤豫備軍	Regular Reserve Forces	Sanggeun yebigun	Sanggŭn yebigun		번역 표준 원칙
1909	상동교회	尙洞敎會	Sangdong Methodist Church	Sangdong gyohoe	Sangdong kyohoe	1888	상동교회 사이트 http://www.sangdong.org/
1910	상동청년회	尙洞靑年會	Sangdong Youth Association	Sangdong cheongnyeonhoe	Sangdong ch'ŏngnyŏnhoe	1897	번역 표준 원칙
1911	상륙기동부대	上陸機動部隊	Amphibious Task Force (ATF)	Sangnyuk gidongbudae	Sangnyuk kidongbudae		번역 표준 원칙
1912	상무부	商務部	Department of Commerce and Industry	Sangmubu	Sangmubu	1945-1948	번역 표준 원칙

NO	용어	한자	영문	RO	MC	시대 및 연도	출전
1913	상무위원회	常務委員會	Standing Committee of the National People's Congress	Sangmu wiwonhoe	Sangmu wiwŏnhoe	현대	번역 표준 원칙
1914	상민수륙무역장정	商民水陸貿易章程	Regulations for Maritime and Overland Trade	Sangmin suryuk muyeok jangjeong	Sangmin suryuk muyŏk changjŏng	1882	Ki-baik Lee, translated by Edward W. Wagner, A New History of Korea, Harvard University Press, 1984,
1915	상병포로교환	傷病捕虜交換	exchange of sick and wounded prisoners of war (POW)	Sangbyeong poro gyohwan	Sangbyŏng poro kyohwan	1953	번역 표준 원칙
1916	상수도시설 확충	上水道施設 擴充	expansion of water supply facilities	Sangsudo siseol hwakchung	Sangsudo sisŏl hwakch'ung		번역 표준 원칙
1917	상품협상그룹	商品協商Group	Group of Negotiations on Goods (GNG)	Sangpum hyeopsang geurup	Sangp'um hyŏpsang kŭ rup		번역 표준 원칙
1918	상해 대한교민단	上海 大韓僑民團	Association of Korean Residents in Shanghai	Sanghae daehan gyomindan	Sanghae taehan kyomindan	1920	번역 표준 원칙
1919	상해 대한민국임시정부	上海 大韓民國臨時政府	Provisional Government of the Republic of Korea in Shanghai	Sanghae daehanminguk imsi jeongbu	Sanghae taehanmin'guk imsi chŏngbu	1919-1945	번역 표준 원칙
1920	상해 독립신문	上海 獨立新聞	The Independent (Dongnip Sinmun), Shanghai	Sanghae dongnipsinmun	Sanghae tongnipsinmun	1919-1925	번역 표준 원칙

NO	용어	한자	영문	RO	MC	시대 및 연도	출전
1921	상해 한인애국부인회	上海 韓人愛國婦人會	Shanghai Korean Patriotic Women's Association	Sanghae hanin aeguk buinhoe	Sanghae hanin aeguk puinhoe	1919-?	번역 표준 원칙
1922	상해사변	上海事變	Shanghai Incident	Sanghae sabyeon	Sanghae sabyŏn	1932, 1937	번역 표준 원칙
1923	상해의거	上海義擧	patriot Yun Bong-gil's bombing of the Japanese colonial government's key figures in Shanghai in 1932	Sanghae uigeo	Sanghae ŭigŏ	1934	번역 표준 원칙
1924	상해정전협정	上海停戰協定	Shanghai Truce Agreement of 1932 (officially, Agreement on the Cessation of Hostilities in Shanghai and Neighborhood and Withdrawal of Japanese Forces, signed between China and Japan on May 5, 1932)	Sanghae jeongjeon hyeopjeong	Sanghae chŏngjŏn hyŏpchŏng	1932	번역 표준 원칙
1925	상해파 고려공산당	上海派 高麗共産黨	Shanghai-based Goryeo Communist Party	Sanghaepa goryeo gongsandang	Sanghaep'a koryŏ kongsandang	1920-1923	번역 표준 원칙
1926	상호운용성	相互運用性	interoperability	Sangho unyongseong	Sangho unyongsŏng		번역 표준 원칙
1927	상호지급보증	相互支給保證	credit guarantee between subsidiaries	Sangho jigeup bojeung	Sangho chigŭp pojŭng		번역 표준 원칙
1928	새나라자동차사건	새나라自動車事件	Saenara Motors Incident	Saenara jadongcha sageon	Saenara chadongch'a sakŏn	1960년대	번역 표준 원칙

NO	용어	한자	영문	RO	MC	시대 및 연도	출전
1929	새마을운동	새마을運動	Saemaeul (New Village) Movement	Saemaeul undong	Saemaŭl undong	1970-?	번역 표준 원칙
1930	새마을운동중앙본부	새마을運動中央本部	Central Headquarters of the Saemaeul (New Village) Movement	Saemaeul undong jungang bonbu	Saemaŭl undong chungang ponbu		번역 표준 원칙
1931	새마을호	새마을號	Saemaeul Train	Saemaeulho	Saemaŭrho	1969-	번역 표준 원칙
1932	새마을훈장	새마을勳章	Order of Saemaeul Service Merit	Saemaeul hunjang	Saemaŭl hunjang	1973	번역 표준 원칙
1933	새만금 간척사업	새만금 干拓事業	Saemangeum Project	saemangeum gancheok saeop	Saemangŭm kanch'ŏk saŏp	1991-?	번역 표준 원칙
1934	새벽별보기운동	새벽별보기運動	"Look at the Early Morning Star" Movement	Saebyeokbyeol bogi undong	Saebyŏkpyŏl pogi undong		번역 표준 원칙
1935	새볍씨 밀양 21호	새볍씨 密陽 21號	rice variety "Milyang No. 21"	Saebyeopssi milyang 21ho	saebyŏpsi miryang 21ho		번역 표준 원칙
1936	새터민	새터民	North Korean defector	Setoemin	Saet'ŏmin		번역 표준 원칙

NO	용어	한자	영문	RO	MC	시대 및 연도	출전
1937	색동회	色동會	Saekdonghoe (Korea's first culture foundation for children)	Saekdonghoe	Saektonghoe	1923-	번역 표준 원칙
1938	샌프란시스코 강화조약	San Francisco 講和條約	San Francisco Peace Treaty (Treaty of Peace with Japan)	Saenpeuransiseuko ganghwa joyak	Saenp'ŭransisŭk'o kanghwa choyak	1951	번역 표준 원칙
1939	생명공학	生命工學	biological engineering	Saengmyeong gonghak	Saengmyŏng konghak		번역 표준 원칙
1940	생활 기반시설	生活 基盤施設	neighborhood facilities	Saenghwal giban siseol	Saenghwal kiban sisŏl		번역 표준 원칙
1941	생활보호대상자	生活保護對象者	welfare recipient	Saenghwal boho daesangja	Saenghwal poho taesangja		번역 표준 원칙
1942	생활협동조합운동	生活協同組合運動	Consumers' Cooperative Movement	Saenghwal hyeopdong johap undong	Saenghwal hyŏptong chohap undong		번역 표준 원칙
1943	서간도	西間島	West Gando (Jiandao)	Seogando	Sŏgando	1392-?	번역 표준 원칙
1944	서경원 의원 방북 사건	徐敬元 議員 訪北 事件	lawmaker Seo Gyeong-won's unauthorized visit to North Korea	Seo Gyeong-won uiwon bangbuk sageon	Sŏ Kyŏng-wŏn ŭiwŏn pangbuk sakŏn	1989	번역 표준 원칙

NO	용어	한자	영문	RO	MC	시대 및 연도	출전
1945	서대문	西大門	Seodaemun Gate (West Gate)	Seodaemun	Sŏdaemun	조선	번역 표준 원칙
1946	서대문형무소	西大門刑務所	Seodaemun Prison	Seodaemun hyeongmuso	Sŏdaemun hyŏngmuso	1923-1946	번역 표준 원칙
1947	서독 간호원 파견	西獨 看護員 派遣	dispatch of Korean nurses to West Germany	Seodok ganhowon pagyeon	Sŏdok kanhowŏn p'agyŏn	1963-?	번역 표준 원칙
1948	서독 광부 파견	西獨 鑛夫 派遣	dispatch of Korean miners to West Germany	Seodok gwangbu pagyeon	Sŏdok kwangbu p'agyŏn	1963-?	번역 표준 원칙
1949	서로군정서	西路軍政署	Western Route Military Command	Seoro gunjeongseo	Sŏro kunjŏngsŏ	1919-1922	번역 표준 원칙
1950	서무처	庶務處	Office of General Affairs	Seomucheo	Sŏmuch'ŏ		번역 표준 원칙
1951	서부영화	西部映畵	Western (movie)	Seobu yeonghwa	Sŏbu yŏnghwa		번역 표준 원칙
1952	서북5도 당대회	西北5道 黨大會	Conference of Highly Important Five Northern Provinces of North Korea	Seobuk 5do dangdaehoe	Sŏbuk 5to tangdaehoe	1945	번역 표준 원칙

NO	용어	한자	영문	RO	MC	시대 및 연도	출전
1953	서북청년회	西北青年會	Northwest Youth Association	Seobuk cheongnyeonhoe	Sŏbuk ch'ŏngnyŏnhoe	1946	번역 표준 원칙
1954	서북학회	西北學會	Northwest Educational Association	Seobuk hakhoe	Sŏbuk hakhoe	1908-1910	번역 표준 원칙
1955	서비스협상그룹	Service協商Group	Group of Negotiations on Services (GNS)	Seobiseu hyeopsang gerup	Sŏbisŭ hyŏpsang kŭrup		번역 표준 원칙
1956	서세동점	西勢東漸	Eastern expansion of Western powers	Seosedongjeom	Sŏsedongjŏm		번역 표준 원칙
1957	서승, 서준식 형제 사건	徐勝, 徐俊植 兄弟 事件	Incident of Brothers Seo Seung-Seo and Seo Jun-sik (1971)	Seo Seung, Seo Seung-sik hyeongje sageon	Sŏ Sŭng, Sŏ Chun-sik hyŏngje sakŏn	1971	번역 표준 원칙
1958	서우학회	西友學會	Western Friends Academic Association	Seou hakhoe	Sŏu hakhoe	1906-1908	Peter H. Lee, Sourcebook of Korean Civilization(Volume 2), Columbia University Press, 1993.
1959	서울 G20 정상회의	서울 G20 頂上會議	2010 G-20 Seoul summit	Seoul G20 jeongsang hoeui	Sŏul G20 chŏngsang hoeŭi	2010	번역 표준 원칙
1960	서울 국제무역박람회	Seoul 國際貿易博覽會	Seoul International Trade Fair (SITRA)	Seoul gukje muyeok bangnamhoe	Sŏul kukche muyŏk pangnamhoe	1982	번역 표준 원칙

NO	용어	한자	영문	RO	MC	시대 및 연도	출전
1961	서울 국제연극제	Seoul 國際演劇祭	Seoul International Theater Festival	Seoul gukje yeongeukje	Sŏul kukche yŏn'gŭkche	1977	번역 표준 원칙
1962	서울 국제음악제	Seoul 國際音樂祭	Seoul International Music Festival	Seoul gukje eumakje	Sŏul gukche ŭmakche	1976-1985, 2009-	번역 표준 원칙
1963	서울 미문화원	Seoul 美文化院	American Cultural Center in Seoul	Seoul mimunhwawon	Sŏul mimunhwawŏn		번역 표준 원칙
1964	서울 민간방송 주식회사	Seoul 民間放送 株式會社	Seoul Private Broadcasting Corp. (now Munhwa Broadcasting Corp., MBC)	Seoul minganbangsong jusikhoesa	Sŏul minganbangdong chusikwoesa	1961	번역 표준 원칙
1965	서울 아시안게임	Seoul Asian Games	1986 Seoul Asian Games	Seoul asian geim	Sŏul asian keim	1986	번역 표준 원칙
1966	서울 에어쇼	Seoul Airshow	Seoul International Aerospace & Defense Exhibition (aka Seoul Air Show)	Seoul eeosyo	Sŏul eŏsyo	1996-	번역 표준 원칙
1967	서울 올림픽 대회	Seoul Olympic 大會	1988 Seoul Olympic Games	Seoul ollimpik daehoe	Sŏul ollimp'ik taehoe	1988	번역 표준 원칙
1968	서울 올림픽 문화예술축전	Seoul Olympic 文化藝術祝典	1988 Olympics Cultural Art Festival	Seoul ollimpik munhwa yesul chukjeon	Sŏul ollimp'ik munwa yesul ch'ukchŏn		번역 표준 원칙

NO	용어	한자	영문	RO	MC	시대 및 연도	출전
1969	서울 프린지 페스티벌		Seoul Fringe Festival	Seoul peurinji peseutibeol	Sŏul p'ŭrunji p'esŭt'ibŏl	1998	번역 표준 원칙
1970	서울경제신문	Seoul經濟新聞	Seoul Gyeongje (Seoul Economic Daily)	Seoul gyeongje	Sŏul kyŏngje	1960-?	번역 표준 원칙
1971	서울대 민족통일연맹	Seoul大 民族統一聯盟	Seoul National University National Reunification League	Seouldae minjok tongil yeonmaeng	Sŏultae minjok t'ongil yŏnmaeng	1960-1961	번역 표준 원칙
1972	서울미문화원점거 농성사건	Seoul美文化院占據籠城事件	sit-in occupation by student protesters at the U.S. Cultural Center in Seoul, 1985	Seoul mimunhwawon jeomgeo nongseong sageon	Seoul mimunhwawŏn chŏmgŏ nongsŏng sagŏn	1985	번역 표준 원칙
1973	서울선언문	Seoul宣言文	G20 Seoul Summit Leaders' Declaration of 2010	Seoul seoneonmun	Sŏul sŏnŏnmun	2010	번역 표준 원칙
1974	서울시티투어버스		Seoul City Tour Bus	Seoul siti tueo beoseu	Sŏul sit'i t'uŏ pŏsŭ	2000-	번역 표준 원칙
1975	서울신문	Seoul新聞	Seoul Shinmun (daily newspaper)	Seoul sinmun	Sŏul sinmun	1945-1998	번역 표준 원칙
1976	서울역 회군	Seoul驛 回軍	turning back of demonstrators at Seoul Station (1980)	Seoulyeok hoegun	Sŏullyŏk hoegun	1980	번역 표준 원칙

NO	용어	한자	영문	RO	MC	시대 및 연도	출전
1977	서울역사박물관	Seoul歷史博物館	Seoul Museum of History	Seoul yeoksa bangmulgwan	Sŏul yŏksa pangmulgwan	2002	번역 표준 원칙
1978	서울예술단	Seoul藝術團	Seoul Performing Arts Company	Seoul yesuldan	Sŏul yesultan	1986-	번역 표준 원칙
1979	서울외곽순환고속도로	Seoul外廓循環高速道路	Seoul Beltway	Seoul oegwak sunhwan gosokdoro	Sŏul oegwak sunhwan kosoktoro		번역 표준 원칙
1980	서울의 봄	Seoul의 봄	Seoul Spring (period of democratization in South Korea)	Seoul-ui bom	Sŏul-ŭi pom	1979-1980	번역 표준 원칙
1981	서울지휘소	Seoul指揮所	Command Post Seoul	Seoul jihwiso	Sŏul jihwiso		번역 표준 원칙
1982	서울청년회	Seoul青年會	Seoul Young Men's Association	Seoul cheongnyeonhoe	Sŏul ch'ŏngnyŏnhoe	1921-1929	번역 표준 원칙
1983	서울춘천고속도로	Seoul春川高速道路	Seoul-Chuncheon Expressway	Seoul chuncheon gosokdoro	Sŏul ch'unch'ŏn kosoktoro		번역 표준 원칙
1984	서울충무로국제영화제	Seoul忠武路國際映畵祭	Chungmuro International Film Festival in Seoul	Seoul chungmuro gukje yeonghwaje	Sŏul ch'ungmuro kukche yŏnghwaje	2007-	번역 표준 원칙

NO	용어	한자	영문	RO	MC	시대 및 연도	출전
1985	서울탈환작전	Seoul奪還作戰	operation to recapture Seoul	Seoul talhwan jakjeon	Sŏul t'arhwan chakchŏn		번역 표준 원칙
1986	서울특별시	Seoul特別市	Seoul Metropolitan City	Seoul teukbyeolsi	Sŏul tŭkpyŏlsi	1946-?	번역 표준 원칙
1987	서울프레스	Seoul Press	The Seoul Press	Seoul peureseu	Sŏul pŭressŭ	1905-1937	번역 표준 원칙
1988	서울함	Seoul艦	ROKS Seoul	Seoulham	Sŏuram	1985	번역 표준 원칙
1989	서원철폐령	書院撤廢令	abolishment of seowon (Confucian academies) in the Joseon Dynasty	Seowon cheolpyeryeong	Sŏwŏn ch'ŏlp'yeryŏng	1868-1871	번역 표준 원칙
1990	서유견문	西遊見聞	Observations on a Journey to the West (Seoyu Gyeonmun)	Seoyugyeonmun	Sŏyugyŏnmun	1895	번역 표준 원칙
1991	서전서숙	瑞甸書塾	Seojeon School	Seojeon seosuk	Sŏjŏn sŏsuk	1906-1907	번역 표준 원칙
1992	서천공주고속도로	舒川公州高速道路	Seocheon-Gongju Expressway	Seocheon gongju gosokdoro	Sŏch'ŏn kongju kosoktoro		번역 표준 원칙

NO	용어	한자	영문	RO	MC	시대 및 연도	출전
1993	서편제	西便制	"Sopyonje," movie directed by Im Kwon-taek, 1993	Seopyeonje	Sŏp'yŏnje	1993	번역 표준 원칙
1994	서학	西學	Western learning (Catholicism)	Seohak	Sŏhak	조선	번역 표준 원칙
1995	서해	西海	West Sea	Seohae	Sŏhae		번역 표준 원칙
1996	서해 5도	西海 5島	Five Islands in the Yellow Sea	Seohae 5do	Sŏhae 5do		번역 표준 원칙
1997	서해교전	西海交戰	Korean naval skirmish in the West Sea	Seohae gyojeon	Sŏhae kyojŏn	1999	번역 표준 원칙
1998	서해안고속도로	西海岸高速道路	Seohaean (West Coast) Expressway	Seohaean gosokdoro	Sŏhaean kosoktoro	2001	번역 표준 원칙
1999	서희부대	徐熙部隊	Seohui Unit (engineering and construction Corp.)	Seohuibudae	Sŏhŭibudae	2003	번역 표준 원칙
2000	석굴암	石窟庵	Seokguram Grotto	Seokgulam	Sŏkulam	통일신라/발해	번역 표준 원칙

NO	용어	한자	영문	RO	MC	시대 및 연도	출전
2001	석유공급원의 다변화	石油供給源의 多邊化	diversification of oil supply sources	Seogyu gonggeubwonui dabyeonhwa	Sŏgyu konggŭbwŏn-ŭi tabyŏnhwa		번역 표준 원칙
2002	석유무기화	石油武器化	weaponization of oil	Seogyu mugihwa	Sŏgyu mugihwa		번역 표준 원칙
2003	석유비상대책회의	石油非常對策會議	emergency meeting on the oil shock	Seogyu bisang daechaekhoeui	Sŏgyu bisang daech'aekkoeŭi		번역 표준 원칙
2004	석유비축계획	石油備蓄計劃	plan to build strategic petroleum reserves	Seogyu bichuk gyehoek	Sŏgyu pich'uk kyehoek		번역 표준 원칙
2005	석유수출국기구	石油輸出國機構	Organization of Petroleum Exporting Countries (OPEC)	Seogyu suchulguk gigu	Sŏgyu such'ulguk kigu	1960	번역 표준 원칙
2006	석유외교	石油外交	oil diplomacy	Seogyu oegyo	Sŏgyu oegyo		번역 표준 원칙
2007	석유파동	石油波動	oil shock	Seogyu padong	Sŏgyu p'adong	1차:1973-1974, 2차:1978-1980	번역 표준 원칙
2008	석유화학공업육성법	石油化學工業育成法	Petrochemical Industry Promotion Act	Seogyu hwahak gongeop yukseongbeop	Sŏgyu hwahak kongŏp yuksŏngpŏp	1970	번역 표준 원칙

NO	용어	한자	영문	RO	MC	시대 및 연도	출전
2009	석유화학콤비나트	石油化學Kombinat	petrochemical complex	Seogyu hwahak kombinateu	Sŏgyu hwahak k'ombinat'ŭ		번역 표준 원칙
2010	석탄	石炭	coal	Seoktan	Sŏkt'an		번역 표준 원칙
2011	선거공보	選擧公報	campaign bulletin	Seongeo gongbo	Sŏn'gŏ kongbo		번역 표준 원칙
2012	선거권	選擧權	voting rights	Seongeogwon	Sŏn'gŏgwŏn		번역 표준 원칙
2013	선거법	選擧法	Electoral Law	Seongeobeop	Sŏn'gŏpŏp		번역 표준 원칙
2014	선거법위반 당선무효제	選擧法違反 當選無效制	invalidation of election results due to violation of the election law	Seongeobeop wiban dangseon muhyoje	Sŏngŏpŏp wiban tangsŏn muhyoje		번역 표준 원칙
2015	선거보조금	選擧補助金	election subsidy	Seongeo bojogeum	Sŏngŏ pojogŭm		번역 표준 원칙
2016	선거유세	選擧遊說	election campaign	Seongeo yuse	Sŏn'gŏ yuse		번역 표준 원칙

NO	용어	한자	영문	RO	MC	시대 및 연도	출전
2017	선거조례	選擧條例	rules for the selection of government officials	Seongeo jorye	Sŏngŏ chorye		번역 표준 원칙
2018	선건설·후통일론	先建設·後統一論	theory of development first, unification later	Seongeonseol·hutongillon	Sŏn'gŏnsŏl·hut'ongillon	1961-?	번역 표준 원칙
2019	선군정치	先軍政治	"Military First" policy (North Korea)	Seongun jeongchi	Sŏn'gun chŏngch'i	1995-	번역 표준 원칙
2020	선단식경영	船團式經營	convoy-style conglomerate management	Seondansik gyeongyeong	Sŏndansik kyŏngyŏng		번역 표준 원칙
2021	선박도하 지점	船舶渡河 地点	ferry crossing sites	Seonbak doha jijeom	Sŏnbak toha chijŏm		번역 표준 원칙
2022	선발대	先發隊	Advance Element	Seonbaldae	Sŏnbaltae		번역 표준 원칙
2023	선전촌	宣傳村	Propaganda Village	Seonjeonchon	Sŏnjŏnch'on		번역 표준 원칙
2024	선제타격계획	先制打擊計劃	Pre-emptive Strike Plan of the North Korean Military	Seonje tagyeok gyehoek	Sŏnje t'agyŏk kyehoek		번역 표준 원칙

NO	용어	한자	영문	RO	MC	시대 및 연도	출전
2025	선진농업	先進農業	advanced agriculture	Seonjin nongeop	Sŏnjin nongŏp	조선	M. Deuchler, The Confucian Transformation of Korea: A Study of Society and Ideology, Harvard
2026	설악산 전투	雪嶽山 戰鬪	Battle of Mt. Seoraksan	Seoraksan jeontu	Sŏraksan chŏnt'u	6·25전쟁	번역 표준 원칙
2027	섬유공업진흥계획	纖維工業振興計劃	Textiles Industry Promotion Plan	Seomnyu gongeop jinheung gyehoek	Sŏmyu kongŏp chinhŭng kyehoek		번역 표준 원칙
2028	성매매방지법	性賣買防止法	Act on the Prevention of Sexual Trafficking and Protection of Victims Thereof	Seongmaemae bangjibeop	Sŏngmaemae pangjipŏp	2004	번역 표준 원칙
2029	성명회	聲明會	National Committee of Korea	Seongmyeonghoe	Sŏngmyŏnghoe	1910	번역 표준 원칙
2030	성명회 선언서	聲鳴會 宣言書	Declaration of the National Committee of Korea	Seongmyeonghoe seoneonseo	Sŏngmyŏnghoe sŏnŏnsŏ	1910	번역 표준 원칙
2031	성수대교 붕괴	聖水大橋 崩壞	collapse of Seongsu Bridge in 1994	Seongsudaegyo bunggoe	Sŏngsudaegyo punggoe	1994	번역 표준 원칙
2032	성장일변도 정책	成長一邊倒 政策	growth-oriented policy	Seongjang ilbyeondo jeongchaek	Sŏngjang ilbyŏndo chŏngch'aek		번역 표준 원칙

NO	용어	한자	영문	RO	MC	시대 및 연도	출전
2033	성차별	性差別	gender discrimination	Seongchabyeol	Sŏngch'abyŏl		번역 표준 원칙
2034	성폭력상담소	性暴力相談所	Korea Sexual Violence Relief Center	Seongpongnyeok sangdamso	Sŏngp'ongnyŏk sangdamso	1991	번역 표준 원칙
2035	성폭력특별법	性暴力特別法	Act on the Punishment of Sexual Crimes and Protection of Victims Thereof	Seongpongnyeok teukbyeolbeop	Sŏngp'ongnyŏk t'ŭkpyŏlpŏp	1994	번역 표준 원칙
2036	세계 경영	世界 經營	global management	Segye gyeongyeong	Segye kyŏngyŏng		번역 표준 원칙
2037	세계경제 개발지표	世界經濟 開發指標	global economic development indicators	Segye gyeongje gaebal jipyo	Segye kyŏngje kaebal chip'yo		번역 표준 원칙
2038	세계기록유산	世界記錄遺産	UNESCO Memory of the World	Segye girok yusan	Segye kirok yusan	1992	번역 표준 원칙
2039	세계노동조합연맹	世界勞動組合聯盟	World Federation of Trade Unions	Segye nodong johap yeonmaeng	Segye nodong chohap yŏnmaeng	1945-	번역 표준 원칙
2040	세계대공황	世界大恐慌	Great Depression	Segye daegonghwang	Segye taegonghwang	1928-1933	번역 표준 원칙

NO	용어	한자	영문	RO	MC	시대 및 연도	출전
2041	세계무역기구설립을 위한 마라케시협정	世界貿易機構設立을 爲한 Marrakesh協定	Marrakesh Agreement Establishing the World Trade Organization	Segye muyeok gigu seollipeul wihan marakesi hyeopjeong	Segye muyŏk kigu sŏllip-ŭl wihan marak'esi hyŏpchŏng		번역 표준 원칙
2042	세계문화유산	世界文化遺産	UNESCO World Cultural Heritage	Segye munhwa yusan	Segye munhwa yusan	1972-	번역 표준 원칙
2043	세계박람회	世界博覽會	International Exposition	Segye bangnamhoe	Segye pangnamhoe		번역 표준 원칙
2044	세계반공연맹	世界反共聯盟	World Anti-Communist League	Segye bangong yeonmaeng	Segye pan'gong yŏnmaeng	1967	번역 표준 원칙
2045	세계보건기구 헌장	世界保健機構 憲章	Constitution of the World Health Organization	Segye bogeongigu heonjang	Segye pogŏngigu hŏnjang	1946	번역 표준 원칙
2046	세계사격선수권대회	世界射擊選手權大會	World Shooting Championships	Segye sagyeok seonsugwon daehoe	Segye sagyŏk sŏnsukwŏn taehoe	1897-	번역 표준 원칙
2047	세계신기록	世界新記錄	new world record	Segye singirok	Segye singirok		번역 표준 원칙
2048	세계유산협약	世界遺産協約	World Heritage Convention	Segye yusan hyeobyak	Segye yusan hyŏbyak	1972	번역 표준 원칙

NO	용어	한자	영문	RO	MC	시대 및 연도	출전
2049	세계은행	世界銀行	International Bank for Reconstruction and Development (IBRD)	Segye eunhaeng	Segye ŭnhaeng	1946-?	번역 표준 원칙
2050	세계일보	世界日報	*Segye Ilbo*, daily newspaper	Segye ilbo	Segye ilbo	1989	번역 표준 원칙
2051	세계자연유산	世界自然遺産	UNESCO World Natural Heritage	Segye jayeon yusan	Segye chayŏn yusan	1972-	번역 표준 원칙
2052	세계청년학생축전	世界靑年學生祝典	World Festival of Youth and Students	Segye cheongnyeon haksaeng chukjeon	Segye ch'ŏngnyŏn haksaeng ch'ukchŏn	1947-	번역 표준 원칙
2053	세계청소년축구 선수권대회	世界靑少年蹴球 選手權大會	FIFA World Youth Championship	Segye cheongsonyeon chukgu seonsugwon daehoe	Segye ch'ŏngsonyŏn ch'ukku sŏnsukwŏn taehoe	1991	번역 표준 원칙
2054	세계탁구선수권대회	世界卓球選手權大會	World Table-Tennis Championships	Segye takgu seonsugwon daehoe	Segye t'akku sŏnsukwŏn taehoe	1926-	번역 표준 원칙
2055	세계한민족축전	世界韓民族祝典	World Koreans Festival	Segye hanminjok chukjeon	Segye hanminjok ch'ukchŏn	1989	번역 표준 원칙
2056	세도정치	勢道政治	in-law government	Sedo jeongchi	Sedo chŏngch'i	조선후기	Ki-baik Lee, translated by Edward W. Wagner, A New History of Korea, Harvard University Press, 1984,

NO	용어	한자	영문	RO	MC	시대 및 연도	출전
2057	세브란스병원	Severance病院	Severance Hospital	Sebeuranseu byeongwon	Sebŭransŭ pyŏngwŏn	1904-?	번역 표준 원칙
2058	세브란스의학전문학교	Severance醫學專門學校	Severance Medical School	Sebeuranseu uihak jeonmun hakgyo	Sebŭransŭ ŭihak chŏnmun hakkyo	1917-	번역 표준 원칙
2059	세제개혁요강	稅制改革要綱	outline of tax reform	Seje gaehyeok yogang	Seje gaehyŏk yogang		번역 표준 원칙
2060	세종문화회관	世宗文化會館	Sejong Center for the Performing Arts	Sejong munhwa hoegwan	Sejong munhwa hoegwan	1978-?	번역 표준 원칙
2061	세종시	世宗市	Sejong (Special Self-Governing) City	Sejong-si	Sejongsi		번역 표준 원칙
2062	세종학당	世宗學堂	King Sejong Institute	Sejong hakdang	Sejong haktang	2011	번역 표준 원칙
2063	소급입법	遡及立法	retroactive legislation	Sogeup ipbeop	Sogŭp ippŏp		번역 표준 원칙
2064	소년	少年	*Sonyeon* (youth magazine)	Sonyeon	Sonyŏn	1908-1911	번역 표준 원칙

NO	용어	한자	영문	RO	MC	시대 및 연도	출전
2065	소년병제도	少年兵制度	military use of children	Sonyeonbyeong Jedo	Sonyŏnbyŏng chedo		번역 표준 원칙
2066	소년운동	少年運動	youth movement	Sonyeon undong	Sonyŏn undong	1923-1925	번역 표준 원칙
2067	소년잡지	少年雜誌	boy's magazines	Sonyeon japji	Sonyŏn chapchi	1910	번역 표준 원칙
2068	소년한국일보	少年韓國日報	Sonyeon Hankook Ilbo (children's newspaper)	Sonyeon hanguk ilbo	Sonyŏn han'guk ilbo	1960-?	번역 표준 원칙
2069	소대	小隊	Platoon	Sodae	Sodae	1950	번역 표준 원칙
2070	소떼 방북	소떼 訪北	sending a herd of cattle to North Korea	Sodde bangbuk	Sotte pangbuk	1998	번역 표준 원칙
2071	소련	蘇聯	Union of Soviet Socialist Republics (USSR)	Soryeon	Soryŏn	1917-1992	번역 표준 원칙
2072	소련 규탄 공동 결의안	蘇聯 糾彈 共同 決議案	joint resolution denouncing the Soviet Union	Soryeon gyutan gongdong gyeoluian	Soryŏn kyut'an kongdong gyŏrŭian		번역 표준 원칙

NO	용어	한자	영문	RO	MC	시대 및 연도	출전
2073	소련군사고문단	蘇聯軍事顧問團	Soviet Union's Military Advisory Group to North Korea	Soryeon gunsa gomundan	Soryŏn kunsa komundan		번역 표준 원칙
2074	소련극동방면군	蘇聯極東方面軍	Far Eastern Front (Soviet Union)	Soryeon geukdong bangmyeongun	Soryŏn kŭktong pangmyŏn'gun		번역 표준 원칙
2075	소련파	蘇聯派	Soviet-Korean Group	Soryeonpa	Soryŏnp'a	1945-1956	번역 표준 원칙
2076	소만국경	蘇滿國境	Soviet-Manchurian Border	Soman gukgyeong	Soman kukkyŏng		번역 표준 원칙
2077	소몰이투쟁	소몰이鬪爭	farmer's cattle driving protest of 1985	Somori tujaeng	Somori t'ujaeng	1985	번역 표준 원칙
2078	소방방재청	消防防災廳	National Emergency Management Agency (NEMA)	Sobang bangjaecheong	Sobang pangjaech'ŏng	2004	번역 표준 원칙
2079	소백산국립공원	小白山國立公園	Sobaeksan National Park	Sobaeksan gungnip gongwon	Sobaeksan kungnip kongwŏn	1987-?	번역 표준 원칙
2080	소비문화	消費文化	consumer culture	Sobi munhwa	Sobi munhwa		번역 표준 원칙

NO	용어	한자	영문	RO	MC	시대 및 연도	출전
2081	소비자 권리	消費者 權利	consumer rights	Sobija gwolli	Sobija kwŏlli		번역 표준 원칙
2082	소비자운동	消費者運動	consumer rights movement	Sobija undong	Sobija undong		번역 표준 원칙
2083	소비절약저축운동	消費節約貯蓄運動	frugality and savings campaign	Sobi jeoryak jeochuk undong	Sobi chŏryak chŏch'uk undong		번역 표준 원칙
2084	소선거구제	小選擧區制	single-member electorate system	Soseongeoguje	Sosŏn'gŏguje		번역 표준 원칙
2085	소양강 다목적댐	昭陽江 多目的dam	Soyanggang River Multipurpose Dam	Soyanggang damokjeok daem	Soyanggang tamokchŏk taem	1973	번역 표준 원칙
2086	소양강 다목적댐 건설계획	昭陽江 多目的dam 建設 計劃	plan to build the Soyanggang River Multipurpose Dam in Chuncheon, Gangwon-do Province	Soyanggang damokjeokdaem geonseol gyehoek	Soyanggang tamokchŏk taem kŏnsŏl kyehoek	1967(?)	번역 표준 원칙
2087	소요진압작전	騷擾鎭壓作戰	suppresion of civil distrubance	Soyo jinap jakjeon	Soyo jinap chakchŏn		번역 표준 원칙
2088	소작노동자대회	小作勞動者大會	Tenant Farmers' Rally of 1922	Sojak nodongja daehoe	Sojak nodongja taehoe	1922	번역 표준 원칙

NO	용어	한자	영문	RO	MC	시대 및 연도	출전
2089	소작농	小作農	tenant farming	Sojangnong	Sojangnong	조선	번역 표준 원칙
2090	소작인조합	小作人組合	Tenant Farmer Organization	Sojagin johap	Sojagin chohap	1920년대 초반	Ki-baik Lee, translated by Edward W. Wagner, A New History of Korea, Harvard University Press, 1984,
2091	소작쟁의	小作爭議	tenancy dispute	Sojak jaengui	Sojak chaengǔi		번역 표준 원칙
2092	소재산업	素材産業	basic materials industries	Sojae saneop	Sojae sanŏp		번역 표준 원칙
2093	소탕전	掃蕩戰	mop-up operation	Sotangjeon	Sot'angjŏn		번역 표준 원칙
2094	속리산국립공원	俗離山國立公園	Songnisan National Park	Songnisan gungnipgongwon	Songnisan kungnipkongwŏn	1970-?	번역 표준 원칙
2095	속전속결	速戰速決	lightening war	Sokjeonsokgyeol	Sokchŏnsokkyŏl		번역 표준 원칙
2096	손원일함	孫元一艦	ROKS Son Won-il (SS 072)	Sonwonilham	Sonwŏnilham		번역 표준 원칙

NO	용어	한자	영문	RO	MC	시대 및 연도	출전
2097	송죽회	松竹會	Songjuk Society (women's independence organization)	Songjukhoe	Songjukhoe	1913-?	번역 표준 원칙
2098	쇄국정책	鎖國政策	policy of isolation	Swaeguk jeongchaek	Swaeguk chŏngch'aek	1864-1873	Ki-baik Lee, translated by Edward W. Wagner, A New History of Korea, Harvard University Press, 1984,
2099	수도고지, 지형능선 전투	首都高地, 指型稜線 戰鬪	Battle of Capital Hill, Fingers Ridge	Sudogyoji, jihyeongneungseon jeontu	Sudogoji, chihyŏngnŭngsŏn chŏnt'u	1953	번역 표준 원칙
2100	수도권 7개 도시 정비계획	首都圈 7個 都市 整備計劃	plan for the advancement of seven cities in the Seoul Metropolitan Area	Sudogwon 7gae dosi jeongbigyehoek	Sudokwŏn 7gae dosi chŏngbigyehoek		번역 표준 원칙
2101	수도권 전철	首都圈 電鐵	metropolitan subway	Sudogwon jeoncheol	Sudogwŏn chŏnch'ŏl	1974-	번역 표준 원칙
2102	수력발전소	水力發電所	hydroelectric power plant	Suryeok baljeonso	Suryŏk palchŏnso	1991-?	번역 표준 원칙
2103	수리안전답	水利安全畓	well-irrigated paddies	Suri anjeondap	Suri anjŏndap		번역 표준 원칙
2104	수리조합	水利組合	irrigation associations	Suri johap	Suri chohap	1906-1962	번역 표준 원칙

NO	용어	한자	영문	RO	MC	시대 및 연도	출전
2105	수리조합반대운동	水利組合反對運動	protest against irrigation associations	Suri johap bandae undong	Suri chohap pandae undong	1920-?	번역 표준 원칙
2106	수몰지역	水沒地域	submerged districts	Sumol jiyeok	Sumol chiyŏk		번역 표준 원칙
2107	수산협동조합	水産協同組合	National Fisheries Cooperative Federation	Susan hyeopdong johap	Susan hyŏptong chohap		번역 표준 원칙
2108	수색격멸작전	搜索擊滅作戰	search-and-destroy operation	Susaek gyeongmyeol jakjeon	Susaek kyŏngmyŏl chakchŏn		번역 표준 원칙
2109	수신사	修信使	special envoy	Susinsa	Susinsa	1876-1894	Ki-baik Lee, translated by Edward W. Wagner, A New History of Korea, Harvard University Press, 1984,
2110	수원 화성	水原 華城	Suwon Hwaseong Fortress	Suwon hwaseong	Suwŏn hwasŏng	1796	번역 표준 원칙
2111	수입선다변화	輸入先多邊化	import source diversification	Suipseon dabyeonhwa	Suipsŏn tabyŏnhwa	1977-1999	번역 표준 원칙
2112	수입자유화	輸入自由化	liberalization of imports	Suip jayuhwa	Suip chayuhwa		번역 표준 원칙

NO	용어	한자	영문	RO	MC	시대 및 연도	출전
2113	수자원종합개발 10개년 계획	水資源綜合開發 10個年 計劃	10-year plan for the development of water resources	Sujawon jonghap gaebal 10gaenyeon gyehoek	Sujawŏn chonghap kaebal 10kaenyŏn kyehoek		번역 표준 원칙
2114	수재민	水災民	flood victims	Sujaemin	Sujaemin		번역 표준 원칙
2115	수출공업화전략	輸出工業化戰略	export-led industrialization strategy	Suchul gongeophwa jeollyak	Such'ul kongŏphwa chŏllyak	1960년대	번역 표준 원칙
2116	수출금융	輸出金融	export financing	Suchul geumyung	Such'ul kŭmyung		번역 표준 원칙
2117	수출목표	輸出目標	export target	Suchul mokpyo	Such'ul mokp'yo		번역 표준 원칙
2118	수출보조금	輸出補助金	export subsidy	Suchul bojogeum	Such'ul pojogŭm		번역 표준 원칙
2119	수출위주의 경공업육성 전략	輸出爲主의 輕工業育成 戰略	export-driven strategy of fostering light industries	Suchul wijuui gyeonggongeop yukseong jeollyak	Such'ul wiju-ŭi kyŏnggongŏp yuksŏng chŏllyak		번역 표준 원칙
2120	수출의 날	輸出의 날	Export Day	Suchului nal	Such'ul-ŭi nal	1964	번역 표준 원칙

NO	용어	한자	영문	RO	MC	시대 및 연도	출전
2121	수출자유지역설치법	輸出自由地域設置法	Act on the Establishment of Free Export Zones	Suchul jayu jiyeok seolchibeop	Such'ul chayu chiyŏk sŏlch'ipŏp	1970	번역 표준 원칙
2122	수출제일주의	輸出第一主義	export-driven policy	Suchul jeiljuui	Such'ul cheiljuǔi		번역 표준 원칙
2123	수출지향공업화정책	輸出指向工業化政策	export-oriented industrialization strategy	Suchul jihyang gongeophwa jeongchaek	Such'ul chihyang kongŏphwa chŏngch'aek	1960년대	번역 표준 원칙
2124	수출진흥종합시책	輸出振興綜合施策	export promotion policies	Suchul jinheung jonghap sichaek	Such'ul chinhǔng chonghap sich'aek	1965	번역 표준 원칙
2125	수출진흥확대회의	輸出振興擴大會議	meeting to promote exports	Suchul jnheung hwakdae hoeui	Such'ul chinhǔng hwaktae hoeǔi		번역 표준 원칙
2126	수피아여학교	Speer女學校	Speer Girls' School	Supia yeohakgyo	Supia yŏhakkyo	1908	번역 표준 원칙
2127	수해상습지	水害常習地	flood-prone areas	Suhae sangseupji	Suhae sangsǔpchi		번역 표준 원칙
2128	수호통상조약	修好通商條約	treaty of protection and trade	Suho tongsang joyak	Suho t'ongsang choyak	1883	번역 표준 원칙

NO	용어	한자	영문	RO	MC	시대 및 연도	출전
2129	수훈십자훈장 (미육군)	殊勳十字勳章 (美陸軍)	Distinguished Service Cross (DSC)	Suhun sipja hunjang (mi yukgun)	Suhun sipcha hunjang (mi yukkun)		번역 표준 원칙
2130	숙명여학교	淑明女學校	Sookmyung Girls' School (now Sookmyung Girls' High School)	Sungmyeong yeohakgyo	Sungmyŏng yŏhakkyo	1906-?	번역 표준 원칙
2131	숙천·순천지역 공수작전	肅川·順天地域 空輸作戰	airbone operations in Sukcheon and Suncheon	Sukcheon suncheon jiyeok gongsujakjeon	Sukch'ŏn sunch'ŏn chiyŏk kongsujakchŏn	1950	번역 표준 원칙
2132	순화교육	純化敎育	"social purification"	Sunhwa gyoyuk	Sunhwa kyoyuk		번역 표준 원칙
2133	순환출자	循環出資	cyclical investment	Sunhwan chulja	Sunhwan ch'ulcha		번역 표준 원칙
2134	숫자로 본 경제성장	숫자로 본 經濟成長	Statistics on Korea's Economic Growth	Sutjaro bon gyeongje seongjang	Sutcha-ro pon kyŏngje sŏngjang	1975.1.	번역 표준 원칙
2135	숭례문 화재	崇禮門 火災	Sungnyemun Gate fire	Sungnyemun hwajae	Sungnyemun hwaje	2008	번역 표준 원칙
2136	숭무학교	崇武學校	Sungmu Independent Army School in Mexico	Sungmu hakgyo	Sungmu hakkyo	1910	번역 표준 원칙

NO	용어	한자	영문	RO	MC	시대 및 연도	출전
2137	숭실전문학교	崇實專門學校	Soongsil College	Sungsil jeonmun hakgyo	Sungsil chŏnmun hakkyo	1925	번역 표준 원칙
2138	숭실학당	崇實學堂	Soongsil Hakdang (Soongsil School)	Sungsil hakdang	Sungsil haktang	1901	번역 표준 원칙
2139	스마트 TV	Smart TV	smart TV	Seumateu TV	Sŭmat'ŭ TV	2011	번역 표준 원칙
2140	스미스 특수 임무부대	Smith 特殊 任務部隊	Task Force Smith	Seumiseu teuksu immu budae	Sŭmisŭ t'ŭksu immu pudae		번역 표준 원칙
2141	스승의 날 제정	스승의 날 制定	enactment of Teachers' Day	Seuseungui nal jejeong	Sŭsŭngŭi nal chejŏng	1960년대	번역 표준 원칙
2142	스탠더드 팝		Standard Pop	pop song	Seutaendeodeu pop	Sŭt'aendŏdŭ p'ap		번역 표준 원칙
2143	승가대학	僧伽大學	sangha university	Seungga daehak	Sŭngga taehak	현대	번역 표준 원칙
2144	승정원일기	承政院日記	Daily Records of the Royal Secretariat (Seungjeongwon Ilgi)	Seungjeongwon ilgi	Sŭngjŏngwŏn ilgi	조선	번역 표준 원칙

NO	용어	한자	영문	RO	MC	시대 및 연도	출전
2145	시간강사	時間講師	part-time lecturer	Sigan gangsa	Sikan kangsa		번역 표준 원칙
2146	시국수습에 관한 특별담화문	時局收拾에 關한 特別談話文	Special Statement to Stabilize the Country	Siguk suseube gwanhan teukbyeol damhwamun	Siguk susŭp-e kwanhan t'ŭkpyŏl tamhwamun	1987	번역 표준 원칙
2147	시노모세키 조약	시노모세키 條約	Treaty of Shimonoseki of 1895	Simonoseki joyak	Simonosek'i choyak	1895	번역 표준 원칙
2148	시드니 올림픽	Sydney Olympics	2000 Sydney Olympics	Sideuni ollimpik	Sidŭni ollip'ik	2000	번역 표준 원칙
2149	시드니 올림픽 개·폐회식 남북공동입장	Sydney Olympic 開·閉會式 南北共同入場	South and North Korea marching together at the opening and closing cermonies of the Sydney Olympics	Sideuni ollimpik gepyehoesik nambuk gongdong ipjang	Sidŭni ollimpik kaepyehoesik nambuk kongtong ipchang	2000	번역 표준 원칙
2150	시립박물관	市立博物館	municipal museum	Sirip bangmulgwan	Sirip pangmulgwan		번역 표준 원칙
2151	시민군	市民軍	militia	Simingun	Simin'gun		번역 표준 원칙
2152	시민아파트	市民Apartment	apartments for low-income earners	Simin apateu	Simin ap'at'ŭ		번역 표준 원칙

NO	용어	한자	영문	RO	MC	시대 및 연도	출전
2153	시민운동	市民運動	civic movement	Simin undong	Simin undong		번역 표준 원칙
2154	시발자동차	始發自動車	Sibal (first Korean-made car)	Sibal jadongcha	Sibal chadongch'a	1955	번역 표준 원칙
2155	시범단지	示範團地	apartments sold before construction	Sibeom danji	Sibŏm tanchi		번역 표준 원칙
2156	시베리아 철도	Siberia 鐵道	Trans-Siberian Railway	Siberia cheoldo	Siberia ch'ŏlto		번역 표준 원칙
2157	시베리아 철병	Siberia 撤兵	withdrawal of troops from Siberia	Siberia cheolbyeong	Siberia ch'ŏlbyŏng		번역 표준 원칙
2158	시위대	侍衛隊	Palace Guard Regiment	Siwidae	Siwidae	1895-1907	번역 표준 원칙
2159	시일야방성대곡	是日也放聲大哭	"Today we cry out in lamentation" (editorial written by Jang Ji-yeon, publisher of the *Hwangseong Shinmun*, in protest	Siiryabangseongdaegok	Siiryabangsŏngdaegok	1905	번역 표준 원칙
2160	시장평균환율제도	市場平均換率制度	exchange rate system based on market average	Sijang pyeonggyun hwannyul jedo	Sijang p'yŏnggyun hwanyul chedo		번역 표준 원칙

NO	용어	한자	영문	RO	MC	시대 및 연도	출전
2161	시티폰	City phone	Cityphone (receive-only mobile phone)	Sitipon	Sit'ip'on	1990년대	번역 표준 원칙
2162	시험관 아기	試驗管 아기	test-tube babies	Siheomgwan agi	Sihŏmgwan agi		번역 표준 원칙
2163	시화지구	始華地區	Sihwa District	Sihwajigu	Sihwajigu	1987-1994	번역 표준 원칙
2164	시흥지구 전투사령부	始興地區 戰鬪司令部	Siheung Area Combat Command	Siheung jigu jeontu saryeongbu	Sihŭng chigu chŏnt'u saryŏngbu		번역 표준 원칙
2165	식량배급표	食糧配給票	food stamps	Singnyang baegeuppyo	Singnyang paegŭpp'yo	1956	번역 표준 원칙
2166	식량자급	食糧自給	food self-sufficiency	Singnyang jageup	Singnyang chagŭp		번역 표준 원칙
2167	식량증산	食糧增産	increased production of food products	Singnyang jeungsan	Singnyang chŭngsan		번역 표준 원칙
2168	식량증산 7개년 계획	食糧增産 7個年 計劃	seven-year plan to boost food production (1965-1971)	Singnyang jeungsan 7gaenyeon gyehoek	Singnyang chŭngsan 7kaenyŏn kyehoek	1965-1971	번역 표준 원칙

NO	용어	한자	영문	RO	MC	시대 및 연도	출전
2169	식량행정처	食糧行政處	National Food Administration	Singnyang haengjeongcheo	Singnyang haengjŏngch'ŏ		번역 표준 원칙
2170	식민사관	植民史觀	colonial historical perspective	Singmin sagwan	Singmin sagwan	1890-1945	번역 표준 원칙
2171	식민지개발론	植民地開發論	modernization theory	Singminji gaeballon	Singminji kaeballon		번역 표준 원칙
2172	식민지공업화론	植民地工業化論	theory of industrialization under colonialism	Singminji gongeophwaron	Singminji kongŏphwaron		번역 표준 원칙
2173	식민지교육정책	植民地教育政策	colonial education policy	Singminji gyoyuk jeongchaek	Singminji kyoyuk chŏngch'aek		번역 표준 원칙
2174	식민지근대화론	植民地近代化論	theory of modernization under colonialism	Singminji geundaehwaron	Singminji kŭndaehwaron		번역 표준 원칙
2175	식민지산업화론	植民地産業化論	theory of industrialization under colonialism	Singminji sangeophwaron	Singminji sanŏphwaron		번역 표준 원칙
2176	식민지수탈론	植民地收奪論	theory of exploitation under colonialism	Singminji sutallon	Singminji sut'allon		번역 표준 원칙

NO	용어	한자	영문	RO	MC	시대 및 연도	출전
2177	식산은행	殖産銀行	Industrial Bank (Shokusan Ginkō)	Siksan eunhaeng	Siksan ŭnhaeng	1918-1952	Ki-baik Lee, translated by Edward W. Wagner, A New History of Korea, Harvard University Press, 1984,
2178	식산흥업	殖産興業	increasing production and promoting new industries	Siksan heungeop	Siksan hŭngŏp	근현대	번역 표준 원칙
2179	식품의약품안전청	食品醫藥品安定廳	Korea Food and Drug Administration (KFDA)	Sikpum uiyakpum anjeongcheong	Sikp'um ŭiyakpum anjŏngch'ŏng	1998	번역 표준 원칙
2180	신간회	新幹會	New Korea Society (Singanhoe)	Singanhoe	Sin'ganhoe	1927-1931	번역 표준 원칙
2181	신경향파문학	新傾向派文學	new tendency literature	Singyeonghyangpa munhak	Sin'gyŏnghyangp'a munhak	1923-?	번역 표준 원칙
2182	신공업도시	新工業都市	new industrial city	Singongeop dosi	Sin'gongŏp tosi		번역 표준 원칙
2183	신교육운동	新教育運動	New Education Movement	Singyoyuk undong	Shin'gyoyuk undong	1946-?	번역 표준 원칙
2184	신군부 세력	新軍部 勢力	new military power	Singunbu seryeok	Sin'gunbu seryŏk	1979-1987	번역 표준 원칙

NO	용어	한자	영문	RO	MC	시대 및 연도	출전
2185	신극운동	新劇運動	Theatrical Reform Movement	Singeuk undong	Sin'gŭk undong	1920년대	번역 표준 원칙
2186	신도시개발	新都市開發	development of new cities	Sindosi gaebal	Sindosi kaebal		번역 표준 원칙
2187	신문지법	新聞紙法	Newspaper Act	Sinmunji beop	Sinmunji pŏp	1907	번역 표준 원칙
2188	신문학	新文學	new literature	Sinmunhak	Sinmunhak	19세기 말	번역 표준 원칙
2189	신미양요	辛未洋擾	Foreign Disturbance of 1871 (Sinmi Yangyo)	Sinmiyangyo	Sinmiyangyo	1871	Ki-baik Lee, translated by Edward W. Wagner, A New History of Korea, Harvard University Press, 1984,
2190	신민당	新民黨	New Democratic Party	Sinmindang	Sinmindang		번역 표준 원칙
2191	신민당 대통령 후보	新民黨 大統領 候補	presidential candidate of the New People's Party	Sinmindang daetongnyeong hubo	Sinmindang taet'ongnyŏng hubo		번역 표준 원칙
2192	신민당전당대회	新民黨全黨大會	national convention of the New People's Party	Sinmindang jeondang daehoe	Sinmindang chŏndang taehoe		번역 표준 원칙

NO	용어	한자	영문	RO	MC	시대 및 연도	출전
2193	신민부	新民府	New People's Government (Sinminbu)	Sinminbu	Sinminbu	1925-1929	한국학중앙연구원,《영문한국백과》-김좌진
2194	신민족주의론	新民族主義論	New Nationalism	Sinminjokjuuiron	Sinminjokjuŭiron		번역 표준 원칙
2195	신민주공화당	新民主共和黨	New Democratic Republican Party	Sinminju gonghwadang	Sinminju konghwadang	1987-1990	한국학중앙연구원,《영문한국백과》-한국
2196	신민회	新民會	New People's Association (Sinminhoe)	Sinminhoe	Sinminhoe		번역 표준 원칙
2197	신민회사건	新民會事件	1911 Incident of the New People's Association (Sinminhoe)	Sinminhoe sageon	Sinminhoe sakŏn	1911	번역 표준 원칙
2198	신사유람단	紳士遊覽團	Korean Courtiers' Observation Mission to Japan (1881)	Sinsa yuramdan	Sinsa yuramdan	1881	번역 표준 원칙
2199	신사참배	神社參拜	worship at Shinto shrines	Sinsa chambae	Sinsa ch'ambae	일제	번역 표준 원칙
2200	신사참배거부운동	神社參拜拒否運動	resistance to worship at Shinto shrines	Sinsa chambae geobu undong	Sinsa ch'ambae kŏbu undong	1930년대 후반-광복	번역 표준 원칙

NO	용어	한자	영문	RO	MC	시대 및 연도	출전
2201	신사회운동	新社會運動	new social movement	Sinsahoe undong	Sinsahoe undong		번역 표준 원칙
2202	신생활운동	新生活運動	New Life Movement	Sinsaenghwal undong	Sinsaenghwal undong	1960	번역 표준 원칙
2203	신소설	新小說	new novel	Sinsoseol	Sinsosŏl		Ki-baik Lee, translated by Edward W. Wagner, A New History of Korea, Harvard University Press, 1984,
2204	신아일보	新亞日報	*Shin-A Ilbo* (daily newspaper)	Sinailbo	Sinailbo	1965-1980	번역 표준 원칙
2205	신용등급	信用等級	credit rating	Sinyong deunggeup	Sinyong tŭnggŭp		번역 표준 원칙
2206	신의주학생사건	新義州學生事件	Sinuiju Students Incident	Sinuiju haksaeng sageon	Sinŭiju haksaeng sakŏn	1945	번역 표준 원칙
2207	신자유주의	新自由主義	neoliberalism	Sinjayujuui	Sinjayujuŭi	1980-?	번역 표준 원칙
2208	신전술	新戰術	new tactics	Sinjeonsul	Sinjŏnsul	1946	번역 표준 원칙

NO	용어	한자	영문	RO	MC	시대 및 연도	출전
2209	신정 동국역사	新訂 東國歷史	A Newly Revised History of Korea (Sinjeong Dongguk Yeoksa)	Sinjeong dongguk yeoksa	Sinjŏng tongguk yŏksa	1906	번역 표준 원칙
2210	신정당	新政黨	new political party	Sinjeongdang	Sinjŏngdang	1963	번역 표준 원칙
2211	신종인플루엔자	新種influenza	Influenza A virus subtype H1N1	Sinjong inpeulluenja	Sinjong inp'ulluenja	2009	번역 표준 원칙
2212	신진 퍼블리카	新進 Publica	Shinjin Publica	Sinjin peobeullika	Sinjin p'ŏbŭllik'a	1967-1971	번역 표준 원칙
2213	신진자동차	新進自動車	Shinjin Motor Co.	Sinjin jadongcha	Sinjin chadongch'a	1961-?	번역 표준 원칙
2214	신진회	新進會	Sinjinhoe	Sinjinhoe	Sinjinhoe		번역 표준 원칙
2215	신찬 소물리학	新撰 小物理學	A New Compilation of Physics Digest (Sinchan So Mullihak)	Sinchan so mullihak	Sinch'an so mullihak	1906	번역 표준 원칙
2216	신체시	新體詩	new style poem	Sinchesi	Sinch'esi	1908-1919	한국학중앙연구원, 《영문한국백과》-해에게서 소년에게

NO	용어	한자	영문	RO	MC	시대 및 연도	출전
2217	신탁통치	信託統治	trusteeship	Sintak tongchi	Sint'ak t'ongchi	1945-1948	번역 표준 원칙
2218	신탁통치반대운동	信託統治反對運動	anti-trusteeship movement	Sintak tongchi bandae undong	Sint'ak t'ongch'i pandae undong	1945-1947	한국학중앙연구원, 《영문한국백과》-신탁통치반대운동
2219	신탁통치안	信託統治案	Moscow Trusteeship Proposal	Sintak tongchian	Sint'ak t'ongch'ian	1945	번역 표준 원칙
2220	신토불이	身土不二	"the body and earth are one"	Sinto buri	Shint'o puri		번역 표준 원칙
2221	신한공사	新韓公社	Sinhan Public Corporation	Sinhan gongsa	Sinhan kongsa	1946-1948	번역 표준 원칙
2222	신한국당	新韓國黨	New Korea Party	Sinhangukdang	Sinhan'guktan	1995-1997	한국학중앙연구원, 《영문한국백과》-대한민국
2223	신한국보	新韓國報	The United Korean News	Sinhangukbo	Sinhan'gukpo	1909	번역 표준 원칙
2224	신한민보	新韓民報	Sinhan Minbo (New Korea)	Sinhanminbo	Sinhanminbo	1909-1945	번역 표준 원칙

NO	용어	한자	영문	RO	MC	시대 및 연도	출전
2225	신한민주당	新韓民主黨	New Korea Democratic Party	Sinhan minjudang	Sinhan minjudang	1985-1987	번역 표준 원칙
2226	신한청년단	新韓靑年黨	New Korea Youth Party	Sinhan cheongnyeondang	Sinhan ch'ŏngnyŏndan	1918-?	번역 표준 원칙
2227	신한촌	新韓村	New Korea Village (Sinhanchon, Korean community in Vladivostok)	Sinhanchon	Sinhanch'on	일제	번역 표준 원칙
2228	신한혁명단	新韓革命黨	New Korea Revolutionary Party	Sinhan hyeongmyeongdang	Sinhan hyŏngmyŏngdang	1915	번역 표준 원칙
2229	신한회	新韓會	New Korea Association (Sinhanhoe)	Sinhanhoe	Sinhanhoe	1918	번역 표준 원칙
2230	신해혁명	辛亥革命	Chinese Revolution of 1911	Sinhaehyeongmyeong	Sinhaehyŏngmyŏng	1911	번역 표준 원칙
2231	신행정수도	新行政首都	New Administrative Capital	Sinhaengjeongsudo	Sinhaengjŏngsudo		번역 표준 원칙
2232	신흥강습소	新興講習所	Sinheung Military School	Sinheung gangseupso	Sinhŭng kangsŭpso	1911-1919	번역 표준 원칙

NO	용어	한자	영문	RO	MC	시대 및 연도	출전
2233	신흥공업국(NIES)	新興工業國	newly industrializing countries (NIES)	Sinheung gongeopguk (NIES)	Sinhŭng kongŏpkuk (NIES)	1960-1970년대	번역 표준 원칙
2234	신흥무관학교	新興武官學校	Sinheung Military Academy	Sinheung mugwan hakgyo	Sinhŭng mugwan hakkyo	1919-1920	번역 표준 원칙
2235	신흥학우단	新興學友團	Alumni Association of Sinheung Military Academy	Sinheung hagudan	Sinhŭng hagudan	1913-1919	번역 표준 원칙
2236	실력양성운동	實力養成運動	Capacity-enhancing Movement (as a way to gain Korea's independence)	Sillyeok yangseong undong	Sillyŏk yangsŏng undong	일제	번역 표준 원칙
2237	실미도 사건	實尾島 事件	Silmido Incident	Silmido sageon	Silmido sakŏn	1971	번역 표준 원칙
2238	실버타운	silver town	"silver town" for senior citizens	Silbeo taun	Silbŏ t'aun		번역 표준 원칙
2239	실사구시	實事求是	seeking truth from facts	Silsagusi	Silsagusi		번역 표준 원칙
2240	실업고등전문학교	實業高等專門學校	vocational college	Sileop godeung jeonmun hakgyo	Sirŏp kodŭng chŏnmun hakkyo	1960년대	번역 표준 원칙

NO	용어	한자	영문	RO	MC	시대 및 연도	출전
2241	실업교육	實業教育	vocational training	Sileop gyoyuk	Sirŏp kyoyuk		번역 표준 원칙
2242	실업급여	失業給與	unemployment benefits	Sireop geubyeo	Sirŏp kŭbyŏ		번역 표준 원칙
2243	실업보험	失業保險	unemployment insurance	Sileop boheom	Sirŏp pohŏm		번역 표준 원칙
2244	실업팀	實業team	company-sponsored teams	Sileoptim	Sirŏpt'im		번역 표준 원칙
2245	실종자	失踪者	Missing in Action (MIA)	Siljongja	Silchongja		번역 표준 원칙
2246	실증주의사학	實證主義史學	positivist historiography	Siljeungjuui sahak	Siljŭngjuŭi sahak	?-?	번역 표준 원칙
2247	실학	實學	Silhak ("practical learning")	Silhak	Silhak		번역 표준 원칙
2248	실향난민 귀향협조 위원회	失鄕離民 歸鄕協助 委員會	Coordination Committee for Repatriation of Displaced People	Silhyang nanmin gwihyang hyeopjo wiwonhoe	Sirhyang nanmin kwihyang hyŏpcho wiwŏnhoe	17세기 후반-19세기 전반	번역 표준 원칙

NO	용어	한자	영문	RO	MC	시대 및 연도	출전
2249	심리전	心理戰	Psychological Operations (PSYOPS)	Simnijeon	Shimnijŏn		번역 표준 원칙
2250	심전개발운동	心田開發運動	Millitaristic Mind Cultivation Movement	Simjeon gaebal undong	Simjŏn kaebal undong	1930년대	번역 표준 원칙
2251	십삼도의군	十三道義軍	Righteous Army of the 13 Provinces	Sipsamdo uigun	Sipsamdo ŭigun	1910	한국학중앙연구원, 《영문한국백과》-대한민국의회
2252	쌀소동	쌀騷動	Rice Riots of 1918	Ssalsodong	Ssalsodong	1918	번역 표준 원칙
2253	쌍룡83훈련	雙龍83訓鍊	Ssangyong 83 Military Exercise	Ssangnyong 83 hullyeon	Sangnyong 83 hullyŏn		번역 표준 원칙
2254	쓰레기 종량제	쓰레기 從量制	volume-rate garbage disposal system	Sseuregi jongnyangje	Ssŭregi chongnyangje		번역 표준 원칙
2255	씨알의 소리	씨알의 소리	Ssial-ui Sori (The Voice of the People)	Ssial-ui sori	Ssial-ŭi sori	1970-1980, 1989-?	번역 표준 원칙
2256	아관파천	俄館播遷	Emperor Gojong's refuge at the Russian Legation (Agwan Pacheon)	Agwanpacheon	Agwanp'ach'ŏn	1896	번역 표준 원칙

NO	용어	한자	영문	RO	MC	시대 및 연도	출전
2257	아동보육정책	兒童保育政策	childcare policy	Adong boyuk jeongchaek	Adong boyuk chŏngch'aek		번역 표준 원칙
2258	아랍석유수출국기구 (OAPEC)	Arab石油輸出國機構	Organization of Arab Petroleum Exporting Countries (OAPEC)	Arap seogyu suchulguk gigu (OAPEC)	Arap sŏgyu such'ulguk kigu (OAPEC)	1968-	번역 표준 원칙
2259	아리랑	아리랑	*Arirang* (magazine)	Arirang	Arirang	1955-1980	번역 표준 원칙
2260	아리랑TV	아리랑TV	Arirang TV (English-language network)	Arirang TV	ArirangTV	1997-	번역 표준 원칙
2261	아시아개발은행	Asia開發銀行	Asia Development Bank	Asia gaebal eunhaeng	Asia kaebal ŭnhaeng	1966-?	번역 표준 원칙
2262	아시아나 여객기 추락	Asiana 旅客機 墜落	crash of Asiana Airlines' passenger jet in 1993	Asiana yeogaekgi churak	Asiana yŏgaekki ch'urak	1993	번역 표준 원칙
2263	아시아연대주의	Asia連帶主義	Pan-Asianism	Asia yeondaejuui	Asia yŏndaejuŭi		번역 표준 원칙
2264	아시아영화제	Asia映畵祭	Asian Film Festival	Asia yeonghwaje	Asia yŏnghwaje		번역 표준 원칙

NO	용어	한자	영문	RO	MC	시대 및 연도	출전
2265	아시아주의	Asia主義	Asianism	Asiajuui	Asiajuŭi		번역 표준 원칙
2266	아시안게임	Asian Games	Asian Games	Asian geim	Asian keim	1951-	번역 표준 원칙
2267	아웅산사건	Aung San事件	Rangoon Bombing of October 1983 (assassination attempt on President Chun Doo-hwan)	Aungsan sageon	Oungsan sakŏn	1983	번역 표준 원칙
2268	아이훈조약	Aihun 條約	Treaty of Aigun	Aihun joyak	Aihun choyak	1858	번역 표준 원칙
2269	아파트	apartment	apartment (complex)	Apateu	Ap'at'ŭ		번역 표준 원칙
2270	아파트문화	apartment文化	apartment lifestyle	Apateu munhwa	Ap'at'ŭ munhwa		번역 표준 원칙
2271	아편전쟁	阿片戰爭	Opium War (1839-1842)	Apyeon jeonjaeng	Ap'yŏn chŏnjaeng	1840-1842	번역 표준 원칙
2272	안강 전투	安康 戰鬪	Battle of Angang	Angang jeontu	An'gang chŏnt'u	1950	번역 표준 원칙

NO	용어	한자	영문	RO	MC	시대 및 연도	출전
2273	안동 전투	安東 戰鬪	Battle of Andong	Andong jeontu	Andong chŏnt'u		번역 표준 원칙
2274	안동 하회마을	安東 河回마을	Andong Hahoe Village	Andong hahoe maeul	Andong hahoe maŭl		번역 표준 원칙
2275	안악사건	安岳事件	Anak Conspiracy	Anak sageon	Anak sakŏn	1910	번역 표준 원칙
2276	안중근 의거	安重根 義擧	An Jung-geun's assassination of Ito Hirobumi in Harbin, Manchuria in 1909	An Jung-geun uigeo	An Chung-kŭn ŭigŏ	1909	번역 표준 원칙
2277	안중근전	安重根傳	Biography of An Jung-geun	An Jung-geun jeon	An Chung-kŭn chŏn	1914	번역 표준 원칙
2278	알뜨르 비행장	알뜨르 飛行場	Alddeureu Airfield	Altteureu bihaengjang	Alttŭrŭ pihaengjang	1930년대	번역 표준 원칙
2279	알려지지 않은 전쟁	알려지지 않은 戰爭	the Unknown War	Allyeojiji aneun jeonjaeng	Allyŏjiji anŭn chŏnjaeng	1953	번역 표준 원칙
2280	암태도소작쟁의	巖泰島小作爭議	Amtaedo Island Tenancy Strike	Amtaedo sojak jaengui	Amt'aedo sojak chaengŭi	1923-1924	번역 표준 원칙

NO	용어	한자	영문	RO	MC	시대 및 연도	출전
2281	압록강	鴨綠江	Yalu (Amnok) River	Amnokgang	Amnokkang		번역 표준 원칙
2282	압록강 진격	鴨綠江 進擊	Advance to the Yalu River	Amnokgang jingyeok	Amnokkang chingyŏk		번역 표준 원칙
2283	압록강철교	鴨綠江鐵橋	Yalu River Railway Bridge	Amnokgang cheolgyo	Amnokkang ch'ŏlgyo	1911-?	번역 표준 원칙
2284	압축성장	壓縮成長	accelerated growth	Apchuk seongjang	Apch'uk sŏngjang		번역 표준 원칙
2285	애국가	愛國歌	Korean National Anthem	Aegukga	Aegukka	1936-?	한국학중앙연구원, 《영문한국백과》-한국환상곡
2286	애국계몽운동	愛國啓蒙運動	Patriotic Enlightenment Movement	Aeguk gyemong undong	Aeguk kyemong undong	1904-1910	Ki-baik Lee, translated by Edward W. Wagner, A New History of Korea, Harvard University Press, 1984,
2287	애국열사	愛國烈士	patriots	Aeguk yeolsa	Aeguk yŏlsa		번역 표준 원칙
2288	애국열사릉	愛國烈士陵	Patriotic Martyrs' Cemetery	Aegugyeolsareung	Aegugyŏlsarŭng	1986	번역 표준 원칙

NO	용어	한자	영문	RO	MC	시대 및 연도	출전
2289	애국창가	愛國唱歌	patriotic songs	aeguk changga	Aeguk ch'angga		번역 표준 원칙
2290	애국채권	愛國債券	patriotic bonds	Aeguk chaegwon	Aeguk ch'aekwon		번역 표준 원칙
2291	애플 아이폰		Apple iPhone	Apple iPhone	Apple aipon	Aep'ŭl aip'on	2007-	번역 표준 원칙
2292	야간 구급진료 센터	夜間 救急診療 center	nighttime emergency medical center	Yagan gugeup jillyo senteo	Yagan kugŭp chillyo sent'ŏ		번역 표준 원칙
2293	야간통행금지	夜間通行禁止	night curfew	Yagan tonghaeng geumji	Yagan t'onghaeng kŭmji	1945-1983	번역 표준 원칙
2294	야간통행금지 해제	夜間通行禁止 解除	lifting of the night curfew	Yagan tonghaeng geumji haeje	Yagan t'onghaeng kŭmji haeje		번역 표준 원칙
2295	야당성회복투쟁 동지회	野黨性回復鬪爭 同志會	Comrades Association for the Restoration of Identity as Opposition Party	Yadangseong hoebok tujaeng dongjihoe	Yadangsŏng hoebok t'ujaeng dongjihoe		번역 표준 원칙
2296	야전교범	野戰敎範	Field Manual (FM)	Yajeongyobeom	Yajŏngyobŏm		번역 표준 원칙

NO	용어	한자	영문	RO	MC	시대 및 연도	출전
2297	야학	夜學	night school for laborers	Yahak	Yahak		번역 표준 원칙
2298	얄타밀약설	Yalta密約說	rumor of a secret agreement at the Yalta Conference	Yalta milyakseol	Yalt'a milyaksŏl		번역 표준 원칙
2299	얄타회담	Yalta會談	Yalta Conference	Yalta hoedam	Yalt'a hoedam	1945	번역 표준 원칙
2300	양곡관리법	糧穀管理法	Grain Control Act	Yanggok gwallibeop	Yanggok kwallipŏp	1950	번역 표준 원칙
2301	양국정상	兩國頂上	leaders from both countries	Yangguk jeongsang	Yangguk chŏngsang		번역 표준 원칙
2302	양극화	兩極化	polarization	Yanggeukhwa	Yanggŭkhwa		번역 표준 원칙
2303	양동	陽動	demonstration	Yangdong	Yangdong		번역 표준 원칙
2304	양무운동	洋務運動	Chinese Self-Strengthening Movement in the late 19th century	Yangmu undong	Yangmu undong	19세기 후반	번역 표준 원칙

NO	용어	한자	영문	RO	MC	시대 및 연도	출전
2305	양비교환법안	糧肥交換法案	Bill on Exchanging Grain and Fertilizer for Spot Goods	Yangbi gyohwan beoban	Yangbi gyohwan bŏban		번역 표준 원칙
2306	양심과 종교의 자유	良心과 宗敎의 自由	freedom of conscience and religion	Yangsimgwa jonggyoui jayu	Yangsimgwa chonggyoŭi chayu		번역 표준 원칙
2307	양심선언문	良心宣言文	Declaration of Conscience	Yangsim seoneonmun	Yangshim sŏnŏnmun		Wi Jo Kang, Christ and Caesar in Modern Korea: A History of Christianity and Politics, State University of
2308	양원제	兩院制	bicameral system	Yangwonje	Yangwŏnje	1960-1961	번역 표준 원칙
2309	양전사업	量田事業	land surveys	Yangjeon saeop	Yangjŏn saŏp	조선	James B. Palais, Politics and Policy in Traditional Korea, Harvard University Press, 1991, p.29.
2310	양정의숙	養正義塾	Yangchung School (now Yangchung High School)	Yangjeong uisuk	Yangjŏng ŭisuk	1905-1913	번역 표준 원칙
2311	양화진	楊花津	Yanghwajin Ferry Dock	Yanghwajin	Yanghwajin		번역 표준 원칙
2312	어뢰정	魚雷艇	torpedo boat	Eoroejeong	Ŏroejŏng		번역 표준 원칙

NO	용어	한자	영문	RO	MC	시대 및 연도	출전
2313	어린이 날	어린이 날	Children's Day	Eorini nal	Ŏrini nal	1922-1939, 1946-?	번역 표준 원칙
2314	어린이보호구역	어린이保護區域	school zone	Eorini boho guyeok	Ŏrini poho kuyŏk		번역 표준 원칙
2315	어린이운동	어린이運動	Children's Movement	Eorini undong	Ŏrini undong		번역 표준 원칙
2316	어업 문제	漁業 問題	fishing issues (between Korea and Japan)	Eoeop munje	Ŏŏp munje		번역 표준 원칙
2317	어용노동조합	御用勞動組合	company-dominated unions	Eoyong nodong johap	Ŏyong nodong chohap		번역 표준 원칙
2318	어용노조의 민주화	御用勞組의 民主化	democratization of company-dominated unions	Eoyong nojoui minjuhwa	Ŏyong nojo-ŭi minjuhwa		번역 표준 원칙
2319	억제전략	抑制戰略	deterrence strategy	Eokje jeollyak	Ŏkche chŏllyak		번역 표준 원칙
2320	언론개혁시민연대	言論改革市民連帶	People's Coalition for Media Reform	Eollon gaehyeok simin yeondae	Ŏllon kaehyŏk simin yŏndae	1998	번역 표준 원칙

NO	용어	한자	영문	RO	MC	시대 및 연도	출전
2321	언론검열	言論檢閱	press censorship	Eollon geomyeol	Ŏllon kŏmyŏl		번역 표준 원칙
2322	언론기관통폐합	言論機關統廢合	forced merger of mass media organizations	Eollon gigwan tongpyehap	Ŏllon kigwan t'ongp'yehap	1980	번역 표준 원칙
2323	언론기본법	言論基本法	Press Act	Eollon gibonbeop	Ŏllon gibonpŏp	1980	번역 표준 원칙
2324	언론노조운동	言論勞組運動	movement to establish a media union	Eollon nojo undong	Ŏllon nojo undong	1960-1961	번역 표준 원칙
2325	언론운동	言論運動	media movement	Eollon undong	Ŏllon undong		번역 표준 원칙
2326	언론자유수호운동	言論自由守護運動	movement to protect freedom of speech	Eollon jayu suho undong	Ŏllon chayu suho undong	1967-1975	번역 표준 원칙
2327	언론집회압박탄핵회	言論集會壓迫彈劾會	Association for Denunciating Imperialist Japan's Suppression of the Freedom of Speech and Assembly	Eollon jiphoe apbak tanhaekhoe	Ŏllon chiphoe appak t'anhaekhoe	1924	번역 표준 원칙
2328	언론탄압	言論彈壓	supression of the press	Eonnon tanap	Ŏllon t'anap		번역 표준 원칙

NO	용어	한자	영문	RO	MC	시대 및 연도	출전
2329	언론통제	言論統制	control of the media	Eollon tongje	Ŏllon t'ongje		번역 표준 원칙
2330	엄호부대	掩護部隊	covering forces	Eomho budae	Ŏmho pudae		번역 표준 원칙
2331	에너지 대책위원회	energy 對策委員會	National Committee on Energy	Eneoji daechaek wiwonhoe	Enŏji taech'aek wiwonhoe		번역 표준 원칙
2332	에너지 소비절약	energy 消費節約	energy saving	Eneoji sobi jeolyak	Enŏji sobi chŏryak		번역 표준 원칙
2333	에너지 안보	energy 安保	energy security	Eneoji anbo	Enŏji anbo		번역 표준 원칙
2334	엔터프라이즈호	Enterprise號	USS Enterprise	Enteopeuraijeu ho	Ent'ŏp'ŭraijŭ ho	1960년대	번역 표준 원칙
2335	여권신장	女權伸張	expansion of women's rights	Yeogwon sinjang	Yŏgwŏn sinjang		번역 표준 원칙
2336	여단	旅團	Brigade	Yeodan	Yŏdan	1950	번역 표준 원칙

NO	용어	한자	영문	RO	MC	시대 및 연도	출전
2337	여성가족부	女性家族部	Ministry of Gender Equality and Family	Yeoseong gajokbu	Yŏsŏng kajokpu	2001	http://www.mogef.go.kr
2338	여성노동운동	女性勞動運動	women's labor movement	Yeoseong nodong undong	Yŏsŏng nodong undong		번역 표준 원칙
2339	여성노동자회	女性勞動者會	Korean Women Workers Association	Yeoseong nodongjahoe	Yŏsŏng nodongjahoe		번역 표준 원칙
2340	여성단체의 설립	女性團體의 設立	establishment of women's associations	Yeoseong dancheui seollip	Yŏsŏng tanch'e-ŭi sŏllip		번역 표준 원칙
2341	여성문제	女性問題	women's issues	Yeoseong munje	Yŏsŏng munje		번역 표준 원칙
2342	여성민우회	女性民友會	Korean Womenlink	Yeoseong minuhoe	Yŏsŏng minuhoe	1987-	번역 표준 원칙
2343	여성발전기본법	女性發展基本法	Framework Act on Women's Development	Yeoseong baljeon gibonbeop	Yŏsŏng palchŏn kibonpŏp	1995	번역 표준 원칙
2344	여성부	女性部	Ministry of Gender Equality	Yeoseongbu	Yŏsŏngbu	2001-?	번역 표준 원칙

NO	용어	한자	영문	RO	MC	시대 및 연도	출전
2345	여성운동	女性運動	women's movement	Yeoseong undong	Yŏsŏng undong	근대	번역 표준 원칙
2346	여성유권자연맹	女性有權者聯盟	Korean League of Women Voters	Yeoseong yugwonja yeonmaeng	Yŏsŏng yukwŏnja yŏnmaeng		번역 표준 원칙
2347	여성평우회	女性平友會	Association for Women's Equality and Peace	Yeoseong pyeonguhoe	Yŏsŏng p'yŏnguhoe		번역 표준 원칙
2348	여성학	女性學	women's studies	Yeoseonghak	Yŏsŏnghak		번역 표준 원칙
2349	여성해방운동	女性解放運動	women's liberation movement	Yeoseong haebang undong	Yŏsŏng haebang undong		번역 표준 원칙
2350	여수·순천 사건	麗水·順天 事件	Yeosu-Suncheon Incident	Yeosu·Suncheon sageon	Yŏsu·Sunch'ŏn sakŏn	1948	번역 표준 원칙
2351	여수엑스포	麗水Expo	Expo 2012 Yeosu Korea	Yeosu ekseupo	Yŏsu eksŭp'o	2012	번역 표준 원칙
2352	여신학자협의회	女神學者協議會	Korean Association of Women Theologians	Yeosinhakja hyeobuihoe	Yŏsinhakcha hyŏbŭihoe	1980	번역 표준 원칙

NO	용어	한자	영문	RO	MC	시대 및 연도	출전
2353	여운형	呂運亨	Yun Woon-hyung	Yeo Un-hyeong	Yŏ Un-hyŏng	1886-1947	번역 표준 원칙
2354	여의도 농민시위	汝矣島 農民示威	farmers rally in Yeouido	Yeouido nongminsiwi	Yŏŭido nongminsiwi	1980년대	번역 표준 원칙
2355	여자근로정신대	女子勤勞挺身隊	Women Labor Corps, (female laborers conscripted by imperialist Japan)	Yeoja geullo jeongsindae	Yŏja kŭllo chŏngsindae		번역 표준 원칙
2356	여자기독교청년회연합회	女子基督敎靑年會聯合會	YWCA of Korea	Yeoja gidokgyo cheongnyeonhoe yeonhaphoe	Yŏja kidokkyo ch'ŏngnyŏnhoe yŏnhaphoe	1922-1939	번역 표준 원칙
2357	여자정신대	女子挺身隊	Women Labor Corps	Yeoja jeongsindae	Yŏja chŏngsindae	?-1945	번역 표준 원칙
2358	여자정신대 근무령	女子挺身隊 勤務令	Ordinance for Women Labor Corps Service	Yeoja jeongsindae geunmuryeong	Yŏja chŏngsindae kŭmmuryŏng	1944	번역 표준 원칙
2359	여자탁구 남북단일팀	女子卓球 南北單一team	women's single inter-Korean table tennis team	Yeoja takgu nambuk daniltim	Yŏja t'akku nambuk tanilt'im	1991	번역 표준 원칙
2360	여천석유화학공단	麗川石油化學工團	Yeocheon Petrochemical Industrial Complex	Yeocheon seogyu hwahak gongdan	Yŏch'ŏn sŏgyu hwahak kongdan		번역 표준 원칙

NO	용어	한자	영문	RO	MC	시대 및 연도	출전
2361	역사 바로 세우기	歷史 바로 세우기	rectification of history	Yeoksa baro se-ugi	Yŏksa paro seugi		번역 표준 원칙
2362	역사학	歷史學	history	Yeoksahak	Yŏksahak		번역 표준 원칙
2363	역청구권	逆請求權	Japan's property claims against Korea	Yeokchunggugwon	Yŏkch'ŏnggukwŏn		번역 표준 원칙
2364	연대	聯隊	Regiment	Yeondae	Yŏndae	1950	번역 표준 원칙
2365	연대전투단	聯隊戰鬪團	Regimental Combat Team	Yeondae jeontudan	Yŏndae chŏnt'udan		번역 표준 원칙
2366	연락장교회담	連絡將校會談	Liaison Officers' Conference	Yeollak janggyo hoedam	Yŏllak changgyo hoedam		번역 표준 원칙
2367	연립정부	聯立政府	coalition government	Yeollip jeongbu	Yŏllip chŏngbu		번역 표준 원칙
2368	연변조선족자치주	延邊朝鮮族自治州	Yanbian Korean Autonomous Prefecture	Yeonbyeon joseonjok jachiju	Yŏnbyŏn chosŏnjok chach'Iju	1952-?	번역 표준 원칙

NO	용어	한자	영문	RO	MC	시대 및 연도	출전
2369	연불수출금융	延拂輸出金融	finance for deferred payment exports	Yeonbul suchul geumnyung	Yŏnbul such'ul kŭmyung		번역 표준 원칙
2370	연안	延安	Yeonan (in Hwanghae-do Province)	Yeonan	Yŏnan		번역 표준 원칙
2371	연안계	延安系	Yeonan Faction	Yeonangye	Yŏnan'gye	1945-1956	번역 표준 원칙
2372	연좌데모	連坐示威	sit-down demonstration	Yeonjwa demo	Yŏnjwa temo		번역 표준 원칙
2373	연좌제	連坐制	guilt by association	Yeonjwaje	Yŏnjwaje	?-1894	번역 표준 원칙
2374	연탄파동	煉炭波動	shortage of coal briquettes (1967)	Yeontan padong	Yŏnt'an p'adong	1966	번역 표준 원칙
2375	연통제	聯通制	Yeontongje (communication network of the Provisional Government of the Republic of Korea)	Yeontongje	Yŏnt'ongje	1919-1921	번역 표준 원칙
2376	연합 권한 위임사항	聯合 權限 委任事項	Combined Delegated Authority (CODA)	Yeonhap gwonhan wiimsahang	Yŏnhap kwŏnhan wiimsahang		번역 표준 원칙

NO	용어	한자	영문	RO	MC	시대 및 연도	출전
2377	연합고사	聯合考查	Standardized High School Admission Test	Yeonhapgosa	Yŏnhapkosa		번역 표준 원칙
2378	연합국환영준비회	聯合國歡迎準備會	Preparation Committee for Welcoming Allied Nations	Yeonhapguk hwannyeong junbihoe	Yŏnhapkuk hwanyŏng chunbihoe		번역 표준 원칙
2379	연합군 총사령부	聯合軍 總司令部	General Headquarters, UN Forces	Yeonhapgun chongsaryeongbu	Yŏnhapkun ch'ongsaryŏngbu		번역 표준 원칙
2380	연합방어증강계획	聯合防禦增强計劃	Combined Defense Improvement Projects (CDIP)	Yeonhap bangeo jeunggang gyehoek	Yŏnhap pangŏ chŭnggang kyehoek		번역 표준 원칙
2381	연합숭실대학 (숭실대학)	聯合崇實大學 (崇實大學)	Union Christian College	Yeonhap sungsil daehak (sungsil daehak)	Yŏnhap sungsil taehak (sungsil taehak)		번역 표준 원칙
2382	연합의병운동	聯合義兵運動	United Righteous Army Movement	Yeonhap uibyeong undong	Yŏnhap ŭibyŏng undong		번역 표준 원칙
2383	연합전시증원 연습	聯合戰時增員 鍊習	Reception, Staging, Onward Movement & Integration (RSOI) Practices	Yeonhap jeonsi jeungwon yeonseup	Yŏnhap chŏnsi chŭngwŏn yŏnsŭp		번역 표준 원칙
2384	연합특수전사령부	聯合特殊戰司令部	Combined Unconventional Warfare Task Force (CUWTF)	Yeonhap teuksujeon saryeongbu	Yŏnhap t'ŭksujŏn saryŏngbu		번역 표준 원칙

NO	용어	한자	영문	RO	MC	시대 및 연도	출전
2385	연합해병대사령부	聯合海兵隊司令部	Combined Marine Forces Command (CMFC)	Yeonhap haebyeongdae saryeongbu	Yŏnhap haebyŏngdae saryŏngbu		번역 표준 원칙
2386	연해주	沿海州	Maritime Province of Siberia	Yeonhaeju	Yŏnhaeju		번역 표준 원칙
2387	연해주 13도의군	沿海州 13道義軍	Righteous Army of the 13 Provinces in the Maritime Province of Siberia	Yeonhaeju 13douigun	Yŏnhaeju 13doŭigun		번역 표준 원칙
2388	연해주 의병	沿海州 義兵	Righteous Army in the Maritime Province of Siberia	Yeonhaeju uibyeong	Yŏnhaeju ŭibyŏng		번역 표준 원칙
2389	연해주 한인사회	沿海州 韓人社會	Korean Community in the Maritime Province of Siberia	Yeonhaeju haninsahoe	Yŏnhaeju haninsahoe		번역 표준 원칙
2390	연희전문학교	延禧專門學校	Yeonhui College	Yeonhui jeonmun hakgyo	Yŏnhŭi chŏnmun hakkyo	1915-1946	번역 표준 원칙
2391	열린교육사회	열린敎育社會	society with open access to education	Yeollin gyoyuk sahoe	Yŏllin kyoyuk sahoe		번역 표준 원칙
2392	염군사	焰群社	Yeomgunsa (Korea's first proletariat literary association)	Yeomgunsa	Yŏmgunsa	1922-1925	번역 표준 원칙

NO	용어	한자	영문	RO	MC	시대 및 연도	출전
2393	영광원자력발전소	靈光原子力發電所	Yeonggwang Nuclear Power Plant	Yeonggwang wonjaryeok baljeonso	Yŏnggwang wŏnjaryŏk palchŏnso	1986-?	번역 표준 원칙
2394	영국공사관	英國公使館	British Legation	Yeongguk gongsagwan	Yŏngguk kongsagwan		번역 표준 원칙
2395	영남만인소	嶺南萬人疏	Appeal to the King by Ten Thousand Men of Gyeongsang Province (Yeongnam Maninso)	Yeongnam maninso	Yŏngnam maninso	1881	번역 표준 원칙
2396	영남부인실업동맹회	嶺南婦人實業同盟會	Youngnam Women's Association	Yeongnam buin sileop dongmaenghoe	Yŏngnam puin silŏp tongmaenghoe	1928-?	번역 표준 원칙
2397	영동고속도로	嶺東高速道路	Yeongdong Expressway	Yeongdong gosokdoro	Yŏngdong kosoktoro	1971	번역 표준 원칙
2398	영릉가성전투	永陵街城戰鬪	Battle of Yonglingjie	Yeongneunggaseong jeontu	Yŏngnŭnggasŏng chŏnt'u	1932	번역 표준 원칙
2399	영변원자력 단지	寧邊原子力 團地	Yongbyon Nuclear Power Plant	Yeongbyeon wonjaryeok danji	Yŏngbyŏn wŏnjaryŏk tanji	1964	번역 표준 원칙
2400	영사재판권	領事裁判權	consular jurisdiction	Yeongsa jaepangwon	Yŏngsa chaep'an'gwŏn	1876-?	번역 표준 원칙

NO	용어	한자	영문	RO	MC	시대 및 연도	출전
2401	영산 전투	靈山 戰鬪	Battle of Yeognsan	Yeongsan jeontu	Yŏngsan chŏnt'u	1950	번역 표준 원칙
2402	영산재	靈山齋	Yeongsanjae (rite reenacting Buddha's delivery of the Lotus Sutra on Vulture Peak)	Yeongsanjae	Yŏngsanjae		번역 표준 원칙
2403	영선사	領選使	emissary dispatched to the Qing Dynasty, China	Yeongseonsa	Yŏngsŏnsa	1895-1907	한국학중앙연구원, 《영문한국백과》-고종
2404	영세민보호	零細民保護	protection of low-income families	Yeongsemin boho	Yŏngsemin poho	현대	Kim Chongho, Korean Shamanism: The Cultural Paradox, Aldershot, Hants, and Burlington, Vt.:
2405	영세중립	永世中立	permanent neutrality	Yeongse jungnip	Yŏngse chungnip		번역 표준 원칙
2406	영세중립국	永世中立國	permanently neutral country	yeongse jungnipguk	Yŏngse chungnipguk		번역 표준 원칙
2407	영어공교육	英語公敎育	public English education	Yeongeo gonggyoyuk	Yŏngŏ konggyoyuk		번역 표준 원칙
2408	영연방여단	英聯邦旅團	British Commonwealth Brigade	Yeongyeonbangyeodan	Yŏngyŏnbangyŏdan		번역 표준 원칙

NO	용어	한자	영문	RO	MC	시대 및 연도	출전
2409	영월 제2 화력발전소	寧越 第2 火力發電所	second thermal power plant in Yeongwol, Gangwon-do Province	Yeongwol je2hwaryeok baljeonso jungong ginyeompae	Yŏngwŏl che2hwaryŏk palchŏnso chun'gong kinyŏmp'ae	1965	번역 표준 원칙
2410	영유권 분쟁	領有權 紛爭	territorial dispute	Yeongyugwon bunjaeng	Yŏngyukwŏn punjaeng		번역 표준 원칙
2411	영유아보육법	嬰幼兒保育法	Infant Care Act	Yeongyua boyukbeop	Yŏngyua poyukpŏp	1991	번역 표준 원칙
2412	영은문	迎恩門	Yeongeunmun Gate (Gate of Welcoming Imperial Grace)	Yeongeunmun	Yŏngŭnmun	1539-?	번역 표준 원칙
2413	영일동맹	英日同盟	Anglo-Japanese Alliance	Yeongil dongmaeng	Yŏngil tongmaeng	1902-1921	Ki-baik Lee, translated by Edward W. Wagner, A New History of Korea, Harvard University Press, 1984,
2414	영종진	永宗鎭	Yeongjongjin Garrison	Yeongjongjin	Yŏngjongjin		번역 표준 원칙
2415	영천 전투	永川 戰鬪	Battle of Yeongcheon	Yeongcheon jeontu	Yŏngch'ŏn chŏnt'u	1950	번역 표준 원칙
2416	영화단체	映畵團體	film organizations	Yeonghwa danche	Yŏnghwa tanch'e		번역 표준 원칙

NO	용어	한자	영문	RO	MC	시대 및 연도	출전
2417	영환지략	瀛環志略	A Short Account of the Maritime Circuit (Yinghuan Zhilue)	Yeonghwanjiryak	Yŏnghwanjiryak	1848 완성 1850 간행	번역 표준 원칙
2418	예비군	豫備軍	Reserve Forces	Yebigun chochanggi wanjang mit yebigun jihwigwanyong sucheop	Yebigun ch'och'anggi wanjang mit yebigun chihwigwannyong such'ŏp	1960년대	번역 표준 원칙
2419	예비역	豫備役	Reserve Forces	Yebiyeok	Yebiyŏk		번역 표준 원칙
2420	예비후보자 등록	豫備候補者 登錄	registration of preliminary candidates	Yebi huboja deungnok	Yebi Huboja dŭngnok		번역 표준 원칙
2421	예술의 전당 개관	藝術의 殿堂 開館	opening of Seoul Arts Center	Yesului jeondang gaegwan	Yesurŭi chŏndang kaegwan	1988 1단계 1990 2단계 1993 3단계	번역 표준 원칙
2422	예술의전당	藝術의殿堂	Seoul Arts Center(SAC)	Yesurui jeondang	Yesurŭi chŏndang		번역 표준 원칙
2423	오대산국립공원	五臺山國立公園	Odaesan National Park	Odaesan gungnip gongwon	Odaesan kungnip kongwŏn	1975	번역 표준 원칙
2424	오라리 방화사건	吾羅里 放火事件	Orari Arson Incident	Orari banghwa sageon	Ora-ri panghwa sakŏn	1948	번역 표준 원칙

NO	용어	한자	영문	RO	MC	시대 및 연도	출전
2425	오산전투(죽미령 전투)	烏山戰鬪 (竹美嶺 戰鬪)	Battle of Osan	Osan jeontu (jukmiryeong jeontu)	Osan chŏnt'u (chungmiryŏng chŏnt'u)	1950	번역 표준 원칙
2426	오산학교	五山學校	Osan Middle School (now Osan Middle School and Osan High School)	Osan hakgyo	Osan hakkyo	1907-1926	번역 표준 원칙
2427	오일 달러		Oil dollar	oil dollar	Oil dalleo	Oil talla		번역 표준 원칙
2428	오일 쇼크		Oil shock	oil shock	Oil syokeu	Oil syok'ŭ		번역 표준 원칙
2429	오작교 작전	烏鵲橋 作戰	Operation Ojakgyo	Ojakgyo jakjeon	Ojakkyo chakchŏn	1967	번역 표준 원칙
2430	오적암살단	五賊暗殺團	squad to assassinate five ministers who signed the Korea-Japan Treaty of 1905	5jeok amsaldan	5chŏk amsaltan	1905	번역 표준 원칙
2431	오존 주의보	ozone 注意報	ozone warning	Ojon juuibo	Ojon chuŭibo		번역 표준 원칙
2432	오쿠보 형무소	大久保 刑務所	Okubo Prison	Okubo hyeongmuso	Ok'ubo hyŏngmuso		번역 표준 원칙

NO	용어	한자	영문	RO	MC	시대 및 연도	출전
2433	오키나와 전투	沖繩 戰鬪	Battle of Okinawa	Okinawa jeontu	Ok'inawa chŏnt'u	1945	번역 표준 원칙
2434	옥호루	玉壺樓	Okhoru Pavilion (in Gyeongbokgung Palace)	Okhoru	Okhoru	1873-1929	번역 표준 원칙
2435	온건개화파	穩健開化派	Moderate Progressive Faction (in the Englightenment Party	Ongeon gaehwapa	On'gŏn kaehwap'a	1876-1910	번역 표준 원칙
2436	올림픽 복권	Olympics 福券	Olympics lottery	Ollimpik bokgwon	Ollimp'ik pokkwŏn	1947-?	번역 표준 원칙
2437	올림픽 작전	Olympics 作戰	Operation Olympics	Ollimpik jakjeon	Ollimp'ik chakchŏn	1945	번역 표준 원칙
2438	올림픽대교 개통	Olympic大橋 開通	opening of the Olympic Bridge	Ollimpik daegyo gaetong	Ollimp'ik taegyo kaet'ong	1989	번역 표준 원칙
2439	와우아파트 붕괴사건	臥牛아파트 崩壞事件	collapse of Wow Apartment building	Wau apateu bunggoe sageon	Wau ap'at'ŭ punggoe sagŏn	1970	번역 표준 원칙
2440	와이파이폰 상용화 서비스	Wi-Fi phone 常用化 service	commercialization of WiFi phones	Waipaipon sangyonghwa seobiseu	Waip'aip'on sangyonghwa sŏbisŭ		번역 표준 원칙

NO	용어	한자	영문	RO	MC	시대 및 연도	출전
2441	완충지대	緩衝地帶	buffer zone	Wanchung jidae	Wanch'ung chidae		번역 표준 원칙
2442	왜관 전투	倭館 戰鬪	Battle of Waegwan	Waegwan jeontu	Waegwan chŏnt'u	1950	번역 표준 원칙
2443	왜양일체	倭洋一體	"Japan and the West are equally barbaric"	Waeyangilche	Waeyangilch'e		번역 표준 원칙
2444	왜양일체론	倭洋一體論	view that Japan and the West are equally barbaric	Waeyangilcheron	Waeyangilch'eron		번역 표준 원칙
2445	왜척세력	外戚勢力	political forces formed by the clans of the Queen Dowager or the Queen	Oecheok seryeok	Waech'ŏk seryŏk		번역 표준 원칙
2446	외교관 밀수사건	外交官 密輸事件	Diplomat Contraband Incident	Oegyogwan milsu sageon	Oegyogwan milsu sakŏn	1976	번역 표준 원칙
2447	외교권 박탈	外交權 剝奪	Japan's stripping of Korea's diplomatic rights	Oegyogwon baktal	Oekyokwŏn pakt'al		번역 표준 원칙
2448	외교독립론	外交獨立論	theory of diplomatic independence	Oegyo dongnipnon	Oegyo tongnimnon	1919-?	번역 표준 원칙

NO	용어	한자	영문	RO	MC	시대 및 연도	출전
2449	외교통상부	外交通商部	Ministry of Forign Affairs and Trade	Oegyo tongsangbu	Oegyo t'ongsangbu	1998-?	번역 표준 원칙
2450	외국군 철수	外國軍 撤收	withdrawal of foreign troops	Oegukgun cheolsu	Oegukkun ch'ŏlsu		번역 표준 원칙
2451	외국인 등록증	外國人 登錄證	certificate of alien registration	Oegugin deungnokjeung	Oegugin tŭngnokchŭng		번역 표준 원칙
2452	외국인 지문날인 제도	外國人 指紋捺印 制度	foreigner fingerprint registration system	Oegugin jimunnalin jedo	Oegugin chimunnarin chedo		번역 표준 원칙
2453	외국인 직접투자	外國人 直接投資	Foreign Direct Investment (FDI)	Oegugin jikjeop tuja	Oegugin chikchŏp t'uja		번역 표준 원칙
2454	외국환관리법 시행령	外國換管理法 施行令	Enforcement Decree of the Foreign Exchange Management Act	Oegukhwan gwallibeop sihaengnyeong	Oegukhwan gwallipŏp sihaengnyŏng	1961	번역 표준 원칙
2455	외래어 표기	外來語 表記	orthography of loan words	Oeraeeo pyogi	Oeraeŏ p'yogi		번역 표준 원칙
2456	외무국방위원회	外務國防委員會	Foreign Affairs and National Defense Committee	Oemu gukbang wiwonhoe	Oemu kukpang wiwŏnhoe	1948	번역 표준 원칙

NO	용어	한자	영문	RO	MC	시대 및 연도	출전
2457	외자	外資	foreign capital	Oeja	Oeja		번역 표준 원칙
2458	외자도입교섭단	外資導入交涉團	negotiating team for attracting foreign investment	Oeja doip gyoseopdan	Oeja toip kyosŏptan		번역 표준 원칙
2459	외자도입법	外資導入法	Foreign Capital Inducement Act	Oeja doipbeop	Oeja toippŏp	1966	번역 표준 원칙
2460	외채상환문제	外債償還問題	issue of repayment of foreign debts	Oechae sanghwan munje	Oech'ae sanghwan munje		번역 표준 원칙
2461	외환위기	外換危機	foreign currency crisis	Oehwan wigi	Oehwan wigi		번역 표준 원칙
2462	외환종합수급계획	外換綜合受給計劃	comprehensive plan for the supply and demand of foreign currency	Oehwan jonghap sugeup gyehoek	Oehwan jonghap sugŭp kyehoek		번역 표준 원칙
2463	요녕성	遼寧省	Liaoning Province	Yonyeongseong	Yonyŏngsŏng		번역 표준 원칙
2464	요요 작전	Yo-yo 作戰	Operation Yo-yo	Yoyo jakjeon	Yoyo chakchŏn	1950	번역 표준 원칙

NO	용어	한자	영문	RO	MC	시대 및 연도	출전
2465	요인 납북	要人 拉北	kidnap of high-profile figures to North Korea	Yoinnapbuk	Yoinnappuk		번역 표준 원칙
2466	용문산 전투	龍門山 戰鬪	Battle of Yongmunsan Mountain	Yongmunsan jeontu	Yongmunsan chŏnt'u	1951	국사편찬위원회
2467	용산 미군기지	龍山 美軍基地	US Army Garrison, Yongsan	Yongsan migun giji	Yongsan migun kiji		번역 표준 원칙
2468	용수댐	用水Dam	multipurpose dam	Yongsu daem	Yongsu taem		번역 표준 원칙
2469	용암포사건	龍巖浦事件	Yongampo Incident	Yongampo sageon	Yongamp'o sagŏn	1903	번역 표준 원칙
2470	용인서울고속도로	龍仁Seoul高速道路	Yongin-Seoul Expressway	Yongin seoul gosokdoro	Yongin sŏul kosoktoro		번역 표준 원칙
2471	우금치 전투	牛金峙 戰鬪	Battle of Ugeumchi	Ugeumchi jeontu	Ugŭmch'i chŏnt'u	1894	번역 표준 원칙
2472	우라키	The Rocky	*The Rocky*	Uraki	Urak'i	1925 ~ 1936	번역 표준 원칙

NO	용어	한자	영문	RO	MC	시대 및 연도	출전
2473	우루과이라운드 협정	Uruguay Round 協定	Uruguay Round Agreement	Urugwai raundeu hyeopjeong	Urugwai raundŭ hyŏpchŏng	1993	번역 표준 원칙
2474	우리 농산물 살리기운동	우리 農産物 살리기 運動	campaign for the consumption of homegrown products	Uri nongsanmul salligi undong	Uri nongsanmul salligi undong	1994-	번역 표준 원칙
2475	우리말 큰사전	우리말 큰辭典	A Comprehensive Dictionary of the Korean Language (Urimal Keunsajeon)	Urimal keunsajeon	Urimal k'ŭnsajŏn	1991	번역 표준 원칙
2476	우리별1호 (KITSAT-1)	우리별1號	Uribyeol No. 1, Korea's first satellite	Uribyeol 1ho (KITSAT-1)	Uribyŏl 1ho (KITSAT-1)	1992	번역 표준 원칙
2477	우발사태	偶發事態	contingencies	Ubalsatae	Ubalsat'ae		번역 표준 원칙
2478	우수리 강	Ussuri 江	Ussuri River	Usurigang	Usurigang		번역 표준 원칙
2479	우익	右翼	right-wing	Uik	Uik		번역 표준 원칙
2480	우정총국	郵征總局	Central Office of the modern Korean Postal Service	Ujeongchongguk	Ujŏngch'ongguk	1884	번역 표준 원칙

NO	용어	한자	영문	RO	MC	시대 및 연도	출전
2481	우회기동	迂廻機動	flank movement	Uhoegidong	Uhoegidong		번역 표준 원칙
2482	운수부	運輸部	Department of Transportation	Unsubu	Unsubu	1945-1948	번역 표준 원칙
2483	운영기획위원회	運營企劃委員會	operation and planning committee	Unnyeong gihoek wiwonhoe	Unyŏng kihoek wiwonhoe		번역 표준 원칙
2484	운요호	雲揚號	Japanese warship Unyo	Unyoho	Unyoho		번역 표준 원칙
2485	운요호사건	雲揚號事件	Japanese Warship Unyo Incident	Unyoho sageon	Unyoho sakŏn	1875	번역 표준 원칙
2486	울산 석유화학 콤플렉스	蔚山 石油化學Complex	Ulsan Petrochemical Industrial Complex	Ulsan seokyu hwahak kompeullekseu	Ulsan sŏgyu hwahak k'omp'ŭllleksŭ	1972	번역 표준 원칙
2487	울산고속도로	蔚山高速道路	Ulsan Expressway	Ulsan gosokdoro	Ulsan kosoktoro	1969	번역 표준 원칙
2488	울산공업단지	蔚山工業團地	Ulsan Industrial Complex	Ulsan gongeop danji	Ulsan kongŏp tanji	1962-1973	번역 표준 원칙

NO	용어	한자	영문	RO	MC	시대 및 연도	출전
2489	울산광역시	蔚山廣域市	Ulsan Metropolitan City	Ulsan gwangyeoksi	Ulsan kwangyŏksi		번역 표준 원칙
2490	울진·삼척지구 무장공비 침투사건	蔚珍·三陟地區 武裝共匪 浸透事件	Uljin-Samcheok Guerilla Landing	Uljin·samcheok jigu mujang gongbi chimtu sageon	Uljin·samch'ŏk chigu mujang kongbi ch'imt'u sakŏn	1968	번역 표준 원칙
2491	울진원자력발전소	蔚珍原子力發電所	Uljin Nuclear Power Plant	Uljin wonjaryeok baljeonso	Ulchin wŏnjaryŏk palchŏnso	1982-?	번역 표준 원칙
2492	워싱턴회의 (태평양회의)	Washington會議 (太平洋會議)	Washington Conference	Wosingteon hoeui (taepyeongyang hoeui)	Wŏsingt'ŏn hoeŭi (t'aep'yŏngyang hoeŭi)	1921	번역 표준 원칙
2493	워커힐 사건	Walkerhill 事件	Walkerhill Hotel Scandal	Wokeohil sageon	Wŏk'ŏhil sakŏn	1961-1963	번역 표준 원칙
2494	원각사	圓覺社	Wongaksa Theater	Wongaksa	Wŏn'gaksa	1908-1909	번역 표준 원칙
2495	원격의료진단시스템	遠隔醫療診斷system	tele-diagnosis system	Wongyeok uiryo jindan siseutem	Wŏnkyŏk ŭiryo chindan sisŭtem		번역 표준 원칙
2496	원동공화국	遠東共和國	Far Eastern Republic	Wondong gonghwaguk	Wondong konghwaguk		번역 표준 원칙

NO	용어	한자	영문	RO	MC	시대 및 연도	출전
2497	원동임야주식회사	遠東林野株式會社	Far East Woodland Corp. (in Vladivostok)	Wondong imnya jusikhoesa	Wŏndong imya chusikhoesa	1906	번역 표준 원칙
2498	원불교	圓佛敎	Won Buddhism	Wonbulgyo	Wŏnbulgyo	1916-?	번역 표준 원칙
2499	원산노동자총파업	元山勞動者總罷業	general strike of Wonsan factory workers	Wonsan nodongja chongpaeop	Wŏnsan nodongja ch'ongp'aŏp	1929	번역 표준 원칙
2500	원산탈환전투	元山奪還戰鬪	Wonsan Recapture Battle	Wonsan talhwan jeontu	Wŏnsan t'arhwan chŏnt'u	1950	번역 표준 원칙
2501	원산학사	元山學舍	Wonsan Academy	Wonsan haksa	Wŏnsan haksa	1883-1945	Ki-baik Lee, translated by Edward W. Wagner, A New History of Korea, Harvard University Press, 1984,
2502	원산해관	元山海關	Wonsan Maritime Customs	Wonsan haegwan geupbal chulgu hwaseheomdan	Wŏnsan haegwan kŭ ppalch'ulgu hwasehŏmdan	1883	번역 표준 원칙
2503	원외자유당	院外自由黨	extra-parliamentary Liberal Party	Wonoe jayudang	Wŏnoe chayudang	1951	번역 표준 원칙
2504	원자력발전소	原子力發電所	nuclear power plant	Wonjaryeok baljeonso	Wŏnjaryŏk palchŏnso		번역 표준 원칙

NO	용어	한자	영문	RO	MC	시대 및 연도	출전
2505	원자력법	原子力法	Atomic Energy Act	Wonjaryeok beop	Wŏnjaryŏk pŏp	1958	번역 표준 원칙
2506	원자력안전위원회	原子力安全委員會	Nuclear Safety and Security Commission	Wonjaryeok anjeon wiwonhoe	Wŏnjaryŏk anjŏn wiwŏnhoe	1997 발족 2011 공식 출범	번역 표준 원칙
2507	원자력연구소	原子力硏究所	Korea Atomic Energy Research Institute	Wonjaryeok yeonguso	Wŏnjaryŏk yŏn'guso	1959	번역 표준 원칙
2508	원자력의 비군사적 이용에 관한 한미협력협정	原子力의 非軍事的 利用에 關한 韓美協力協定	Agreement for Cooperation Between the Government of the Republic of Korea and the Government of the United States of America Concerning Civil Uses of Atomic	Wonjaryeogui bigunsajeok iyonge gwanhan hanmi hyeomnyeok hyeopjeong	Wŏnjaryŏk-ŭi pigunsajŏk iyong-e kwanhan hanmi hyŏmnyŏk hyŏpchŏng		번역 표준 원칙
2509	원자력의 평화적 이용	原子力의 平和的 利用	peaceful use of atomic energy	Wonjaryeogui pyeonghwajeok iyong	Wŏnjaryŏk-ŭi p'yŏnghwajŏk iyong		번역 표준 원칙
2510	원자력청	原子力廳	Atomic Energy Administration (1967-1973, under the Ministry of Science and Technology)	Wonjaryeokcheong	Wŏnjaryŏkch'ŏng	1967-1973	번역 표준 원칙
2511	원자로	原子爐	nuclear reactor	Wonjaro	Wŏnjaro		번역 표준 원칙
2512	원자폭탄	原子爆彈	atomic bomb	Wonja poktan	Wŏnja p'okt'an		번역 표준 원칙

NO	용어	한자	영문	RO	MC	시대 및 연도	출전
2513	원자폭탄투하	原子爆彈投下	dropping of atomic bomb(s)	Wonja poktan tuha	Wŏnja p'okt'an t'uha	1945	국사편찬위원회
2514	원조	援助	aid	Wonjo	Wŏnjo		번역 표준 원칙
2515	원조공여국	援助供與國	donor countries	Wonjo gongyeoguk	Wŏnjo kongyŏguk		번역 표준 원칙
2516	원조물자도입	援助物資導入	distribution of aid goods	Wonjo mulja doip	Wŏnjo mulcha toip	1950년대	번역 표준 원칙
2517	원조수여국	援助授與國	aid-recipient country	Wonjo suyeoguk	Wŏnjo suyŏguk		번역 표준 원칙
2518	월간지	月刊誌	monthly magazine	Wolganji	Wŏlganji		번역 표준 원칙
2519	월남	越南	defection to South Korea	Wollam	Wŏlnam		번역 표준 원칙
2520	월남공화국	越南共和國	Republic of Vietnam	Wolnam gonghwaguk	Wŏllam konghwaguk	1964	번역 표준 원칙

NO	용어	한자	영문	RO	MC	시대 및 연도	출전
2521	월남망국사	越南亡國史	The Decay of Vietnam	Wollam mangguksa	Wŏllam mangguksa	1906	한국학중앙연구원, 《영문한국백과》-교과서
2522	월남전	越南戰	Vietnam War (1961-1975)	Wolnamjeon	Wŏllamjŏn	1960-1975	번역 표준 원칙
2523	월남전 전상자	越南戰 戰傷者	wounded veterans of the Vietnam War (WIA)	Wolnamjeon jeonsangja	Wŏllamjŏn chŏnsangja	1969	번역 표준 원칙
2524	월남전 참전용사	越南戰 參戰勇士	Vietnam War veterans	Wolnamjeon chamjeon yongsa	Wŏllamjŏn ch'amjŏn yongsa	1960~70년대	번역 표준 원칙
2525	월남파병	越南派兵	dispatch of troops to Vietnam	Wolnam pabyeong	Wŏlnam p'abyŏng	1964-1973	번역 표준 원칙
2526	월드컵 길거리 응원	World Cup 길거리 應援	street cheering for the World Cup Finals	Woldeuceop gilgeori eungwon	Wŏltŭk'ŏp kilgŏri ŭngwŏn		번역 표준 원칙
2527	월드프렌즈 코리아	World Friends Korea	World Friends Korea (WFK)	Woldeu peurenjeu koria	Wŏltŭ p'ŭrenjŭ k'oria	2009	번역 표준 원칙
2528	월맹 군사시설 폭격	越盟 軍事施設 爆擊	bombing of North Vietnamese military facilities	Wolmaeng gunsa siseol pokgyeok	Wŏlmaeng kunsa sisŏl p'okkyŏk	1964	번역 표준 원칙

NO	용어	한자	영문	RO	MC	시대 및 연도	출전
2529	월북	越北	defection to North Korea	Wolbuk	Wŏlbuk		번역 표준 원칙
2530	월북작가	越北作家	writer who has defected to North Korea	Wolbuk jakga	Wŏlbuk chakka		번역 표준 원칙
2531	월비산 전투	月飛山 戰鬪	Battle of Wolbisan Mountain	Wolbisan jeontu	Wŏlbisan chŏnt'u	1951	번역 표준 원칙
2532	월성 원자력발전소	月城 原子力發電所	Wolseong Nuclear Power Plant	Wolseong wonjaryeok baljeonso	Wŏlsŏng wŏnjaryŏk palchŏnso	1977-?	번역 표준 원칙
2533	월악산국립공원	月岳山國立公園	Woraksan National Park	Woraksan gungnip gongwon	Wŏraksan kungnip konwŏn	1984 국립공원 지정	번역 표준 원칙
2534	월출산국립공원	月出山國立公園	Wolchulsan National Park	Wolchulsan gungnip gongwon	Wŏlch'ulsan kungnip kongwŏn	1988 국립공원 지정	번역 표준 원칙
2535	위대한 인공강	偉大한 人工江	Great Man-made River	Widaehan inponggang	Widaehan in'gonggang		번역 표준 원칙
2536	위력수색	威力搜索	reconnaissance-in-force	Wiryeok susaek	Wiryŏk susaek		번역 표준 원칙

NO	용어	한자	영문	RO	MC	시대 및 연도	출전
2537	위성 DMB	衛星 DMB	satellite digital multimedia broadcasting (S-DMB)	Wiseong DMB	Wisŏng DMB		번역 표준 원칙
2538	위성도시	衛星都市	satellite town	Wiseong dosi	Wisŏng tosi		번역 표준 원칙
2539	위임통치 청원	委任統治 請願	Petition for the Mandate of Korea	Wieomtongchi cheongwon	Wiimt'ongch'I ch'ŏngwon	1905-1919	번역 표준 원칙
2540	위장취업	僞裝就業	covert employment of student activists in the factories	Wijang chwieop	Wijang ch'wiŏp		번역 표준 원칙
2541	위장취업 노동운동	僞裝就業 勞動運動	labor action by students covertly employed in the factories	Wijang chwieop nodong undong	Wijang ch'wiŏp nodong undong		번역 표준 원칙
2542	위정척사	衛正斥邪	defending orthodoxy and rejecting heterodoxy	Wijeongcheoksa	Wijŏngch'ŏksa		Ki-baik Lee, translated by Edward W. Wagner, A New History of Korea, Harvard University Press, 1984,
2543	위정척사사상	衛正斥邪思想	doctrine of defending orthodoxy and rejecting heterodoxy	Wijeongcheoksa sasang	Wijŏngch'ŏksa sasang		한국학중앙연구원,《영문한국백과》-유인석
2544	위정척사운동	衛正斥邪運動	Defending Orthodoxy and Rejecting Heterodoxy Movement	Wijeongcheoksa undong	Wijŏngch'ŏksa undong	?-1910	번역 표준 원칙

NO	용어	한자	영문	RO	MC	시대 및 연도	출전
2545	유격전	遊擊戰	guerrilla operations / guerrilla warfare	Yugyeokjeon	Yukyŏkchŏn		번역 표준 원칙
2546	유교구신론	儒敎求新論	Doctrine of the Reformation of Confucianism	Yugyo gusinnon	Yugyo kusinnon	1909	번역 표준 원칙
2547	유년필독	幼年必讀	Required Readings for Juveniles	Yunyeonpildok	Yunyŏnp'iltok	1907-1909	번역 표준 원칙
2548	유럽연합(EU)	Europe聯合	European Union	Yureob yeonhap	Yurŏp yŏnhap		번역 표준 원칙
2549	유림	儒林	Confucian scholars	Yurim	Yurim	조선	번역 표준 원칙
2550	유물사관	唯物史觀	historial materialism / materialist view of history	Yumulsagwan	Yumulsagwan		번역 표준 원칙
2551	유선티비 시범방송	有線TV 示範放送	pilot broadcasting of cable TV	Yuseontibi sibeom bangsong	Yusŏnt'ibi sibŏm pangsong		번역 표준 원칙
2552	유신정우회	維新政友會	Yushin Fraternity (association of lawmakers selected by President Park Chung-hee)	Yusin jeonguhoe	Yusin chŏnguhoe	1973-1980	번역 표준 원칙

NO	용어	한자	영문	RO	MC	시대 및 연도	출전
2553	유신철폐운동	維新撤廢運動	Yushin (Revitalizing Reforms) Abolition Movement	Yusin cheolpye undong	Yusin ch'ŏlp'ye undong		번역 표준 원칙
2554	유신헌법	維新憲法	Yushin (Revitalizing Reforms) Constitution	Yusin heonbeop	Yusin hŏnpŏp	1972	번역 표준 원칙
2555	유심	唯心	*Yusim (Mind-Only)*, Buddhist magazine launched in 1918	Yusim	Yusim	1918	번역 표준 원칙
2556	유언비어	流言蜚語	black rumor	Yueonbieo	Yuŏnbiŏ		번역 표준 원칙
2557	유엔 기념공원	UN 紀念公園	UN Memorial Cemetery in Korea	Yuen ginyeomgongwon	Yuen kinyŏmgongwon	1952	사이버 유엔기념공원 (http://www.unmck.or.kr/)
2558	유엔 사무총장	UN 事務總長	UN Secretary General	Yuen samu chongjang	Yuen samu ch'ongjang	1953	번역 표준 원칙
2559	유엔 소총회	UN 小總會	Little (Sub, Minor) Assembly of the United Nations	Yuen sochonghoe	Yuen soch'onghoe		번역 표준 원칙
2560	유엔 아동권리협약	UN 兒童權利協約	Convention on the Rights of the Child (CRC)	Yuen adong gwolli hyeobyak	Yuen adong gwŏlli hyŏbyak	1989-?	번역 표준 원칙

NO	용어	한자	영문	RO	MC	시대 및 연도	출전
2561	유엔 안전보장이사회 결의문	UN 安全保障理事會 決議文	Resolutions of the United Nations Security Council	Yuen anjeon bojang isahoe gyeoluimun	Yuen anjŏn pojang isahoe kyŏrŭimun	1950	번역 표준 원칙
2562	유엔 총회	UN 總會	General Assembly of the United Nations (1945)	Yuen chonghoe	Yuen ch'onghoe	1945	번역 표준 원칙
2563	유엔 총회 한국문제 자동상정	UN 總會 韓國問題 自動上程	the Korean question being mechanically placed on the provisional agenda of the UN General Assembly	Yuen chonghoe hanguk munje jadong sangjeong	Yuen ch'onghoe han'guk munje chadong sangjŏng		번역 표준 원칙
2564	유엔 특사	UN 特使	special envoy to the United Nations	Yuen teuksa	Yuen t'ŭksa		번역 표준 원칙
2565	유엔 한국부흥위원회 (UNKRA)	UN 韓國復興委員會 (UNKRA)	United Nations Korean Reconstruction Agency (UNKRA)	Yuen hanguk buheung wiwonhoe (UNKRA)	Yuen han'guk puhŭng wiwŏnhoe (UNKRA)	1950-1973	번역 표준 원칙
2566	유엔 한국위원단	UN 韓國委員團	United Nations Commission on Korea (UNCOK)	Yuen hanguk wiwondan jeonbomun	Yuen han'guk wiwŏndan chŏnbomun	1950	번역 표준 원칙
2567	유엔 한국임시위원단	UN 韓國臨時委員團	United Nations Temporary Commission on Korea (UNTCOK)	Yuen hanguk imsi wiwondan	Yuen han'guk imsi wiwŏndan	1947-1948	번역 표준 원칙
2568	유엔군	UN軍	UN Forces / United Nations forces	Yuengun	Yuengun	1950	번역 표준 원칙

NO	용어	한자	영문	RO	MC	시대 및 연도	출전
2569	유엔군 참전	UN軍 參戰	Participation of the UN Forces	Yuengun chamjeon	Yuengun ch'amjŏn	1950	번역 표준 원칙
2570	유엔군과 공산군	UN軍과 共産軍	UN and Communist Forces	Yuengungwa gongsangun	Yuengungwa kongsangun	1950	번역 표준 원칙
2571	유엔군총사령관	UN軍總司令官	Commander-in-Chief, UN Forces	Yuengun chongsaryeonggwan	Yuen'gun ch'ongsaryŏnggwan		번역 표준 원칙
2572	유엔기	UN旗	Flag of the United Nations	Yuengi	Yuen'gi	1946	번역 표준 원칙
2573	유엔사 군사정전위원회	UN司 軍事停戰委員會	United Nations Command Military Armistice Commission (UNCMAC)	Yuensa gunsajeongjeon wiwonhoe	Yuensa kunsajŏngjŏn wiwŏnhoe		번역 표준 원칙
2574	유엔안전보장이사회	UN安全保障理事會	United Nations Security Council	Yuen anjeon bojang isahoe	Yuen anjŏn pojang isahoe	1945	번역 표준 원칙
2575	유엔의 참전과 지연작전	UN의 參戰과 遲延作戰	United Nation Forces Particiation and Delaying Operations	Yuenui chamjeongwa jiyeon jakjeon	Yuenŭi chamjŏngwa chiyŏk chakchŏn	1950	번역 표준 원칙
2576	유엔정치위원회	UN政治委員會	United Nations Political Commission	Yuen jeongchi wiwonhoe	Yuen chŏngch'i wiwŏnhoe		번역 표준 원칙

NO	용어	한자	영문	RO	MC	시대 및 연도	출전
2577	유엔평화유지군	UN平和維持軍	UN Peacekeeping Forces	Yuen pyeonghwa yujigun	Yuen p'yŏnghwa yujigun	1948-?	번역 표준 원칙
2578	유적지	遺跡地	historic site	Yujeokji	Yujŏkchi		번역 표준 원칙
2579	유행성 출혈열 예방백신 개발	流行性 出血熱 豫防 Vaccine 開發	development of vaccine for epidemic hemorrhagic fever	Yuhaengseong chulhyeolyeol yebang baeksin gaebal	Yuhaengsŏng ch'uryŏryŏl yebang baeksin kaebal	1990	번역 표준 원칙
2580	유혈시위	流血示威	bloody demonstration	Yuhyeol siwi	Yuhyŏl siwi		번역 표준 원칙
2581	유호한국독립운동자동맹	留滬韓國獨立運動者同盟	Alliance of Korean Independence Activists in Shanghai	Yuho hanguk dongnip undongja dongmaeng	Yuho han'guk tongnip undongja tongmaeng	1929	번역 표준 원칙
2582	육군사관학교	陸軍士官學校	Korea Military Academy	Yukgun sagwan hakgyo	Yukkun sagwan hakkyo	1948-?	번역 표준 원칙
2583	육군성	陸軍省	Department of the Army	Yukgunseong	Yukkunsŏn		번역 표준 원칙
2584	육군중앙군관학교	陸軍中央軍官學校	Central Military Academy in Nanjing, China	Yukgun jungang gungwan hakgyo	Yukkun chungang kun'gwan hakkyo		번역 표준 원칙

NO	용어	한자	영문	RO	MC	시대 및 연도	출전
2585	육군특별지원병령	陸軍特別志願兵令	Special Army Volunteer Ordinance	Yukgun teukbyeol jiwonbyeongnyeong	Yukkun t'ŭkpyŏl chiwŏnbyŏngnyŏng	1938	번역 표준 원칙
2586	육십만세운동	六十萬歲運動	June 10 Manse Independence Movement	Yuksip manse undong	Yuksip manse undong	1926	번역 표준 원칙
2587	육영공원	育英公院	Royal Institute of Language Education	Yugyeong gongwon	Yugyŏng kongwŏn	1886-1894	한국학중앙연구원,《영문한국백과》-대학
2588	육영수여사 피격사건	陸英修女史 被擊事件	assassination of Yuk Young-soo	Yuk Young-soo yeosa pigyeok sageon	Yuk Yŏng-su yŏsa p'igyŏk sakŏn	1974	번역 표준 원칙
2589	윤봉길 의거	尹奉吉 義擧	Martyr Yun Bong-gil's bombing of Hongkou Park, Shanghai in 1932	Yun Bong-gil uigeo	Yun Pong-kil ŭigŏ	1932	번역 표준 원칙
2590	율곡사업	栗谷事業	Yulgok Project - ROK Military Modernization Plan	Yulgok saeop	Yulgok saŏp	1974-1986	번역 표준 원칙
2591	융단폭격	絨緞爆擊	carpet bombing	Yungdan pokgyeok	Yungdan p'okkyŏk		번역 표준 원칙
2592	융희황제	隆熙皇帝	Emperor Yunghui	Yunghui hwangje	Yunghŭi hwangje	1907-1910	번역 표준 원칙

NO	용어	한자	영문	RO	MC	시대 및 연도	출전
2593	은둔의 나라 한국	隱遁의 나라 韓國	Corea, the Hermit Nation (by Willam Elliot Griffis, 1882)	Eundun-ui nara hanguk	Ŭndun-ŭi nara han'guk	1882	번역 표준 원칙
2594	을미개혁	乙未改革	Reform of 1895 (Eulmi Gaehyeok)	Eulmigaehyeok	Ŭlmigaehyŏk	1895-1896	번역 표준 원칙
2595	을미사변	乙未事變	assassination of Empress Myeongseong by the Japanese	Eulmisabyeon	Ŭlmisabyŏn	1895	번역 표준 원칙
2596	을미의병	乙未義兵	Eulmi Righteous Army of 1895	Eulmiuibyeong	Ŭlmiŭibyŏng	1895	번역 표준 원칙
2597	을사늑약조약문	乙巳勒約條約文	text of the Eulsa Treaty of 1905	Eulsaneugyak joyakmun	Ŭlsanŭgyak choyangmun	1905	번역 표준 원칙
2598	을사오적	乙巳五賊	five treacherous ministers who signed the Eulsa Treaty of 1905	Eulsa ojeok	Ŭlsa ojŏk	1905	번역 표준 원칙
2599	을사조약	乙巳條約	Eulsa Treaty of 1905 (forced by Japan)	Eulsajoyak	Ŭlsajoyak	1905	번역 표준 원칙
2600	을지연습	乙支演習	Eulji Exercise	Euljiyeonseup	Ŭljiyŏnsŭp		번역 표준 원칙

NO	용어	한자	영문	RO	MC	시대 및 연도	출전
2601	을지포커스렌즈 지휘소(UFL)연습	乙支focus lens指揮所演習	Ulchi Focus Lens Command Post Exercise	Eulji pokeoseu renjeu jihwiso yeonseup	Ŭlji p'ok'ŏsŭ lensŭ chihwiso yŏnsŭp	1960-?	번역 표준 원칙
2602	음성 전투	陰城戰鬪	Battle of Eumseong	Eumseong jeontu	Ŭmsŏng chŏnt'u	1950	번역 표준 원칙
2603	음주문화	飮酒文化	drinking culture	Eumju munhwa	Ŭmju munhwa		번역 표준 원칙
2604	의군부	義軍府	Righteous Army Headquarters	Uigunbu	Ŭigunbu		번역 표준 원칙
2605	의궤(조선왕조의궤)	儀軌(朝鮮王朝儀軌)	*uigwe* (records of state ceremonies of the Joseon Dynasty)	Uigwe (joseon wangjo uigwe)	Ŭigwe (chosŏn wangjo ŭigwe)	조선	번역 표준 원칙
2606	의료관광사업	醫療觀光事業	medical tourism	Uiryo gwangwang saeop	Ŭiryo kwangwang saŏp		Daily Mail (http://www.dailymail.co.uk/news/article-1030947/Every-NHS-patient-given-right-abroad-FREE-
2607	의료보험제도	醫療保險制度	medical insurance system	Uiryo boheom jedo	Ŭiryo pohŏm chedo		번역 표준 원칙
2608	의료분업 파동	醫療分業 波動	controversy over government medical service reform	Uiryo buneop padong	Ŭiryo punŏp p'adong		번역 표준 원칙

NO	용어	한자	영문	RO	MC	시대 및 연도	출전
2609	의료제도	醫療制度	healthcare system	Uiryo jedo	Ŭiryo chedo		번역 표준 원칙
2610	의무교육	義務敎育	compulsory education	Uimugyoyuk	Ŭimugyoyuk		번역 표준 원칙
2611	의문사	疑問死	suspicious death	Uimunsa	Ŭimunsa	?-?	번역 표준 원칙
2612	의문사진상규명위원회	疑問死眞相糾明委員會	Presidential Truth Commission on Suspicious Deaths	Uimunsa jinsang gyumyeong wiwonhoe	Ŭimunsa chinsang kyumyŏng wiwŏnhoe	2000-2002	번역 표준 원칙
2613	의병	義兵	Righteous Army	Uibyeong	Ŭibyŏng	?-?	국사편찬위원회
2614	의병봉기	義兵蜂起	Uprising of the Righteous Armies	Uibyeong bonggi	Ŭibyŏng ponggi		번역 표준 원칙
2615	의병부대	義兵部隊	Righteous Army troops	Uibyeong budae	Ŭibyŏng pudae		번역 표준 원칙
2616	의병전쟁	義兵戰爭	Righteous Army battles	Uibyeong jeonjaeng	Ŭibyŏng chŏnjaeng		번역 표준 원칙

NO	용어	한자	영문	RO	MC	시대 및 연도	출전
2617	의식개혁운동	意識改革運動	campaign for the people's enlightenment	Uisik gaehyeok undong	Ŭisik kaehyŏk undong		번역 표준 원칙
2618	의열단	義烈團	Righteous Patriots Corps	Uiyeoldan	Ŭiyŏltan	1919-1929	Peter H. Lee, Sourcebook of Korean Civilization(Volume 2), Columbia University Press, 1993,
2619	의열투쟁	義烈鬪爭	independence struggles of the Righteous Patriots Corps	Uiyeoltujaeng	Ŭiyŏlt'ujaeng		번역 표준 원칙
2620	의정부 전투	議政府 戰鬪	Battle of Uijeongbu	Uijeongbu jeontu	Ŭijŏngbu chŏnt'u	1950	번역 표준 원칙
2621	의학전문대학원	醫學專門大學院	graduate school of medicine	Uihak jeonmun daehagwon	Ŭihak chŏnmun taehagwŏn		번역 표준 원칙
2622	의화단운동	義和團運動	Boxer Rebellion	Uihwadan undong	Ŭihwadan undong	1900-1901	Ki-baik Lee, translated by Edward W. Wagner, A New History of Korea, Harvard University Press, 1984,
2623	의회설립운동	議會設立運動	Independence Club's campaign for the establishment of a parliament	Uihoe seollip undong	Ŭihoe sŏllip undong	1898	번역 표준 원칙
2624	이권침탈	利權侵奪	foreign concessions	Igwonchimtal	Ikwŏnch'imt'al		번역 표준 원칙

NO	용어	한자	영문	RO	MC	시대 및 연도	출전
2625	이기붕 일가 변사사건	李起鵬 一家 變死事件	death of Yi Ki-bung and family in a suicide pact	Yi Gi-bung ilga byeonsa sageon	Yi Ki-pung ilga pyŏnsa sakŏn	1960	번역 표준 원칙
2626	이농현상	離農現象	rural exodus	Inong hyeonsang	Inong hyŏnsang		번역 표준 원칙
2627	이동 탄약보급소	移動 彈藥補給所	Mobile Ammunition Supply Point (MASP)	Idong tanyak bogeupso	Idong t'anyak pogŭpso		번역 표준 원칙
2628	이동외과병원	移動外科病院	Mobile Army Surgical Hospital (MASH)	Idong oegwa byeongwon	Idong oekwa pyŏngwŏn		번역 표준 원칙
2629	이라크 파병	Iraq 派兵	dispatch of troops to Iraq	Irakeu pabyeong	Irakŭ p'abyŏng		번역 표준 원칙
2630	이란의 석유전면수출 금지조치	Iran의 石油全面輸出禁止措置	Iran's oil embargo	Iranui seogyu jeonmyeon suchul geumji jochi	Iran-ŭi sŏgyu chŏnmyŏn such'ul kŭmji choch'i		번역 표준 원칙
2631	이륭양행	怡隆洋行	Shaw Brothers Co. (which housed the office of the Transportation Bureau of the Provisional Government of the	Iryung yanghaeng	Iryung yanghaeng	1920-?	번역 표준 원칙
2632	이르쿠츠크파 고려공산당	Irkutsk派 高麗共産黨	Irkutsk Faction of the Goryeo Communist Party	Ireukucheukeupa goryeo gongsandang	Irŭk'uch'ŭk'ŭp'a koryŏ kongsandang	1919-1922	번역 표준 원칙

NO	용어	한자	영문	RO	MC	시대 및 연도	출전
2633	이리역 화약수송열차 폭발	裡里驛 火藥輸送列車 爆發	blowing up of a freight train carrying explosives at Iri Station (now Iksan Station)	Iriyeok hwayak susong yeolcha pokbal	Iriŏk hwayak susong yŏlch'a p'okpal	1977	번역 표준 원칙
2634	이봉창 의거	李奉昌 義擧	Martyr Yi Bong-chang's assassination attempt on the Japanese emperor	Yi Bong-chang uigeo	Yi Pong-ch'ang ŭigŏ	1932	번역 표준 원칙
2635	이산가족 상봉	離散家族 相逢	reunion of separated families	Isangajok sangbong	Isankajok sangbong	1985-	번역 표준 원칙
2636	이산가족 상설면회소	離散家族 常設面會所	permanent venue for meeting of separated families	Isangajok sangseol myeonhoeso	Isankajok sangsŏl myŏnhoeso		번역 표준 원칙
2637	이순신 성웅화	李舜臣 聖雄化	hero worship of Admiral Yi Sun-sin	Yi Sun-sin seongunghwa	Yi Sun-sin sŏngunghwa		번역 표준 원칙
2638	이승만 대통령 대국민 담화문	李承晩 大統領 對國民 談話文	President Syngman Rhee's Address to the Nation	Yi Seung-man daetongnyeong daegungmin damhwamun	Yi Sŭng-man taet'ongnyŏng taegungmin tamhwamun	1960	번역 표준 원칙
2639	이승만 대통령 사임서	李承晩 大統領 辭任書	President Syngman Rhee's letter of resignation	Yi Seung-man daetongnyeong saimseo	Yi Sŭng-man taet'ongnyŏng saimsŏ	1960	번역 표준 원칙
2640	이승만 암살미수사건	李承晩 暗殺未遂事件	assassination attempt on President Syngman Rhee	Yi Seung-man amsal misu sageon	Yi Sŭng-man amsal misu sakŏn	1952	번역 표준 원칙

NO	용어	한자	영문	RO	MC	시대 및 연도	출전
2641	이승만 하야성명	李承晩 下野聲明	resignation statement of President Syngman Rhee	Yi Seung-man haya seongmyeong	Yi Sŭng-man haya sŏngmyŏng	1960	번역 표준 원칙
2642	이승만 하와이망명	李承晩 Hawaii亡命	Syngman Rhee's exile to Hawaii	Yi Seung-man hawai mangmyeong	Yi Sŭng-man hawai mangmyŏng	1960	번역 표준 원칙
2643	이승만의 정읍발언	李承晩의 井邑發言	Syngman Rhee's Jeongeup Speech (June 3, 1946)	Yi Seung-man-ui Jeongeup bareon	Yi Sŭng-man-ŭi Chŏngŭp parŏn	1946	번역 표준 원칙
2644	이양선	異樣船	foreign ships	Iyangseon	Iyangsŏn		번역 표준 원칙
2645	이오지마 전투	硫黃島 戰鬪	Battle of Iwo Jima	Iojima jeontu	Iojima chŏnt'u	1945	번역 표준 원칙
2646	이원집정부제	二元執政府制	dual executive system	Iwon jipjeongbuje	Iwŏn chipchŏngbuje		번역 표준 원칙
2647	이이제이	以夷制夷	"using barbarians to control barbarians"	Iijei	Iijei		Jai-Keun Choi, The Origin of the Roman Catholic Church in Korea, The Hermit Kingdom Press, 2006, p.215.
2648	이자제한법	利子制限法	Interest Ceiling Act	Ijajehanbeop	Ijajehanpŏp	1962-1998 2007-	번역 표준 원칙

NO	용어	한자	영문	RO	MC	시대 및 연도	출전
2649	이재명 의거	李在明 義擧	Martyr Yi Jae-Myung's assassinatation attempt on Yi Wan-Yong, pro-Japanese Korean minister	Yi Jae-myeong uigeo	Yi Chae-myŏng ŭigŏ	1909	번역 표준 원칙
2650	이재민	罹災民	disaster victims	Ijaemin	Ijaemin		번역 표준 원칙
2651	이중곡가제	二重穀價制	dual grain price system	Ijung gokgaje	Ijung kokkaje	1969-?	번역 표준 원칙
2652	이지스구축함	Aegis驅逐艦	Aegis destoryer	Ijiseu guchukham	Ijisŭ kuch'ukham		번역 표준 원칙
2653	이천함	李阡艦	ROKS Lee Chun, first Korean made submarine	Icheonham	Ich'ŏnam		번역 표준 원칙
2654	이화장	梨花莊	Ewhajang (private residence of the first Korean President Syngman Rhee)	Ihwajang	Ihwajang		번역 표준 원칙
2655	이화학당	梨花學堂	Ewha Hakdang (school for girls)	Ihwa hakdang	Ihwa haktang	1886-1925	번역 표준 원칙
2656	이후락-김영주 회담	李厚洛-金英柱 會談	Secret talks between Lee Hu-rak (South Korea) and Kim Yeong-ju (North Korea)	Yi Hu-rak - Kim Yeong-ju hoedam	Yi Hu-rak - Kim Yŏng-chu hoedam	1972	번역 표준 원칙

NO	용어	한자	영문	RO	MC	시대 및 연도	출전
2657	익산포항고속도로	益山浦項高速道路	Iksan-Pohang Expressway	Iksan pohang gosokdoro	Iksan p'ohang kosoktoro		번역 표준 원칙
2658	인간 배아줄기 세포	人間 胚芽줄기 細胞	embryonic stem cell	Ingan baea julgi sepo	Ingan baea chulgi sep'o		번역 표준 원칙
2659	인간유전자	人間遺傳子	human genome	Ingan yujeonja	Ingan yujŏnja		번역 표준 원칙
2660	인간정보	人間情報	human intelligence (HUMINT)	Inganjeongbo	Inganjŏngbo		번역 표준 원칙
2661	인감증명 제도	印鑑證明 制度	seal certification system	Ingam jeungmyeong jedo	Ingam chŭngmyŏng chedo		번역 표준 원칙
2662	인공강우	人工降雨	artificial rain making	Ingong gangu	Ingong kangu		번역 표준 원칙
2663	인공위성연구센터	人工衛星硏究Center	Satellite Technology Research Center (SaTReC)	Ingong wiseong yeongu senteo	Ingong wisŏng yŏn'gu sent'ŏ	1989	번역 표준 원칙
2664	인구 공동화 현상 (도넛 현상)	人口 空洞化 現象 (doughnut 現象)	donut effect (urban flight and suburbanization)	Ingu gongdonghwa hyeonsang (doneot hyeonsang)	Ingu kongdonghwa hyŏnsang (tonŏt hyŏnsang)		번역 표준 원칙

NO	용어	한자	영문	RO	MC	시대 및 연도	출전
2665	인구억제정책	人口抑制政策	population control policy	Ingu eokje jeongchaek	In'gu ŏkche chŏngch'aek	1962-1989	번역 표준 원칙
2666	인권보호	人權保護	protection of human rights	Ingwon boho	Ingwŏn poho		번역 표준 원칙
2667	인권선언	人權宣言	declaration of human rights	Ingwon seoneon	Ingwon sŏnŏn		번역 표준 원칙
2668	인권실천시민연대	人權實踐市民連帶	Citizens' Solidarity for Human Rights	Ingwon silcheon simin yeondae	Inkwŏn silch'ŏn simin yŏndae	1999-	번역 표준 원칙
2669	인권외교	人權外交	human rights diplomacy	Ingwon oegyo	Inkwŏn oegyo		번역 표준 원칙
2670	인권운동사랑방	人權運動舍廊房	Sarangbang Group for Human Rights	Ingwon undong sarangbang	Inkwŏn undong sarangbang	1992-	번역 표준 원칙
2671	인권재단	人權財團	Korea Human Rights Foundation	Ingwon jaedan	Inkwŏn chaedan	1999-	번역 표준 원칙
2672	인도-버마전구	印度-Burma戰區	India - Burma Theater (IBT)	indo beoma jeongu	Indo pŏma chŏngu		국가보훈처,「NAPKO Project OF OSS」2001

NO	용어	한자	영문	RO	MC	시대 및 연도	출전
2673	인도차이나 전쟁	Indochina 戰爭	Indochina Wars	Indochaina jeonjaeng	Indoch'aina chŏnjaeng	1946-1954	번역 표준 원칙
2674	인디 포럼98	Indie Forum98	Indie Forum 1998	Indiporeom 98	Indip'orŏm 98	1998-	번역 표준 원칙
2675	인력수탈	人力收奪	exploitation of human labor	Illyeok sutal	Illyŏk sut'al		번역 표준 원칙
2676	인류무형문화유산	人類無形文化遺産	Masterpieces of the Oral and Intangible Heritage of Humanity	Illyu muhyeong munhwa yusan	Illyu muhyŏng munhwa yusan	2001	번역 표준 원칙
2677	인면전구공작대	印緬戰區工作隊	Indian-Burma (Myanmar) Theater Operations Unit	Inmyeon jeongu gongjakdae	Inmyŏn chŏn'gu kongjaktae	1943-1945	번역 표준 원칙
2678	인민군최고사령관	人民軍最高司令官	Supreme Commander, North Korean People's Army	Inmingun choego saryeonggwan	Inmin'gun ch'oego saryŏnggwan	1948-	번역 표준 원칙
2679	인민무력부	人民武力部	Ministry of the People's Armed Forces (MPAF)	Inmin muryeokbu	Inmin muryŏkpu	1978-1998	번역 표준 원칙
2680	인민위원회	人民委員會	people's committee	Inmin wiwonhoe	Inmin wiwŏnhoe	1945	한국학중앙연구원, 《영문한국백과》-농민운동

- 355 -

NO	용어	한자	영문	RO	MC	시대 및 연도	출전
2681	인민재판	人民裁判	people's courts	Inmin jaepan	Inmin chaep'an		번역 표준 원칙
2682	인민전선노선	人民戰線路線	People's Front Line	Inmin jeonseon noseon	Inmin chŏnsŏn nosŏn		번역 표준 원칙
2683	인민혁명단 사건	人民革命黨 事件	People's Revolutionary Party Incident	Inmin hyeongmyeongdang sageon	Inmin hyŏngmyŏngdan sakŏn	1964	번역 표준 원칙
2684	인사청문회	人事聽聞會	confirmation hearing	Insa cheongmunhoe	Insa ch'ŏngmunhoe	2000-	번역 표준 원칙
2685	인신구속 등에 관한 임시특례법	人身拘束 等에 關한 臨時特例法	Provisional Special Law on the Personal Arrest	Insin gusok deunge gwanhan imsi teungnyebeop	Insin kusok tŭng-e kwanhan imsi t'ŭngnyepŏp	1961-1963	번역 표준 원칙
2686	인원수송장갑차	人員輸送裝甲車	Armored Personnel Carrier (APC)	Inwon susong janggapcha	Inwŏn susong janggapch'a		번역 표준 원칙
2687	인제 전투	麟蹄 戰鬪	Battle of Inje	Inje jeontu	Inje chŏnt'u	1951	번역 표준 원칙
2688	인종론	人種論	racial ideology	Injongnon	Injongnon		번역 표준 원칙

NO	용어	한자	영문	RO	MC	시대 및 연도	출전
2689	인종주의	人種主義	racism	Injongjuui	Injongjuǔi		번역 표준 원칙
2690	인종차별	人種差別	racial discrimination	Injong chabyeol	Injong ch'abyǒl		번역 표준 원칙
2691	인종학	人種學	ethnology	Injonghak	Injonghak		번역 표준 원칙
2692	인천 국제공항 고속도로	仁川 國際空航 高速道路	Incheon International Airport Expressway	Incheon gukje gonghang gosokdoro	Inch'ǒn kukche konghang kosoktoro	2000	번역 표준 원칙
2693	인천 내리교회	仁川 내리教會	Naeri Methodist Church in Incheon	Incheon naeri gyohoe	Inch'ǒn naeri kyohoe	1885	번역 표준 원칙
2694	인천공항	仁川空港	Incheon International Airport	Incheon gonghang	Inchǒn konghang	2001	번역 표준 원칙
2695	인천광역시	仁川廣城市	Incheon Metropolitan City	Incheon gwangyeoksi	Inch'ǒn kwangyǒksi		번역 표준 원칙
2696	인천대교 고속도로	仁川大橋 高速道路	Incheon Bridge Expressway	Incheon daegyo gosokdoro	Inch'ǒn taegyo kosoktoro		번역 표준 원칙

NO	용어	한자	영문	RO	MC	시대 및 연도	출전
2697	인천상륙작전	仁川上陸作戰	Incheon Amphibious Landing Operation	Incheon sangnyuk jakjeon	Inch'ŏn sangnyuk chakchŏn	1950	번역 표준 원칙
2698	인천집회	仁川集會	Incheon anti-government protest of 1986	Incheon jiphoe	Inch'ŏn chiphoe	1986	번역 표준 원칙
2699	인천항	仁川港	Incheon Port	Incheonhang	Inch'ŏnhang	1883-?	번역 표준 원칙
2700	인터넷 전자신문	Internet 電子新聞	Internet newspapers	Inteonet jeonjasinmun	Intŏnet chŏnjasinmun		번역 표준 원칙
2701	인해전술	人海戰術	human-wave tactics	Inhae jeonsul	Inhae chŏnsul		번역 표준 원칙
2702	인혁당재건위 사건	人革黨再建委 事件	People's Revolutionary Party Reconstruction Committee Incident	Inhyeokdang jaegeonwi sageon	Inhyŏktang chaegŏnwi sakŏn	1974	번역 표준 원칙
2703	일간지	日刊紙	daily newspaper	Ilganji	Ilganji		번역 표준 원칙
2704	일관제철소	一貫製鐵所	integrated steelworks	Ilgwan jecheolso	Ilgwan chech'ŏlso		번역 표준 원칙

NO	용어	한자	영문	RO	MC	시대 및 연도	출전
2705	일민주의	一民主義	Ideology of United People (to establish the foundation of democracy)	Ilminjuui	Ilminjuǔi	1949	번역 표준 원칙
2706	일반농지	一般農地	general farm land	Ilban nongji	Ilban nongji		번역 표준 원칙
2707	일반명령 1호	一般命令 1號	General Order No. 1	Ilban myeongnyeong 1ho	Ilban myǒngnyǒng 1ho	1945	번역 표준 원칙
2708	일본 문부과학성	日本 文部科學省	Ministry of Education, Culture, Sports, Science and Technology of Japan	Ilbon munbu gwahakseong	Ilbon munbu kwahaksǒng	2001-	번역 표준 원칙
2709	일본 외무성	日本 外務省	Ministry of Foreign Affairs of Japan	Ilbon oemuseong	Ilbon oemusǒng	1885	번역 표준 원칙
2710	일본 육군성	日本 陸軍省	Army Ministry of Japan	Ilbon yukgunseong	Ilbon yukkunsǒng		번역 표준 원칙
2711	일본 제국주의	日本 帝國主義	Japanese imperialism	Ilbon jegukjuui	Ilbon jegukjuǔi		번역 표준 원칙
2712	일본 항복문서	日本 降伏文書	statement of Japanese Surrender in 1945	Ilbon hangbok munseo	Ilbon hangbok munsǒ	1945	번역 표준 원칙

NO	용어	한자	영문	RO	MC	시대 및 연도	출전
2713	일본 해군성	日本 海軍省	Navy Ministry of Japan	Ilbon haegunseong	Ilbon haegunsŏng		번역 표준 원칙
2714	일본공사관	日本公使館	Japanese Legation	Ilbon gongsagwan	Ilbon kongsagwan		번역 표준 원칙
2715	일본군 성노예전범 국제법정	日本軍 性奴隷戰犯 國際 法廷	Women's International War Crimes Tribunal on Japan's Military Sexual Slavery	Ilbongun seongnoye jeonbeom gukje beopjeong	Ilbongun sŏngnoye chŏnbŏm kukche pŏpchŏng	2000	번역 표준 원칙
2716	일본군 위안부	日本軍 慰安婦	women forced into sexual slavery by the Japanese military (aka "comfort women")	Ilbongun wianbu	Ilbon'gun wianbu	?-1945	번역 표준 원칙
2717	일본군 위안부 문제	日本軍 慰安婦 問題	controversy over Japan's military sexual slavery	Ilbongun wianbu munje	Ilbon'gun wianbu munje		번역 표준 원칙
2718	일본역사교과서왜곡사건	日本歷史敎科書歪曲事件	1982 case of distortion of history in Japanese textbooks	Ilbon yeoksa gyogwaseo waegok sageon	Ilbon yŏksa kyogwasŏ waegok sagŏn	1982	번역 표준 원칙
2719	일본조합교회	日本組合敎會	Japanese Congregational Church	Ilbon johap gyohoe	Ilbon chohap kyohoe	1878	번역 표준 원칙
2720	일선동조	日鮮同祖	theory of common origin of Japanese and Koreans	Ilseondongjo	Ilsŏndongjo		번역 표준 원칙

NO	용어	한자	영문	RO	MC	시대 및 연도	출전
2721	일선동조론	日鮮同祖論	propaganda of common origin of Japanese and Koreans	Ilseondongjoron	Ilsŏndongjoron		번역 표준 원칙
2722	일성록	日省錄	Records of Daily Reflections (Ilseongnok)	Ilseongnok	Ilsŏngnok	1932	한국학중앙연구원,《영문한국백과》-일성록
2723	일소불가침조약	日蘇不可侵條約	Japan-Soviet Nonaggression Pact	Ilso bulgachim joyak	Ilso pulgach'im choyak	1941-1945	번역 표준 원칙
2724	일월회	日月會	Day-Month Society January Society, (socialist organization comprising Korean students in Tokyo, formed in January	Ilwolhoe	Ilwolhoe	1925	번역 표준 원칙
2725	일일연속극	日日連續劇	daily soap opera	Ilil yeonsokgeuk	Iril yŏnsokkŭk		번역 표준 원칙
2726	일자리 창출	일자리 創出	job creation	Iljari changchul	Iljari ch'angch'ul		번역 표준 원칙
2727	일장기말소 사건	日章旗抹消 事件	erasure of the Japanese flag in a photo of Sohn Kee-jung at the 1936 Berlin Olympics medal ceremony	Iljanggi malso sageon	Iljanggi malso sagŏn	1936	번역 표준 원칙
2728	일제 식민지시대	日帝 植民地時代	period of Japanese colonial rule	Ilje sikminji sidae	Ilje sikminji sidae	1910-1945	번역 표준 원칙

NO	용어	한자	영문	RO	MC	시대 및 연도	출전
2729	일제 패망	日帝 敗亡	collapse of Imperial Japan	Ilje paemang	Ilche p'aemang	1945	번역 표준 원칙
2730	일제시기 농민운동	日帝時期 農民運動	peasant movements of the Japanese colonial period	Iljesigi nongmin undong	Iljesigi nongmin undong	1910-1945	번역 표준 원칙
2731	일진회	一進會	Iljinhoe (pro-Japan society)	Iljinhoe	Ilchinhoe	1904-1910	번역 표준 원칙
2732	일해재단	日海財團	Ilhae Foundation (now Sejong Foundation)	Ilhae jaedan	Ilhae chaedan	1983	번역 표준 원칙
2733	임무형보호태세	任務型保護態勢	Mission Oriented Protective Poture (MOPP)	Immuhyeong bohotaese	Immuhyŏng pohot'aese		번역 표준 원칙
2734	임수경 방북사건	林秀卿 訪北事件	college student Im Su-gyeong's unauthorized visit to North Korea	Im Su-gyeong bangbuk sageon	Im Su-kyŏng pangbuk sakŏn	1989	번역 표준 원칙
2735	임시국무회의	臨時國務會議	extraordinary cabinet meeting	Imsi gungmu hoeui	Imsi kungmu hoeŭi		번역 표준 원칙
2736	임시국회	臨時國會	provisional session of the National Assembly	Imsi gukhoe	Imsi kukhoe		번역 표준 원칙

NO	용어	한자	영문	RO	MC	시대 및 연도	출전
2737	임시사료편찬위원회	臨時史料編纂委員會	Provisional Committee for the Compilation of Historical Materials	Imsi saryo pyeonchan wiwonhoe	Imsi saryo p'yŏnch'an wiwonhoe	1919	번역 표준 원칙
2738	임시정부 요인	臨時政府 要人	key figures of the Provisional Government of the Republic of Korea	Imsi jeongbu yoin	Imsi chŏngbu yoin		번역 표준 원칙
2739	임시정부 채권	臨時政府 債券	bonds issued by the Provisional Government of the Republic of Korea	Imsi jeongbu chaegwon	Imsi chŏngbu ch'aekwŏn	1923	번역 표준 원칙
2740	임시조선민주주의정부	臨時朝鮮民主主義政府	Korean Democratic Provisional Government	Imsi joseon minjujuui jeongbu	Imsi chosŏn minjujuŭi chŏngbu	1945	번역 표준 원칙
2741	임시학교	臨時學校	temporary schools	Imsi hakgyo	Imsi hakkyo		번역 표준 원칙
2742	임야조사령	林野調査令	Woodlands Survey Order of 1918	Imnya josaryeong	Imya chosaryŏng	1918	번역 표준 원칙
2743	임오군란	壬午軍亂	Military Uprising of 1882	Imogullan	Imogullan	1882	번역 표준 원칙
2744	임오군변	壬午軍變	Military Uprising of 1882	Imogunbyeon	Imogunbŏn	1882	James B. Palais, Politics and Policy in Traditional Korea, Harvard University Press, 1991, p.177.

NO	용어	한자	영문	RO	MC	시대 및 연도	출전
2745	임전보국단	臨戰報國團	Korean Wartime Patriotic Corps	Imjeon bogukdan	Imjŏn poguktan	1941-1942	번역 표준 원칙
2746	임정환국	臨政還國	return of the Provisional Government of the Republic of Korea	Imjeonghwanguk	Imjŏnghwan'guk	1945	번역 표준 원칙
2747	임진왜란	壬辰倭亂	Imjin War (1592-1598)	Imjinwaeran	Imjinwaeran	1592-1598	번역 표준 원칙
2748	임팔전투	Imphal戰鬪	Battle of Imphal	Impal jeontu	Imp'al chŏnt'u	1944	번역 표준 원칙
2749	임해공업단지	臨海工業團地	coastal industrial complex	Imhae gongeop danji	Imhae kongŏp tanji		번역 표준 원칙
2750	입법의원	立法議員	member of the legislative assembly	Ipbeop uiwon	Ippŏp ŭiwŏn	1946	번역 표준 원칙
2751	입헌군주제	立憲君主制	constitutional monarchy	Ipheon gunjuje	Iphŏn kunjuje		번역 표준 원칙
2752	입헌정치	立憲政治	constitutional government / parliamentary politics	Ipheon jeongchi	Iphŏn chŏngch'i		번역 표준 원칙

NO	용어	한자	영문	RO	MC	시대 및 연도	출전
2753	입헌주의	立憲主義	constitutionalism	Ipheonjuui	Iphŏnjuŭi	1800-	국사편찬위원회
2754	잉여농산물	剩餘農産物	agricultural surplus	Ingyeo nongsanmul	Ingyŏ nongsanmul	1954-	번역 표준 원칙
2755	잉여농산물 도입협정	剩餘農産物 導入協定	Surplus Agricultural Commodity Agreement	Ingyeo nongsanmul doip hyeopjeong	Ingyŏ nongsanmul toip hyŏpchŏng	1954-	번역 표준 원칙
2756	잉여농산물 판매대금	剩餘農産物 販賣代金	payment for the sale of agricultural surpluses	Ingyeo nongsanmul panmae daegeum	Ingyŏ nongsanmul p'anmae taegŭm		번역 표준 원칙
2757	자강운동	自强運動	reform movement of Korea 1905-1910	Jagang undong	Chagang undong	1905-1910	번역 표준 원칙
2758	자급비료증산요강	自給肥料增産要綱	guidelines for increasing production of fertilizer	Jageup biryo jeungsan yogang	Chagŭp piryo chŭngsan yogang	1946	번역 표준 원칙
2759	자동금리제	自動金利制	automatic interest-rate adjustment mechanism	Jadong geumnije	Chadong gŭmnije		번역 표준 원칙
2760	자동차 공장	自動車 工場	automobile plant	Jadongcha gongjang	Chadongch'a kongjang		번역 표준 원칙

NO	용어	한자	영문	RO	MC	시대 및 연도	출전
2761	자동차 수송체계	自動車 輸送體系	motor vehicle transportation system	Jadongcha susong chegye	Chadongch'a susong ch'egye		번역 표준 원칙
2762	자립갱생	自立更生	self-reliance	Jarip gaengsaeng	Charip kaengsaeng		번역 표준 원칙
2763	자립마을	自立마을	self-reliant villages	Jarip maeul	Charip maŭl		번역 표준 원칙
2764	자본자유화	資本自由化	liberalization of capital	Jabon jayuhwa	Chabon chayuhwa		번역 표준 원칙
2765	자본주의맹아론	資本主義萌芽論	theory on the rise of capitalism in Joseon (arguing that signs of capitalism had already appeared in the late Joseon period)	Jabonjuui maengaron	Chabonjuŭi maengaron		번역 표준 원칙
2766	자선사업	慈善事業	charity work	Jaseon saeop	Chasŏn saŏp		번역 표준 원칙
2767	자연보호헌장	自然保護憲章	Charter for the Conservation of Nature	Jayeon boho heonjang	Chayŏn poho hyŏnjang	1978	번역 표준 원칙
2768	자원민족주의	資源民族主義	resource nationalism	Jawon minjokjuui	Chawŏn minjokjuŭi		번역 표준 원칙

NO	용어	한자	영문	RO	MC	시대 및 연도	출전
2769	자원봉사활동	自願奉仕活動	volunteer work	Jawon bongsa hwaldong	Chawŏn pongsa hwaltong		번역 표준 원칙
2770	자유경제	自由經濟	free economy	Jayu gyeongje	Chayu kyŏngje		번역 표준 원칙
2771	자유당	自由黨	Liberal Party	Jayudang	Chayudang	1951-1960	한국학중앙연구원, 《영문한국백과》-사회보장제도
2772	자유당 본부	自由黨 本部	Headquarters of the Liberal Party	Jayudang bonbu	Chayudang ponbu		번역 표준 원칙
2773	자유무역지역	自由貿易地域	free trade zone	Jayu muyeok jiyeok	Chayu muyŏk chiyŏk	1932-	번역 표준 원칙
2774	자유민주연합 (자민련)	自由民主聯合 (自民聯)	United Liberal Democrats	Jayu minju yeonhap (jamillyeon)	Chayu minju yŏnhap (chamillyŏn)	1995-	번역 표준 원칙
2775	자유민주주의	自由民主主義	liberal democracy	Jayu minjujuui	Chayu minjujuŭi		번역 표준 원칙
2776	자유민주파	自由民主派	Liberal Democratic Faction	Jayu minjupa	Chayu minjup'a	1955	번역 표준 원칙

NO	용어	한자	영문	RO	MC	시대 및 연도	출전
2777	자유부인	自由婦人	"A Lady of Freedom" (Jayu Buin), movie directed by Han Hyeong-mo, 1956	Jayu buin	Chayu puin	1956	번역 표준 원칙
2778	자유세계	自由世界	World of Liberty (Jayu Segye)	Jayu segye	Chayu segye	1952-1953	번역 표준 원칙
2779	자유시참변	自由市慘變	Free City (Svobodny) Incident of 1921	Jayusi chambyeon	Chayusi ch'ambyŏn	1921	번역 표준 원칙
2780	자유실천문인협의회	自由實踐文人協議會	Literary Council for the Realization of Freedom	Jayu silcheon munin hyeobuihoe	Chayu silch'ŏn munin hyŏbŭihoe	1974-?	번역 표준 원칙
2781	자유언론실천선언	自由言論實踐宣言	Free Press Declaration of 1974	Jayu eollon silcheon seoneon	Chayu ŏllon silch'ŏn sŏnŏn	1974	번역 표준 원칙
2782	자유월남	自由越南	Free Vietnam (South Vietnam)	Jayu wolnam	Chayu wŏllam	1954-1975	번역 표준 원칙
2783	자유의 다리	自由의 다리	Freedom Bridge	Jayu-ui dari	Chayu-ŭi tari	1953-?	번역 표준 원칙
2784	자유의 마을	自由의 마을	Freedom Village	Jayu-ui maeul	Chayu-ŭi maŭl	1953-?	번역 표준 원칙

NO	용어	한자	영문	RO	MC	시대 및 연도	출전
2785	자유의사에 의한 포로송환원칙	自由意思에 依한 捕虜送還原則	principle of voluntary repatriation of prisoners of war	Jayu uisae uihan poro songhwan wonchik	Chayu ŭisa-e ŭihan p'oro songhwan wŏnch'ik		번역 표준 원칙
2786	자유종	自由鐘	Liberty Bell	Jayujong	Chayujong	1910	Ki-baik Lee, translated by Edward W. Wagner, A New History of Korea, Harvard University Press, 1984,
2787	자유주의연대	自由主義連帶	Liberty Union	Jayujuui yeondae	Chayujuŭi yŏndae	2004-	번역 표준 원칙
2788	자유한인대회	自由韓人大會	First Korean Congress of 1919	Jayu hanindaehoe	Chayu hanintaehoe	1919	번역 표준 원칙
2789	자이툰 부대	Zaytun 部隊	Zaytun Division	Jaitun budae	Chaitun pudae	2004-2008	번역 표준 원칙
2790	자작회	自作會	Self-Production Association	Jajakhoe	Chajakhoe	1922-1923	번역 표준 원칙
2791	자정순국	自靖殉國	committing suicide as a form of anti-Japanese resistance	Jajeongsunguk	Chajŏngsun'guk		번역 표준 원칙
2792	자조마을	自助마을	Self-sufficient village	Jajo maeul	Chajo maŭl		번역 표준 원칙

NO	용어	한자	영문	RO	MC	시대 및 연도	출전
2793	자주국방 강화기	自主國防 强化期	strengthening self-reliant national defense	Jajugukbang ganghwagi	Chajukukpang kanghwagi	1981-1990	번역 표준 원칙
2794	자주국방 기반조성기	自主國防 基盤造成期	building self-reliant national defense	Jaju gukbang giban joseonggi	Chaju kukpang kiban chosŏnggi	1974-1989	번역 표준 원칙
2795	자주국방체제 확립	自主國防體制 確立	establishment of self-reliant national defense system	Jaju gukbang cheje hwangnip	Chaju kukpang ch'eje hwangnip		번역 표준 원칙
2796	자주노선	自主路線	self-reliance policy	Jaju noseon	Chaju nosŏn		번역 표준 원칙
2797	자주독립	自主獨立	independence	Jajudongnip	Chajudongnip		번역 표준 원칙
2798	자주부강	自主富强	independence and prosperity	Jajubugang	Chajubugang		번역 표준 원칙
2799	자주포	自走砲	self-propelled howitzer	Jajupo	Chajup'o		번역 표준 원칙
2800	자치론	自治論	theory of Korean autonomy	Jachiron	Chach'iron		번역 표준 원칙

NO	용어	한자	영문	RO	MC	시대 및 연도	출전
2801	자치운동	自治運動	movement for Korean autonomy	Jachi undong	Chach'i undong		번역 표준 원칙
2802	자혜의원	慈惠醫院	Jahye Medical Center	Jahye uiwon	Chahye ŭiwŏn	1909-?	번역 표준 원칙
2803	작전개념	作戰槪念	concept of operations (CONOP)	Jakjeongaenyeom	Chakchŏn'gyenyŏm		번역 표준 원칙
2804	작전통제권	作戰統制權	operational control (OPCON) authority	Jakjeon tongjegwon	Chakchŏn t'ongjekwŏn		번역 표준 원칙
2805	잠수교	潛水橋	Jamsugyo ("submerged bridge")	Jamsugyo	Chamsugyo	1976	번역 표준 원칙
2806	잠실 서울올림픽 주경기장	蠶室 Seoul Olympic 主競技場	Jamsil Olympic Main Stadium in Seoul	Jamsil seoul ollimpik jugyeonggijang	Chamsil sŏul ollimp'ik chugyŏnggijang	1984	번역 표준 원칙
2807	잠실종합운동장	蠶室綜合運動場	Jamsil Sports Complex	Jamsil jonghap undongjang	Chamsil chonghap undongjang	1979	번역 표준 원칙
2808	장기기증	臟器寄贈	organ donation	Janggi gijeung	Changgi Kijŭng		번역 표준 원칙

NO	용어	한자	영문	RO	MC	시대 및 연도	출전
2809	장기수	長期囚	long-term prisoner	Janggisu	Changgisu		번역 표준 원칙
2810	장기수 북송	長期囚 北送	repatriation of long-term prisoners to North Korea	Janggisu buksong	Changgisu puksong		번역 표준 원칙
2811	장기수출계획안	長期輸出計劃案	long-term export plan	Janggi suchul gyehoegan	Changgi such'ul kyehoegan	1967	번역 표준 원칙
2812	장기에너지수급계획	長期Energy需給計劃	Long-term Energy Supply Plan of 1967	Janggi eneoji sugeup gyehoek	Changgi enŏji sugŭp kyehoek	1967	번역 표준 원칙
2813	장기자동차공업진흥계획	長期自動車工業振興計劃	long-term plan for promotion of the automobile industry	Janggi jadongcha gongeop jinheung gyehoek	Changgi chadongch'a gongŏp chinhŭng kyehoek	1973	번역 표준 원칙
2814	장기집권	長期執權	prolonged autocratic rule	Janggi jipgwon	Changgi chipkwŏn		번역 표준 원칙
2815	장면 부통령 저격 사건	張勉 副統領 狙擊 事件	assassination attempt on Vice President Chang Myon	Jang Myeon butongnyeong jeogyeok sageon	Chang Myŏn put'ongnyŏng chŏgyŏk sakŏn	1956	번역 표준 원칙
2816	장면 정권	張勉 政權	Chang Myon government	Jang Myeon jeonggwon	Chang Myŏn chŏngkwŏn	1960-1961	번역 표준 원칙

NO	용어	한자	영문	RO	MC	시대 및 연도	출전
2817	장발	長髮	long hair	Jangbal	Changbal		번역 표준 원칙
2818	장발단속	長髮團束	crackdowns on men with long hair	Jangbal dansok	Changbal tansok	1969-1980	번역 표준 원칙
2819	장보고함	張保皐艦	ROKS Chang Bogo submarine	Jangbogoham	Changbogoham	1993	번역 표준 원칙
2820	장애인 차별 금지법	障碍人 差別 禁止法	Act Against Discrimination of Disabled Persons	Jangaein chabyeol geumjibeop	Changaein ch'abyŏl kŭmjipŏp	2009-	번역 표준 원칙
2821	장애인복지	障碍人福祉	welfare for the disabled	Jangaein bokji	Changaein pokchi		번역 표준 원칙
2822	장인환·전명운 의거	張仁煥·田明雲 義擧	assasination of Durham Stevens by Jang In-whan and Jeon Myeong-hun	Jang In-hwan·Jeon Myeong-un uigeo	Chang In-hwan·Chŏn Myŏng-un ŭigŏ	1942	번역 표준 원칙
2823	장진호 전투	長津湖 戰鬪	Battle of Jangjinho Lake	Jangjinho jeontu	Changjinho chŏnt'u	1950	번역 표준 원칙
2824	장학제도	奬學制度	scholarship system	Janghak jedo	Changhak chedo		번역 표준 원칙

NO	용어	한자	영문	RO	MC	시대 및 연도	출전
2825	재2차 석유파동	第2次 石油波動	second oil shock	Je2cha seogyu padong	Che2ch'a sŏgyu p'adong	1978-1981	번역 표준 원칙
2826	재개발지역	再開發地域	redevelopment area	Jaegaebal jiyeok	Chaegaebal chiyŏk		번역 표준 원칙
2827	재건국민운동본부	再建國民運動本部	Headquarters of the National Reconstruction Movement	Jaegeon gungmin undong bonbu	Chaegŏn kungmin undong ponbu	1961-1963	번역 표준 원칙
2828	재건복	再建服	"reconstruction suits" (worn by public servants and teachers under the military dictatorship in the 1960s)	Jaegeonbok	Chaegŏnbok	1965-1970	번역 표준 원칙
2829	재건학교	再建學校	"reconstruction schools" (reference to night schools established after the military coup of May 16, 1961)	Jaegeon hakgyo	Chaegŏn hakkyo		번역 표준 원칙
2830	재건한국독립당	再建韓國獨立黨	Korean Independence Party	Jaegeon hanguk dongnipdang	Chaegŏn han'guk tongniptang	1930-1970	번역 표준 원칙
2831	재난 구호 지원활동	災難 救護 支援活動	disaster relief supporting activities	Jaenan guho jiwon hwaldong	Chaenan kuho chiwon hwaldong	2010	번역 표준 원칙
2832	재난구호작전	災難救護作戰	disaster relief operations (DRO)	Jaenan guho jakjeon	Chenan kuho chakchŏn		번역 표준 원칙

NO	용어	한자	영문	RO	MC	시대 및 연도	출전
2833	재독일 동포연합회	在獨逸 同胞聯合會	Korean People's Association in Germany	Jaedogil dongpo yeonhaphoe	Chaedogil tongp'o yŏnhaphoe	1963-	번역 표준 원칙
2834	재래식무기	在來式武器	conventional weapons (non-nuclear weapons)	Jaeraesik mugi	Chaeraesik mugi		번역 표준 원칙
2835	재만한인사회	在滿韓人社會	Korean community in Manchuria	Jaeman hanin sahoe	Chaeman hain sahoe		번역 표준 원칙
2836	재만한인조국광복회	在滿韓人祖國光復會	Korean Fatherland Restoration Association in Manchuria (KFRAM)	Jaeman hanin joguk gwangbokhoe	Chaeman hanin choguk kwangbokhoe	1936-?	Peter H. Lee, Sourcebook of Korean Civilization(Volume 2), Columbia University Press, 1993,
2837	재무부	財務部	Department of Finance	Jaemubu	Chaemubu	1919-1945	번역 표준 원칙
2838	재미동포 전국연합회	在美同胞 全國聯合會	National Association of Korean Americans	Jaemi dongpo jeonguk yeonhaphoe	Chaemi tongp'o chŏn'guk yŏnhaphoe	1997-	번역 표준 원칙
2839	재미한인50년사	在美韓人50年史	The 50-year History of Korean Americans	Jaemi hanin 50nyeonsa	Chaemi hanin 50yŏnsa	1958	번역 표준 원칙
2840	재미한족연합회	在美韓族聯合會	United Korean Committee in America	Jaemi hanjok yeonhaphoe	Chaemi hanjok yŏnhaphoe	1941	번역 표준 원칙

NO	용어	한자	영문	RO	MC	시대 및 연도	출전
2841	재반격작전	再反擊作戰	counter-offensive operation	Jjaebangyeok jakjeon	Chaebangyŏk chakchŏn	1951-1953	번역 표준 원칙
2842	재벌	財閥	*chaebol* (Korea's family-owned conglomerates)	Jaebeol	Chaebŏl	현대	번역 표준 원칙
2843	재벌개혁	財閥改革	reform of the *chaebol*	Jaebeol gaehyeok	Chaebŏl kaehyŏk		번역 표준 원칙
2844	재북평화통일촉진협의회	在北平和統一促進協議會	(North Korean) Committee for the Peaceful Unification of the Fatherland	Jaebuk pyeonghwa tongil chokjin hyeobuihoe	Chaebuk p'yŏnghwa t'ongil ch'okchin hyŏbŭihoe	1956-	번역 표준 원칙
2845	재산청구권	財産請求權	property claim rights	Jaesan chunggugwon	Chaesan ch'ŏnggukwŏn		번역 표준 원칙
2846	재야운동	在野運動	anti-governmet civil opposition movement	Jaeya undong	Chaeya undong		번역 표준 원칙
2847	재외국민투표권	在外國民投票權	voting rights for overseas Koreans	Jaeoe gungmin tupyogwon	Chaeoe kungmin t'up'yokwŏn	2009-	번역 표준 원칙
2848	재일동포	在日同胞	Korean residents in Japan	Jaeil dongpo	Cheil tongp'o		번역 표준 원칙

NO	용어	한자	영문	RO	MC	시대 및 연도	출전
2849	재일동포 북송	在日同胞北送	repatriation of Korean residents of Japan to North Korea	Jaeil dongpo buksong	Chaeil tongp'o puksong	1959-1967	번역 표준 원칙
2850	재일동포 북송 반대 궐기대회	在日同胞 北送 反對 蹶起大會	rally against the repatriation of Korean residents of Japan to North Korea	Jaeildongpo buksong bandae gwolgidaehoe	Chaeildongp'o puksong pandae kwŏlgidaehoe	1959	번역 표준 원칙
2851	재일본조선노동총동맹	在日本朝鮮勞動總同盟	General Federation of Korean Laborers in Japan	Jaeilbon joseon nodong chongdongmaeng	Chaeilbon chosŏn nodong ch'ongdongmaeng	1925-1929	번역 표준 원칙
2852	재일본조선청년동맹	在日本 朝鮮青年同盟	League of Korean Youth in Japan	Jaeilbon joseon cheongnyeon dongmaeng	Chaeilbon chosŏn chŏngnyŏn tongmaeng	1928	번역 표준 원칙
2853	재일유학생	在日留學生	Koreans studying in Japan	Jaeil yuhaksaeng	Chaeil yuhaksaeng		번역 표준 원칙
2854	재일조선거류민단	在日朝鮮居留民團	Pro-Seoul Federation of Korean Residents in Japan (Mindan)	Jaeil joseon georyumindan	Chaeil chosŏn kŏ ryumindan	1946	번역 표준 원칙
2855	재일조선인연맹	在日朝鮮人聯盟	League of Koreans Residing in Japan (predecessor of Chochongryon)	Jaeil joseonin yeonmaeng	Chaeil chosŏnin yŏnmaeng	1945-1955	번역 표준 원칙
2856	재일한국인의 법적 지위문제	在日韓國人의 法的 地位問題	issues on the legal status of Koreans residing in Japan	Jaeil hanguginui beopjeok jiwi munje	Chaeil han'gugin-ŭi pŏpchŏk chiwi munje		번역 표준 원칙

NO	용어	한자	영문	RO	MC	시대 및 연도	출전
2857	재입국허가제도	再入國許可制度	reentrance admission system	Jaeipguk heoga jedo	Chaeipkuk hŏga chedo		번역 표준 원칙
2858	재정경제위원회	財政經濟委員會	Finance and Economy Committee	Jaejeong gyeongje wiwonhoe	Chaejŏng kyŏngje wiwŏnhoe	현대	기획재정위원회 사이트 http://finance.assembly.go.kr
2859	재중국조선 무정부주의자연맹	在中國朝鮮 無政府主義者聯盟	Korean Anarchist Communist Federation in China	Jaejunggguk joseon mujeongbujuuija yeonmaeng	Chaejungguk chosŏn mujŏngbujuŭija yŏnmaeng	1924	번역 표준 원칙
2860	재중조선공민 총연합회	在中朝鮮公民總聯合會	Korean Citizen's General Association in China	Jaejung joseon gongmin chongyeonhaphoe	Chaejung chosŏn kongmin ch'ongyŏnhaphoe	1991-	번역 표준 원칙
2861	재중조선인총연합회 (재중 조총련)	在中朝鮮人總聯合會(在中 朝總聯)	Korean Citizen's General Association in China	Jaejung joseonin chongyeonhaphoe (jaejung jochongnyeon)	Chaejung chosŏnin ch'ongyŏnhaphoe (chaejung choch'ongnyŏn)	1991-	번역 표준 원칙
2862	재택근무	在宅勤務	telecommuting	Jaetaek geunmu	Chaet'aek kŭnmu		번역 표준 원칙
2863	재향군인회부녀부	在鄉軍人會婦女部	Women's Society of the Korean Veterans Association	Jaehyang guninhoe bunyeobu	Chaehyang kuninhoe punyŏbu		번역 표준 원칙
2864	쟁의권 부활투쟁	爭議權 復活鬪爭	protests for restoration of the right to strike	Jaenguigwon buhwal tujaeng	Chaengŭikwŏn puhwal t'ujaeng	1962	번역 표준 원칙

NO	용어	한자	영문	RO	MC	시대 및 연도	출전
2865	저가항공	低價航空	low-cost airlines	Jeoga hanggong	Chŏka hanggong		번역 표준 원칙
2866	저격여단	狙擊旅團	sniper brigade (of North Korea)	Jeogyeok yeodan	Chŏgyŏk yŏdan		번역 표준 원칙
2867	저곡가정책	低穀價政策	agricultural products price-control policy	Jeogokga jeongchaek	Chŏgokka chŏngch'aek	1970-?	번역 표준 원칙
2868	저공해자동차	低公害自動車	low-emission vehicles	Jeogonghae jadongcha	Chŏgonghae chadongch'a		번역 표준 원칙
2869	저농산물가격정책	低農産物價格政策	low-price policy for farm products	Jeonongsanmul gagyeok jeongchaek	Chŏnongsanmul kakyŏk chŏngch'aek		번역 표준 원칙
2870	저임금정책	低賃金政策	low-wage policy	Jeoimgeum jeongchaek	Chŏimgŭm chŏngch'aek	1970-?	번역 표준 원칙
2871	저축생활	貯蓄生活	"Savings in Everyday Life" (booklet designed to promote savings)	Jeochuk saenghwal	Chŏch'uk saenghwal	1961	번역 표준 원칙
2872	저출산	低出産	low birth rate	Jeochulsan	Chŏch'ulsan		번역 표준 원칙

NO	용어	한자	영문	RO	MC	시대 및 연도	출전
2873	적색노동운동	赤色勞動運動	left-wing labor movement	Jeoksaek nodong undong	Chŏksaek nodong undong		번역 표준 원칙
2874	적색노동조합	赤色勞動組合	left-wing labor Union	Jeoksaek nodongjohap	Chŏksaek nodongjohap	1920	번역 표준 원칙
2875	적색농민조합운동	赤色農民組合運動	Socialist Peasant Association Movement	Jeoksaeng nongmin johap undong	Chŏksaek nongmin chohap undong	1930년대	번역 표준 원칙
2876	적색해안	赤色海岸	Red Beach	Jeoksaek haean	chŏksaek haean		번역 표준 원칙
2877	적화통일	赤化統一	unification under Communism	Jeokhwa tongil	Chŏkhwa t'ongil	1948-?	번역 표준 원칙
2878	전교조 투쟁	全敎組 鬪爭	struggles of the Korean Teachers and Education Workers Union	Jeongyojo tujaeng	chŏngyojo t'ujaeng		번역 표준 원칙
2879	전구 유도탄 방어	戰區 誘導彈 防禦	Theater Missile Defense (TMD)	Jeongu yudotan bangeo	Chŏn'gu yudot'an pangŏ		번역 표준 원칙
2880	전국경제인연합회	全國經濟人聯合會	Korea Businessmen's Association (predecessor of the Korean Federation of Industries)	Jeonguk gyeongjein hyeophoe	Chŏn'guk kyŏngjein hyŏp'oe	1961-1968	번역 표준 원칙

NO	용어	한자	영문	RO	MC	시대 및 연도	출전
2881	전국경제인협회	全國經濟人協會	Association of Korean Industries	Jeonguk gyeongjein hyeophoe	Chŏn'guk kyŏngjein hyŏphoe	1961-1968	번역 표준 원칙
2882	전국구의원	全國區議員	national constituency lawmakers	Jeongukgu uiwon	Chŏngukku ŭiwon		번역 표준 원칙
2883	전국기능경기대회	全國技能競技大會	National Skills Competition	Jeonguk gineung gyeonggi daehoe	Chŏn'guk kinŭng kyŏnggi taehoe	1966-	번역 표준 원칙
2884	전국노동조합협의회	全國勞動組合協議會	National Council of Trade Unions	Jeonguk nodong johap hyeobuihoe	Chŏn'guk nodong chohap hyŏbŭihoe	1959	번역 표준 원칙
2885	전국농민조합총연맹	全國農民組合總聯盟	National Federation of Peasant Unions	Jeonguk nongmin johap chongyeonmaeng	Chŏn'guk nongmin chohap ch'ongyŏnmaeng	1945-	번역 표준 원칙
2886	전국농민회총연맹	全國農民會總聯盟	Korean Peasants League	Jeonguk nongminhoe chongyeonmaeng	Chŏn'guk nongminhoe ch'ongyŏnmaeng	1990-?	번역 표준 원칙
2887	전국대학생대표자 협의회(전대협)	全國大學生代表者 協議會(全大協)	National Council of Korean College Students (Jeondaehyeop)	Jeonguk daehaksaeng daepyoja hyeobuihoe (jeondaehyeop)	Chŏn'guk taehaksaeng taep'yoja hyŏbŭihoe (chŏndaehyŏp)	1987-1993	번역 표준 원칙
2888	전국문화단체 총연합회	全國文化團體 總聯合會	Federation of Korean Cultural Associations	Jeonguk munhwa danche chongyeonhaphoe	Chŏn'guk munhwa tanch'e ch'ongyŏnhap'oe	1947-?	번역 표준 원칙

NO	용어	한자	영문	RO	MC	시대 및 연도	출전
2889	전국민족민주운동연합	全國民族民主運動聯合	National Democratic Movement Federation of Korea	Jeonguk minjok minju undong yeonhap	Chŏn'guk minjok minju undong yŏnhap	1989-1997	번역 표준 원칙
2890	전국민주노동조합총연맹	全國民主勞動組合總聯盟	Korean Confederation of Trade Unions	Jeonguk minju nodong johap chongnyeonmaeng	Chŏn'guk minju nodong chohap ch'ongyŏnmaeng	1995-?	번역 표준 원칙
2891	전국민주청년학생총연맹	全國民主青年學生總聯盟	Democratic Youth League of Korea	Jeonguk minju cheongnyeon haksaeng chongyeonmaeng	Chŏn'guk minju ch'ŏngnyŏn haksaeng ch'ongyŏnmaeng	1974	번역 표준 원칙
2892	전국빈민연합	全國貧民聯合	National Alliance of the Urban Poor	Jeonguk binmin yeonhap	Chŏn'guk pinmin yŏnhap	1989-?	번역 표준 원칙
2893	전국소비자상담망	全國消費者相談網	Consumer Gateway (Internet portal of Korea Consumer Agency)	Jeonguk sobija sangdammang	Chŏnguk sobija sangdammang	2004-	번역 표준 원칙
2894	전국언론노동조합연맹	全國言論勞動組合聯盟	National Union of Media Workers	Jeonguk eollon nodong johap yeonmaeng	Chŏnguk ŏllon nodong johap yŏnmaeng	1988-?	번역 표준 원칙
2895	전국여성농민위원회	全國女性農民委員會	Korean Women Peasant Association	Jeonguk yeoseong nongmin wiwonhoe	Chŏnguk yŏsŏng nongmin wiwŏnhoe	1989	번역 표준 원칙
2896	전국연합진선협회	全國聯合陣線協會	Korean Restoration Movement Federation	Jeonguk yeonhap jinseon hyeophoe	Chŏn'guk yŏnhap chinsŏn hyŏphoe	1939	번역 표준 원칙

NO	용어	한자	영문	RO	MC	시대 및 연도	출전
2897	전국은행노동조합 연합회	全國銀行勞動組合 聯合會	National Federation of Bank Workers' Unions	Jeonguk eunhaeng nodongjohap yeonhaphoe	Chŏn'guk ŭnhaeng nodongjohap yŏnhap'oe	1960-?	번역 표준 원칙
2898	전국청년단체대표자협 의회	全國靑年團體代表者協 議會	National Council of Representatives of Youth Organizations	Jeonguk cheongnyeon danche daepyoja hyeobuihoe	Chŏnguk ch'ŏngnyŏ ndanch'e taep'yoja hyŏb ŭihoe	1987	번역 표준 원칙
2899	전국청년단체총동맹	全國靑年團體總同盟	National Alliance of Youth Organizations	Jeonguk cheongnyeon danche chongdongmaeng	Chŏnguk ch'ŏngnyŏn danch'e ch'ongdongmaeng	1945	번역 표준 원칙
2900	전국체육대회	全國體育大會	National Sports Festival	Jeonguk cheyuk daehoe	Chŏn'guk ch'eyuk taehoe	1920-	번역 표준 원칙
2901	전국토의 요새화	全國土의 要塞化	"fortifying the entire country" (one of Kim Il-sung's Four Military Lines)	Jeonguktoui yosaehwa	Chŏn'gukt'o-ŭi yosaehwa	1962-	번역 표준 원칙
2902	전국학생총동맹	全國學生總同盟	National Students' Alliance	Jeonguk haksaeng chongdongmaeng	Chŏnguk haksaeng ch'ongdongmaeng	1946-1949	번역 표준 원칙
2903	전국환경자원조사	全國環境資源調査	nationwide natural resources survey	Jeonguk hwangyeong jawon josa	Chŏnguk hwangyŏng chawŏn chosa		번역 표준 원칙
2904	전군의 간부화	全軍의 幹部化	"covert all members of the military into cadres" (one of Kim Il-sung's Four Military Lines)	Jeongunui kanbuhwa	Chŏn'gun-ŭi kanbuhwa	1962-?	번역 표준 원칙

NO	용어	한자	영문	RO	MC	시대 및 연도	출전
2905	전군의 현대화	全軍의 現代化	"modernize weaponry" (one of Kim Il-sung's Four Military Lines)	Jeongunui hyeondaehwa	Chŏn'gun-ŭi hyŏndaehwa	1962-	번역 표준 원칙
2906	전권공사	全權公使	minister plenipotentiary	Jeongwon gongsa	Chŏnkwŏn kongsa		번역 표준 원칙
2907	전당대회	全黨大會	national party convention	Jeondang daehoe	Chŏndang taehoe		번역 표준 원칙
2908	전라남도	全羅南道	Jeollanam-do Province	Jeollanam-do	Chŏllanamdo	1896	번역 표준 원칙
2909	전라북도	全羅北道	Jeollabuk-do Province	Jeollabuk-do	Chŏllabukto	1896	번역 표준 원칙
2910	전략무기감축협정	戰略武器減縮協定	Strategic Arms Reduction Talks	Jeollyak mugi gamchuk hyeopjeong	Chŏllyak mugi kamch'uk hyŏpchŏng	1982-?	번역 표준 원칙
2911	전력증강사업	戰力增强事業	Force Improvement Plans (FIP)	Jeonryeok jeunggang saeop	Chŏllyŏk chŭnggang saŏp		번역 표준 원칙
2912	전로한족회	全露韓族會	Association of Ethnic Koreans in Russia	Jeonno hanjokhoe	Chŏllo hanjokhoe	1917-1919	번역 표준 원칙

NO	용어	한자	영문	RO	MC	시대 및 연도	출전
2913	전민족대단결10대강령	全民族大團結10大綱領	Ten-point Program of Great Unity of the Whole Nation for Reunification of the Country	Jeon minjok daedangyeol 10dae gangnyeong	Chŏn minjok taedan'gyŏl 10tae kangnyŏng	1993	번역 표준 원칙
2914	전반적 11년제 의무교육	全般的 11年制 義務敎育	North Korea's universal 11-year compulsory education	Jeonbanjeok 11nyeonje uimugyoyuk	Chŏnbanjŏk 11nyŏnje ŭimugyoyuk	1972-	번역 표준 원칙
2915	전반적 9년제 기술 의무교육	全般的 9年制 技術 義務敎育	North Korea's universal 9-year compulsory technical education	Jeonbanjeok 9nyeonje gisul uimugyoyuk	Chŏnbanjŏk 9nyŏnje kisul ŭimugyoyuk	1967-1974	번역 표준 원칙
2916	전반적 무상치료제	全般的 無償治療制	North Korea's free, uiversal health care system	Jeonbanjeok musang chiryoje	Chŏnbanjŏk musang ch'iryoje	1947-?	번역 표준 원칙
2917	전방무장 및 재급유 지역	前方武裝 및 再給油地域	forward arming and refueling point (FARP)	Jeonbang mujang mit jaegeubyu jiyeok	Chŏnbang mujang mit chaegŭbyu jiyŏk		번역 표준 원칙
2918	전방지휘소 연락반	前方指揮所 連絡班	Advance Command and Liaison Group in Korea (ADCOM)	Jeonbang jihwiso yeollakban	Chŏnbang chihwiso yŏllakpan		번역 표준 원칙
2919	전보국	電報局	Telegraph Bureau	Jeonboguk	Chŏnboguk	1885-1897	번역 표준 원칙
2920	전사자	戰死者	Killed in Action (KIA)	Jeonsaja	Chŏnsaja		번역 표준 원칙

NO	용어	한자	영문	RO	MC	시대 및 연도	출전
2921	전사자확인증	戰死者確認證	letter of confirmation of death in battle	Jeonsaja hwaginjeung	Chŏnsaja hwaginchŭng	1956	번역 표준 원칙
2922	전선교착	戰線膠着	stalemate	Jeonseon gyochak	Chŏnsŏn kyoch'ak		번역 표준 원칙
2923	전술책임지역	戰術責任地域	tactical area of responsibility (TAOR)	Jeonsul chaegim jiyeok	Chŏnsul chaegim chiyŏk		번역 표준 원칙
2924	전시연합대학	戰時聯合大學	Wartime United University	Jeonsi yeonhap daehak	Chŏnsi yŏnhap taehak	1951	한국학중앙연구원,《영문한국백과》-서울대학교
2925	전시작전통제권	戰時作戰統制權	Wartime Operational Control of South Korea's Armed Forces	Jeonsi jakjeon tongjegwon	Chŏnsi chakchŏn t'ongjegwŏn		번역 표준 원칙
2926	전시채권	戰時債券	war bonds	Jeonsi chaegwon	Chŏnsi ch'aekwon		번역 표준 원칙
2927	전시총동원체제	戰時總動員體制	wartime general mobilization	Jeonsi chongdongwon cheje	Chŏnsi ch'ongdongwŏn ch'eje	1938-1945	번역 표준 원칙
2928	전우조	戰友組	buddy system	Jeonujo	Chŏnujo		번역 표준 원칙

NO	용어	한자	영문	RO	MC	시대 및 연도	출전
2929	전인민의 무장화	全人民의 武裝化	"arm the entire people" (one of Kim Il-sung's Four Military Lines)	Jeoninminui mujanghwa	Chŏninmin-ŭi mujanghwa	1962	번역 표준 원칙
2930	전자개표	電子開票	electronic ballot count	Jeonja gaepyo	Chŏnja kaep'yo	2002-	번역 표준 원칙
2931	전자공업육성방안	電子工業育成方案	Electronics Industry Development Plan (1968)	Jeonja gongeop yukseong bangan	Chŏnja kongŏp yuksŏng pangan	1968	번역 표준 원칙
2932	전자공업진흥법	電子工業振興法	Electronics Industry Promotion Act	Jeonja gongeop jinheungbeop	Chŏnja kongŏp chinhŭngpŏp	1968	번역 표준 원칙
2933	전자공업진흥회	電子工業振興會	Electronics Industries Association of Korea (EIAK)	Jeonja gongeop jinheunghoe	Chŏnja kongŏp chinhŭnghoe	1976	번역 표준 원칙
2934	전자산업	電子産業	electronics industry	Jeonja saneop	Chŏnja sanŏp		번역 표준 원칙
2935	전장 가시화	戰場 可視化	visualization of the battlefield	Jeokjang gasihwa	Chŏnjang kasihwa		번역 표준 원칙
2936	전쟁 이외의 작전	戰爭 以外의 作戰	Military Operations Other than War (MOOTW)	Jeonjaeng ioeui jakjeon	Chŏnjaeng ioeŭi chakchŏn		번역 표준 원칙

NO	용어	한자	영문	RO	MC	시대 및 연도	출전
2937	전쟁기념관	戰爭記念館	War Memorial of Korea	Jeonjaeng ginyeomgwan	Chŏnjaeng kinyŏmgwan	1994	번역 표준 원칙
2938	전쟁의 배경과 원인	戰爭의 背景과 原因	background and causes of war	Jeonjaengui baegyeonggwa wonin	Chŏnjaengŭi paegyŏnggwa wonin	1945	번역 표준 원칙
2939	전쟁포로송환	戰爭捕虜送還	Repatriation of POWs	Jeonjaeng poro songhwan	Chŏnjaeng p'oro songhwan	1953	번역 표준 원칙
2940	전쟁회복기	戰爭回復期	war recovery period	Jeonjaeng hoebokgi	Chŏnjaeng hoebokki	1954-1955	번역 표준 원칙
2941	전조선기자대회	全朝鮮記者大會	National Reporters' Rally of 1925	Jeonjoseon gija daehoe	Chŏnjosŏn kija daehoe	1925	번역 표준 원칙
2942	전조선정당사회단체지도자협의회	全朝鮮政黨社會團體指導者協議會	All-Korea Political-Social Parties' Leaders Association	Jeon joseon jeongdang sahoedanche jidoja hyeobuihoe	Chŏn chosŏn chŏngdang sahoedanch'e chidoja hyŏbŭihoe	1948	번역 표준 원칙
2943	전조선제정당사회단체대표자연석회의	全朝鮮諸政黨社會團體代表者連席會議	All-Korea Political-Social Parties' Representatives Joint Coference	Jeon joseon jejeongdang sahoedanche daepyoja yeonseokhoeui	Chŏn chosŏn chejŏngdang sahoedanch'e taep'yoja yŏnsŏkhoeŭi	1948	번역 표준 원칙
2944	전주화약	全州和約	Jeonju Peace Agreement of 1894	Jeonju hwayak	Chŏnju hwayak	1894	번역 표준 원칙

NO	용어	한자	영문	RO	MC	시대 및 연도	출전
2945	전천후농업차관	全天候農業借款	general loan for agricultural development (from IBRD in 1969)	Jeoncheonhu nongeop chagwan	Chŏnch'ŏnhu nongŏp ch'agwan		번역 표준 원칙
2946	전태일분신자살사건	全泰壹焚身自殺事件	self-immolation of labor activist Jeon Tae-il in 1970	Jeon Tae-il bunsin jasal sageon	Chŏn T'ae-il punsin chasal sakŏn	1970	번역 표준 원칙
2947	전투부대	戰鬪部隊	combat unit	Jeontu budae	Chŏnt'u pudae		번역 표준 원칙
2948	전투지역전단	戰鬪地域前端	forward edge of battle area (FEBA)	Jeontujiyeok jeondan	Chŏnt'ujiyŏk chŏndan		번역 표준 원칙
2949	전투지원협조반	戰鬪支援協調班	Combat Support Coordination Team (CSCT)	Jeontujiwon hyeopjoban	Chŏntujiwŏn hyŏpchoban		번역 표준 원칙
2950	전투편성	戰鬪編成	task organization	Jeontu pyeonseong	Chŏntu p'yŏnsŏng		번역 표준 원칙
2951	전투피해평가	戰鬪被害評價	Battle Damage Assessment (BDA)	Jeontu pihae pyeongga	Chŏnt'u pihae p'yongka		번역 표준 원칙
2952	전환국	典圜局	Royal Mint	Jeonhwanguk	Chŏnhwan'guk	1883-1904	한국학중앙연구원, 《영문한국백과》-경제

NO	용어	한자	영문	RO	MC	시대 및 연도	출전
2953	전후 정비기	前後 整備期	post-war reconstruction	Jeonhu jeongbigi	Chŏnhu chŏngbigi	1954	번역 표준 원칙
2954	전후인민경제복구 발전 3개년계획	戰後人民經濟復舊 發展 3個年計劃	North Korea's Three-Year Plan (1954-1956) for Post-War Reconstruction	Jeonhu inmin gyeongje bokgu baljeon 3gaenyeon gyehoek	Chŏnju inmin kyŏngje pokku paljŏn 3gaenyŏn kyehoek	1954-1956	번역 표준 원칙
2955	절대적빈곤	絶對的貧困	absolute poverty	Jeoldaejeok bingon	Chŏldaejŏk pingon		번역 표준 원칙
2956	절량농가	絶糧農家	farming families short of food	Jeollyang nongga	Chŏllyang nongga		번역 표준 원칙
2957	접근로	接近路	avenues of approach	Jepgeullo	Chŏpkŭllo		번역 표준 원칙
2958	정경유착	政經癒着	cozy relations between politics and business	Jeonggyeong yuchak	Chŏnggyŏng yuch'ak		번역 표준 원칙
2959	정군운동	整軍運動	anti-corruption campaign in the military	Jeonggun undong	Chŏnggun undong	1960	번역 표준 원칙
2960	정규직	正規職	permanent employment	Jeonggyujik	Ch'ŏnggyujik		번역 표준 원칙

NO	용어	한자	영문	RO	MC	시대 및 연도	출전
2961	정당공천제	政黨公薦制	party nomination	Jeongdang gongcheonje	Chŏngdang kongch'ŏnje	1954-	번역 표준 원칙
2962	정당대회	政黨大會	party convention	Jeongdang daehoe	Chŏngdang taehoe		번역 표준 원칙
2963	정당명부제	政黨名簿制	party list system	Jeongdang myeongbuje	Chŏngdang myŏngbuje		번역 표준 원칙
2964	정당정치	政黨政治	party politics	Jeongdang jeongchi	Chŏngdang chŏngch'i		번역 표준 원칙
2965	정동구락부	貞洞俱樂部	Chongdong Club	Jeongdong gurakbu	Chŏngdong kurakpu	1894-1910	번역 표준 원칙
2966	정동극장	貞洞劇場	Chongdong Theater	Jeongdong geukjang	Chŏngdong gŭkchang	1995	번역 표준 원칙
2967	정리해고	整理解雇	layoff	Jeongri haego	Chŏngni haego		번역 표준 원칙
2968	정면공격	正面攻擊	frontal attack	Jeongmyeon gonggyeok	Chŏngmyŏn gonggŏk		번역 표준 원칙

NO	용어	한자	영문	RO	MC	시대 및 연도	출전
2969	정무원	政務院	Administration Council	Jeongmuwon	Chŏngmuwŏn	1972-1998	번역 표준 원칙
2970	정무총감	政務總監	Japanese administrative superintendent	Jeongmu chonggam	Chŏngmu ch'onggam	1910-1945	Ki-baik Lee, translated by Edward W. Wagner, A New History of Korea, Harvard University Press, 1984,
2971	정미7조약	丁未7條約	Korea-Japan Protocol of 1907	Jeongmi7joyak	Chŏngmi7choyak	1907	번역 표준 원칙
2972	정미의병	丁未義兵	Righteous Army Struggle of 1907 (following the forced dethronement of Emperor Gojong)	Jeongmi uibyeong	Chŏngmi ŭibyŏng	1907-1910	번역 표준 원칙
2973	정보사회	情報社會	information society	Jeongbo sahoe	Chŏngbo sahoe		번역 표준 원칙
2974	정보준비태세	情報準備態勢	Watch Readiness Condition (WATCHCON)	Jeongbo junbitaese	Chŏngbo junbit'aese		번역 표준 원칙
2975	정보통신기금	情報通信基金	information and telecommunications fund	Jeongbo tongsin gigeum	Chŏngbo t'ongsin gigŭm		번역 표준 원칙
2976	정부 조직법	政府 組織法	Government Organization Act	Jeongbu jojikbeop	Chŏngbu chojikpŏp	1948-	번역 표준 원칙

NO	용어	한자	영문	RO	MC	시대 및 연도	출전
2977	정부 차관	政府 借款	government loans	Jeongbu chagwan	Chŏngbu ch'agwan		번역 표준 원칙
2978	정부미	政府米	government rice stocks	Jeongbumi	Chŏngbumi		번역 표준 원칙
2979	정부주도형 경제개발	政府主導形 經濟開發	government-led economic development	Jeongbu judohyeong gyeongje gaebal	Chŏngbu chudohyŏng kyŏngje kaebal		번역 표준 원칙
2980	정신여학교	貞信女學校	Chungsin Girls' School (now Chungshin Girls' High School)	Jeongsin yeohakgyo	Chŏngsin yŏhakkyo	1909	번역 표준 원칙
2981	정우회	政友會	Pro-Japanese Political Friends Association (Jeonguhoe)	Jeonguhoe	Chŏnguhoe	1910	번역 표준 원칙
2982	정우회선언	正友會宣言	Declaration of the Political Friends Association	Jeonguhoe seoneon	Chŏnguhoe sŏnŏn	1926	번역 표준 원칙
2983	정유공장	精油工場	oil refinery	Jeongyu gongjang	Chŏngyu kongjang		번역 표준 원칙
2984	정의부	正義府	Jeonguibu (pro-independence armed unit)	Jeonguibu	Chŏngŭibu	1925-1927	번역 표준 원칙

NO	용어	한자	영문	RO	MC	시대 및 연도	출전
2985	정전3인단	停戰3人團	Three-man Group on the Armistice	Jeongjeon 3indan	Chŏngjŏn 3indan	1950	번역 표준 원칙
2986	정전협정	停戰協定	Armistice Agreement	Jeongjeon hyeopjeong	Chŏngjŏn hyŏpchŏng	1953	번역 표준 원칙
2987	정전협정 위반	停戰協定 違反	Violation of the Armistice Agreement	Jeongjeon hyeopjeong wiban	Chŏngjŏn hyŏpchŏng wiban		First Korean Congress 회의록
2988	정전협정서	停戰協定書	Armistice Agreement	Jeongjeon hyeopjeongseo	Chŏngjŏn hyŏpchŏngsŏ	1953	번역 표준 원칙
2989	정족산성	鼎足山城	Jeongjok-sanseong Mountain Fortress	Jeongjok sanseong	Chŏngjok sansŏng		번역 표준 원칙
2990	정찰국	偵察局	reconnaissance division	Jeongchalguk	Chŏngch'alguk	1948-	번역 표준 원칙
2991	정찰여단	偵察旅團	reconnaissance brigade	Jeongchal yeodan	Chŏngch'al yŏdan		번역 표준 원칙
2992	정체성론	停滯性論	stagnation theory	Jeongcheseongnon	Chŏngch'esŏngnon	1890년대-1945	번역 표준 원칙

NO	용어	한자	영문	RO	MC	시대 및 연도	출전
2993	정치	政治	politics	Jeongchi	Chŏngch'i		한국학중앙연구원, 《영문한국백과》-정치
2994	정치간부회의	政治幹部會議	political executive council	Jeongchi ganbu hoeui	Chŏngch'i kanbu hoeŭi		번역 표준 원칙
2995	정치국	政治局	politburo	Jeongchiguk	Chŏngch'iguk		번역 표준 원칙
2996	정치보복	政治報復	political retaliation	Jeongchi bobok	Chŏngch'i popok		번역 표준 원칙
2997	정치사령부	政治司令部	political command	Jeongchi saryeongbu	Chŏngch'i saryŏngbu		번역 표준 원칙
2998	정치위원제	政治委員制	political representative system	Jeongchi wiwonje	Chŏngch'i wiwŏnje	1960년대 후반	번역 표준 원칙
2999	정치인 연금 해제	政治人 軟禁 解除	release of politicians under house arrest	Jeongchiin yeongeum haeje	Chŏngch'iin yŏngŭm haeje		번역 표준 원칙
3000	정치자금	政治資金	political funds	Jeongchi jageum	Chŏngch'i chagŭm		번역 표준 원칙

NO	용어	한자	영문	RO	MC	시대 및 연도	출전
3001	정치자금 수수금지	政治資金 授受禁止	prohibition of illegal political funding	Jeongchi jageum susu geumji	Chŏngch'i chagŭm susu kŭmji		번역 표준 원칙
3002	정치지도부	政治指導部	political leadership	Jeongchi jidobu	Chŏngch'I chidobu		번역 표준 원칙
3003	정치풍토쇄신을 위한 특별 조치법	政治風土刷新을 위한 特別 措置法	Special Act on Reform of the Political Culture	Jeongchi pungto swaesin-eul wihan teukbyeol jochibeop	Chŏngch'i p'ungt'o swaesin-ŭl wihan t'ŭkpyŏl choch'ibŏp	1980-1988	번역 표준 원칙
3004	정치활동금지해제	政治活動禁止解除	lifting of prohibition on political activity	Jeongchi hwaldong geumji haeje	Chŏngch'i hwaltong kŭmji haeje		번역 표준 원칙
3005	정치활동정화법	政治活動淨化法	Political Activity Purification Act	Jeongchi hwaldong jeonghwabeop	Chŏngch'i hwaltong chŏnghwapŏp	1962	번역 표준 원칙
3006	정판사 위폐 사건	精版社 僞幣 事件	Korean Communist Party's issue of counterfeit notes	Jeongpansa wipye sageon	Chŏngp'ansa wip'ye sakŏn	1946	번역 표준 원칙
3007	정평 적색농민조합	定平 赤色農民組合	Jeongpyeong Red Peasant Union	Jeongpyeong jeoksaek nongmin johap	Chŏngp'yŏng chŏksaek nongmin chohap	1930-1934	번역 표준 원칙
3008	정한론	征韓論	Seikanron (debate on conquering Korea)	Jeonghannon	Chŏnghannon	1870-1873	번역 표준 원칙

NO	용어	한자	영문	RO	MC	시대 및 연도	출전
3009	정화운동	淨化運動	"social purification" movement (1980s)	Jeonghwa undong	Chŏnghwa undong		번역 표준 원칙
3010	제1차 남북체육회담	第1次 南北體育會談	Frist Inter-Korean Sports Talks (1963)	Je 1cha nambuk cheyuk hoedam	Che 1ch'a nambuk ch'eyuk hoedam	1963	번역 표준 원칙
3011	제1차 민간경제 교섭단	第1次 民間經濟 交涉團	Frist Private-sector Economic Negotiation Delegation (formed to seek loans from the U.S. and Europe in 1961)	Je 1cha mingan gyeongje gyoseopdan	Che 1ch'a mingan gyŏngje gyosŏptan	1961	번역 표준 원칙
3012	제1호 땅굴 발견	第1號 땅窟 發見	discovery of first North Korean infiltration tunnel in the Demilitarized Zone (DMZ) in 1974	Je 1ho ttanggul balgyeon	Che 1ho ttanggul palgyŏn	1974	번역 표준 원칙
3013	제1회 전국 음악 경연대회	第1回 全國 音樂 競演 大會	Frist National Music Competition (held by the Culture Ministry in 1946)	Je 1hoe jeonguk eumak gyeongyeon daehoe	Che 1hoe chŏnguk ŭmak kyŏngyŏn taehoe	1946	번역 표준 원칙
3014	제2차 남북조절 위원회	第2次 南北調節 委員會	second Inter-Korean Arbitration Board	Je 2cha nambuk jojeol wiwonhoe	Che 2ch'a nambuk chojŏl wiwŏnhoe	1972	번역 표준 원칙
3015	제13대 대통령선거	第13代 大統領選擧	13th president election	Je13dae daetongnyeong seongeo	Che13dae taet'ongnyŏng sŏngŏ	1987	번역 표준 원칙
3016	제1공수여단	第1空輸旅團	First Airborne Troops Brigade	Je1 gongsuyeodan	Che1 kongsuyŏdan		번역 표준 원칙

NO	용어	한자	영문	RO	MC	시대 및 연도	출전
3017	제1공화국	第1共和國	First Republic	Je1 gonghwaguk	Che1 konghwaguk	1948-1960	번역 표준 원칙
3018	제1극동 전선군 (소련)	第1極東 戰線軍 (蘇聯)	First Far Eastern Front (Soviet Union)	Je1 geukdong jeonseongun (soryeon)	Che1 kŭktong chŏnsŏn'gun (soryŏn)		번역 표준 원칙
3019	제1기 고로	第1期 高爐	(Korea's) first blast furnace	Je1gi goro	Che1ki koro	1973	번역 표준 원칙
3020	제1야전군	第1野戰軍	First Republic of Korea Field Army (FROKA)	Je1yajeongun	Che1yajŏn'gun	1953	번역 표준 원칙
3021	제1차 경제개발계획	第1次 經濟開發計劃	First Five-Year Economic Development Plan	Je1cha gyeongje gebal gyehoek	Che1ch'a kyŏngje kaebal kyehoek	1962-1966	번역 표준 원칙
3022	제1차 광부협정	第1次 鑛夫協定	First Agreement on the Dispatch of Korean Men to German Mines (1963)	Je1cha gwangbu hyeopjeong	Che1ch'a kwangbu hyŏpchŏng	1963	번역 표준 원칙
3023	제1차 국공합작	第1次 國共合作	First United Front (between Nationalist and Communist Parities of China)	Je1cha gukgong hapjak	Che1ch'a kukkong hapchak	1924	번역 표준 원칙
3024	제1차 상해사변	第1次 上海事變	First Battle of Shanghai of 1932	Je1cha sanghaesabyeon	Che1ch'a sanghaesabyŏn	1932	번역 표준 원칙

NO	용어	한자	영문	RO	MC	시대 및 연도	출전
3025	제1차 석유파동	第1次 石油波動	first oil shock (1973)	Je1cha seogyu padong	Che1ch'a sŏgyu p'adong	1973	번역 표준 원칙
3026	제1차 세계대전	第1次 世界大戰	First World War	Je1cha segye daejeon	Che1ch'a segye taejŏn	1914-1918	번역 표준 원칙
3027	제1차 연평해전	第1次 延坪海戰	First Yeonpyeong Naval Battle (1999)	Je1cha yeonpyeong haejeon	Che1ch'a yŏnpyŏng haejŏn	1999.6	번역 표준 원칙
3028	제1차 조선공산당 사건	第1次 朝鮮共産黨 事件	First Korean Communist Party Incident of 1925	Je1cha joseon gongsandang sageon	Che1ch'a chosŏn kongsandang sakŏn	1925	번역 표준 원칙
3029	제1차 한인회의	第1次 韓人會議	First Korean Congress	Je1cha haninhoeyui	Che1ch'a haninhoeŭi	1919	번역 표준 원칙
3030	제1차 한일협약	第1次 韓日協約	First Korea-Japan Protocol of 1904	Je1cha hanil hyeobyak	Che1ch'a hanil hyŏbyak	1904	번역 표준 원칙
3031	제1차 휴전회담	第1次 休戰會談	First Truce Talks	Je1cha hyujeonhoedam	Che1ch'a hyujŏnhoedam	1951	번역 표준 원칙
3032	제1회 수출의 날 기념식	第1回 輸出의 날 紀念式	First Export Day Ceremony	Je1hoe suchului nal ginyeomsik	Che1hoe such'urŭi nal kinyŏmsik	1964	번역 표준 원칙

NO	용어	한자	영문	RO	MC	시대 및 연도	출전
3033	제1회 영일동맹(영일동맹)	第1會 英日同盟(英日同盟)	First Anglo-Japanese Alliance of 1902	Je1hoe yeongildongmaeng (yeongildongmaeng)	Che1hoe yŏngiltongmaeng (yŏngiltongmaeng)	1902	번역 표준 원칙
3034	제1회 한국광고인 대상	第1回 韓國廣告人 大賞	First Korea Advertising Awards	Je1hoe hanguk gwanggoin daesang	Che1hoe han'guk kwanggoin daesang	1974	번역 표준 원칙
3035	제1회 한국무역 박람회	第1回 韓國貿易 博覽會	First Korean Trade Fair (1968)	Je1hoe hanguk muyeok bangnamhoe	Che1hoe han'guk muyŏk pangnamhoe	1968	번역 표준 원칙
3036	제2 극동전선군	第2 極東戰線軍	Second Far Eastern Front Units (Soviet Union)	Je2 geukdong jeonseongun	Che2 kŭktong chŏnsŏn'gun		번역 표준 원칙
3037	제2 중부고속도로	第2 中部高速道路	Second Jungbu Expressway	Je2 Jungbu gosokdoro	Che2 chungbu kosoktoro	2001	번역 표준 원칙
3038	제27 보병연대 지휘소	第27 步兵聯隊 指揮所	Command Post of the 27th Infantry Regiment	Je27 bobyeong yeondae jihwiso	Che27 bobyŏng yŏndae jihwiso		번역 표준 원칙
3039	제2경인고속도로	第2京仁高速道路	Second Gyeongin Expressway	Je2 gyeongin gosokdoro	Che2 kyŏngin kosoktoro	1994	번역 표준 원칙
3040	제2공화국	第2共和國	Second Republic	Je2 gonghwaguk	Che2 konghwaguk	1960-1961	번역 표준 원칙

NO	용어	한자	영문	RO	MC	시대 및 연도	출전
3041	제2대 군정청 장관	第2代 軍政廳 長官	Second Military Government Minister	Je2dae gunjeongcheong janggwan	Che2dae kunchŏngch'ŏng changgwan		번역 표준 원칙
3042	제2의 천리마 대진군 운동	第2의 千里馬 大進軍 運動	Second Great Chollima Movement	Je2ui cheollima daejingun undong	Che2-ŭi ch'ŏllima taejin'gun undong	1999-?	번역 표준 원칙
3043	제2정유공장	第2精油工場	Oil Refinery No. 2	Je2 jeongyu gongjang	Che2 chŏngyu gongjang	1966	번역 표준 원칙
3044	제2차 경제개발5개년 계획 1967-1971	第2次 經濟開發5個年計劃 1967-1971	Second Five-Year Economic Development Plan 1967-1971	Je2cha gyeongje gaebal 5gaenyeon gyehoek 1967-1971	Che2ch'a kyŏngje kaebal 5kaenyŏn kyehoek 1967-1971	1966	번역 표준 원칙
3045	제2차 국공합작	第2次 國共合作	Second United Front (between Nationalist and Communist Parities of China)	Je2cha gukgong hapjak	Che2ch'a gukkong hapchak	1937-1945	번역 표준 원칙
3046	제2차 대학정비방안	第2次 大學整備方案	Second University Restructuring Plan (August 1961)	Je2cha daehak jeongbibangan	Che2ch'a taehak chŏngbibangan	1961	번역 표준 원칙
3047	제2차 마산사건	第2次 馬山事件	Second Masan Democratic Protest (April 11, 1960)	Je2cha masan sageon	Che2ch'a masan sakkŏn	1960	번역 표준 원칙
3048	제2차 상해사변	第2次 上海事變	Second Battle of Shanghai (1937)	Je2cha sanghae sabyeon	Che2ch'a sanghae sabyŏn	1937	번역 표준 원칙

NO	용어	한자	영문	RO	MC	시대 및 연도	출전
3049	제2차 세계대전	第2次 世界大戰	Second World War	Je2cha segye daejeon	Che2ch'a segye taejŏn	1939-1945	번역 표준 원칙
3050	제2차 연평해전	第2次 延坪海戰	Second Yeonpyeong Naval Battle (2002)	Je2cha yeonpyeong haejeon	Che2ch'a yŏnpyŏng haejŏn	2002.6	번역 표준 원칙
3051	제2차 조선공산당 사건	第2次 朝鮮共産黨 事件	Second Communist Party of Korea Incident of 1926 (attempt at reviving independence protests of 1919)	Je2cha joseon gongsandang sageon	Che2ch'a chosŏn kongsandang sakŏn	1926	번역 표준 원칙
3052	제2차 코민테른대회	第2次 코민테른大會	2nd World Congress of the Comintern (1920)	Je2cha komintereun daehoe	Che2ch'a kŏmintern taehoe	1920. 7. 19	번역 표준 원칙
3053	제3공화국	第3共和國	Third Republic	Je3 gonghwaguk	Che3 konghwaguk	1961-1972	번역 표준 원칙
3054	제3대 민의원선거	第3代 民議員選擧	third House of Representatives election	Je3dae minuiwon seongeo	Che3dae minŭiwŏn sŏngŏ	1954	번역 표준 원칙
3055	제3세계	第3世界	Third World	Je3segye	Che3segye		번역 표준 원칙
3056	제3세계 국가에 대한 다변외교	第3世界 國家에 對한 多邊外交	multilaterial diplomacy toward Third World countries	Je3segye gukgae daehan dabyeon oegyo	Che3segye kukka-e taehan tabyŏn oegyo		번역 표준 원칙

NO	용어	한자	영문	RO	MC	시대 및 연도	출전
3057	제3야전군	第3野戰軍	Third ROK Field Army (TROKA)	Je3yajeongun	Che3yajŏn'gun		번역 표준 원칙
3058	제3자 개입금지	第3者 介入禁止	prohibition of third-party intervention in labor-management relations	Je3ja gaeip geumji	Che3ja kaeip kŭmji	1980	번역 표준 원칙
3059	제3제철 건설계획	第3製鐵 建設計劃	Steel Mill No. 3 construction plan	Je3 jecheol geonseol gyehoek	Che3 chech'ŏl kŏnsŏl kyehoek		번역 표준 원칙
3060	제3차 7개년 경제계획	第3次 7個年 經濟計劃	North Korea's Third Seven-Year Economic Plan (1987-93)	Je3cha 7gaenyeon gyeongje gyehoek	Che3ch'a 7gaenyŏn kyŏngje kyehoek	1987-1993	번역 표준 원칙
3061	제3차 경제개발5개년계획	第3次 經濟開發五個年 計劃	Third Five-Year Economic Development Plan 1972-1976	Je3cha gyeongje gaebal 5gaenyeon gyehoek	Che3ch'a kyŏngje kaebal 5kaenyŏn kyehoek	1971	번역 표준 원칙
3062	제3차 범시민궐기대회	第3次 汎市民蹶起大會	third popular rally for democracy (May 25, 1980)	Je3cha beomsimin gwolgi daehoe	Che3ch'a pŏmsimin kwŏlgi taehoe	1980	번역 표준 원칙
3063	제3차 세계종교의회 개최	第3次 世界宗教議會 開催	hosting the Third Congress of the World's Religions	Je3cha segye jonggyo uihoe gaechoe	Che3ch'a segye jonggyo ŭihoe kaech'oe	1992	번역 표준 원칙
3064	제3차 조선공산당 사건	第3次 朝鮮共產黨 事件	Third Communist Party of Korea Incident of 1928	Je3cha joseon gongsandang sageon	Che3ch'a chosŏn kongsandang sakŏn	1928	번역 표준 원칙

NO	용어	한자	영문	RO	MC	시대 및 연도	출전
3065	제3차 한일협약(정미7조약)	第3次 韓日協約(丁未7條約)	Korea-Japan Abdication Agreement of 1907	Je3cha hanil hyeobyak (jeongmi 7joyak)	Che3ch'a hanil hyŏbyak (chŏngmi 7choyak)	1907	번역 표준 원칙
3066	제4공화국	第4共和國	Fourth Republic	Je4 gonghwaguk	Che4 konghwaguk	1972-1981	번역 표준 원칙
3067	제4대 민의원선거	第4代 民議員選擧	fourth House of Representatives election	Je4dae minuiwon seongeo	Che4dae minŭiwŏn sŏngŏ	1958	번역 표준 원칙
3068	제5공화국	第5共和國	Fifth Republic	Je5 gonghwaguk	Che5 konghwaguk	1981-1988	번역 표준 원칙
3069	제5공화국 헌법	第5共和國 憲法	Constitution of the Fifth Republic	Je5 gonghwaguk heonbeop	Che5 konghwaguk hŏnpŏp	1980	번역 표준 원칙
3070	제5차 개헌	第5次 改憲	fifth constitutional amendment	Je5cha gaeheon	Che5ch'a kaehŏn	1962	번역 표준 원칙
3071	제5차 아세아민족 반공대회	第5次 亞細亞民族 反共大會	Fifth Congress of the Asian Peoples' Anti-Communist League	Je5cha asea minjok bangong daehoe aelbeom	Che5ch'a asea minjok pan'gong taehoe aelbŏm	1959	번역 표준 원칙
3072	제6공화국	第6共和國	Sixth Republic	Je6 gonghwaguk	Che6 konghwaguk	1988-?	번역 표준 원칙

NO	용어	한자	영문	RO	MC	시대 및 연도	출전
3073	제7대 국회의원선거(6·8 총선)	第7代 國會議員選擧(6·8 總選)	June 8 general election (1967)	Je7dae gukhoeuiwon seongeo (6·8 chongseon)	Che7dae kukhoeŭiwŏn sŏngŏ (6·8 chongsŏn)	1967	번역 표준 원칙
3074	제7차 개헌 (유신헌법)	第7次 改憲 (維新憲法)	Seventh Constitutional Amendment (Yushin Constitution)	Je7cha gaeheon (yusin heonbeop)	Che7ch'a kaehŏn (yusin hŏnpŏp)	1972.12.27	번역 표준 원칙
3075	제8차 개헌	第8次 改憲	eighth constitutional amendment	Je8cha gaeheon	Che8ch'a kaehŏn	1980	번역 표준 원칙
3076	제8특수군단사령부	第8特殊軍團司令部	Eighth Special Forces Command	Je8 teuksugundan saryeongbu	Che8 t'ŭksukundan saryŏngbu	1969	번역 표준 원칙
3077	제공권	制空權	Air Force supremacy	Jegonggwon	Chegongkwŏn		번역 표준 원칙
3078	제국신문	帝國新聞	*Jeguk Shinmun* (*Imperial Post*)	Jeguksinmun	Cheguksinmun	1898-1910	번역 표준 원칙
3079	제국주의	帝國主義	imperialism	Jegukjuui	Chegukjuŭi		번역 표준 원칙
3080	제네럴서만호	General Sherman號	the *General Sherman*	Jeneoreol syeomon ho	Chenerŏl syŏman ho	1866	번역 표준 원칙

NO	용어	한자	영문	RO	MC	시대 및 연도	출전
3081	제네럴셔먼호 사건	General Sherman號 事件	General Sherman Incident	Jeneoreol syeomeon ho sageon	Chenerŏl syŏman ho sakŏn	1866	번역 표준 원칙
3082	제네바협정	Geneva協定	Geneva Conventions	Jeneba hyeopjeong	Cheneba hyŏpchŏng	1954	번역 표준 원칙
3083	제네바회담	Geneva會談	Geneva Conference (1954)	Jeneba hoedam	Cheneba hoedam	1954	번역 표준 원칙
3084	제니스라디오	Zenith Radio	Zenith Radio	Jeniseu radio	Chenisŭ radio		번역 표준 원칙
3085	제당공업	製糖工業	sugar manufacturing	Jedang gongeop	Chedang kongŏp		번역 표준 원칙
3086	제마부대	濟馬部隊	Jema Unit, the 320th Medical Assistance Unit	Jemabudae	Chemabudae	2003	번역 표준 원칙
3087	제물포조약	濟物浦條約	Treaty of Jemulpo of 1882	Jemulpo joyak	Chemulp'o choyak	1882	번역 표준 원칙
3088	제병협동부대	諸兵協同部隊	combined arms unit	Jebyeong hyeopdong budae	Chebyŏng hyŏptong pudae		번역 표준 원칙

NO	용어	한자	영문	RO	MC	시대 및 연도	출전
3089	제분공업	製粉工業	milling industry	Jebun gongeop	Chebun kongŏp		번역 표준 원칙
3090	제암리학살사건	堤巖里虐殺事件	Jeam-ri Massacre	Jeamni haksal sageon	Cheam-ri haksal sakŏn	1919	번역 표준 원칙
3091	제주 4·3사건	濟州 4·3事件	April 3 Jeju Incident (1948)	Jeju 4·3sageon	Cheju 4·3sakŏn	1948	번역 표준 원칙
3092	제주 4·3사건 진상 규명 및 희생자 명예 회복에 관한 특별법	濟州 4·3事件 眞像 糾明 및 犧牲者 名譽回 復에 關한 特別法	Special Act on Fact Finding of the April 3 Jeju Incident and Restoring the Honor of Victims	Jeju 4·3sageon jinsang gumyeong mit huisaengja myeongye hoeboge gwanhan teukbyeolbeop	Cheju 4·3sakŏn chinsang kyumyŏng mit hŭisaengja myŏngye hoebok-e kwanhan t'ŭkpyŏlpŏp	2000	번역 표준 원칙
3093	제주 올레길	濟州 올레길	Jeju Olle trails	Jeju ollegil	Cheju ollegil		번역 표준 원칙
3094	제주 칠머리당굿	濟州 칠머리당굿	Jeju Chilmeori Dang-gut (Worship Rite for the Tutelary Deities of Land and of Sea at Chilmeori Shrine, Geonip-dong, Jeju Island)	Jeju chilmeoridanggut	Cheju ch'ilmŏridanggut		국사편찬위원회
3095	제주 화산섬, 용암동굴	濟州 火山섬, 熔岩洞窟	Jeju Hwasanseom, Yongamdonggul (Jeju Volcanic Island and Lava Tubes)	Jeju hwasanseom, yongam donggul	Cheju hwasansŏm, yongam tonggul		번역 표준 원칙
3096	제주도	濟州島	Jeju Island / Jeju-do	Jeju-do	Chejudo	1946-?	번역 표준 원칙

NO	용어	한자	영문	RO	MC	시대 및 연도	출전
3097	제주도 비상경비 사령부	濟州道 非常警備 司令部	Jeju-do Garrison Command	Jejudo bisang gyeongbi saryeongbu	Cheju-to pisang kyŏngbi saryŏngbu	1948-1949	번역 표준 원칙
3098	제주도 지구전투 사령부	濟州道 地區戰鬪 司令部	Jeju-do Area Command Post	Jejudo jigu jeontu saryeongbu	Cheju-to chigu chŏnt'u saryŏngbu	1949	번역 표준 원칙
3099	제주도지구 계엄 선포에 관한건 공포 (대통령령제31호)	濟州道地區 戒嚴 宣布에 關한件 公布 (大統領令第31號)	Announcement of the Declaration of Martial Law over Jeju-do (Presidential Decree No. 31)	Jejudo jigu gyeum seonpoe gwanhan geon gongpo (daetongnyeongnyeong je31ho)	Cheju-do chigu kyeŏm sŏnp'o-e kwanhan kŏn kongp'o (taet'ongnyŏngnyŏng che31ho)	1948	번역 표준 원칙
3100	제중원	濟衆院	Jejungwon (now Severance Hospital)	Jejungwon	Jejungwon	1885-1904	번역 표준 원칙
3101	제폭구민	除暴救民	"Expel the tyrants and save the people" (slogan of the Donghak Peasant Movement)	Jepokgumin	Chep'okkumin	1894-1895	번역 표준 원칙
3102	제해권	制海權	command of the sea	Jehaegwon	Chehaekwŏn		번역 표준 원칙
3103	제헌 국새	制憲 國璽	Great Seal of Korea	Jeheon guksae	Chehŏn kuksae	1949-1962	번역 표준 원칙
3104	제헌국회	制憲國會	Constituent Legislatives	Jeheon gukhoe	Chehŏn kukhoe	1948-1950	번역 표준 원칙

NO	용어	한자	영문	RO	MC	시대 및 연도	출전
3105	조·로밀약	朝·露密約	Korea-Russia Secret Treaties of 1885-1886	Joro miryak	Choro miryak	1885-1886	번역 표준 원칙
3106	조·로수호통상조약	朝·露修好通商條約	Treaty of Friendship and Commerce between Korea and Russia, 1884	Joro suho tongsang joyak	Choro suho t'ongsang choyak	1884	번역 표준 원칙
3107	조·소 우호협조 및 호상원조 조약	朝·蘇 友好協調 및 互相援助 條約	Treaty of Friendship, Cooperation and Mutual Assistance between the Democratic People's Republic of Korea and the Soviet Union	Jo·so uho hyeopjo mit hosang wonjo joyak	Cho·So uho hyŏpcho mit hosang wŏnjo choyak	1961-?	번역 표준 원칙
3108	조경모귀	朝耕暮歸	"Farming (in Gando) in the morning, returning home (to Korea) in the evening"	Jogyeongmogwi	Chogyŏngmogwi		번역 표준 원칙
3109	조계종	曹溪宗	Jogye Order of Korean Buddhism	Jogyejong	Chogyejong		번역 표준 원칙
3110	조공관계	朝貢關係	tributary relations	Jogong gwangye	Chogong kwan'gye		번역 표준 원칙
3111	조국근대화	祖國近代化	"modernization of the fatherland"	Joguk geundaehwa	Choguk kŭndaehwa		번역 표준 원칙
3112	조국의 평화통일을 지향하는 헌법개정안	祖國의 平和統一을 指向하는 憲法改正案	Proposal for Constitutional Amendment for Peaceful National Unification	Jogugui pyeonghwa tongileul jihyanghaneun heonbeop gaejeongan	Chogugŭi p'yŏnghwa t'ongirŭl chihyanghanŭn hŏnpŏp kaechŏngan	1972	번역 표준 원칙

NO	용어	한자	영문	RO	MC	시대 및 연도	출전
3113	조국통일5대강령	祖國統一5大綱領	North Korea's Five-point Policy for National Unification	Joguk tongil 5dae gangnyeong	Choguk tʻǒngil 5tae kangnyǒng	1973	번역 표준 원칙
3114	조국통일민주주의전선	祖國統一民主主義戰線	Democratic Front for Reunification of the Fatherland	Joguk tongil minjujuui jeonseon	Choguk tʻongil minjujuǔi chǒnsǒn	1949	번역 표준 원칙
3115	조국통일범민족연합	祖國統一汎民族聯合	Pan-Korean Alliance for National Reunification	Joguk tongil beomminjok yeonhap	Choguk tʻongil pǒmminjok yǒnhap	1990-	번역 표준 원칙
3116	조국평화통일위원회	祖國平和統一委員會	Committee for the Peaceful Reunification of the Fatherland	Joguk pyeonghwa tongil wiwonhoe	Choguk pʻyǒnghwa tʻongil wiwǒnhoe	1961	번역 표준 원칙
3117	조국해방전쟁	祖國解放戰爭	National Liberation War	Joguk haebang jeonjaeng	Choguk haebang chǒnjaeng	1950-1953	번역 표준 원칙
3118	조기유학	早期留學	study abroad at an early age	Jogiyuhak	Chogiyuhak		번역 표준 원칙
3119	조달청	調達廳	Public Procurement Service (PPS)	Jodalcheong	Chodalchʻǒng	1949-?	번역 표준 원칙
3120	조먹수호통상조약	朝德修好通商條約	Treaty of Amity and Commerce between Korea and Germany, 1883	Jodeok suho tongsang joyak	Chodǒk suho tʻongsang choyak	1883	번역 표준 원칙

NO	용어	한자	영문	RO	MC	시대 및 연도	출전
3121	조력발전소	潮力發電所	tidal power plant	Joryeok baljeonso	Choryŏk paljŏnso		번역 표준 원칙
3122	조로육로통상조약	朝露陸路通商條約	Overland Trade Agreement between Korea and Russia, 1888	Joro yungno tongsang joyak	Choro yungno t'ongsang choyak	1888	번역 표준 원칙
3123	조류인플루엔자 사태	鳥類influenza 事態	avian flu outbreak	Joryu inpeulluenja satae	Choryu inp'ŭlluenja satae		번역 표준 원칙
3124	조미수호통상조약	朝美修好通商條約	Treaty of Peace, Amity, Commerce and Navigation between Korea and the United States, 1882	Jomi suho tongsang joyak	Chomi suho t'ongsang choyak	1882	번역 표준 원칙
3125	조법수호통상조약	朝法修好通商條約	Treaty of Amity, Commerce and Navigation between Korea and France, 1886	Jobeop suho tongsang joyak	Chobŏp suho t'ongsang choyak	1886	번역 표준 원칙
3126	조사시찰단	朝士視察團	Korean Courtiers' Observation Mission to Japan in 1881	Josa sichaldan	Chosa sich'altan	1881	번역 표준 원칙
3127	조선YMCA연합회	朝鮮YMCA聯合會	YMCA Korea	Joseon YMCA yeonhaphoe	Chosŏn YMCA yŏnhaphoe	1903-?	번역 표준 원칙
3128	조선건국준비위원회	朝鮮建國準備委員會	Prepatory Committee for Nation Building	Joseon geonguk junbi wiwonhoe	Chosŏn kŏn'guk chunbi wiwŏnhoe	1945	번역 표준 원칙

NO	용어	한자	영문	RO	MC	시대 및 연도	출전
3129	조선공산당	朝鮮共産黨	Korean Communist Party	Joseon gongsandang	Chosŏn kongsandang	1925-1928	번역 표준 원칙
3130	조선공산당 북조선 분국	朝鮮共産黨 北朝鮮 分局	North Korea Bureau of the Korean Communist Party	Joseon gongsandang bukjoseon bunguk	Chosŏn kongsandang pukchosŏn pun'guk	1945-1946	번역 표준 원칙
3131	조선공산당 재건운동	朝鮮共産黨 再健運動	Korean Communist Party Reconstruction Movement	Joseon gongsandang jaegeon undong	Chosŏn kongsandang chaegŏn undong	1925-1928	국사편찬위원회
3132	조선공산당선언	朝鮮共産黨宣言	Declaration of the Korean Communist Party (1926)	Joseon gongsandang seoneon	Chosŏn kongsandang sŏnŏn	1926	번역 표준 원칙
3133	조선공업육성방안	造船工業育成方案	measures to foster the shipbuilding industry	Joseon gongeop yukseong bangan	Chosŏn kongŏp yuksŏng pangan		번역 표준 원칙
3134	조선공업육성법	造船工業育成法	Shipbuilding Industry Promotion Act	Joseon gongeop yukseongbeop	Chosŏn kongŏp yuksŏngpŏp	1969	번역 표준 원칙
3135	조선공업진흥기본계획	造船工業振興基本計劃	master plan for fostering the shipbuilding industry	Joseon gongeop jinheung gibon gyehoek	Chosŏn kongŏp chinhŭng kibon kyehoek	1970	번역 표준 원칙
3136	조선광문회	朝鮮光文會	Korean Association for Cultural Enlightenment	Joseon gwangmunhoe	Chosŏn kwangmunhoe	1910-?	번역 표준 원칙

NO	용어	한자	영문	RO	MC	시대 및 연도	출전
3137	조선광업령	朝鮮鑛業令	Mining Ordinance of 1915	Joseon gwangeomnyeong	Chosŏn kwangŏmnyŏng	1915	번역 표준 원칙
3138	조선교육령	朝鮮教育令	Ordinance on Korean Education	Joseon gyoyungnyeong	Chosŏn kyoyungnyŏng	1911-1945	한국학중앙연구원,《영문한국백과》-대학
3139	조선교육심의회	朝鮮教育審議會	Korean Committee on Educational Planning (KCEP)	Joseon gyoyuk simuihoe	Chosŏn kyoyuk simŭihoe	1945-1946	번역 표준 원칙
3140	조선교통전도	朝鮮交通全圖	map of Korea's transportation network	Joseon gyotong jeondo	Chosŏn kyot'ong chŏndo	1910	번역 표준 원칙
3141	조선교회사	朝鮮教會史	*Histoire de l'Église de Corée (The History of the Church of Korea)*, by Charles Dallet, 1874	Joseon gyohoesa	Chosŏn kyohoesa	1947	번역 표준 원칙
3142	조선국권회복단	朝鮮國權恢復團	Society for the Restoration of Korea's National Sovereignty	Joseon gukgwon hoebokdan	Chosŏn kukkwŏn hoeboktan	1915-?	번역 표준 원칙
3143	조선국민당	朝鮮國民黨	Korean National Party	Joseon gungmindang	Chosŏn kungmindang	1945-?	번역 표준 원칙
3144	조선국제합영 총회사	朝鮮國際合營 總會社	Korea International Joint Cooperation	Joseon gukje habyeong chonghoesa	Chosŏn kukche habyŏng ch'onghoesa	1986-?	번역 표준 원칙

NO	용어	한자	영문	RO	MC	시대 및 연도	출전
3145	조선군주차사령부	朝鮮軍駐箚司領部	headquarters of Japanese forces stationed in Korea	Joseongun jucha saryeongbu	Chosŏn'gun chuch'a saryŏngbu	1904-1918	번역 표준 원칙
3146	조선기독교연맹	朝鮮基督敎聯盟	Korean Christians Federation	Joseon gidokgyo yeonmaeng	Chosŏn kidokkyo yŏnmaeng	1946-?	번역 표준 원칙
3147	조선노농총동맹	朝鮮勞農總同盟	Alliance of Korean Labor and Farmers Unions	Joseon nonong chongdongmaeng	Chosŏn nonong ch'ongdongmaeng	1924-1927	번역 표준 원칙
3148	조선노동공제회	朝鮮勞動共濟會	Korean Workers Mutual Fund Association	Joseon nodong gongjehoe	Chosŏn nodong kongjehoe	1920	번역 표준 원칙
3149	조선노동당	朝鮮勞動黨	Workers' Party of Korea	Joseon nodongdang	Chosŏn nodongdang	1949-?	번역 표준 원칙
3150	조선노동당 비서국	朝鮮勞動黨 秘書局	Secretariat of the Workers' Party of Korea	Joseon nodongdang biseoguk	Chosŏn nodongdang pisŏguk	1966-?	번역 표준 원칙
3151	조선노동당 중앙위원회 제6차 전원회의	朝鮮勞動黨 中央委員會 第6次 全員會議	Sixth Plenary Session of the Korean Communist Party's Central Committee	Joseon nodongdang jungang wiwonhoe je6cha jeonwon hoeui	Chosŏn nodongdang chungang wiwŏnhoe che6ch'a chŏnwŏn hoeŭi	1953	번역 표준 원칙
3152	조선노동당 총비서	朝鮮勞動黨 總秘書	General Secretariat of the Workers' Party of Korea	Joseon nodongdang chongbiseo	Chosŏn nodongdang ch'ongbisŏ		번역 표준 원칙

NO	용어	한자	영문	RO	MC	시대 및 연도	출전
3153	조선노동연맹회	朝鮮勞動聯盟會	Korean Workers League	Joseon nodong yeonmaenghoe	Chosŏn nodong yŏnmaenghoe	1922	번역 표준 원칙
3154	조선노동조합전국평의회	朝鮮勞動組合全國評議會	Korean National Assembly of Labor Unions	Joseon nodong johap jeonguk pyeonguihoe	Chosŏn nodong chohap chŏn'guk p'yŏngŭihoe	1945-1950	번역 표준 원칙
3155	조선노동총동맹	朝鮮勞動總同盟	Korean Federation of Workers	Joseon nodong chongdongmaeng	Chosŏn nodong ch'ongdongmaeng	1927-1929	번역 표준 원칙
3156	조선농민사	朝鮮農民社	Korean Farmers' Association	Joseon nongminsa	Chosŏn nongminsa	1925-1936	번역 표준 원칙
3157	조선농민총동맹	朝鮮農民總同盟	Korean Farmers' Union	Joseon nongmin chongdongmaeng	Chosŏn nongmin ch'ongdongmaeng	1927-1929	번역 표준 원칙
3158	조선농업근로자동맹	朝鮮農業勤勞者同盟	Korean Farmers' Alliance	Joseon nongeop geulloja dongmaeng	Chosŏn nongŏp kŭlloja tongmaeng	1965-?	번역 표준 원칙
3159	조선농지령	朝鮮農地令	Korean Farmland Ordinance	Joseon nongji-ryeong	Chosŏn nongji-ryŏng	일제	번역 표준 원칙
3160	조선농회	朝鮮農會	Agricultural Association of Korea	Joseon nonghoe	Chosŏn nonghoe	1926-1952	번역 표준 원칙

NO	용어	한자	영문	RO	MC	시대 및 연도	출전
3161	조선독립군가	朝鮮獨立軍歌	Song of the Korean Independence Army	Joseon dongnip gunga	Chosŏn tongnip kun'ga	1920-?	번역 표준 원칙
3162	조선무정부주의자연맹	朝鮮無政府主義者聯盟	Korean Anarchists' League	Joseon mujeongbujuuija yeonmaeng	Chosŏn mujŏngbujuŭija yŏnmaeng	?-?	번역 표준 원칙
3163	조선문인협회	朝鮮文人協會	Joseon Writers' Association	Joseon munin hyeophoe	Chosŏn munin hyŏp'oe	1939-1943	번역 표준 원칙
3164	조선문화단체총연맹	朝鮮文化團體總聯盟	National Federation of Cultural Organizations	Joseon munhwa danche chongyeonmaeng	Chosŏn munhwa tanch'e ch'ongyŏnmaeng	1946-?	번역 표준 원칙
3165	조선물산장려운동	朝鮮物産獎勵運動	campaign for the promotion of Korean products	Joseon mulsan jangnyeo undong	Chosŏn mulsan changnyŏ undong	1923-?	번역 표준 원칙
3166	조선물산장려회	朝鮮物産獎勵會	committee for the promotion of Korean products	Joseon mulsan jangnyeohoe	Chosŏn mulsan changnyŏhoe	1920-1923	번역 표준 원칙
3167	조선민속학회	朝鮮民俗學會	Korean Folklore Society	Joseon minsok hakhoe	Chosŏn minsok hakhoe	1932-1940	번역 표준 원칙
3168	조선민족당	朝鮮民族黨	Joseon National Party	Joseon minjokdang	Chosŏn minjoktang	1945-?	번역 표준 원칙

NO	용어	한자	영문	RO	MC	시대 및 연도	출전
3169	조선민족전선연맹	朝鮮民族戰線聯盟	Korean National Front Alliance	Joseon minjok jeonseon yeonmaeng	Chosŏn minjok chŏnsŏn yŏnmaeng	1937-?	번역 표준 원칙
3170	조선민족제일주의	朝鮮民族第一主義	Korea-First nationalism	Joseon minjok jeiljuui	Chosŏn minjok cheiljuŭi	1986-	번역 표준 원칙
3171	조선민족청년단 (족청)	朝鮮民族青年團 (族青)	Korean National Youth Corps	Joseon minjok cheongnyeondan (jokcheong)	Chosŏn minjok ch'ŏngnyŏndan (chokch'ŏng)	1946-1954	번역 표준 원칙
3172	조선민족해방동맹	朝鮮民族解放同盟	Korean National Liberation Alliance	Joseon minjok haebang dongmaeng	Chosŏn minjok haebang tongmaeng	1936-?	번역 표준 원칙
3173	조선민족혁명당	朝鮮民族革命黨	Korean National Revolutionary Party	Joseon minjok hyeongmyeongdang	Chosŏn minjok hyŏngmyŏngdang	1935-1946	국사편찬위원회
3174	조선민주당	朝鮮民主黨	Joseon Democratic Party	Joseon minjudang	Chosŏn minjudang	1945-1961	번역 표준 원칙
3175	조선민주여성동맹	朝鮮民主女性同盟	Korean Democratic Women's Union	Joseon minju yeoseong dongmaeng	Chosŏn minju yŏsŏng tongmaeng	1951-	번역 표준 원칙
3176	조선민주주의인민공화국	朝鮮民主主義人民共和國	Democratic People's Republic of Korea	Joseon minjujuui inmin gonghwaguk	Chosŏn minjujuŭi inmin konghwaguk	1948-?	번역 표준 원칙

NO	용어	한자	영문	RO	MC	시대 및 연도	출전
3177	조선민주주의인민공화국 사회주의 노동법	朝鮮民主主義人民共和國 社會主義 勞動法	Socialist Labor Law of the Democratic People's Republic of Korea	Joseon minjujuui inmin gonghwaguk sahoejuui nodongbeop	Chosŏn minjujuŭi inmin konghwaguk sahoejuŭi nodongpŏp	1978-?	번역 표준 원칙
3178	조선민주주의인민공화국 토지법	朝鮮民主主義人民共和國 土地法	Land Law of the Democratic People's Republic of Korea	Joseon minjujuui inmin gonghwaguk tojibeop	Chosŏn minjujuŭi inmin konghwaguk t'ojipŏp	1977-?	번역 표준 원칙
3179	조선민주주의인민공화국 헌법	朝鮮民主主義人民共和國 憲法	Constitution of the Democratic People's Republic of Korea	Joseon minjujuui inmin gonghwaguk heonbeop	Chosŏn minjujuŭi inmin konghwaguk hŏnpŏp	1972-?	번역 표준 원칙
3180	조선민흥회	朝鮮民興會	People's Prosperity Society of Korea	Joseon minheunghoe	Chosŏn minhŭnghoe	1926-1927	번역 표준 원칙
3181	조선반도사편찬위원회	朝鮮半島史編纂委員會	Korean History Compilation Committee	Joseon bandosa pyeonchan wiwonhoe	Chosŏn pandosa p'yŏnch'an wiwŏnhoe	1916-1945	번역 표준 원칙
3182	조선방공협회	朝鮮防共協會	Korean Anti-Communist Association	Joseon banggong hyeophoe	Chosŏn panggong hyŏphoe	1938	번역 표준 원칙
3183	조선불교도연맹	朝鮮佛敎徒聯盟	Korean Buddhist Federation	Joseon bulgyodo yeonmaeng	Chosŏn pulgyodo yŏnmaeng	1955-	번역 표준 원칙
3184	조선불교유신론	朝鮮佛敎維新論	*Treatise on the Revitalization of Korean Buddhism*	Joseon bulgyo yusinnon	Chosŏn pulgyo yusinnon	1913	번역 표준 원칙

NO	용어	한자	영문	RO	MC	시대 및 연도	출전
3185	조선사	朝鮮史	History of Korea (Joseonsa)	Joseonsa	Chosŏnsa	1932~1938	번역 표준 원칙
3186	조선사상범보호관찰령	朝鮮思想犯保護觀察令	Decree for the Probation of Korean Political Offenders	Joseon sasangbeom boho gwanchallyeong	Chosŏn sasangbŏm poho kwanch'allyŏng	1936	번역 표준 원칙
3187	조선사연구초	朝鮮史研究草	Exploratory Studies on Korean History (Joseonsa Yeongucho)	Joseonsa yeongucho	Chosŏnsa yŏn'guch'o	1929	Ki-baik Lee, translated by Edward W. Wagner, A New History of Korea, Harvard University Press, 1984,
3188	조선사정조사연구회	朝鮮事情調査研究會	Korean Affairs Research Society	Joseonsajeong josa yeonguhoe	Chosŏnsajŏng chosa yŏnguhoe	1925-?	번역 표준 원칙
3189	조선사편수회	朝鮮史編修會	Joseon History Committee	Joseonsa pyeonsuhoe	Chosŏnsa p'yŏnsuhoe	1925-1945	한국학중앙연구원, 《영문한국백과》-최남선
3190	조선사회민주당	朝鮮社會民主黨	Korean Social Democratic Party	Joseon sahoe minjudang	Chosŏn sahoe minjudang	1981-?	번역 표준 원칙
3191	조선사회주의헌법	朝鮮社會主義憲法	Socialist Constitution of the Democratic People's Republic of Korea	Joseon sahoejuui heonbeop	Chosŏn sahoejuŭi hŏnpŏp	1992-?	번역 표준 원칙
3192	조선산미증식계획	朝鮮産米增殖計畵	plan for increasing Korean rice production	Joseon sanmi jeungsik gyehoek	Chosŏn sanmi chŭngshik kyehoek	일제	번역 표준 원칙

NO	용어	한자	영문	RO	MC	시대 및 연도	출전
3193	조선산업 합리화조치	造船産業 合理化措置	measures for rationalization of the shipbuilding industry (1989)	Joseon saneop hamnihwa jochi	Chosŏn sanŏp hamnihwa choch'i	1989	번역 표준 원칙
3194	조선상고사	朝鮮上古史	Ancient History of Korea (Joseon Sanggosa)	Joseon sanggosa	Chosŏn sanggosa	1948	Peter H. Lee, Sourcebook of Korean Civilization(Volume 2), Columbia University Press, 1993,
3195	조선상업은행	朝鮮商業銀行	Joseon Commercial Bank	Joseon sangeop eunhaeng	Chosŏn sangŏp ŭnhaeng	1911-1950	번역 표준 원칙
3196	조선성악연구회	朝鮮聲樂硏究會	Korean Vocal Music Research Society	Joseon seongak yeonguhoe	Chosŏn sŏngak yŏn'guhoe	1933-1936	번역 표준 원칙
3197	조선소	造船所	shipyard	Joseonso	Chosŏnso		번역 표준 원칙
3198	조선소년군	朝鮮少年軍	Joseon Youth Corps (Korea's first Boy Scout organization formed in 1922)	Joseon sonyeongun	Chosŏn sonyŏn'gun	1922-?	번역 표준 원칙
3199	조선소년단	朝鮮少年團	Joseon Boys' Association	Joseon sonyeondan	Chosŏn sonyŏndan	1946-	번역 표준 원칙
3200	조선소년연합회	朝鮮少年聯合會	Federation of Korean Youth	Joseon sonyeon yeonhaphoe	Chosŏn sonyŏn yŏnhaphoe	1927-1928	번역 표준 원칙

NO	용어	한자	영문	RO	MC	시대 및 연도	출전
3201	조선소년척후대	朝鮮少年斥候隊	Joseon Youth Scouts (religious group founded under Japanese colonial rule)	Joseon sonyeon choekhudae	Chosŏn sonyŏn ch'ŏ khudae	1922-1937	번역 표준 원칙
3202	조선시대왕릉40기	朝鮮時代王陵40基	40 royal tombs of the Joseon Dynasty	Joseon sidae wangneung 40gi	Chosŏn sidae wangnŭng 40gi	조선	번역 표준 원칙
3203	조선식산은행	朝鮮殖産銀行	Joseon Industrial Bank	Joseon siksan eunhaeng	Chosŏn siksan ŭnhaeng	1918-1952	번역 표준 원칙
3204	조선신궁	朝鮮神宮	Chosen Jingu (main Shinto shrine in Korea)	Joseon singung	Chosŏn sin'gung	1924-?	번역 표준 원칙
3205	조선신민당	朝鮮新民黨	Joseon New People's Party	Joseon simindang	Chosŏn simindang	1946	번역 표준 원칙
3206	조선아시아태평양평화위원회	朝鮮Asia太平洋平和委員會	North Korea's Asia Pacific Peace Committee	Joseon asia taepyeongnyang pyeonghwa wiwonhoe	Chosŏn asia t'aep'yŏngyang p'yŏnghwa wiwŏnhoe	1994-	번역 표준 원칙
3207	조선어사전편찬회	朝鮮語事典編纂會	Society for the Compilation of a Korean Language Dictionary	Joseoneo sajeon pyeonchanhoe	Chosŏnŏ sajŏn p'yŏnch'anhoe	1929-?	번역 표준 원칙
3208	조선어연구회	朝鮮語研究會	Korean Language Research Society	Joseoneo yeonguhoe	Chosŏnŏ yŏn'guhoe	1921-1931	번역 표준 원칙

NO	용어	한자	영문	RO	MC	시대 및 연도	출전
3209	조선어학회	朝鮮語學會	Korean Language Society	Joseoneohakhoe	Chosŏnŏhakhoe	1931-1949	Ki-baik Lee, translated by Edward W. Wagner, A New History of Korea, Harvard University Press, 1984,
3210	조선어학회사건	朝鮮語學會事件	Korean Language Society Incident of 1942	Joseoneo hakhoe sageon	Chosŏnŏ hakhoe sakŏn	1942	번역 표준 원칙
3211	조선여성동우회	朝鮮女性同友會	Association of Korean Women Comrades	Joseon yeoseong donguhoe	Chosŏn yŏsŏng tonguhoe	1924-1927	번역 표준 원칙
3212	조선여성청년동맹	朝鮮女性青年同盟	Korean Young Women's League	Joseon yeoseong cheongnyeon dongmaeng	Chosŏn yŏsŏng ch'ŏngnyŏn tongmaeng		번역 표준 원칙
3213	조선여자교육협회	朝鮮女子教育協會	Korean Women's Education Association	Joseon yeoja gyoyuk hyeophoe	Chosŏn yŏja kyoyuk hyŏphoe	1920-?	번역 표준 원칙
3214	조선여자청년회	朝鮮女子青年會	Korean Young Women's Association	Joseon yeoja cheongnyeonhoe	Chosŏn yŏja ch'ŏngnyŏnhoe	1921-?	번역 표준 원칙
3215	조선역사	朝鮮歷史	The History of Joseon (Joseon Yeoksa)	Joseon yeoksa	Chosŏn yŏksa	1895	번역 표준 원칙
3216	조선왕조실록	朝鮮王朝實錄	Annals of the Joseon Dynasty (Joseon wangjo sillok)	Joseon wangjo sillok	Chosŏn wangjo sillok	조선	번역 표준 원칙

NO	용어	한자	영문	RO	MC	시대 및 연도	출전
3217	조선유기상회	朝鮮鍮器商會	Joseon Brassware Trading Company	Joseon yugi sanghoe	Chosŏn yugi sanghoe	?-?	번역 표준 원칙
3218	조선은행	朝鮮銀行	Bank of Joseon	Joseon eunhaeng	Chosŏn ŭnhaeng	1911-1945	번역 표준 원칙
3219	조선의용군	朝鮮義勇軍	Korean Volunteer Corps	Joseon uiyonggun	Chosŏn ŭiyonggun		Peter H. Lee, Sourcebook of Korean Civilization(Volume 2), Columbia University Press, 1993,
3220	조선의용대	朝鮮義勇隊	Korean National Volunteer Corps	Joseon uiyongdae	Chosŏn ŭiyongdae	1938-1942	번역 표준 원칙
3221	조선의용대 미주후원회	朝鮮義勇隊 美洲後援會	American Supporters' Association for the Korean National Volunteer Corps	Joseon uiyongdae miju huwonhoe	Chosŏn ŭiyongdae miju huwŏnhoe	1939	번역 표준 원칙
3222	조선의용대 화북지대	朝鮮義勇隊 華北支隊	North China Unit of the Korean Volunteer Corps	Joseon uiyongdae hwabuk jidae	Chosŏn ŭiyongdae hwabuk chidae	1941	번역 표준 원칙
3223	조선인민공화국	朝鮮人民共和國	Korean People's Republic	Joseon inmin gonghwaguk	Chosŏn inmin konghwaguk	1945	Ki-baik Lee, translated by Edward W. Wagner, A New History of Korea, Harvard University Press, 1984,
3224	조선인민군	朝鮮人民軍	North Korean People's Army	Joseon inmingun	Chosŏn inmin'gun	1948-	번역 표준 원칙

NO	용어	한자	영문	RO	MC	시대 및 연도	출전
3225	조선인민혁명군	朝鮮人民革命軍	Korean People's Revolutionary Army	Joseon inmin hyeongmyeonggun	Chosŏn inmin hyŏngmyŏnggun	1932-1945	번역 표준 원칙
3226	조선일보	朝鮮日報	The Chosun Ilbo (daily newspaper)	Joseonilbo	Chosŏnilbo	1920-?	번역 표준 원칙
3227	조선적십자회	朝鮮赤十字會	North Korea Red Cross	Joseon jeoksipjahoe	Chosŏn chŏksipchahoe	1948-?	번역 표준 원칙
3228	조선전업주식회사	朝鮮電業株式會社	Chosun Electric Co.	Joseon jeoneop jusikhoesa	Chosŏn chŏnŏp chusikhoesa	1943-?	번역 표준 원칙
3229	조선주차군사령부	朝鮮駐箚軍司令部	headquarters of the Japanese forces stationed in Korea	Joseon juchagun saryeongbu	Chosŏn chuch'agun saryŏngbu	1904-1945	번역 표준 원칙
3230	조선중앙방송	朝鮮中央放送	Korean Central Broadcasting Station	Joseon jungang bangsong	Chosŏn chungang pangsong	1948-	번역 표준 원칙
3231	조선중앙은행 화폐	朝鮮中央銀行 貨幣	Joseon Central Bank banknotes	Joseon jungang eunhaeng hwapye	Chosŏn chungang ŭnhaeng hwap'ye	1947	번역 표준 원칙
3232	조선중앙일보	朝鮮中央日報	Joseon Jungang Ilbo (Korean Central Daily Newspaper)	Joseon jungangilbo	Chosŏn chungangilbo	1933-1937	번역 표준 원칙

NO	용어	한자	영문	RO	MC	시대 및 연도	출전
3233	조선지지	朝鮮地誌	Joseon Jiji (Korea's first geography textbook)	Joseon jiji	Chosŏn chiji	1895	번역 표준 원칙
3234	조선직업총동맹	朝鮮職業總同盟	General Federation of Trade Unions	Joseon jigeop chongdongmaeng	Chosŏn chigŏp ch'ongdongmaeng	1951-?	번역 표준 원칙
3235	조선징병독본	朝鮮徵兵讀本	Joseon Compulsory Military Service	Joseon jingbyeong dokbon	Chosŏn chingbyŏng tokpon	1943	번역 표준 원칙
3236	조선책략	朝鮮策略	A Policy for Korea (Joseon Chaengnyak)	Joseon chaengnyak	Chosŏn ch'aengnyak	1880	번역 표준 원칙
3237	조선천도교중앙지도위원회	朝鮮天道教中央指導委員會	Joseon Cheondogyo Central Guiding Committee	Joseon cheondogyo jungang jido wiwonhoe	Chosŏn ch'ŏndogyo chungang chido wiwŏnhoe	1946-	번역 표준 원칙
3238	조선청년독립단	朝鮮青年獨立團	Korean Youth Independence Corps	Joseon cheongnyeon dongnipdan	Chosŏn ch'ŏngnyŏn tongniptan	1918-1919	한국학중앙연구원, 《영문한국백과》-이팔독립선언
3239	조선청년회연합회	朝鮮青年會聯合會	Association of Korean Youth Corps	Joseon cheongnyeonhoe yeonhaphoe	Chosŏn ch'ŏngnyŏnhoe yŏnhaphoe	1920-1924	한국학중앙연구원, 《영문한국백과》-조선물산장려운동
3240	조선체육회	朝鮮體育會	Joseon Amateur Sports Association	Joseon cheyukhoe	Chosŏn ch'eyukhoe	1920-1938	번역 표준 원칙

NO	용어	한자	영문	RO	MC	시대 및 연도	출전
3241	조선총독부	朝鮮總督府	Japanese Government General of Korea	Joseon chongdokbu	Chosŏn ch'ongdokpu	1910-1945	번역 표준 원칙
3242	조선총독부 항복조인식	朝鮮總督府 降伏調印式	surrender ceremony of the Japanese Government General of Korea	Joseon chongdokbu hangbok joinsik	Chosŏn ch'ongdokpu hangbok choinsik	1945	번역 표준 원칙
3243	조선카톨릭교협회	朝鮮Catholic敎協會	(North) Korean Roman Catholics Association	Joseon katollikgyo hyeophoe	Chosŏn k'at'ollikkyo hyŏphoe	1988	번역 표준 원칙
3244	조선통신사	朝鮮通信使	Joseon's diplomatic mission to Japan	Joseon tongsinsa	Chosŏn t'ongsinsa	1413-1876	번역 표준 원칙
3245	조선학운동	朝鮮學運動	Korean Studies Movement	Joseonhak undong	Chosŏnhak undong	1930년대	번역 표준 원칙
3246	조선혁명군	朝鮮革命軍	Korean Revolutionary Army	Joseon hyeongmyeonggun	Chosŏn hyŏngmyŏnggun	1929-1938	한국학중앙연구원, 《영문한국백과》-간도
3247	조선혁명군사정치 간부학교	朝鮮革命軍事政治 幹部學校	Korean Revolutionary Cadres School	Joseon hyeongmyeong gunsa jeongchi ganbu hakgyo	Chosŏn hyŏngmyŏng kunsa chŏngch'i kanbu hakkyo	1932-1935	번역 표준 원칙
3248	조선혁명당	朝鮮革命黨	Joseon Revolutionary Party	Joseon hyeongmyeongdang	Chosŏn hyŏngmyŏngdang	1930-1937	번역 표준 원칙

NO	용어	한자	영문	RO	MC	시대 및 연도	출전
3249	조선혁명선언	朝鮮革命宣言	Declaration of Korean Revolution	Joseon hyeongmyeong seoneon	Chosŏn hyŏngmyŏng sŏnŏn	1923	번역 표준 원칙
3250	조선형평사	朝鮮衡平社	Korean Society for Equality	Joseon hyeongpyeongsa	Chosŏn hyŏngp'yŏngsa	1927	번역 표준 원칙
3251	조세지원정책	租稅支援政策	tax support policies	Jose jiwon jeongchaek	Chose chiwŏn chŏngch'aek		번역 표준 원칙
3252	조영수호통상조약	朝英修好通商條約	Treaty of Friendship and Commerce between Korea and the United Kingdom, 1883	Joyeong suho tongsang joyak	Choyŏng suho t'ongsang choyak	1883	번역 표준 원칙
3253	조오수호통상조약	韓墺修好通商條約	Treaty of Amity and Commerce between Korea and Austria, 1892	Hano suho tongsangjoyak	Hano suho t'ongsang choyak	1892	번역 표준 원칙
3254	조의수호통상조약	朝意修好通商條約	Treaty of Amity and Commerce between Korea and Italy, 1884	Joui suho tongsang joyak	Choŭi suho t'ongsang choyak	1884	번역 표준 원칙
3255	조일수호조규	朝日修好條規	articles of the Treaty of Amity between Korea and Japan (aka the Ganghwa Treaty), 1876	Joil suho jogyu	Choil suho chogyu	1876	번역 표준 원칙
3256	조일수호조규 비준서	朝日修好條規 批准書	ratification statement of articles of the Treaty of Amity between Korea and Japan (aka the Ganghwa Treaty), 1876	Joil suho jogyu bijunseo	Choil suho chogyu pijunsŏ	1876	번역 표준 원칙

NO	용어	한자	영문	RO	MC	시대 및 연도	출전
3257	조일수호조규 속약	朝日修好條規 續約	Agreement between Korea and Japan for Maritime and Inland Trade (aka Treaty of Jemulpo), 1882	Joil suho jogyu sogyak	Choil suho chogyu sogyak	1882	번역 표준 원칙
3258	조일통상장정	朝日通商章程	Korea-Japan Commerical Agreement of 1883	Joil tongsang jangjeong	Choil t'ongsang changjŏng	1883	번역 표준 원칙
3259	조청상민수륙무역 장정	朝淸商民水陸貿易 章程	Regulations for Maritime and Overland Trade between Korea and China, 1882	Joseon sangmin suryuk muyeok jangjeong	Chochʻŏng sangmin suryuk muyŏk changjŏng	1882	번역 표준 원칙
3260	조청통상조약	朝淸通商條約	Treaty of Commerce between Korea and China, 1899	Jocheong tongsang joyak	Chochʻŏng tʻongsang choyak	1899	번역 표준 원칙
3261	조총련	朝總聯	Pro-Pyeongyang General Association of Korean Residents in Japan (Chochongryon)	Jochongnyeon	Chochʻongnyŏn	1955-?	번역 표준 원칙
3262	졸업정원제	卒業定員制	graduate quota system	Joreop jeongwonje	Chorŏp chŏngwŏnje	1980-?	번역 표준 원칙
3263	종두법	種痘法	vaccination for small pox	Jongdubeop	Chongdupŏp	1796	번역 표준 원칙
3264	종묘	宗廟	Jongmyo Shrine	Jongmyo	Chongmyo	조선	번역 표준 원칙

NO	용어	한자	영문	RO	MC	시대 및 연도	출전
3265	종묘제례악	宗廟祭禮樂	Jongmyo Jeryeak (Rite to Royal Ancestors)	Jongmyo jeryeak	Chongmyo cheryeak	조선	번역 표준 원칙
3266	종신집권	終身執權	power for life	Jongsin jipgwon	Chongsin chipkwŏn		번역 표준 원칙
3267	종심방어	縱深防禦	Defense in Depth	Jongsimbangeo	Chongsimbangŏ		번역 표준 원칙
3268	종주권	宗主權	suzerainty	Jongjugwon	Chongjukwŏn		James B. Palais, Politics and Policy in Traditional Korea, Harvard University Press, 1991, p.9.
3269	종친	宗親	member of the royal family	Jongchin	Chongch'in		번역 표준 원칙
3270	종합군수지원	綜合軍需支援	Integrated Logistic Support (ILS)	Jonghap gunsu jiwon	Chonghap kunsu jiwŏn		번역 표준 원칙
3271	종합금융회사	綜合金融會社	merchant bank	Jonghap geumnyung hoesa	Chonghap kŭmyung hoesa		Shin Myung-ho, Translated by Timothy V. Atkinson, Joseon Royal Court Culture, Dolbegae Publishers,
3272	종합물가대책	綜合物價對策	comprehensive measures for price control	Jonghap mulga daechaek	Chonghap mulka taech'aek		번역 표준 원칙

NO	용어	한자	영문	RO	MC	시대 및 연도	출전
3273	종합부동산세	綜合不動産稅	comprehensive real estate holding tax	Jonghap budongsanse	Chonghap pudongsanse	2005-?	번역 표준 원칙
3274	종합상사	綜合商社	integrated trading company	Jonghap sangsa	Chonghap sangsa	1975-?	번역 표준 원칙
3275	종합제철	綜合製鐵	integrated steelworks	Jonghap jechul	Chonghap chech'ŏl		번역 표준 원칙
3276	종합제철소	綜合製鐵所	integrated steelworks	Jonghap jecheolso	Chonghap chech'ŏlso		번역 표준 원칙
3277	종합제철추진위원회	綜合製鐵推進委員會	Commission for the Construction of Integrated Steelworks	Jonghap jecheol chujin wiwonhoe	Chonghap chech'ŏl ch'ujin wiwŏnhoe		번역 표준 원칙
3278	종합주가지수 2백선 돌파	綜合株價指數 2百線 突破	Korea Composite Stock Price Index (KOSPI) hitting the 200 mark	Jonghap juga jisu 2baekseon dolpa	Chonghap chuka jisu 2paeksŏn tolp'a		번역 표준 원칙
3279	종합편성채널사업	綜合編成Channel 事業	plan for new cable TV broadcasters (to air a variety of programs including news, entertainment as with existing terrestrial	Jonghap pyeonseong chaeneol saeop	Chonghap p'yŏnsŏng chaenŏl saŏp	2009-?	번역 표준 원칙
3280	좌우통일전선운동	左右統一戰線運動	Left-Right United Front movement	Jwau tongil jeonseon undong	Chwau t'ongil chŏnsŏn undong		번역 표준 원칙

NO	용어	한자	영문	RO	MC	시대 및 연도	출전
3281	좌우합작	左右合作	Left-Right Coalition	Jwau hapjak	Chwau hapchak	1946-1947	번역 표준 원칙
3282	좌우합작위원회	左右合作委員會	Left-Right Coalition Committee	Jwau hapjak wiwonhoe	Chwau hapchak wiwŏnhoe	1946	번역 표준 원칙
3283	좌익	左翼	left-wing	Jwaik	Chwaik		번역 표준 원칙
3284	좌파 헌법안	左派 憲法案	Draft of the Constitution by the left	Jwapa heonbeoban	Chwap'a hŏnpŏban	1946	번역 표준 원칙
3285	주5일 근무제	週5日 勤務制	five-day work week	Ju5il geunmuje	Chu5il kŭnmuje		번역 표준 원칙
3286	주간지	週刊誌	weekly magazine	Juganji	Chuganji		번역 표준 원칙
3287	주력부대	主力部隊	main force unit	Juryeok budae	Churyŏk pudae		번역 표준 원칙
3288	주물선공장	鑄物銑工場	continuous casting plant	Jumulseon gongjang	Chumulsŏn kongjang		번역 표준 원칙

NO	용어	한자	영문	RO	MC	시대 및 연도	출전
3289	주미 한인국민 총회	駐美 韓人國民 總會	Korean National Association in the U.S.	Jumi hanin gungmin chonghoe	Chumi hanin kungmin ch'onghoe	1919	번역 표준 원칙
3290	주미공사관	駐美公使館	Korean Legation in the U.S.	Jumi gongsagwan	Chumi kongsagwan		번역 표준 원칙
3291	주미외교위원부	駐美外交委員部	Korean Commission in the U.S.	Jumi oegyo wiwonbu	Chumi oegyo wiwŏnbu		번역 표준 원칙
3292	주민등록제	住民登錄制	resident registration system	Jumin deungnokje	Chumin tŭngnokche		번역 표준 원칙
3293	주민등록증	住民登錄證	resident registration card	Jumin deungnokjeung	Chumin tŭngnkjŭng		번역 표준 원칙
3294	주민센터	住民center	community center	Jumin senteo	Chumin sent'ŏ		번역 표준 원칙
3295	주방어진지	主防禦陣地	main defense position	Jubangeojinji	Chubangŏjinji		번역 표준 원칙
3296	주베일항만공사	Al-Jubayl港灣工事	harbor construction in Jubail, Saudi Arabia	Jubeil hangman gongsa	Chubeil hangman kongsa	1976	번역 표준 원칙

NO	용어	한자	영문	RO	MC	시대 및 연도	출전
3297	주보급로	主補給路	main supply route (MSR)	Jubogeumno	Chubogŭmno		번역 표준 원칙
3298	주사파	主思派	sympathizers of North Korea's Juche ("self reliance") ideoglogy	Jusapa	Chusap'a		번역 표준 원칙
3299	주상복합	住商複合	mixed-use building / mixed commercial-residential building	Jusang bokhap	Chusang pokhap		번역 표준 원칙
3300	주석	主席	premier	Juseok	Chusŏk	1927	번역 표준 원칙
3301	주왕산국립공원	周王山國立公園	Juwangsan National Park	Juwangsan gungnip gongwon	Chuwangsan kungnip kongwŏn	1976	번역 표준 원칙
3302	주월 한국군사원조단	駐越 韓國軍事援助團	Korean Military Aid Coprs in Vietnam	Juwol hanguk gunsa wonjodan	Chuwŏl han'guk kunsa wŏnjodan	1965	번역 표준 원칙
3303	주월군철수	駐越軍撤收	evacuation of ROK Troops from Vietnam	Juwolgun cheolsu	Chuwŏlgun ch'ŏlsu	1973	번역 표준 원칙
3304	주월한국군	駐越韓國軍	ROK Armed Forces, Vietnam	Juwol hangukgun	Chuwol hangukkun	1964-1973	번역 표준 원칙

NO	용어	한자	영문	RO	MC	시대 및 연도	출전
3305	주작전기지	主作戰基地	main operation base (MOB)	Jujakjeongiji	Chujakchŏngiji		번역 표준 원칙
3306	주저항선	主抵抗線	Main Line of Resistance	Jujeohangseon	Chujŏhangsŏn		번역 표준 원칙
3307	주체노선	主體路線	Juche (self-reliance) doctrine	Juche noseon	Chuch'e nosŏn		번역 표준 원칙
3308	주체사상	主體思想	the Juche Idea (North Korea's philosophy of self-reliance)	Juchesasang	Chuch'esasang	1967-?	번역 표준 원칙
3309	주택 5백만 채 건설계획	住宅 5百萬 채 建設計劃	plan for building five million housing units	Jutaek 5baekman chae geonseol gyehoek	Chutaek 5paengman chae kŏnsŏl kyehoek		번역 표준 원칙
3310	주택가격 안정대책	住宅價格 安定對策	measures to stabilize house prices	Jutaek gagyeok anjeong daechaek	Chutaek kagyŏk anjŏng taechaek		번역 표준 원칙
3311	주택난	住宅難	housing shortage crisis	Jutaeknan	Chut'aengnan		번역 표준 원칙
3312	주택복권	住宅福券	housing lottery	Jutaek bokgwon	Chut'aek pokkwŏn		번역 표준 원칙

NO	용어	한자	영문	RO	MC	시대 및 연도	출전
3313	주택자금	住宅資金	housing funds	Jutaek jageum	Chut'aek chagŭm		번역 표준 원칙
3314	주한미국경제협조처	駐韓美國經濟協調處	United States Operations Mission to Korea	Juhan miguk gyeongje hyeopjocheo	Chuhan miguk kyŏngje hyŏpchoch'ŏ		번역 표준 원칙
3315	주한미군	駐韓美軍	United States Armed Forces in Korea	Juhan migun	Chuhan migun	1945-?	번역 표준 원칙
3316	주한미군공사	駐韓美軍工事	construction works commissioned by the U.S. Army stationed in Korea	Juhan migun gongsa	Chuhan migun kongsa		번역 표준 원칙
3317	주한미군방송	駐韓美軍放送	American Forces in Korea Network (AFKN)	Juhan migun bangsong	Chuhan migun pangsong		번역 표준 원칙
3318	주한미군철수	駐韓美軍撤收	withdrawal of U.S. troops from Korea	Juhan miguk cheolsu	Chuhan miguk ch'ŏlsu		번역 표준 원칙
3319	주한미군철수론	駐韓美軍撤收論	idea of evacuation of U.S. troops from Korea	Juhan migun cheolsuron	Chuhan migun ch'ŏlsuron		번역 표준 원칙
3320	주한미제 8군	駐韓美第 8軍	Eighth United States Army (EUSA)	Juhan mije 8gun	Chuhan miche 8kun	1950-	번역 표준 원칙

- 435 -

NO	용어	한자	영문	RO	MC	시대 및 연도	출전
3321	주한미합동군사 지원단	駐韓美合同軍事 支援團	Joint U.S. Military Affairs Group, Korea (JUSMAG-K)	Juhan mihapdong gunsa jiwondan	Chuhan mihaptong gunsajiwŏndan		번역 표준 원칙
3322	준비명령	準備命令	warning order	Junbi myeongnyeong	Chunbi myŏngnyŏng		번역 표준 원칙
3323	준전시상태명령	準戰時常態命令	quasi-war condition order	Junjeonsi sangtae myeongnyeong	Chunjŏnsi sangt'ae myŏngnyŏng		번역 표준 원칙
3324	중·소 등거리외교	中·蘇 等距離外交	(North Korea's) policy of equidistance with the Soviet Union and China	Jung-so deunggeori oegyo	Chung-So tŭnggŏri oegyo		번역 표준 원칙
3325	중간교역	中間交易	intermediate trade	Junggan gyoyeok	Chunggan kyoyŏk		번역 표준 원칙
3326	중간평가	中間評價	mid-term evaluation	Junggan pyeongga	Chunggan p'yŏngga		번역 표준 원칙
3327	중경 대한민국 임시정부	重慶 大韓民國 臨時政府	Provisional Government of the Republic of Korea in Chongqing (Sept. 1940-Nov. 1945)	Junggyeong daehanminguk imsi jeongbu	Chunggyŏng teahanmin'guk imsi chŏngbu	1940-1945	p.17
3328	중공군	中共軍	Chinese Communist Forces (CCF)	Junggonggun	Chunggonggun	1950	번역 표준 원칙

NO	용어	한자	영문	RO	MC	시대 및 연도	출전
3329	중공군 서울점령	中共軍 Seoul占領	CCF occupation of Seoul	Junggonggun seoul jeomnyeong	Chunggonggun sŏul chŏmnyŏng	1951	번역 표준 원칙
3330	중공군 제1차 공세	中共軍 第1次 攻勢	CCF First Phase Offensive	Junggonggun je1cha gongse	Chunggonggun ch1ch'a kongse	1950	번역 표준 원칙
3331	중공군 최후공세	中共軍 最後攻勢	CCF Final Phase Offensive	Junggonggun choehugongse	Chunggonggun ch'oehugongse		번역 표준 원칙
3332	중공업육성방안	重工業育成方案	Measures for the Fostering of Heavy Industry of 1969	Junggongeop yukseong bangan	Chunggongŏp yuksŏng pangan	1969	번역 표준 원칙
3333	중광단	重光團	Liberation Corps (formed by believers of an indigenous Korean religion in Manchuria in 1911)	Junggwangdan	Chunggwangdan	1911-1918	번역 표준 원칙
3334	중국공산당	中國共産黨	Chinese Communist Party	Jungguk gongsandang	Chungguk kongsandang	1921-?	번역 표준 원칙
3335	중국국민당	中國國民黨	Chinese Nationalist Party	Jungguk gungmindang	Chungguk kungmindang	1921-	번역 표준 원칙
3336	중국군관학교	中國軍官學校	Chinese military academies	Jungguk gungwan hakgyo	Chungguk kun'gwan hakkyo		번역 표준 원칙

NO	용어	한자	영문	RO	MC	시대 및 연도	출전
3337	중국-베트남전쟁	中國·越南戰爭	China-Vietnam War	Jungguk-beteunam jeonjaeng	Chungguk-pet'ŭnam chŏnjaeng	1979	번역 표준 원칙
3338	중대	中隊	company	Jungdae	Chungdae	1950	번역 표준 원칙
3339	중대전술기지	中隊戰術基地	company tactical bases	Jungdae junsul giji	Chungdae chŏnsul kiji		번역 표준 원칙
3340	중도파	中道派	moderate faction	Jungdopa	Chungdop'a		번역 표준 원칙
3341	중동건설	中東建設	(Korean) construction projects in the Middle East	Jungdong geonseol	Chungdong kŏnsŏl	1973	번역 표준 원칙
3342	중동붐	中東boom	construction boom in the Middle East in the 1970s	Jungdongbum	Chungdongbum	1970년대	번역 표준 원칙
3343	중동시장	中東市場	Middle East market	Jungdong sijang	Chungdong sijang		번역 표준 원칙
3344	중동전쟁	中東戰爭	Arab-Israeli conflict	Jungdong jeonjaeng	Chungdong chŏnjaeng	1948-1974	번역 표준 원칙

NO	용어	한자	영문	RO	MC	시대 및 연도	출전
3345	중동철도	中東鐵道	railways in the Middle East	Jungdong cheoldo	Chungdong ch'ŏldo		번역 표준 원칙
3346	중립국	中立國	neutral nation	Jungnipguk	Chungnipkuk		번역 표준 원칙
3347	중립국감시위원단	中立國監視委員團	Neutral Nations Supervisory Commission	Jungnipguk gamsi wiwondan	Chungnipkuk kamsi wiwŏndan	1953-?	번역 표준 원칙
3348	중립국송환위원회	中立國送還委員會	Neutral Nations Repatriation Committee	Jungnipguk songhwan wiwonhoe	Chungnipkuk songhwan wiwŏnhoe	1953	번역 표준 원칙
3349	중립국외교	中立國外交	neutral nation diplomacy	Jungnipguk oegyo	Chungnipkuk oegyo		번역 표준 원칙
3350	중립화 통일연맹	中立化 統一聯盟	Unification under Neutralization League	Jungniphwa tongilyeonmaeng	Chungniphwa t'ongilyŏnmaeng	1961	번역 표준 원칙
3351	중립화정책	中立化政策	policies toward a neutral Korea	Jungniphwa jeongchaek	Chungniphwa chŏngch'aek		번역 표준 원칙
3352	중부고속도로	中部高速道路	Jungbu Expressway	Jungbu gosokdoro	Chungbu kosoktoro	1987	번역 표준 원칙

NO	용어	한자	영문	RO	MC	시대 및 연도	출전
3353	중석불사건	重石弗事件	Tungsten Dollar Scandal of 1952	Jungseokbul sageon	Chungsŏkpul sagŏn	1952	번역 표준 원칙
3354	중소기업 부흥계획	中小企業 復興計劃	Revitaliztion Plan for Small- and Medium-Sized Business	Jungso gieop buheung gyehoek	Chungso kiŏp puhŭng kyehoek		번역 표준 원칙
3355	중소기업계열화 촉진법	中小企業系列化 促進法	Promotion of Alliance between Small and Medium Enterprises Act (Repealed)	Jungso gieop gyeyeolhwa chokjinbeop	Chungso kiŏp kyeyŏlhwa ch'okchinpŏp	1975-?	번역 표준 원칙
3356	중소기업진흥법	中小企業振興法	Small and Medium Enterprises Promotion Act (Repealed)	Jungso gieop jinheungbeop	Chungso kiŏp chinhŭngpŏp	1982	번역 표준 원칙
3357	중소기업청	中小企業廳	Small and Medium Business Administration (SMBA)	Jungso gieopcheong	Chungso kiŏpch'ŏng	1996-?	번역 표준 원칙
3358	중수로 원자력 발전소	重水爐 原子力 發電所	heavy water reactor	Jungsuro wonjaryeok baljeonso	Chungsuro wŏnjaryŏk palchŏnso		번역 표준 원칙
3359	중앙고속도로	中央高速道路	Jungang Expressway	Jungang gosokdoro	Chungang kosoktoro	1995	번역 표준 원칙
3360	중앙관제소	中央官制所	control and reporting center (CRC)	Jungang gwanjeso	Chungang gwanjeso		번역 표준 원칙

NO	용어	한자	영문	RO	MC	시대 및 연도	출전
3361	중앙당집중지도사업	中央黨集中指導事業	Central Party's Intensive Guiding Enterprise	Jungangdang jipjung jido saeop	Chungangdang chipchung chido saŏp	1958-?	번역 표준 원칙
3362	중앙민방위협의회	中央民防衛協議會	Central Council for the Civil Defense Corps	Jungang minbangwi hyeobuihoe	Chungang minbangwi hyŏbŭihoe	1976-?	번역 표준 원칙
3363	중앙선거관리위원회	中央選擧管理委員會	National Election Commission	Jungang seongeo gwalli wiwonhoe	Chung'ang sŏn'gŏ kwalli wiwŏnhoe	현대	중앙선거관리위원회 사이트 http://www.nec.go.kr
3364	중앙아시아 강제이주	中央Asia 强制移住	forced relocation to Central Asia by the Soviet Union	Jungangasia gangjeiju	Chungangasia kangjeiju	1937	번역 표준 원칙
3365	중앙인민위원회	中央人民委員會	Central People's Committee	Jungang inmin wiwonhoe	Chungang inmin wiwŏnhoe	1972-1998	번역 표준 원칙
3366	중앙일보	中央日報	*JoongAng Ilbo* (daily newspaper)	Jungang ilbo	Chungang ilbo		번역 표준 원칙
3367	중앙정보부	中央情報部	Korean Central Intelligence Agency (CIA)	Jungang jeongbobu	Chungang chŏngbobu	1961-1980	번역 표준 원칙
3368	중앙풍수해대책위원회	中央風水害對策委員會	Central Committee for Natural Disaster Relief	Jungang pungsuhae daechaek wiwonhoe	Chungang p'ungsuhae taech'aek wiwŏnhoe		번역 표준 원칙

NO	용어	한자	영문	RO	MC	시대 및 연도	출전
3369	중요산업국유화	重要産業國有化	nationalization of key industries	Jungyo saneop gugyuhwa	Chungyo sanŏp kugyuhwa		번역 표준 원칙
3370	중요지형지물	重要地形地物	key terrain feature	Jungyo jihyeong jimul	Chungyo jihyŏng jimul		번역 표준 원칙
3371	중일전쟁	中日戰爭	Second Sino-Japanese War (1937-45)	Jungil jeonjaeng	Chungil chŏnjaeng	1937-1945	번역 표준 원칙
3372	중장기수출금융	中長期輸出金融	mid- to long-term export financing	Jungjanggi suchul geumyung	Chungjanggi such'ul kŭmyung		번역 표준 원칙
3373	중장기자문단	中長期諮問團	World Friends Advisers Program (WFA)	Jungjanggi jamundan	Chungjanggi chamundan	2010-?	번역 표준 원칙
3374	중추원	中樞院	Advisory Council to the Government General	Jungchuwon	Chungch'uwŏn	1894-1910	번역 표준 원칙
3375	중학교 의무교육 확대	中學校 義務敎育 擴大	extension of compulsory education to middle school	Junghakgyo uimu gyoyuk hwakdae	Chunghakkyo ŭimu kyouk hwaktae		번역 표준 원칙
3376	중학교무시험진학 제도	中學校無試驗進學 制度	policy to abolish middle-school entrance exams	Junghakgyo musiheom jinha kjedo	Chunghakkyo musihŏm chinhak chedo	1968	번역 표준 원칙

NO	용어	한자	영문	RO	MC	시대 및 연도	출전
3377	중한민중동맹단	中韓民衆同盟團	Sino-Korean People's League	Junghan minjung dongmaengdan	Chunghan minjung tongmaengdan	1935	번역 표준 원칙
3378	중화민국	中華民國	Republic of China (Taiwan)	Junghwaminguk	Chunghwamin'guk	1911-?	번역 표준 원칙
3379	중화인민공화국	中華人民共和國	People's Republic of China	Junghwa inmin gonghwaguk	Chunghwa inmin konghwaguk	1949-?	번역 표준 원칙
3380	중화주의	中華主義	Sinocentrism	Junghwajuui	Chunghwajuŭi		번역 표준 원칙
3381	중화학공업 육성정책	重化學工業 育成政策	policy for fostering heavy and chemical industry	Junghwahak gongeop yukseong jeongchaek	Chunghwahak kongŏp yuksŏng chŏngch'aek	1973-1979	번역 표준 원칙
3382	중화학공업추진 위원회	重化學工業推進 委員會	Heavy and Chemical Industry Promotion Council	Junghwahak gongeop chujin wiwonhoe	Chunghwahak kongŏp ch'ujin wiwŏnhoe	1973	번역 표준 원칙
3383	중화학공업화선언	重化學工業化宣言	President Park Chung-hee's announcement of the Heavy and Chemical Industrialization Program	Junghwahak gongeophwa seoneon	Chunghwahak kongŏphwa sŏnŏn	1973	번역 표준 원칙
3384	중화학투자조정	重化學投資調整	shift away from heavy and chemical industry focus	Junghwahak tuja jojeong	Chunghwahak t'uja chojŏng	1979	번역 표준 원칙

NO	용어	한자	영문	RO	MC	시대 및 연도	출전
3385	즉결처분	卽決處分	summary conviction	Jeukgyeol cheobun	Chŭkkyŏl ch'ŏbun		번역 표준 원칙
3386	증권거래법	證券去來法	Act on Securities Transactions	Jeunggwon georaebeop	Chŭngkwŏn kŏraepŏp	1962-?	번역 표준 원칙
3387	증권파동	證券波動	stock market crisis	Jeunggwon padong	Chŭngkwŏn p'adong		번역 표준 원칙
3388	지가상승	地價上乘	land price hike	Jiga sangseung	Chiga sangsŭng		번역 표준 원칙
3389	지계사업	地契事業	project to clarify land ownership (1898-1904)	Jigyesaeop	Chigyesaŏp	1898-1904	번역 표준 원칙
3390	지구온난화	地球溫暖化	global warming	Jigu onnanhwa	Chigu onnanhwa		번역 표준 원칙
3391	지급보증	支給保證	payment guarantee	Jigeup bojeung	Chigŭp pojŭng		번역 표준 원칙
3392	지대공유도탄	地對空誘導彈	Surface to Air Missile (SAM)	Jidaegongyudotan	Chidaegongyudot'an		번역 표준 원칙

NO	용어	한자	영문	RO	MC	시대 및 연도	출전
3393	지리산국립공원	智異山國立公園	Jirisan National park	Jirisan gungnip gongwon	Chirisan kungnip kongwŏn	1967-?	번역 표준 원칙
3394	지리학	地理學	geography	Jirihak	Chirihak		번역 표준 원칙
3395	지문날인제도	指紋捺印制度	fingerprint sealing system	Jimun nalin jedo	Chimun narin chedo		번역 표준 원칙
3396	지방교육자치제	地方敎育自治制	local educational autonomy system	Jibang gyoyuk jachije	Chibang kyouk chach'ije		번역 표준 원칙
3397	지방기능경기대회	地方技能競技大會	regional skills competition	Jibang gineung gyeonggi daehoe	Chibang kinŭng kyŏnggi taehoe	1966-?	번역 표준 원칙
3398	지방세	地方稅	local taxes	Jibangse	Chibangse		James B. Palais, Politics and Policy in Traditional Korea, Harvard University Press, 1991, p.100.
3399	지방인민위원회	地方人民委員會	Local People's Committee	Jibang inmin wiwonhoe	Chibang inmin wiwŏnhoe	1945-?	번역 표준 원칙
3400	지방인민회의	地方人民會議	Local People's Assembly	Jibang inmin hoeui	Chibang inmin hoeŭi	1949-	번역 표준 원칙

NO	용어	한자	영문	RO	MC	시대 및 연도	출전
3401	지방자치제	地方自治制	local autonomy	Jibang jachije	Chibang chach'ije	1952-1961, 1991-?	번역 표준 원칙
3402	지상관제요격	地上管制邀擊	Ground Controlled Interjection (GCI)	Jisang gwanjeyogyeok	Chisang gwanjeyogyŏk		번역 표준 원칙
3403	지식경제부	智識經濟部	Ministry of Knowledge Economy(MKE)	Jisik gyeongjebu	Chisik kyŏngjebu	2008-?	번역 표준 원칙
3404	지역감정	地域感情	regional antagonism	Jiyeok gamjeong	Chiyŏk kamjŏng		번역 표준 원칙
3405	지역균형발전	地域均衡發展	balanced regional development	Jiyeok gyunhyeong baljeon	Chiyŏk kyunhyŏng paljŏn		번역 표준 원칙
3406	지역민방위대	地域民防衛隊	Regional Civil Defense Forces	Jiyeok minbangwidae	Chiyŏk minbangwidae	1975-?	번역 표준 원칙
3407	지역예비군	地域豫備軍	Regional Reserve Forces	Jiyeok yebigun	Chiyŏk yebigun		번역 표준 원칙
3408	지역이기주의	地域利己主義	regional favoritism	Jiyeok igijuui	Chiyŏk igijuŭi		번역 표준 원칙

NO	용어	한자	영문	RO	MC	시대 및 연도	출전
3409	지역-직장 건강보험 재정 통합	地域-職場 健康保險 財政 統合	integration of regional and workplace health insurance funds	Jiyeok Jikjang geongang boheom jaejeong tonghap	Chiyŏk chikchang kŏngang bohŏm chaejŏng t'onghap		번역 표준 원칙
3410	지역통합전략	地域統合戰略	regional integration strategy	Jiyeok tonghap jeollyak	Chiyŏk t'onghap chŏllyak		번역 표준 원칙
3411	지연전	遲延戰	delaying operations	Jiyeonjeon	Chiyŏnjŏn		번역 표준 원칙
3412	지원병제도	志願兵制度	volunteer soldier system	Jiwonbyeong jedo	Chiwŏnbyŏng chedo	1938-1945	번역 표준 원칙
3413	지하경제	地下經濟	underground economy	Jiha gyeongje	Chiha kyŏngje		번역 표준 원칙
3414	지하철 개통	地下鐵 開通	opening of the subway	Jihacheol gaetong	Chihach'ŏl kaet'ong	1974-	번역 표준 원칙
3415	지형격실	地形隔室	compartment of terrain	Jihyeong gyeoksil	Chihyŏng kyŏksil		번역 표준 원칙
3416	지휘소 연습	指揮所 演習	Command Post Exercise (CPX)	Jihwiso yeonseup	Chihwiso yŏnsŭp		번역 표준 원칙

NO	용어	한자	영문	RO	MC	시대 및 연도	출전
3417	직무대행	職務代行	acting / locum tenens	Jingmu daehaeng	Chingmu taehaeng		번역 표준 원칙
3418	직선제	直選制	direct presidential election system	Jikseonje	Chiksŏnje	1987-?	번역 표준 원칙
3419	직선제 개헌	直選制 改憲	Constitutional Amendment for Direct Presidential Elections	Jikseonje gaeheon	Chiksŏnje kaehŏn	1987, 1988	번역 표준 원칙
3420	직업훈련제도	職業訓練制度	vocational training	Jigeop hullyeon jedo	Chigŏp hullyŏn chedo		번역 표준 원칙
3421	직장민방위대	職場民防衛隊	Workplace Civil Defense Forces	Jikjang minbangwidae	Chikchang minbangwidae	1975-?	번역 표준 원칙
3422	직장새마을운동	職場새마을運動	Saemaeul (New Village) Movement in the workplace	Jikjang saemaeul undong	Chikchang saemaŭl undong	1972-?	번역 표준 원칙
3423	직장예비군	職場豫備軍	Workplace Reserve Forces	Jikjang yebigun	Chikchang yebigun		번역 표준 원칙
3424	직접세 감면	直接稅 減免	direct tax reduction	Jikjeopse gammyeon	Chikchŏpse kammyŏn		번역 표준 원칙

NO	용어	한자	영문	RO	MC	시대 및 연도	출전
3425	직접투자	直接投資	direct investment	Jikjeop tuja	Chikchŏp t'uja		번역 표준 원칙
3426	직접투표	直接投票	direct election	jikjeop tupyo	Chikchŏp t'up'yo		번역 표준 원칙
3427	직지심체요절	直指心體要節	Selected Sermons of Buddhist Sages and Seon Masters (Jikjisimche yojeol)	Buljo jikji simche yojeol	Puljo chikchi shimch'e yojŏl	고려	번역 표준 원칙
3428	직할시	直轄市	Jikhalsi (major cities under the direct control of the central government)	Jikhalsi	Chikhalsi	1964-1994	번역 표준 원칙
3429	진단학보	震檀學報	Jindan Hakbo (Journal of the Chintan Society)	Jindanhakbo	Chindanhakpo	1934-?	번역 표준 원칙
3430	진보당	進步黨	Progressive Party	Jinbodang	Chinbodang	1956-1958	번역 표준 원칙
3431	진보당사건	進步黨事件	Progressive Party Incident of 1958	Jinbodang sageon	Chinbodang sakŏn	1958	번역 표준 원칙
3432	진실과 화해를 위한 과거사정리위원회	眞實과 和解를 爲한 過去事整理委員會	Truth and Reconciliation Commission	Jinsilgwa hwahaereul wihan gwageosa jeongni wiwonhoe	Chinsil-kwa hwahae-rŭl wihan kwagŏsa chŏngni wiwŏnhoe	2005-?	번역 표준 원칙

NO	용어	한자	영문	RO	MC	시대 및 연도	출전
3433	진위대	鎭衛隊	garrisons	Jinwidae	Chinwidae	1895-1907년	번역 표준 원칙
3434	진주만기습(진주만 공격)	眞珠灣奇襲(眞珠灣 攻擊)	Japanese attack on Pearl Harbor (1941)	Jinjuman giseup (jinjuman gonggyeok)	Chinjuman kisŭp (chinjuman konggyŏk)	1941	번역 표준 원칙
3435	진지	陣地	strongholds position	Jinji	Chinji		번역 표준 원칙
3436	진지강화	陣地强化	consolidation of position	Jinji ganghwa	Chinji ganghwa		번역 표준 원칙
3437	진해화학	鎭海化學	Chinhae Chemical Co.	Jinhae hwahak	Chinhae hwahak		번역 표준 원칙
3438	집강소	執綱所	local directorates	Jipgangso	Chipkangso	1894-?	Ki-baik Lee, translated by Edward W. Wagner, A New History of Korea, Harvard University Press, 1984,
3439	집단이주	集團移住	mass migration	Jipdaniju	Chiptaniju		번역 표준 원칙
3440	집단적 조치위원회	集團的 措置委員會	Collective Action Committee	Jipdanjeok jochiwiwonhoe	Chiptanjŏk choch'iwiwŏnhoe	1953	번역 표준 원칙

- 450 -

NO	용어	한자	영문	RO	MC	시대 및 연도	출전
3441	집중호우	集中豪雨	torrential rain	Jipjung hou	Chipjung hou		번역 표준 원칙
3442	집회에 관한 임시조치법	集會에 關한 臨時措置法	Provisional Act on Political Rallies	Jiphoee gwanhan imsi jochibeop	Chiphoe-e kwanhan imsi choch'ipŏp	1961	번역 표준 원칙
3443	징병제도	徵兵制度	conscription	Jingbyeong jedo	Chingbyŏng chedo		번역 표준 원칙
3444	징용제	徵用制	labor conscription	Jingyongje	Chingyongche	1944	번역 표준 원칙
3445	짜빈동 전투	Tra Binh Dong 戰鬪	Battle of Tra Binh Dong	Jjabindong jeontu	Tchabindong chŏnt'u	1967	번역 표준 원칙
3446	쪽방	쪽房	*jjokbang* (tiny rentable rooms)	Jjokbang	Tchokpang		번역 표준 원칙
3447	쪽방촌	쪽房村	*jjokbang* town	Jjokbangchon	Tchokpangch'on		번역 표준 원칙
3448	차관	借款	government loans	Chagwan	Ch'agwan		번역 표준 원칙

NO	용어	한자	영문	RO	MC	시대 및 연도	출전
3449	차관정치	次官政治	governance by Japanese vice-ministers during the Great Han Empire	Chagwan jeongchi	Ch'agwan chŏngch'i	1907-1910	번역 표준 원칙
3450	차단터널	遮斷Tunnel	blocked tunnel	Chadan teoneol	Ch'adan t'ŏnŏl		번역 표준 원칙
3451	차상위계층	次上位階層	potential welfare recipients	Chasangwi gyecheung	Ch'asangwi kyechŭng		번역 표준 원칙
3452	찬탁	贊託	pro-trusteeship	Chantak	Ch'ant'ak		번역 표준 원칙
3453	찰스 B. 스미스 중령	Charles B. Smith 中領	LTC Charles B. Smith	Chalseu B. seumiseu jungnyeong	Ch'alsŭ B. sŭmisŭ chungnyŏng	1950	번역 표준 원칙
3454	참교육	參教育	True Education Movement	Chamgyoyuk	Ch'amgyoyuk		번역 표준 원칙
3455	참여민주사회 시민연대(참여연대)	參與民主社會 市民連帶 (參與連帶)	People's Solidarity for Participatory Democracy	Chamyeo minjusahoe simin yeondae (chamyeo yeondae)	Ch'amyŏ minjusahoe simin yŏndae (ch'amyŏ yŏndae)	1994-?	번역 표준 원칙
3456	참의부	參議府	General Staff Headquarters (in Manchuria)	Chamuibu	Ch'amŭibu	1923-1927	한국학중앙연구원, 《영문한국백과》-정의부

NO	용어	한자	영문	RO	MC	시대 및 연도	출전
3457	참의원	參議院	House of (Legislative) Councilors	Chamuiwon	Ch'amŭiwŏn	1960-1963	한국학중앙연구원, 《영문한국백과》-신민부
3458	참정권청원운동	參政權請願運動	Suffrage Petition Movement	Chamjeonggwon cheongwon undong	Ch'amjŏngkwŏn ch'ŏngwŏn undong	1920년대 초	번역 표준 원칙
3459	참정론	參政論	arguments in favor of suffrage	Chamjeongnon	Ch'amjŏngnon		번역 표준 원칙
3460	창경궁	昌慶宮	Changgyeonggung Palace	Changgyeonggung	Ch'anggyŏnggung	1483	번역 표준 원칙
3461	창당준비위원회	創黨準備委員會	preparatory committee for the establishment of a political party	Changdang junbi wiwonhoe	Ch'angdang chunbi wiwŏnhoe		번역 표준 원칙
3462	창덕궁	昌德宮	Changdeokgung Palace	Changdeokgung	Ch'angdŏkkung	1405	번역 표준 원칙
3463	창동방어선	倉洞防禦線	Changdong Defense Line	Changdong bangeoseon	Changdong pangŏsŏn		번역 표준 원칙
3464	창씨개명	創氏改名	forced adoption of Japanese names	Changssi gaemyeong	Ch'angssi kaemyŏng	1939-1945	번역 표준 원칙

- 453 -

NO	용어	한자	영문	RO	MC	시대 및 연도	출전
3465	창씨개명 호적부	創氏改名 戶籍簿	family register showing Korean names changed to Japanese names	Changssi gaemyeong hojeokbu	Ch'angssi kaemyŏng hojŏkpu	1943	번역 표준 원칙
3466	창원종합기계공업기지	昌原綜合機械工業基地	Changwon Machine Building Industrial Complex	Changwon jonghap gigye gongeop giji	Ch'angwŏn chonghap kigye kongŏp tanji	1978	번역 표준 원칙
3467	창작과 비평 (계간 종합문예지)	創作과 批評 (季刊 綜合文藝誌)	Creation and Criticism (Changjakgwa bipyeong)	Changjak-gwa bipyeong (gyegan jonghap munyeji)	Ch'angjak-kwa pip'yŏng (kyegan chonghap munyeji)	1966-?	번역 표준 원칙
3468	창조 (최초 문예동인지)	創造 (最初 文藝同人誌)	Creation (Changjo), Korea's first literary coterie magazine	Changjo (choecho munye donginji)	Ch'angjo (ch'oech'o munye tonginji)	1919-1921	번역 표준 원칙
3469	창조파	創造派	Changjo Faction (group advocating the creation of the Provisional Government of the Republic of Korea)	Changjopa	Ch'angjop'a	1923	번역 표준 원칙
3470	처용무	處容舞	Cheoyongmu (Dance of Cheoyong, son the Dragon King of the East Sea)	Cheoyongmu	Ch'ŏyongmu		번역 표준 원칙
3471	척화비	斥和碑	steles installed to keep out foreigners	Cheokhwabi	Ch'ŏkhwabi	1871	번역 표준 원칙
3472	척화주전론	斥和主戰論	theory of "anti-negotiation, pro-war"	Cheokhwa jujeonnon	Ch'ŏkhwa chujŏnnon		번역 표준 원칙

NO	용어	한자	영문	RO	MC	시대 및 연도	출전
3473	천도교	天道敎	Cheondogyo (Religion of the Heavenly Way)	Cheondogyo	Ch'ŏndogyo	1905-?	번역 표준 원칙
3474	천도교 구파	天道敎 舊派	old school of Cheondogyo (Religion of the Heavenly Way)	Cheondogyo gupa	Ch'ŏndogyo kup'a	1926-1953?	번역 표준 원칙
3475	천도교 농민공생조합	天道敎 農民共生照合	Farmers' Mutual Aid Association of Cheondogyo (Religion of the Heavenly Way)	Cheondogyo nongmin gongsaeng johap	Ch'ŏndogyo nongmin kongsaeng chohap	1931	번역 표준 원칙
3476	천도교 신파	天道敎 新派	new school of Cheondogyo (Religion of the Heavenly Way)	Cheondogyo sinpa	Ch'ŏndogyo sinp'a	1926-1953?	번역 표준 원칙
3477	천도교소년회	天道敎少年會	Youth Association of Cheondogyo (Religion of the Heavenly Way)	Cheondogyo sonyeonhoe	Ch'ŏndogyo sonyŏnhoe	1921-?	번역 표준 원칙
3478	천도교중앙총부	天道敎中央總部	Central Headquarters of Cheondogyo (Religion of the Heavenly Way)	Cheondogyo jungang chongbu	Ch'ŏndogyo chungang ch'ongbu	1906-?	번역 표준 원칙
3479	천도교청년당	天道敎靑年黨	Youth Party of Cheondogyo (Religion of the Heavenly Way)	Cheondogyo cheongnyeondang	Ch'ŏndogyo ch'ŏngnyŏndang	1923-?	번역 표준 원칙
3480	천리마운동	千里馬運動	Chollima Movement	Cheollimaundong	Ch'ŏllimaundong	1957-	번역 표준 원칙

NO	용어	한자	영문	RO	MC	시대 및 연도	출전
3481	천마	天馬	Cheonma surface-to-air missile	Cheonma	Ch'ŏnma	1997-?	번역 표준 원칙
3482	천문학	天文學	astronomy	Cheonmunhak	Ch'ŏnmunhak		번역 표준 원칙
3483	천삽뜨고 허리한번 펴기 운동	千삽뜨고 허리한番 펴기 運動	campaign to balance labor and exercise (instructions to "straighten back once for every thousand shovel lifts")	Cheonsap tteugo heori hanbeon pyeogi undong	Ch'ŏnsap ttŭgo hŏri hanbŏn p'yŏgi undong		번역 표준 원칙
3484	천안논산고속도로	天安論山高速道路	Cheonan-Nonsan Expressway	Cheonan nonsan gosokdoro	Ch'ŏnan nonsan kosoktoro	2002	번역 표준 원칙
3485	천안함 폭침사건	天安艦 爆沈事件	sinking of the Cheonan warship	Cheonanham pokchim sageon	Ch'ŏnanam p'okch'im sakŏn	2010	번역 표준 원칙
3486	천연가스 도입	天然gas 導入	introduction of natural gas	Cheonyeon gaseu doip	Ch'ŏnyŏn kasŭ toip		번역 표준 원칙
3487	천주교	天主敎	the Catholic Church	Cheonjugyo	Ch'ŏnjugyo		번역 표준 원칙
3488	천주교정의구현전국사제단	天主敎正義具現全國司祭團	Catholic Priests' Association for Justice	Cheonjugyo jeongui guhyeon jeonguk sajedan	Ch'ŏnjugyo chŏngŭi kuhyŏn chŏnkuk sachaedan	1974-?	번역 표준 원칙

NO	용어	한자	영문	RO	MC	시대 및 연도	출전
3489	천진조약	天津條約	Convention of Tianjin	Cheonjin joyak	Ch'ŏnjin choyak	1885	번역 표준 원칙
3490	철강공업육성법	鐵鋼工業育成法	Steel Industry Promotion Act	Cheolgang gongeop yukseongbeop	Ch'ŏlgang kongŏp yuksŏngpŏp	1970	번역 표준 원칙
3491	철도보안대	鐵道保安隊	Railway Security Guards Units	Cheoldo boandae	Chŏlto poandae	1946	번역 표준 원칙
3492	철도부설권	鐵道敷設權	railway building concession	Cheoldo buseolgwon	Ch'ŏlto pusŏlkwŏn	1896-1904	번역 표준 원칙
3493	철도연맹	鐵道聯盟	railway workers' union	Cheoldo yeonmaeng	Chŏlto yŏnmaeng		번역 표준 원칙
3494	철도총파업	鐵道總罷業	Great Railway Workers' Strike (September 1946)	Cheoldo chongpaeop	Ch'ŏlto ch'ongp'aŏp	1946	번역 표준 원칙
3495	철원 땅굴 (제2호 땅굴)	鐵原 땅窟 (第2號 땅窟)	Second Underground Tunnel at Cheorwon	Cheolwon ddanggul (je2ho ddanggul)	Ch'ŏrwŏn ttangkul (che2ho ttanggul)	1975	번역 표준 원칙
3496	첨단기술 개발	尖端技術 開發	development of high technology	Cheomdan gisul gaebal	Ch'ŏmdan kisul kaebal		번역 표준 원칙

NO	용어	한자	영문	RO	MC	시대 및 연도	출전
3497	첩보함	諜報艦	spy ships	Cheopboham	Ch'ŏppoham		번역 표준 원칙
3498	청계천 복원	淸溪川 復元	restoration of Cheonggyecheon Stream	Cheonggyecheon bogwon	Ch'ŏnggyech'ŏn pogwŏn	2003-2005	번역 표준 원칙
3499	청계피복노조 노동교실사수투쟁	淸溪被服勞組 勞動敎室死守鬪爭	Cheonggye Garment Union workers' struggle to keep the "labor school" open	Cheonggye pibok nojo nodong gyosil sasu tujaeng	Ch'ŏnggye p'ibok nojo nodong kyosil sasu t'ujaeng	1970-1984	번역 표준 원칙
3500	청구권	請求權	claim	Cheonggugwon	Ch'ŏnggukwŏn		번역 표준 원칙
3501	청구학회	靑丘學會	Cheonggu Society	Cheonggu hakhoe	Ch'ŏnggu hakhoe	1930-?	번역 표준 원칙
3502	청국	淸國	Qing Dynasty	Cheongguk	Ch'ŏngguk		번역 표준 원칙
3503	청년문화	靑年文化	youth culture	Cheongnyeon munhwa	Ch'ŏngnyŏn munhwa		번역 표준 원칙
3504	청년학우회	靑年學友會	Association of Young Students	Cheongnyeon haguhoe	Ch'ŏngnyŏn haguhoe	1909	한국학중앙연구원, 《영문한국백과》-신민회

NO	용어	한자	영문	RO	MC	시대 및 연도	출전
3505	청도회의	靑島會議	Qingdao Convention (of the members of the New People's Association [Sinminhoe] in 1910)	Cheongdo hoeui	Ch'ŏngdo hoeŭi	1910	번역 표준 원칙
3506	청룡부대	靑龍部隊	Blue Dragon Unit	Cheongryeong budae	Ch'ŏngnyong pudae	1965-?	번역 표준 원칙
3507	청산리대첩	靑山里大捷	Battle of Cheongsalli (Battle of Qingshanli)	Cheongsalli daecheop	Ch'ŏngsalli taech'ŏp	1920	번역 표준 원칙
3508	청상어	靑상어	Blue Shark, Korean anti-Submarine, lightweight torpedo	Cheongsangeo	Ch'ŏngsangŏ	1995	번역 표준 원칙
3509	청소년보호법	靑少年保護法	Youth Protection Act	Cheongsonyeon bohobeop	Ch'ŏngsonyŏn pohopŏp	1999-?	번역 표준 원칙
3510	청소년헌장	靑少年憲章	Charter of Youth	Cheongsonyeon heonjang	Ch'ŏngsonyŏn hŏnjang	1990	번역 표준 원칙
3511	청일전쟁	淸日戰爭	Sino-Japanese War	Cheongil jeonjaeng	Ch'ŏngil chŏnjaeng	1894-1895	Ki-baik Lee, translated by Edward W. Wagner, A New History of Korea, Harvard University Press, 1984,
3512	청정부	淸政府	Qing Government	Cheongjeongbu	Ch'ŏngjŏngbu		번역 표준 원칙

NO	용어	한자	영문	RO	MC	시대 및 연도	출전
3513	청조	淸朝	Qing Dynasty of China (1644-1911)	Chungjo	Ch'ŏngjo	1636-1912	번역 표준 원칙
3514	청천강 교두보	淸川江 橋頭堡	Cheongcheongang River bridgehead	Cheongcheongang gyodubo	Ch'ŏngch'ŏn'gang kyodubo		번역 표준 원칙
3515	청춘	靑春	Bloom of Youth (Cheongchun), Korea's first monthly magazine	Cheongchun	Ch'ŏngch'un	1914-1918	번역 표준 원칙
3516	체신부	遞信部	Ministry of Postal Service and Communications	Chesinbu	Ch'esinbu	1976-?	번역 표준 원칙
3517	체육관 선거	體育館 選擧	indirect electoral college system	Cheyukgwan seongeo	Ch'eyukkwan sŏngŏ		번역 표준 원칙
3518	체육단체	體育團體	sports organization	Cheyuk danche	Ch'eyuk tanch'e		번역 표준 원칙
3519	체육대회	體育團體	athletics competition	Cheyuk daehoe	Ch'eyuk taehoe		번역 표준 원칙
3520	체육행사 지원활동	體育行事 支援活動	support for sports events	Cheyuk haengsa jiwon hwaldong	Ch'eyuk haengsa chiwon hwaldong	2010	번역 표준 원칙

NO	용어	한자	영문	RO	MC	시대 및 연도	출전
3521	체육훈장	體育勳章	Order of Sports Merit	Cheyuk hunjang	Cheyuk hunjang	1973-?	번역 표준 원칙
3522	초고령사회	超高齡社會	super-aging society	Chogoryeong sahoe	Ch'ogoryŏng sahoe		번역 표준 원칙
3523	초고속 인터넷	超高速 Internet	broadband Internet	Chogosok inteonet	Ch'ogosok int'ŏnet	1998-?	번역 표준 원칙
3524	초대형 유조선	超大型 油槽船	very-large crude carrier (VLCC)	Chodaehyeong yujoseon	Ch'odaehyŏng yujosŏn		번역 표준 원칙
3525	초등학교	初等學校	elementary school	Chodeunghakgyo	Ch'odŭnghakkyo	1995-?	번역 표준 원칙
3526	초산 전투	楚山 戰鬪	Battle of Chosan	Chosan jeontu	Ch'osan chŏnt'u	1950	번역 표준 원칙
3527	초음속 고등훈련기(T-50)	超音速 高等訓鍊機(T-50)	T-50 supersonic trainer jet	Choeumsok godeung hullyeongi (T-50)	Ch'oŭmsok kodŭng hullyŏn'gi (T-50)		번역 표준 원칙
3528	촛불집회	촛불集會	candlelight rally	Chotbuljipoe	Ch'otpulchiphoe		번역 표준 원칙

NO	용어	한자	영문	RO	MC	시대 및 연도	출전
3529	총력안보중앙협의회	總力安保中央協議會	National Security Central Council	Chongnyeok anbo jungang hyeobuihoe	Ch'ongnyŏk anbo chungang hyŏbŭihoe	1975-1997	번역 표준 원칙
3530	총인구조사	總人口調査	national population census	Chongingu josa	Ch'ongin'gu chosa	1949	번역 표준 원칙
3531	최고인민회의	最高人民會議	Supreme People's Assembly	Choego inmin hoeui	Ch'oego inmin hoeŭi	1948-?	번역 표준 원칙
3532	최루탄	催淚彈	tear gas canister	Choerutan	Ch'oerut'an	1980년대	번역 표준 원칙
3533	최루탄 추방 결의대회	催淚彈 追放 決意大會	national rally for banishment of tear gas grenades (1987)	Choerutan chubang gyeolui daehoe	Ch'oerut'an ch'ubang kyŏrŭi taehoe	1987	번역 표준 원칙
3534	최은희, 신상옥 납북사건	崔恩喜, 申相玉 拉北事件	North Korea's abduction of director Shin Sang-ok and actress Choi Eun-hui	Choe Eun-hui, Sin Sang-ok napbuksageon	Ch'oe Ŭn-hŭi, Sin Sang-ok nappuksakŏn	1978	번역 표준 원칙
3535	최저생계비	最低生計費	minimum cost of living	Choejeo saenggyebi	Ch'oejŏ saenggyebi		번역 표준 원칙
3536	최저임금	最低賃金	minimum wage	Choejeo imgeum	Ch'oejŏ imgŭm		번역 표준 원칙

NO	용어	한자	영문	RO	MC	시대 및 연도	출전
3537	최초의 군함 백두산함(PC-701)	最初의 軍艦 白頭山艦(PC-701)	Baekdusan (PC-701), Korea's first battleship	Choechoui gunham baekdusanham (PC-701)	Ch'oech'o-ŭi kunham paektusanham (PC-701)	1950	번역 표준 원칙
3538	최혜국대우	最惠國待遇	most-favored-nation treatment	Choehyeguk daeu	Ch'oehyeguk taeu		번역 표준 원칙
3539	추격 및 전과확대	追擊 및 戰果擴大	pursuit and exploitation	Chugyeok mit jeongwa hwakdae	Ch'ugyŏk mit chŏnkwa hwaktae		번역 표준 원칙
3540	축음기	蓄音機	gramophone	Chugeumgi	Ch'ugŭmgi	1905	번역 표준 원칙
3541	축첩방지법 제정에 관한 건	蓄妾防止法 制定에 關한 件	presidential instruction on banning concubines	Chukcheop bangjibeop jejeonge gwanhan geot	Ch'ukch'ŏp pangjipŏp chejŏng-e kwanhan kŏn	1949	번역 표준 원칙
3542	춘경추귀	春耕秋歸	"farming (in Gando) in spring, returning home (in Korea) in fall"	Chungyeongchugwi	Ch'un'gyŏngch'ugwi		번역 표준 원칙
3543	춘궁기	春窮期	spring lean season	Chungunggi	Ch'un'gunggi		번역 표준 원칙
3544	춘천 방어전투	春川 防禦戰鬪	Battle of Chuncheon	Chuncheon bangeo jeontu	Ch'unch'ŏn bangŏ chŏnt'u	1950	번역 표준 원칙

NO	용어	한자	영문	RO	MC	시대 및 연도	출전
3545	출구조사	出口調査	exit polls	Chulgu josa	Ch'ulgu chosa		번역 표준 원칙
3546	출판 지도부	出版 指導部	Publication Guidance Division	Chulpan jidobu	Ch'ulp'an chidobu		번역 표준 원칙
3547	출판법	出版法	Publication Law	Chulpanbeop	Ch'ulp'anpŏp	1909	한국학중앙연구원, 《영문한국백과》-언론
3548	충주비료공장	忠州肥料工場	Chungju Fertilizer Plant	Chungju biryo gongjang	Ch'ungju piryo kongjang	1961-?	번역 표준 원칙
3549	충주호 화재	忠州湖 火災	fire on the *Chungju* cruise ship	Chungjuho hwajae	Ch'ugjuho hwajae	1994	번역 표준 원칙
3550	충청남도	忠淸南道	Chungcheongnam-do Province	Chungcheongnam-do	Ch'ungch'ŏngnamdo	1896	번역 표준 원칙
3551	충청북도	忠淸北道	Cungcheongbuk-do Province	Chungcheongbuk-do	Ch'ungch'ŏngbukto	1896	번역 표준 원칙
3552	취약계층	脆弱階層	socially vulnerable groups	Chwiyak gyecheung	Ch'wiyak kyech'ŭng		번역 표준 원칙

NO	용어	한자	영문	RO	MC	시대 및 연도	출전
3553	치산녹화계획	治山綠化計劃	afforestation plan	Chisan nokhwa gyehoek	Ch'isan nokhwa kyehoek	1973-1988	번역 표준 원칙
3554	치산치수	治山治水	forestry and water management	Chisan chisu	Ch'isan ch'isu		번역 표준 원칙
3555	치악산국립공원	雉岳山國立公園	Chiaksan National Park	Chiaksan gungnip gongwon	Ch'iaksan kungnip kongwŏn	1984	번역 표준 원칙
3556	치안유지법	治安維持法	Internal Security Law	Chian yujibeop	Ch'ian yujipŏp	1925	번역 표준 원칙
3557	치외법권	治外法權	extraterritoriality	Chioe beopgwon	Ch'ioe pŏpkwŏn	1876-?	번역 표준 원칙
3558	칙명지보	勅命之寶	seal of the royal command	Chingmyeongjibo	Ch'ingmyŏngjibo	1897	번역 표준 원칙
3559	친러세력	親露勢力	pro-Russian faction	Chilleo seryeok	Ch'illo seryŏk		번역 표준 원칙
3560	친미개화파	親美開化派	pro-American progressives	Chinmigaehwapa	Ch'inmikaehwap'a		번역 표준 원칙

NO	용어	한자	영문	RO	MC	시대 및 연도	출전
3561	친일내각	親日內閣	pro-Japanese cabinet	Chinillaegak	Ch'inilnaegak		번역 표준 원칙
3562	친일문학론	親日文學論	Theory of Pro-Japanese Literature	Chinil munhangnon	Ch'inil munhangnon	1930년대 후반 -1945	번역 표준 원칙
3563	친일청산	親日淸算	movement to identify and punish pro-Japanese collaborators	Chinil cheongsan	Ch'inil ch'ŏngsan		번역 표준 원칙
3564	친정	親政	direct royal rule	Chinjeong	Ch'injŏng		번역 표준 원칙
3565	친환경녹색성장	親環境綠色成長	green growth	Chinhwangyeong noksaek seongjang	Ch'inhwan'gyŏng noksaek sŏngjang		번역 표준 원칙
3566	칭제건원	稱帝建元	declaring an empire and assuming the title of emperor	Chingje geonwon	Ch'ingje kŏnwŏn		번역 표준 원칙
3567	카이로 선언	Cairo 宣言	Cairo Declaration of 1943	Kairo seoneon	K'airo sŏnŏn	1943	번역 표준 원칙
3568	카이로 회담	Cairo 會談	Cairo Conference	Kairo hoedam	K'airo hoedam	1943	번역 표준 원칙

NO	용어	한자	영문	RO	MC	시대 및 연도	출전
3569	카투사 제도	KATUSA 制度	Korean Augmentation to the US Army (KATUSA) System	Katusa jedo	Katusa chedo	1950	번역 표준 원칙
3570	카프 (조선프롤레타리아 예술가동맹)	KAPF(朝鮮proletariat藝術家同盟)	Korea Artists Proletarian Federation (KAPF)	Kapeu (joseon peurolletaria yesulga dongmaeng)	K'ap'ŭ (chosŏn p'ŭ rollet'aria yesulga tongmaeng)	1925-1935	번역 표준 원칙
3571	칼빈 소총	Carbine 小銃	carbine rifle	Kalbin sochong	K'albin soch'ong	1950-1953	번역 표준 원칙
3572	캄보디아 내전	Cambodia 內戰	Cambodian Civil Wars	Kambodia naejeon	K'ambodia naejŏn	1970-1975	번역 표준 원칙
3573	코리언 리포지터리	Korean Repository	*The Korean Repository*	Korieon ripojiteori	K'orian rip'ojit'ŏri	1892-1899	번역 표준 원칙
3574	코민테른 '12월테제'	Comintern '12月 These'	Comintern December Thesis (1928)	Komintereun '12wol teje'	K'omint'erŭn '12wŏl t'eje'	1928	번역 표준 원칙
3575	코민테른 고려총국	코민테른 高麗總局	Korean Bureau of Far Eastern Section of Comintern	Komintereun goryeo chongguk	K'ominterŭn koryŏ ch'ongguk	1922-1924	번역 표준 원칙
3576	코스닥	KOSDAQ	Korean Securities Dealers Automated Quotation	Koseudak	K'osŭdak	1996-?	번역 표준 원칙

NO	용어	한자	영문	RO	MC	시대 및 연도	출전
3577	콜로라도 호	Colorado 號	the USS Colorado	Kolloradoho	K'olloradoho	1871	번역 표준 원칙
3578	콜론 보고서	Colon 報告書	Colon Report	Kollon bogoseo	K'ollon pogosŏ	1959	번역 표준 원칙
3579	콜롬보 계획	Colombo 計劃	Colombo Plan for Cooperative Economic and Social Development in Asia and the Pacific	Collombo gyehoek	K'ollombo kyehoek	1951-1957	번역 표준 원칙
3580	큰사전	큰辭典	A Comprehensive Dictionary of Korean (Joseonmal Keunsajeon)	Keunsajeon	K'ŭnsajŏn	1957	번역 표준 원칙
3581	클래어몬트 학생양성소	Claremont 學生養成所	Claremont Korean Student Training Center	Keullaemonteu haksaeng yangseongso	K'ŭllaeŏmont'ŭ haksaeng yangsŏngso	1908	번역 표준 원칙
3582	킬링 필드	Killing Field	the Killing Fields	Killing pildeu	K'illing p'iltŭ		번역 표준 원칙
3583	타스카 보고서	Tasca 報告書	Tasca Report	Taseuka bogoseo	T'asŭk'a pogosŏ	1953	번역 표준 원칙
3584	타스카 사절단	Tasca 使節團	Henry J. Tasca Delegation	Taseuka sajeoldan	T'asŭk'a sajŏltan	1953	번역 표준 원칙

NO	용어	한자	영문	RO	MC	시대 및 연도	출전
3585	탁지부	度支部	Finance Ministry	Takjibu	T'akchibu	1910-1920	Ki-baik Lee, translated by Edward W. Wagner, A New History of Korea, Harvard University Press, 1984,
3586	탁지아문	度支衙門	Department of Finance	Takjiamun	T'akchiamun	1894-1895	번역 표준 원칙
3587	탁치반대국민총동원위원회	託治反對國民總動員委員會	Nationwide Anti-Trusteeship Movement Mobilization Committee	Takchi bandae gungmin chongdongwon wiwonhoe	T'akch'i pandae kungmin ch'ongdongwŏn wiwŏnhoe	1945-1946	번역 표준 원칙
3588	탄원서	歎願書	petition	Tanwonseo	T'anwŏnsŏ		번역 표준 원칙
3589	탄핵소추	彈劾訴追	motion of impeachment	Tanhaek sochu	T'anhaek soch'u		번역 표준 원칙
3590	탈냉전	脫冷戰	detente	Talnaengjeon	T'alnaengjŏn	1989-?	번역 표준 원칙
3591	탈북자	脫北者	North Korean defector	Talbukja	T'albukcha		번역 표준 원칙
3592	탈석유정책	脫石油政策	policy for reducing fuel dependency	Talseogyu jeongchaek	T'alsŏgyu chŏngch'aek		번역 표준 원칙

NO	용어	한자	영문	RO	MC	시대 및 연도	출전
3593	탐관오리	貪官汚吏	corrupt officials	Tamgwanori	T'amgwanori		번역 표준 원칙
3594	탑골공원	塔골公園	Tapgol Park (aka Pagoda Park)	Tapgol gongwon	T'apkol kongwŏn	1987	번역 표준 원칙
3595	태권도 교관단	跆拳道 敎官團	Taekwondo Instructors' Corps	Taegwondo gyogwandan	T'aekwŏndo kyogwandan		번역 표준 원칙
3596	태권도평화봉사단	跆拳道平和奉仕團	Korea Taekwondo Peace Corps (TP Corps)	Taegwondo pyeonghwa bongsadan	T'aekwŏndo p'yŏnghwa pongsadan	2008-?	번역 표준 원칙
3597	태극기	太極旗	Taegeukgi (Korean national flag)	Taegeukgi	T'aegŭkki	1883-?	번역 표준 원칙
3598	태극무공훈장	太極武功勳章	Taegeuk Order of Military Merit	Taegeuk mugong hunjang	T'aegŭk mukong hunjang		번역 표준 원칙
3599	태극서관	太極書館	Taeguk Bookstore	Taegeuk seogwan	T'aegŭk sŏgwan	1905-1911	번역 표준 원칙
3600	태릉선수촌	泰陵選手村	National Training Center in Taereung, Seoul	Taereung seonsuchon	T'aerŭng sŏnsuch'on	1966-?	번역 표준 원칙

NO	용어	한자	영문	RO	MC	시대 및 연도	출전
3601	태서신사	泰西新史	Taeseosinsa (Western history textbook)	Taeseosinsa	T'aesŏsinsa	1896	번역 표준 원칙
3602	태아 성감별 금지법	胎兒 性鑑別 禁止法	Act Prohibiting Embryo Sex Screening	Taea seonggambyeol geumjibeop	T'aea sŏnggambyŏl kŭmjipŏp	1987	번역 표준 원칙
3603	태안 기름유출 사건	泰安 기름流出 事件	Taean oil spill of 2007	Taean gireum yuchul sageon	T'aean kirŭm yuch'ul sakŏn	2007	번역 표준 원칙
3604	태안 해상국립공원	泰安 害想國立公園	Taeanhaean National Park	Taean haesang gungnip gongwon	T'aean haesang kungnip kongwŏn	1978	번역 표준 원칙
3605	태양광 자동차	太陽光 自動車	solar-powered vehicles	Taeyanggwang jadongcha	T'aeyanggwang chadongch'a		번역 표준 원칙
3606	태양광발전소	太陽光發電所	solar power plant	Ttaeyanggwang baljeonso	T'aeyanggwang paljŏnso		번역 표준 원칙
3607	태양력	太陽曆	Gregorian calender	Taeyangnyeok	T'aeyangnyŏk		번역 표준 원칙
3608	태평양 미육군 총사령부 포고	太平洋 美陸軍 總司令部 布告	Proclamation of Commander-in-Chief, United States Army Forces, Pacific	Taepyeongyang miyukgun chongsaryeongbu pogo	T'aep'yŏngyang miyukkun ch'ongsaryŏngbu p'ogo	1945	번역 표준 원칙

NO	용어	한자	영문	RO	MC	시대 및 연도	출전
3609	태평양시사	太平洋時事	The Pacific Times	Taepyeongyangsisa	T'aep'yŏngyangsisa	1918 - 1927	번역 표준 원칙
3610	태평양잡지	太平洋雜誌	The Pacific Magazine	Taepyeongyang japji	T'aep'yŏngyang chapchi	1913 - 1930	번역 표준 원칙
3611	태평양전쟁	太平洋戰爭	Pacific War	Taepyeongnyang jeonjaeng	T'aep'yŏngyang chŏnjaeng	1941 - 1945	번역 표준 원칙
3612	태평양회의 외교후원회	太平洋會議 外交後援會	Diplomatic Support Association for Washington Conference	Taepyeongnyang hoeui oegyo huwonhoe	T'aep'yŏngyang hoeŭi oegyo huwŏnhoe	1921 - 1922	번역 표준 원칙
3613	태풍 곤파스	颱風 Kompasu	Typhoon Kompasu	Taepung gonpaseu	T'ae'ung konp'asŭ	2010	번역 표준 원칙
3614	태풍 매미	颱風 매미	Typhoon Maemi	Taepung maemi	T'aep'ung maemi	2003	번역 표준 원칙
3615	태풍 브렌다 피해	颱風 Brenda 被害	damage caused by Typhoon Brenda	Taepung beurenda pihae	T'aep'ung pŭrenda p'ihae	1985	번역 표준 원칙
3616	태형	笞刑	flogging	Taehyeong	T'aehyŏng		번역 표준 원칙

NO	용어	한자	영문	RO	MC	시대 및 연도	출전
3617	택지소유 상한제	宅地所有 上限制	ceiling on the ownership of housing sites	Taekji soyu sanghanje	T'aekchi soyu sanghanje	1990-?	번역 표준 원칙
3618	테러국	Terror國	terrorist nation	Tereoguk	T'erŏguk		번역 표준 원칙
3619	테헤란로	Teheran路	Tehran-ro	Teheranno	T'eherallo	1977	번역 표준 원칙
3620	텍스트 폰		text phone	text phone	Tekseuteupon	T'eksŭt'ŭp'on	번역 표준 원칙
3621	토막	土幕	"The Mud Hut" (Tomak), play by Yu Chi-jin, 1931	Tomak	T'omak	1931	번역 표준 원칙
3622	토문강	土門江	Tumen River	Tomungang	T'omungang	?-?	번역 표준 원칙
3623	토산애용부인회	土産愛用婦人會	Women's Association for the Promotion of Indigenous Products	Tosan aeyong buinhoe	T'osan aeyong puinhoe	1921-?	번역 표준 원칙
3624	토월회	土月會	Towolhoe (drama troupe of he 1920s)	Towolhoe	T'owŏrhoe	1920년대	번역 표준 원칙

NO	용어	한자	영문	RO	MC	시대 및 연도	출전
3625	토지	土地	The Land (Toji), novel by Park Kyong-ni	Toji	T'oji	1969-1994	번역 표준 원칙
3626	토지개혁	土地改革	land reform	Toji gaehyeok	T'oji kaehyŏk	1946	번역 표준 원칙
3627	토지거래허가제	土地去來許可制	land transaction approval system	Toji georae heogaje	T'oji kŏrae hŏgaje	1978	번역 표준 원칙
3628	토지공개념	土地公槪念	concept of public ownership of land	Toji gonggenyeom	T'oji gonggaenyŏm		번역 표준 원칙
3629	토지대장	土地臺帳	land register	Toji daejang	T'oji taejang		번역 표준 원칙
3630	토지세	土地稅	land taxes	Tojise	T'ojise		번역 표준 원칙
3631	토지조사령	土地調査令	Land Survey Law	Toji josaryeong	T'oji chosaryŏng	1910	Ki-baik Lee, translated by Edward W. Wagner, A New History of Korea, Harvard University Press, 1984,
3632	토지조사사업	土地調査事業	cadastral survey project	Toji josa saeop	T'oji chosa saŏp	1910-1918	번역 표준 원칙

NO	용어	한자	영문	RO	MC	시대 및 연도	출전
3633	토지초과이득세	土地超過利得稅	Land Excess-Profits Tax Act (Repealed)	Toji chogwa ideukse	T'oji ch'ogwa idŭkse		번역 표준 원칙
3634	통감부	統監府	Japanese Residency-General in Korea	Tonggambu	T'onggambu	1906-1910	번역 표준 원칙
3635	통감부 간도파출소	統監府 間島派出所	branch office of the Japanese Residency-General of Korea in Gando (Ch. Jiandao)	Tonggambu gando pachulso	T'onggambu kando p'ach'ulso		번역 표준 원칙
3636	통계청	統計廳	Statistics Korea	Tonggyecheong	T'onggyech'ong	1948-?	번역 표준 원칙
3637	통기타	筒guitar	acoustic guitar	Tonggita	T'onggit'a		번역 표준 원칙
3638	통리교섭통상사무아문	統理交涉通商事務衙門	Office for General Control of Diplomatic and Commercial Matters	Tongnigyoseop tongsangsamu-amun	T'ongnigyosŏp t'ongsangsamu-amun	1882-1885	번역 표준 원칙
3639	통리기무아문	統理機務衙門	Office for Extraordinary State Affairs	Tongnigimu-amun	T'ongnigimu-amun	1880-1882	Ki-baik Lee, translated by Edward W. Wagner, A New History of Korea, Harvard University Press, 1984,
3640	통상개화론	通商開化論	argument in favor of opening ports	Tongsang gaehwaron	T'ongsang kaehwaron		번역 표준 원칙

NO	용어	한자	영문	RO	MC	시대 및 연도	출전
3641	통상교섭	通商交涉	trade negotiations	Tongsang gyoseop	T'ongsang kyosŏp		번역 표준 원칙
3642	통상조약	通商條約	trade treaty	Tongsang joyak	T'ongsang choyak		번역 표준 원칙
3643	통수식	通水式	ceremony for opening of water channel	Tongsusik	T'ongsusik		번역 표준 원칙
3644	통신사	通信使	Joseon envoy to Japan	Tongsinsa	T'ongsinsa	1899-1905	번역 표준 원칙
3645	통신원	通信院	Telecommunications Department	Tongsinwon	T'ongsinwŏn		번역 표준 원칙
3646	통영 국제음악제	統營 國際音樂祭	Tongyeong International Music Festival	Tongyeong gukje eumakje	T'ong'yŏng gukche ŭmakche	1999-?	번역 표준 원칙
3647	통영 상륙작전	統營上陸作戰	Tongyeong Landing Operation	Tongyeong sangnyuk jakjeon	T'ongyŏng sangnyuk chakchŏn	1950	번역 표준 원칙
3648	통위부	統衛部	Department of National Defense	Tongwibu	T'ongwibu	1946-1948	번역 표준 원칙

NO	용어	한자	영문	RO	MC	시대 및 연도	출전
3649	통일 쌀 증산단지 재배력	統一 쌀 增産團地 栽培力	chart on Tongil rice production volumes	Tongil ssal jeungsan danji jaebaeryeok	T'ongil ssal chŭngsan tanji chaebaeryŏk	1972	번역 표준 원칙
3650	통일로	統一路	Tongil-ro (Unification Road)	Tongillo	T'ongillo	1972	번역 표준 원칙
3651	통일론 필화사건	統一論 筆禍事件	indictment of MBC President for alleged pro-Communist writing on unification (1964)	Tongillon pilhwa sageon	T'ongillon p'irwa sakŏn	1964	번역 표준 원칙
3652	통일민주당	統一民主黨	Democratic Reunification Party	Tongil minjudang	T'ongil minjudang	1987-1990	번역 표준 원칙
3653	통일벼(IR667)	統一벼	Korean rice variety "IR 667" (aka "unification rice")	Tongilbyeo (IR667)	T'ongilbyŏ (IR667)	1971-?	번역 표준 원칙
3654	통일부	統一部	Ministry of Unification	Tongilbu	T'ongilbu	1969-?	번역 표준 원칙
3655	통일안보 보고회의	統一安保 報告會議	meetings for reporting unification and national security issues	Tongilanbo bogohoeui	T'ongiranbo pogohoeŭi		번역 표준 원칙
3656	통일운동(4월혁명기)	統一運動 (4月革命期)	Unification Movement of 1960-1961	Tongil undong (4wol hyeongmyeonggi)	T'ongil undong (4wŏl hyŏngmyŏnggi)	1960-1961	번역 표준 원칙

NO	용어	한자	영문	RO	MC	시대 및 연도	출전
3657	통일음악회	統一音樂會	Unification Music Festival	Tongil eumakhoe	T'ongil ŭmakhoe		번역 표준 원칙
3658	통일전망대	統一展望臺	Unification Observatory	Tongil jeonmangdae	T'ongil chŏnmangdae	1984-?	번역 표준 원칙
3659	통일주체국민회의	統一主體國民會議	National Congress for Unification (NCU)	Tongil juche gungmin hoeui	T'ongil chuch'e kungmin hoeŭi	1972-1980	번역 표준 원칙
3660	통일촉진민중궐기	統一促進民衆蹶起	rally to promote unification	Tongil chokjin minjung gwolgi	T'ongil ch'okchin minjung kwŏlgi		번역 표준 원칙
3661	통일혁명당(통혁당)	統一革命黨 (統革黨)	Revolutionary Party for Reunification	Tongil hyeongmyeongdang (tonghyeokdang)	T'ongil hyŏngmyŏngdang (t'onghyŏktang)	1968	번역 표준 원칙
3662	통킹만 사건	Tongking灣 事件	Gulf of Tonkin Incident	Tongkingman sageon	T'ongk'ingman sakŏn	1964	번역 표준 원칙
3663	통합임무명령서	統合任務命令書	integrated task order (ITO)	Tonghap immu myeongnyeongseo	T'onghap immu myŏngnyŏngsŏ		번역 표준 원칙
3664	통화 스와프	通貨 swap	currency swaps	Tonghwa seuwapeu	T'onghwa sŭwapŭ		번역 표준 원칙

NO	용어	한자	영문	RO	MC	시대 및 연도	출전
3665	통화개혁	通貨改革	currency reform	Tonghwa gaehyeok	T'onghwa kaehyŏk		번역 표준 원칙
3666	투자 부적격단계	投資 不適格段階	non-investment grade	Tuja bujeokgyeok dangye	T'uja puchŏkkyŏk tan'gye		번역 표준 원칙
3667	투자재원	投資財源	financial resources for investment	Tuja jaewon	T'uja chaewŏn		번역 표준 원칙
3668	투표개산서	投票計算書	vote counting table	Tupyo gaesanseo	T'up'yo gaesansŏ		번역 표준 원칙
3669	투표함 바꿔치기	投票函 바꿔치기	switching ballot boxes	Tupyoham bakkwochigi	T'up'yoham pakkwŏch'igi		번역 표준 원칙
3670	트로트		Trot	trot (old-fashioned style of Korean pop music)	Teuroteu	T'ŭrot'ŭ	번역 표준 원칙
3671	트루만 독트린		Truman Doctrine	Truman Doctrine	Teurumeon dokteurin	T'ŭruman tokt'ŭrin	1947	번역 표준 원칙
3672	특명전권대신	特命全權大臣	minister plenipotentiary	Teungmyeong jeongwon daesin	T'ŭngmyŏng chŏnkwŏn taesin	조선	Ki-baik Lee, translated by Edward W. Wagner, A New History of Korea, Harvard University Press, 1984,

NO	용어	한자	영문	RO	MC	시대 및 연도	출전
3673	특무대	特務隊	Counter Intelligence Corps (CIC)	Teungmudae	T'ŭngmudae	1945	번역 표준 원칙
3674	특별핵사찰	特別核査察	special inspection of nuclear power plants	Teukbyeol haek sachal	T'ŭkpyŏl haek sach'al		번역 표준 원칙
3675	특수강공장	特殊鋼工場	alloy steel plant	Teuksugang gongjang	T'ŭksugang kongjang		번역 표준 원칙
3676	특수군	特殊軍	special forces	Teuksugun	Tŭksugun		번역 표준 원칙
3677	특수정보	特殊情報	sensitive compartmented intelligence (SCI)	Teuksu jeongbo	T'ŭksu jŏngbo		번역 표준 원칙
3678	특허법	特許法	Patent Law	Teukheobeop	Tŭkhŏpŏp	1961-?	번역 표준 원칙
3679	특허청	特許廳	Korean Intellectual Property Office (KIPO)	Teukheocheong	T'ŭkhŏch'ŏng	1949-?	번역 표준 원칙
3680	팀스피리트훈련	TeamSpirit訓鍊	Team Spirit exercise	Tim seupiriteu hullyeon	T'im sŭp'irit'ŭ hullyŏn	1976-1994	번역 표준 원칙

NO	용어	한자	영문	RO	MC	시대 및 연도	출전
3681	파독 간호사	派獨 看護師	Korean nurses dispatched to Germany (1960s and 70s)	Padok ganhosa	P'adok kanhosa	1960, 1970년대	번역 표준 원칙
3682	파독 광부	派獨 鑛夫	Korean miners dispatched to Germany	Padok gwangbu	P'adok kwangbu		번역 표준 원칙
3683	파리강화회의	Paris講和會議	Paris Peace Conference of 1919	Pari ganghwa hoeui	P'ari kanghwa hoeŭi	1919	번역 표준 원칙
3684	파리장서	Paris長書	petition for Korea's independence sent to the Paris Peace Conference of 1919	Pari jangseo	P'ari changsŏ	1919	번역 표준 원칙
3685	파리장서사건	Paris長書事件	Incident of the Petition for Korea's Independence (sent to the Paris Peace Conference of 1919)	Pari jangseo sageon	P'ari changsŏ sakŏn	1919	번역 표준 원칙
3686	파쇄공격	破碎攻擊	spoiling attack	Paswae gonggyeok	P'aswae gonggyŏk		번역 표준 원칙
3687	파업	罷業	strike	Paeop	P'aŏp		번역 표준 원칙
3688	파주나무꾼 피습사건	坡州나무꾼 被襲事件	shooting of woodcutters in Paju (near the DMZ) in 1962	Paju namukkun piseup sageon	P'aju namukkun p'isŭp sakŏn	1962.01.6	번역 표준 원칙

NO	용어	한자	영문	RO	MC	시대 및 연도	출전
3689	판금도서	販禁圖書	banned books	Pangeum doseo	P'angŭm tosŏ		번역 표준 원칙
3690	판문점	板門店	Panmunjeom	Panmunjeom	P'anmunjŏm	1951-	번역 표준 원칙
3691	판문점 도끼만행사건	板門店 도끼蠻行事件	Panmunjeom Axe Murder Incident of 1978	Panmunjeom dokki manhaeng sageon	P'anmunjŏm tokki manhaeng sakŏn	1978	번역 표준 원칙
3692	판문점 땅굴 (제3호 땅굴)	板門店 땅窟 (第3號 땅窟)	Third Underground Tunnel at Panmunjeom	Panmunjeom ddanggul (je3ho ddanggul)	P'anmunjŏm ttanggul (che3ho ttanggul)	1978	번역 표준 원칙
3693	판문점회담	板門店會談	armistice talks at Panmunjeom	Panmunjeom hoedam	P'anmunjŏm hoedam	1951 - 1953	번역 표준 원칙
3694	판소리	판소리	*pansori* (traditional Korean vocal music)	Pansori	P'ansori		번역 표준 원칙
3695	판자촌	板子村	shantytown	Panjachon	P'anjach'on		번역 표준 원칙
3696	판탈롱		Pantalon	bell-bottoms	Pantallong	P'ant'allong	번역 표준 원칙

NO	용어	한자	영문	RO	MC	시대 및 연도	출전
3697	팔공산 전투	八公山 戰鬪	Battle of Palgongsan Mountain	Palgongsan jeontu	P'algongsan chŏnt'u	927	번역 표준 원칙
3698	팔굉일우	八紘一宇	"eight corners, one roof" (Japanese slogan to rationalize its overseas expansion)	Palgoengiru	P'algoengiru		번역 표준 원칙
3699	팔당대교	八堂大橋	Paldang Grand Bridge	Paldangdaegyo	P'altangdaegyo	1995	번역 표준 원칙
3700	팔당댐	八堂dam	Paldang Dam	Paldangdaem	P'altangdaem	1973	번역 표준 원칙
3701	팔도강산	八道江山	mountains and rivers of the eight provinces (of Korea)	Paldogangsan	P'aldogangsan	1967	번역 표준 원칙
3702	팔로군	八路軍	Eighth Route Army of China	Pallogun	P'allogun	1938-?	번역 표준 원칙
3703	패션산업육성대책	Fashion産業育成對策	Fashion Industry Promotion Plan	Paesyeon saneop yukseong daechaek	P'aesyŏn sanŏp yuksŏng taechaek		국사편찬위원회
3704	펀치볼 전투	Punchball 戰鬪	Battle for the Punchbowl	Peonchibol jeontu	P'ŏnch'ibol chŏnt'u	1951	번역 표준 원칙

NO	용어	한자	영문	RO	MC	시대 및 연도	출전
3705	페리 보고서	Perry 報告書	The Perry Report	Peri bogoseo	P'eri pogosŏ	1999	번역 표준 원칙
3706	편성 및 장비표	編成 및 裝備表	Table of Organization and Equipment	Pyeonseong mit jangbipyo	P'yŏnsŏng mit changbip'yo		번역 표준 원칙
3707	평안남도 인민정치위원회	平安南道 人民政治委員會	Pyeongannam-do People's Political Committee	Pyeongannamdo inmin jeongchi wiwonhoe	P'yŏngannam-to inmin chŏngch'i wiwŏnhoe		번역 표준 원칙
3708	평양 군중대회	平壤 群衆大會	mass rally in Pyongyang	Pyeongyang gunjung daehoe	P'yŏngyang kunjung taehoe		번역 표준 원칙
3709	평양 숭실학교	平壤 崇實學校	Pyongyang Soongsil School (predecessor of Soongsil University)	Pyeongyang sungsil hakgyo	P'yŏngyang sungsil hakkyo	1897	번역 표준 원칙
3710	평양 탈환전투	平壤 奪還戰鬪	Battle for the Recapture of Pyongyang	Pyeongyang talhwan jeontu	P'yŏngyang t'arhwan chŏnt'u	1950	번역 표준 원칙
3711	평양과 원산	平壤과 元山	Pyongyang and Wonsan	Pyeongyanggwa wonsan	P'yŏngyanggwa wonsan	1950	번역 표준 원칙
3712	평양물산장려회	平壤物産奬勵會	Pyongyang Society for the Promotion of Korean Products	Pyeongyang mulsan jangnyeohoe	P'yŏngyang mulsan changnyŏhoe	1920-1937	번역 표준 원칙

NO	용어	한자	영문	RO	MC	시대 및 연도	출전
3713	평양방송	平壤放送	Pyongyang Broadcasting Station	Pyeongyang bangsong	P'yŏngyang pangsong	1972	번역 표준 원칙
3714	평양의학전문학교	平壤醫學專門學校	Pyongyang Medical College	Pyeongyang uihak jeonmun hakgyo	P'yŏngyang ŭihak chŏnmun hakkyo	1933-?	번역 표준 원칙
3715	평양축전(제13차 세계청년학생축전)	平壤祝典(第13次 世界靑年學生祝典)	13th World Festival of Youth and Students	Pyeongyang chukjeon (je13cha segye cheongnyeon haksaeng chukjeon)	P'yŏngyang ch'ukchŏn (che13ch'a segye ch'ŏngnyŏn haksaeng ch'ukchŏn)	1989.7	번역 표준 원칙
3716	평양학원	平壤學院	Pyongyang Institute	Pyeongyang hagwon	P'yŏngyang hagwŏn	1946-1947	번역 표준 원칙
3717	평택제천고속도로	平澤堤川高速道路	Pyeongtaek-Jecheon Expressway	Pyeongtaek jecheon gosokdoro	P'yŏngt'aek chech'ŏn kosoktoro	2008 개통	번역 표준 원칙
3718	평택화력 3호기	平澤火力 3號機	Pyeongtaek Thermoelectric Power Plant Unit No. 3	Pyeongtaek hwaryeok 3hogi	P'yŏngt'aek hwaryŏk 3hogi		번역 표준 원칙
3719	평택화성고속도로	平澤華城高速道路	Pyeongtaek-Hwaseong Expressway	Pyeongtaek hwaseong gosokdoro	P'yŏngt'aek hwasŏng kosoktoro		번역 표준 원칙
3720	평화공존	平和共存	peaceful coexistence	Pyeonghwa gongjon	P'yŏnghwa kongjon		번역 표준 원칙

NO	용어	한자	영문	RO	MC	시대 및 연도	출전
3721	평화민주당	平和民主黨	Party for Peace and Democracy	Pyeonghwa minjudang	P'yŏnghwa minjudang	1987-1991	번역 표준 원칙
3722	평화선 선포	平和線 宣布	Presidential Proclamation of Sovereignty over Adjacent Seas (aka "Peace Line" Declaration of 1952)	Pyeonghwaseon seonpo	P'yŏnghwasŏn sŏnp'o	1952	번역 표준 원칙
3723	평화선(이승만라인)	平和線 (李承晩line)	Peace Line (aka Syngman Rhee Line)	Pyeonghwaseon (Yi Seung-man rain)	P'yŏnghwasŏn (Yi Sŭng-man rain)	1952	번역 표준 원칙
3724	평화선언	平和宣言	peace declaration	Pyeonghwa seoneon	P'yŏnghwa sŏnŏn		번역 표준 원칙
3725	평화시장	平和市場	Pyeonghwa Market	Pyeonghwa sijang	P'yŏnghwa sijang	1962-?	번역 표준 원칙
3726	평화유지활동	平和維持活動	peacekeeping operations (PKO)	Pyeonghwa yuji hwaldong	P'yŏnghwa yuji hwaltong		번역 표준 원칙
3727	평화의 댐	平和의 Dam	Peace Dam (built on the Bukhangang River to stave off possible catastrophe from flooding in North Korea)	Pyeonghwaui daem	P'yŏnghwa-ŭi taem	1988 1단계 완공 2005년 준공	번역 표준 원칙
3728	평화의 마을	平和의 마을	Village of Peace	Pyeonghwaui maeul	P'yŏnghwa-ŭi maŭl		번역 표준 원칙

NO	용어	한자	영문	RO	MC	시대 및 연도	출전
3729	평화적 정권교체	平和的 政權交替	peaceful transfer of power	Pyeonghwajeok jeonggwon gyoche	P'yŏnghwajŏk chŏngkwŏn kyoch'e		번역 표준 원칙
3730	평화통일론	平和統一論	theory of peaceful unification between the two Koreas	Pyeonghwa tongillon	Pyŏnghwa t'ongillon	1948-?	번역 표준 원칙
3731	평화통일정책자문회의	平和統一政策諮問會議	National Unification Advisory Council	Pyeonghwa tongil jeongchaek jamun hoeui	P'yŏnghwa t'ongil chŏngch'aek chamun hoeŭi	1981-?	번역 표준 원칙
3732	평화협정	平和協定	peace treaty	Pyeonghwa hyeopjeong	P'yŏnghwa hyŏpchŏng		번역 표준 원칙
3733	평화회담	平和會談	peace talks	Pyeonghwa hoedam	P'yŏnghwa hoedam		번역 표준 원칙
3734	폐정개혁안	弊政改革案	Twelve-point Code for Local Directorates	Pyejeong gaehyeogan	P'yejŏng kaehyŏgan	1894	번역 표준 원칙
3735	폐허	廢墟	ruins	Pyeheo	P'yehŏ	1920-1921	Peter H. Lee, Sourcebook of Korean Civilization(Volume 2), Columbia University Press, 1993,
3736	포드자동차·기아투자협정	Ford自動車·起亞投資協定	Kia-Ford Investment Agreement	Podeu jadongcha-gia tuja hyeopjeong	P'odŭ chadongcha-kia t'uja hyŏpchŏng		번역 표준 원칙

NO	용어	한자	영문	RO	MC	시대 및 연도	출전
3737	포로송환	捕虜送還	repartriation of POWs	Poro songhwan	P'oro songhwan		번역 표준 원칙
3738	포로수용소	捕虜收容所	prisoner of war camp	Poro suyongso	P'oro suyongso	1950-1953	번역 표준 원칙
3739	포로수집소	捕虜收集所	prisoner of war collecting point (PWCOLL)	Poro sujipso	P'oro sujipso		번역 표준 원칙
3740	포츠담 선언	Potsdam 宣言	Potsdam Declaration of 1945	Pocheudam seoneon	P'och'ŭdam sŏnŏn	1945	번역 표준 원칙
3741	포츠머스 조약	Portsmouth 條約	Portsmouth Treaty of 1905	Pocheumeoseu joyak	P'och'ŭmŏsŭ choyak	1905	번역 표준 원칙
3742	포커스 레티나' 한미연합공수훈련	Focus Retina' 韓美聯合空輸訓練	ROK-US Combined Airlift Exercise "Focus Retina"	Pokeoseu retina' hanmiyeonhap gongsu hullyeon	P'ok'ŏsŭ ret'ina hanmiyŏnhap kongsu hullyŏn	1969	번역 표준 원칙
3743	포크송		folf song	folk song	Pokeusong	P'ok'ŭsong	번역 표준 원칙
3744	포항 전투	浦項 戰鬪	Battle of Pohang	Pohang jeontu	P'ohang chŏnt'u	1950	번역 표준 원칙

NO	용어	한자	영문	RO	MC	시대 및 연도	출전
3745	포항종합제철건설계획	浦項綜合製鐵建設計劃	construction plan for Pohang Iron and Steel Company (1969-1975)	Pohang jonghap jechul gunseol gyehoek	P'ohang chonghap chech'ŏl kŏnsŏl kyehoek	1969-1975	번역 표준 원칙
3746	포항종합제철주식회사	浦項綜合製鐵株式會社	Pohang Iron and Steel Company (POSCO)	Pohang jonghap jecheol jusikhoesa	P'ohang chonghap chech'ŏl chusikhoesa	1968-?	번역 표준 원칙
3747	폭발물 처리반	爆發物 處理班	Explosive Ordinance Disposal (EOD) team	Pokbalmul cheoriban	P'okpalmul ch'ŏriban		번역 표준 원칙
3748	퐁니·퐁넛 양민 학살 사건	Phong Nhi·Phong Nut 良民 虐殺 事件	Phong Nhi and Phong Nhat Massacre	Pongni·Pongnut yangmin haksal sageon	P'ongni·P'ongnŏt yangmin haksal sakŏn	1968	번역 표준 원칙
3749	표준어규정	標準語規定	standard language regulations	Pyojuneo gyujeong	P'yojunŏ kyujŏng		번역 표준 원칙
3750	푸에블로호 납치사건	Pueblo號 拉致事件	the Pueblo Incident of 1968	Puebeulloho napchi sageon	P'uebŭlloho napch'i sakŏn	1968	번역 표준 원칙
3751	프랑스 극동함대	France 極東艦隊	French Far Eastern Fleets	Peurangseu geukdong hamdae	P'ŭrangsŭ kŭktong hamdae		번역 표준 원칙
3752	프랑스 조계	France 租界	French concession	Peurangseu jogye	P'ŭrangsŭ chogye		번역 표준 원칙

NO	용어	한자	영문	RO	MC	시대 및 연도	출전
3753	프랑스공사관	France公使館	French Legation	Peurangseu gongsagwan	P'ŭrangsŭ kongsagwan		번역 표준 원칙
3754	프랑스령인도차이나	佛蘭西領Indochina	French Indochina	Peurangseuryeong indochaina	P'ŭrangsŭryŏng indoch'aina	· 수립 - 라오스 - 북베트남 독립 - 남베	번역 표준 원칙
3755	프레온가스 대체물질 개발	freon gas 代替物質 開發	development of Freon alternatives	Peureon gaseu daechaemuljil gaebal	P'ŭreon gasŭ taechaemuljil kaebal		번역 표준 원칙
3756	프로레슬링	pro wrestling	professional wrestling	Peuro reseulling	P'ŭro resŭlling		번역 표준 원칙
3757	프로문학	Pro文學	proletarian literature	Peuro munhak	P'ŭro munhak		번역 표준 원칙
3758	프롤레타리아 계급독재	Proletariat 階級獨裁	class dictatorship of the proletariat	Peurolletaria gyegeup dokjae	P'ŭrolletaria kyegŭp tokchae		번역 표준 원칙
3759	플렌트 수출	Plant 輸出	plant exports	Peulenteu suchul	P'ŭllent'ŭ such'ul		번역 표준 원칙
3760	피난 생활	避難 生活	refugee life	Pinan saenghwal	P'inan saenghwal	1950-1953	번역 표준 원칙

NO	용어	한자	영문	RO	MC	시대 및 연도	출전
3761	피난 중·고등학교	避難 中·高等學校	wartime middle and high schools	Pinan jung-godeung hakgyo	P'inan chung-kodŭng hakkyo		번역 표준 원칙
3762	피난 특설학교	避難 特設學校	schools for war refugees	Pinan teukseol hakgyo	P'inan t'ŭksŏl hakkyo		번역 표준 원칙
3763	피난민	避難民	refugees	Pinanmin	P'inanmin		번역 표준 원칙
3764	피난민증	避難民證	refugee certificate	Pinanminjeung	P'inanminchŭng	1951	번역 표준 원칙
3765	피복노동자	被服勞動者	garment workers	Pibok nodongja	P'ibok nodongja		번역 표준 원칙
3766	피아골	피아골	Piagol Valley	Piagol	P'iagol	1955	번역 표준 원칙
3767	피아식별장비	彼我識別裝備	Identification Friend or Foe (IFF)	Piasikbyeol jangbi	P'iasikpyŏl changbi		번역 표준 원칙
3768	피압박민족 독립운동	被壓迫民族 獨立運動	independence movements by oppressed people	Piapbak minjok dongnip undong	P'iappak minjok tongnip undong		번역 표준 원칙

- 491 -

NO	용어	한자	영문	RO	MC	시대 및 연도	출전
3769	피의 능선 전투	피의 稜線 戰鬪	Battle of Bloody Ridge	Pi-ui neungseon jeontu	P'i-ŭi nŭngsŏn chŏnt'u	1951	번역 표준 원칙
3770	피의 화요일	피의 火曜日	Bloody Tuesday (April 19th Revolution)	Piui hwayoil	P'i-ŭi hwayoil	1960	번역 표준 원칙
3771	필리핀 제10보병 전투단	Philippine 第10步兵戰鬪團	Philippine 10th Infantry Combat Units	Pillipin je10 bobyeong jeontudan	P'illip'in che10 bobyŏng jŏnt'udan		번역 표준 원칙
3772	하극상 사건	下剋上 事件	shooting of a high military officer by his subordinate in 1959	Hageuksang sageon	Hagŭksang sakŏn	1960.05 -	번역 표준 원칙
3773	하나둘학교	하나둘學校	Hana Dul School (prep school for young North Korean defectors)	Hanadul hakgyo	Hanadul hakkyo	2009-?	번역 표준 원칙
3774	하나원	하나院	Hanawon (settlement support center for North Korean defectors)	Hanawon	Hanawŏn	1999-?	번역 표준 원칙
3775	하나회	하나會	Hanahoe (Group of One, an unofficial private group of military officers headed by Chun Doo-hwan)	Hanahoe	Hanahoe	1963-1993	번역 표준 원칙
3776	하미마을 학살사건	하미마을 虐殺事件	Hami Village Massacre	Hami maeul haksal sageon	Hami maŭl haksal sakŏn	1968	번역 표준 원칙

NO	용어	한자	영문	RO	MC	시대 및 연도	출전
3777	하산호 전투	하산호 戰鬪	Battle of Lake Khasan	Hasanho jeontu	Hasanho chŏnt'u	1938	번역 표준 원칙
3778	하이브리드		hybrid	hybrid	Haibeurideu	Haibūridū		번역 표준 원칙
3779	하청계열화	下請系列化	vertical integration of subcontracting system	Hacheong gyeyeolhwa	Hach'ŏng kyeyŏlhwa		번역 표준 원칙
3780	하프 플라자 사건	Half Plaza 事件	Half Plaza Scam (e-commerce fraud)	Hapeu peullaja sageon	Hap'ŭ p'ŭllaja sakŏn	2003	번역 표준 원칙
3781	학내 민주화 요구	學內 民主化 要求	demand for the democratization of schools	Haknae minjuhwa yogu	Hangnae minjuhwa yogu		번역 표준 원칙
3782	학도병	學徒兵	student soldiers (in the Korean War)	Hakdobyeong	Haktobyŏng	1950	번역 표준 원칙
3783	학도의용군의 참전	學徒義勇軍의 參戰	student volunteer soldiers in the war	Hakdo uiyonggunui chamjeon	Hakto ŭiyonggunŭi ch'amjŏn	1950	번역 표준 원칙
3784	학도지원병	學徒志願兵	student volunteer soldiers	Hakdo jiwonbyeong	Hakto chiwŏnbyŏng	1943	번역 표준 원칙

NO	용어	한자	영문	RO	MC	시대 및 연도	출전
3785	학도호국단	學徒護國團	National Student Defense Corps	Hakdo hogukdan	Hakto hoguktan	1949-1960, 1975-1985	번역 표준 원칙
3786	학도호국단설치령폐지	學徒護國團設置令廢止	Abolition of the Decree on the Establishment of National Student Defense Corps	Hakdo hogukdan seolchiryeong pyeji	Hakdo hoguktan sŏlch'iryŏng p'yeji	1960, 1985	번역 표준 원칙
3787	학림사건	學林事件	Hangnim Incident of 1981 (oppression of labor and student democratic activists)	Hangnim sageon	Hangnim sakŏn	1981	번역 표준 원칙
3788	학무아문	學務衙門	Bureau of Education	Hangmuamun	Hangmuamun	1894-1895	번역 표준 원칙
3789	학부모회	學父母會	parent-teacher association	Hakbumohoe	Hakpumohoe	1950-?	번역 표준 원칙
3790	학생군사교육	學生軍事敎育	military education for students	Haksaeng gunsa gyoyuk	Haksaeng kunsa kyoyuk		번역 표준 원칙
3791	학생인권조례	學生人權條例	Student Rights Ordinance	Haksaeng ingwon jorye	Haksaeng ingwŏn chorye	2012-?	번역 표준 원칙
3792	학생회	學生會	students association	Haksaenghoe	Haksaenghoe		번역 표준 원칙

NO	용어	한자	영문	RO	MC	시대 및 연도	출전
3793	학원민주화	學園民主化	democratization of schools	Hagwon minjuhwa	Hagwŏn minjuhwa		번역 표준 원칙
3794	학원민주화운동 (4월혁명기)	學園民主化運動 (4月革命期)	struggles for campus democratization	Hagwon minjuhwa undong (4wol hyeongmyeonggi)	Hagwŏn minjuhwa undong (4wŏl hyŏngmyŏnggi)		번역 표준 원칙
3795	학원안정법 파동	學園安定法 波動	controversy over legislation of the Campus Stabilization Act of 1985	Hagwon anjeongbeop padong	Hagwŏn anjŏngpŏp p'adong	1985	번역 표준 원칙
3796	학원자율화조치	學園自律化措置	"Campus Autonomy" measures of 1983	Hagwon jayulhwa jochi	Hagwŏn chayulhwa choch'i	1983	번역 표준 원칙
3797	한 칠레 FTA	韓 Chile FTA	Korea-Chile Free Trade Agreement	Han chille FTA	Han ch'ille FTA	2004	번역 표준 원칙
3798	한 페루 FTA	韓 Peru FTA	Korea-Peru Free Trade Agreement	Han peru FTA	Han p'eru FTA	2011	번역 표준 원칙
3799	한·미 민간협조협정	韓·美 民間協調協定	Agreement of Civilian Cooperation between the Republic of Korea and the U.S.	Han·mi mingan hyeopjo hyeopjeong	Han·mi min'gan hyŏpcho hyŏpchŏng	1955	번역 표준 원칙
3800	한강	漢江	Hangang River	Hangang	Hangang	1950	번역 표준 원칙

NO	용어	한자	영문	RO	MC	시대 및 연도	출전
3801	한강 전투	漢江 戰鬪	Battle of the Hangang River	Hangang jeontu	Han'gang chŏnt'u	1950	번역 표준 원칙
3802	한강 종합개발사업 완료	漢江 綜合開發事業 完了	completion of the Hangang River Development Plan	Hangang jonghap gaebal saeop wallyo	Han'gang chonghap kaebal saŏp wallyo	1986	번역 표준 원칙
3803	한강대교	漢江大橋	Hangang River Bridge	Hangang daegyo	Hangang taegyo	1917	번역 표준 원칙
3804	한강대교 폭파	漢江大橋 爆破	bombing of the Hangang River Bridge	Hangang daegyo pokpa	Han'gang taegyo pokp'a	1950	번역 표준 원칙
3805	한강방어선	漢江防禦線	Hangang River Defense Line	Hanggang bangeoseon	Han'gang pangŏsŏn	1950	번역 표준 원칙
3806	한강선 방어전투	漢江線 防禦戰鬪	Battle of the Hangang River Defense Line	Hangangseon bangeojeontu	Hangangsŏn pangŏjŏnt'u	1950	번역 표준 원칙
3807	한강시민공원	漢江市民公園	Hangang Riverside Park	Hangang simin gongwon	Hanggang simin kongwŏn		번역 표준 원칙
3808	한강의 기적	漢江의 奇蹟	"Miracle on the Hangang River" (referring to Korea's rapid economic growth)	Hangangui gijeok	Han'gang-ŭi kijŏk		번역 표준 원칙

NO	용어	한자	영문	RO	MC	시대 및 연도	출전
3809	한강종합개발	漢江綜合開發	comprehensive development of the Hangang River	hangang jonghap gaebal	Hangang chonghap kaebal		번역 표준 원칙
3810	한강종합개발사업	漢江綜合開發事業	comprehensive Hangang River development project	Hangang jonghap gaebal saeop	Hangang chonghap kaebal saŏp	1982-1986	번역 표준 원칙
3811	한겨레민주당	한겨레民主黨	One Nation Democratic Party (Hankyoreh Minjudang)	Hangyeore minjudang	Hangyŏrye minjudang	1988-1991	번역 표준 원칙
3812	한겨레신문	한겨레新聞	Hankyoreh Shinmun (daily newspaper)	Hangyeorye sinmun	Hangyŏrye sinmun	1988	번역 표준 원칙
3813	한국 공군	韓國 空軍	ROK Air Force	Hanguk gonggun	Hanguk konggun	1950	번역 표준 원칙
3814	한국 구호원조물품	韓國 救護援助物品	relief aid goods for the ROK	Hanguk guho wonjo mulpum	Han'guk kuho wŏnjo mulpum	1951	번역 표준 원칙
3815	한국 민간 구호계획	韓國 民間 救護計劃	Civilian Relief in Korea (CRIK)	Hanguk mingan guho gyehoek	Han'guk min'gan kuho kyehoek	1950-1954	번역 표준 원칙
3816	한국 육군	韓國 陸軍	ROK Army	Hanguk yukgun	Hanguk yukkun	1950	번역 표준 원칙

NO	용어	한자	영문	RO	MC	시대 및 연도	출전
3817	한국 육군본부	韓國 陸軍本部	ROK Army Headquarters	Hanguk yukgunbonbu	Hanguk yukkunbonbu	1950	번역 표준 원칙
3818	한국 전투작전정보본부	韓國 戰鬪作戰情報本部	Korea Combat Operations Intelligence Center (KCOICK)	Hanguk jeontu jakjeon jeongbo bonbu	Hanguk chŏntu chakchŏn chŏngbo ponbu		번역 표준 원칙
3819	한국 해군	韓國 海軍	ROK Navy	Hanguk haegun	Hanguk haegun	1950	번역 표준 원칙
3820	한국가스공사	韓國Gas公社	Korea Gas Corporation (KOGAS)	Hanguk gaseu gongsa	Han'guk kasŭ kongsa	1983-?	번역 표준 원칙
3821	한국가톨릭노동청년회	韓國Catholic勞動靑年會	Korean Catholic Labor Youth Association	Hanguk gatollik nodong cheongnyeonhoe	Han'guk kat'ollik nodong ch'ŏngnyŏnhoe	1958-?	한국학중앙연구원,《영문한국백과》-농민운동
3822	한국가톨릭농민회	韓國Catholic農民會	Korean Catholic Farmers Union (CFU)	Hanguk gatollik nongminhoe	Han'guk kat'ollik nongminhoe	1966-?	번역 표준 원칙
3823	한국고속철도	韓國高速鐵道	Korea Train Express (KTX)	Hanguk Gosok Cheoldo	Hanguk Kosok Ch'ŏlto	2004-?	번역 표준 원칙
3824	한국과학기술연구원	韓國科學技術硏究院	Korea Institute of Science and Technology (KIST)	Hanguk gwahak gisul yeonguwon	Han'guk kwahak kisul yŏn'guwŏn	1966	번역 표준 원칙

NO	용어	한자	영문	RO	MC	시대 및 연도	출전
3825	한국과학기술원	韓國科學技術院	Korea Advanced Institute of Science and Technology (KAIST)	Hanguk gwahak gisurwon	Han'guk kwahak kisurwŏn	1971-?	번역 표준 원칙
3826	한국과학원	韓國科學院	Korea Advanced Institute of Science (KAIS)	Hanguk gwahagwon	Han'guk kwahagwŏn	1971	번역 표준 원칙
3827	한국과학원 요람	韓國科學院 要覽	Korea Advanced Institute of Science prospectus	Hanguk gwahagwon yoram	Han'guk kwahagwŏn yoram	1971	번역 표준 원칙
3828	한국광복군	韓國光復軍	Korean Restoration Army	Hanguk gwangbokgun	Han'guk kwangbokkun	1940-1945	Peter H. Lee, Sourcebook of Korean Civilization(Volume 2), Columbia University Press, 1993,
3829	한국광복군 제1지대	韓國光復軍 第1支隊	First Detachment of the Korean Restoration Army	Hanguk gwangbokgun je1jidae	Han'guk kwangbokkun che1chidae		번역 표준 원칙
3830	한국광복군총사령부	韓國光復軍總司令部	General Headquarters of the Korean Restoration Army	Hanguk gwangbokgun chongsaryeongbu	Han'guk kwangbokkun ch'ongsaryŏngbu	1940-1945	번역 표준 원칙
3831	한국광복진선청년 공작대	韓國光復陣線靑年 工作隊	Frontline Youth for Korea's Liberation	Hanguk gwangbok jinseon cheongnyeon gongjakdae	Han'guk kwangbok chinsŏn ch'ŏngnyŏn kongjakdae		번역 표준 원칙
3832	한국교원노동조합 연합회	韓國敎員勞動組合 聯合會	National League of Teachers' Labor Unions	Hanguk gyowon nodongjohap yeonhaphoe	Han'guk kyowŏn nodongjohap yŏnhap'oe	1960	번역 표준 원칙

NO	용어	한자	영문	RO	MC	시대 및 연도	출전
3833	한국교원단체총연합회	韓國敎員團體總聯合會	Korean Federation of Teachers' Associations	Hanguk gyowon danche chongyeonhaphoe	Han'guk kyowŏn tanch'e ch'ongyŏnhap'oe	1947-?	번역 표준 원칙
3834	한국국민당	韓國國民黨	Korean National Party	Hanguk gungmindang	Han'guk kungmindang	1981-1988	번역 표준 원칙
3835	한국국제협력단	韓國國際協力團	Korean International Cooperation Agency (KOICA)	Hanguk gukje hyeomnyeokdan	Han'guk kukche hyŏmnyŏktan	1991-?	번역 표준 원칙
3836	한국군 작전권	韓國軍 作戰權	operational authority of the ROK Military	Hangukgun jakjeongwon	Han'gukkun chakchŏnkwŏn		번역 표준 원칙
3837	한국군과 유엔군	韓國軍과 UN軍	ROK and UN forces	Hangukgungwa yuengun	Hangukkungwa yuengun	1950	번역 표준 원칙
3838	한국군철수	韓國軍撤收	withdrawal of ROK troops from the Vietnam War	Hangukgun cheolsu	Han'gukkun ch'ŏlsu	1973	번역 표준 원칙
3839	한국군현대화	韓國軍現代化	modernization of the ROK Military	Hangukgun hyeondaehwa	Han'gukkun hyŏndaehwa		번역 표준 원칙
3840	한국노동자복지협의회	韓國勞動者福祉協議會	Korean Council for Labor Welfare	Hanguk nodongja bokji hyeobuihoe	Han'guk nodongja pokchi hyŏbŭihoe	1984-1989	번역 표준 원칙

NO	용어	한자	영문	RO	MC	시대 및 연도	출전
3841	한국노동조합총연맹	韓國勞動組合總聯盟	Federation of Korean Trade Unions (FKTU)	Hanguk nodong johap chongnyeonmaeng	Han'guk nodong chohap ch'ongyŏnmaeng	1960	번역 표준 원칙
3842	한국노병회	韓國勞兵會	Korean Labor-Soldier Association (Shanghai-based independence activist group formed in 1922)	Hanguk nobyeonghoe	Hanguk nobyŏnghoe	1922	번역 표준 원칙
3843	한국대일전선통일동맹	韓國對日戰線統一同盟	Korean Anti-Japanese Front Unification League	Hanguk daeil jeonseon tongil dongmaeng	Han'guk taeil chŏnsŏn t'ongil tongmaeng	1932	번역 표준 원칙
3844	한국대학생해외봉사단	韓國大學生海外奉仕團	Korea University Volunteer Program (KUV)	Hanguk daehaksaeng haeoe bongsadan	Han'guk taehaksaeng haeoe pongsadan		번역 표준 원칙
3845	한국독립군	韓國獨立軍	Korean Independence Army	Hanguk dongnipgun	Han'guk tongnipkun	1910-1945	한국학중앙연구원, 《영문한국백과》-간도
3846	한국독립당	韓國獨立黨	Korean Independence Party	Hanguk dongnipdang	Han'guk tongniptang	1930-1933	한국학중앙연구원, 《영문한국백과》-김구
3847	한국독립청원서	韓國獨立請願書	Petition for Korean Independence: "The claim of the Korean people and nation for liberation from Japan and the reconstitution of Korea as an	Hanguk dongnip cheongwonseo	Han'guk tongnip ch'ŏngwŏnsŏ	1919	번역 표준 원칙
3848	한국모방노동자투쟁	韓國毛紡勞動者鬪爭	Wonpoong Textiles labor disputes	Hanguk mobang nodongja tujaeng	Han'guk mobang nodongja t'ujaeng	1972-1982	번역 표준 원칙

NO	용어	한자	영문	RO	MC	시대 및 연도	출전
3849	한국무역협회	韓國貿易協會	Korea International Trade Association (KITA)	Hanguk muyeok hyeophoe	Han'guk muyŏk hyŏphoe	1946-?	번역 표준 원칙
3850	한국문학가협회	韓國文學家協會	Korean Literary Association	Hanguk munhakga hyeophoe	Han'gunk munakka hyŏphoe	1949-1961	번역 표준 원칙
3851	한국문화유산	韓國文化遺産	Korean cultural heritage	Hanguk munhwa yusan	Han'guk munhwa yusan		번역 표준 원칙
3852	한국미군정사	韓國美軍政史	History of U.S. Military Government in Korea	Hanguk migunjeongsa	Han'guk migunjŏngsa	1948	번역 표준 원칙
3853	한국민족민주전선	韓國民族民主戰線	Korean National Democratic Front	Hanguk minjok minju jeonseon	Hanguk minjok minju chŏnsŏn	1985-	번역 표준 원칙
3854	한국민족예술인 총연합	韓國民族藝術人 總聯合	Korean People's Artists Federation (Minyechong)	Hanguk minjok yesurin chongyeonhap	Han'guk minjok yesurin ch'ongyŏnhap	1988-?	번역 표준 원칙
3855	한국민족혁명당	韓國民族革命黨	Korean National Revolutionary Party	Hanguk minjok hyeongmyeongdang	Hanguk minjok hyŏngmyŏngdang	1935-1946	번역 표준 원칙
3856	한국민족혁명당 북미 총지부	韓國民族革命黨 北美總 支部	North American Branch of the Korean National Revolutionary Party	Hanguk minjok hyeongmyeongdang bungmi chaongjibu	Hanguk minjok hyŏngmyŏngdang pungmi ch'ongjibu		번역 표준 원칙

NO	용어	한자	영문	RO	MC	시대 및 연도	출전
3857	한국민주당(한민당)	韓國民主黨(韓民黨)	Korea Democratic Party	Hanguk minjudang (hanmindang)	Han'guk minjudang (hanmindang)	1945-1949	번역 표준 원칙
3858	한국민주회복통일촉진국민회(한민통)	韓國民主回復統一促進國民會(韓民統)	Korean People's Organization for Restoring Democracy and Promoting Unification	Hanguk minju hoebok tongil chokjin gungminhoe (hanmintong)	Han'guk minju hoebok t'ongil ch'okchin kungminhoe (hanmint'ong)	1973-?	번역 표준 원칙
3859	한국방송공사	韓國放送公社	Korean Broadcasting System (KBS)	Hanguk bangsong gonsa	Han'guk pangsong kongsa	1969-?	KBS 공식 사이트 www.kbs.co.kr
3860	한국병합	韓國併合	Japan's annexation of Korea	Hanguk byeonghap	Han'guk pyŏnghap	1910	번역 표준 원칙
3861	한국병합령말설	韓國併合令말설	A Report on Japan's Annexation of Korea (written by the Japanese)	Hanguk byeonghapryeong malseol	Han'guk pyŏnghamnyŏng malsŏl	1910	번역 표준 원칙
3862	한국비료공장	韓國肥料工場	Korea Fertilizer (now Samsung Fine Chemicals)	Hanguk biryo gongjang	Han'guk piryo kongjang	1966	번역 표준 원칙
3863	한국사정사	韓國事情社	Korean Affairs Institute	Hanguk sajeongsa	Hanguk sajŏngsa	1943	번역 표준 원칙
3864	한국사회당	韓國社會黨	Korean Socialist Party	Hanguk sahoedang	Han'guk sahoedang	1960-?	번역 표준 원칙

NO	용어	한자	영문	RO	MC	시대 및 연도	출전
3865	한국산업인력공단	韓國産業人力公團	Human Resources Development Service of Korea	Hanguk saneop illyeok gongdan	Han'guk sanŏp illyŏk kongdan	1982-?	번역 표준 원칙
3866	한국수출입은행	韓國輸出入銀行	Export-Import Bank of Korea	Hanguk suchurip eunhaeng	Han'guk such'urip ŭnhaeng	1976-?	번역 표준 원칙
3867	한국에 대한 군사원조	韓國에 對한 軍事援助	military assistance to the Republic of Korea	Hanguge daehan gunsawonjo	Hanguge taehan kunsawoncho	1950	번역 표준 원칙
3868	한국원조물자의 공급	韓國援助物資의 供給	supply of relief aid to the ROK	Hanguk wonjo muljaui gonggeup	Han'guk wŏnjo mulcha-ŭi konggŭp		번역 표준 원칙
3869	한국위원부 (필라델피아)	韓國委員部	Korea Information Bureau in Philadelphia	Hanguk wiwonbu (pilladelpia)	Hanguk wiwonbu (p'illadelp'ia)		번역 표준 원칙
3870	한국유일독립당	韓國唯一獨立黨	Korean Unitary Independence Party	Hanguk yuil dongnipdang	Han'guk yuil tongniptang	1928-?	번역 표준 원칙
3871	한국유일독립당 촉성회	韓國唯一獨立黨促成會	Promotive Association of the Korean Unitary Independence Party	Hanguk yuil dongnipdang chokseonghoe	Han'guk yuil tongniptang ch'oksŏnghoe	1927-1929	번역 표준 원칙
3872	한국은행	韓國銀行	Bank of Korea (BOK)	Hangug eunhaeng	Hanguk ŭnhaeng	1950-?	번역 표준 원칙

NO	용어	한자	영문	RO	MC	시대 및 연도	출전
3873	한국일보	韓國日報	Hankook Ilbo (daily newspaper)	Hanguk ilbo	Hanguk ilbo	1954-?	번역 표준 원칙
3874	한국적 민주주의	韓國的 民主主義	"Korean-style democracy"	Hangukjeok minjujuui	Hangukchŏk minjujuŭi		번역 표준 원칙
3875	한국전쟁	韓國戰爭	Korean War (1950-53)	Hanguk jeonjaeng	Hanguk chŏnjaeng	1950-1953 (휴전협정)	번역 표준 원칙
3876	한국전쟁 종군기자	韓國戰爭 從軍記者	Korean War correspondents	Hanguk jeonjaeng jonggungija	Hanguk chŏnjaeng chonggun Kija		번역 표준 원칙
3877	한국정밀기기센터 (한국산업기술 시험원)	韓國精密器機center (韓國産業技術試驗院)	Fine Instrument Center (now Korea Testing Laboratory)	Hanguk jeongmil gigi senteo (hanguk saneop gisul siheomwon)	Hanguk chŏngmil kigi sent'ŏ (hanguk sanŏp kisul sihŏmwŏn)	1966-?	번역 표준 원칙
3878	한국정전협정전문	韓國停戰協定全文	full text of the Armistice Agreement	Hanguk jeongjeon hyeopjeong jeonmun	Han'guk chŏngjŏn hyŏpchŏng chŏnmun	1953	번역 표준 원칙
3879	한국종단송유관	韓國縱斷送油管	Trans Korea Pipeline (TKP)	Hanguk jongdan songyugwan	han'guk chongdan songyugwan	1970	번역 표준 원칙
3880	한국주차일본군 참모부	韓國駐箚日本軍 參謀部	Staff Section of Japanese Troops Stationed in Korea	Hanguk jucha ilbongun chammobu	Hanguk juch'a ilbongun ch'ammobu		번역 표준 원칙

NO	용어	한자	영문	RO	MC	시대 및 연도	출전
3881	한국청년전지공작대	韓國青年戰地工作隊	Korean Youths Battlefield Mission Corps.	Hanguk cheongnyeon jeonji gongjakdae	Han'guk ch'ŏngnyŏn chŏnji kongjaktae	1938-1940	번역 표준 원칙
3882	한국청년해외봉사단	韓國青年海外奉仕團	Korea Youth Volunteers (KYV)	Hanguk cheongnyeon haeoe bongsadan	Han'guk ch'ŏngnyŏn haeoe pongsadan	1989	번역 표준 원칙
3883	한국총람	韓國總覽	UNESCO Korean survey	Hanguk chongnam	Han'guk ch'ongnam	1957	번역 표준 원칙
3884	한국친우회	韓國親友會	League of Friends of Korea	Hanguk chinuhoe	Han'guk ch'inuhoe	1920	번역 표준 원칙
3885	한국토지주택공사	韓國土地住宅公社	Korea Land and Housing Corporation (LH)	Hanguk toji jutaek gongsa	Han'guk t'oji jut'aek kongsa	2009	번역 표준 원칙
3886	한국통감부(통감부)	韓國統監府 (統監府)	Japanese Residency-General of Korea	Hanguk tonggambu (tonggambu)	Han'guk t'onggambu (t'onggambu)	1906-1910	번역 표준 원칙
3887	한국통사	韓國痛史	The Tragic History of Korea (Hanguk Tongsa)	Hanguk tosinbu	Han'guk t'ongsa	1919	번역 표준 원칙
3888	한국통신부 (파리통신부)	韓國通信部 (Paris通信部)	Bureau of Information of the Republic of Korea in Paris	Hanguk tongsinbu (pari tongsinbu)	Hanguk t'ongsinbu (p'ari t'ongsinbu)		번역 표준 원칙

NO	용어	한자	영문	RO	MC	시대 및 연도	출전
3889	한국통신부 (필라델피아 통신부)	韓國通信部 (Philadelpia通信部)	Bureau of Information of the Republic of Korea in Philadelphia	Hanguk tongsinbu (pilladelpia tongsinbu)	Han'guk t'ŏngsinbu (p'illadelp'ia t'ŏngsinbu)		번역 표준 원칙
3890	한국통일에 관한 14개 원칙안	韓國統一에 關한 14個 原則案	14-Point Proposal for the Unification of Korea	Hanguk tongire gwanhan 14gae wonchigan	Hanguk t'ongire kwanhan 14gae wŏnch'igan		번역 표준 원칙
3891	한국표준연구소	韓國標準硏究所	Korea Research Institute of Standards and Science (KRISS)	Hanguk pyojun yeonguso	Han'guk p'yojun yŏn'guso	1975-?	번역 표준 원칙
3892	한국해군 백두산함	韓國海軍 白頭山艦	ROKS Baekdusan	Hanguk haegun baekdusanham	Hanguk haegun paektusanham	1950	번역 표준 원칙
3893	한국해외개발공사	韓國海外開發公社	Korean Overseas Development Corp.	Hanguk haeoe gaebal gongsa	Han'guk haeoe kaebal kongsa	1975	번역 표준 원칙
3894	한국해외봉사단	韓國海外奉仕團	Korea Overseas Volunteers Program (KOV)	Hanguk haeoe bongsadan	Han'guk haeoe pongsadan	1990-?	번역 표준 원칙
3895	한국핵연료개발공단	韓國核燃料開發工團	Korea Nuclear Fuel Development Institute	Hanguk haek yeonryo gaebal gongdan	Han'guk haek yŏllyo kaebal kongdan	1976-1980 (한국에너지연구소로 흡수 통합)	번역 표준 원칙
3896	한국형 고속열차	韓國型 高速列車	Korean high-speed train	Hangukhyeong gosok yeolcha	Hangukhyŏng kosok yŏlch'a		번역 표준 원칙

NO	용어	한자	영문	RO	MC	시대 및 연도	출전
3897	한국형 대잠경어뢰	韓國形 對潛輕魚雷	Korean antisubmarine light weight torpedo	Hangukhyeong daejamgyeong eoroe	Han'gukhyŏng taejamgyŏng ŏroe		번역 표준 원칙
3898	한국형 슈퍼컴퓨터 개발	韓國型 Supercomputer 開發	development of a Korean supercomputer	Hangukhyeong syupeo keompyuteo gaebal	Han'gukkyŏng syup'ŏ k'ŏmp'yut'ŏ kaebal		번역 표준 원칙
3899	한국형 전투장갑차	韓國型 戰鬪裝甲車	Korean Fighting Vehicle (KFV)	Hangukhyeong juntu janggapcha	Hangukhyŏng chŏnt'u changgapch'a	1999	번역 표준 원칙
3900	한국형 주식회사	韓國形 株式會社	Korean style incorporated companies	Hangukhyeong jusikhoesa	Han'gukhyŏng chusikhoesa		번역 표준 원칙
3901	한글간소화파동	한글簡素化波動	controversy over the simplification of Hangeul	Hangeul gansohwa padong	Han'gŭl kansohwa p'adong	1953-1955	번역 표준 원칙
3902	한글독본	한글讀本	*Hangeul Reader* (Hangeul Dokbeon)	Hangeul dokbon	Han'gŭl tokpon	1946	번역 표준 원칙
3903	한글맞춤법통일안	한글맞춤法統一案	"Proposal for Unified Hangeul Orthography"	Hangeul matchumbeop tongiran	Han'gŭl match'umpŏp t'ongiran	1933	번역 표준 원칙
3904	한글보급운동	한글普及運動	campaign for the propagation of Hangeul (Korean script)	Hangeul bogeub undong	Han'gŭl pogŭp undong		번역 표준 원칙

NO	용어	한자	영문	RO	MC	시대 및 연도	출전
3905	한글의 우수성	한글의 優秀性	strengths of Hangeul, the Korean writing system	Hangeurui ususeong	Hangŭrŭi ususŏng		번역 표준 원칙
3906	한글학회	한글學會	Korean Language Society	Hangeulhakhoe	Han'gŭrhak'oe	1949-?	번역 표준 원칙
3907	한글학회큰사전	한글學會큰辭典	A Comprehensive Dictionary by Korean Language Research Society (Hangeul Hakhoe Keunsajeon)	Hangeul hakgoe keunsajeon	Han'gŭl hakhoe k'ŭnsajŏn	1957-1958	번역 표준 원칙
3908	한단수호통상조약	韓丹修好通商條約	Treaty of Friendship, Commerce and Navigation between Korea and Denmark, 1902	Handan suho tongsang joyak	Handan suho t'ongsang choyak	1902	번역 표준 원칙
3909	한독간 간호요원 협정	韓獨間 看護要員 協定	Agreement on the Hiring of Nurses between Korea and West Germany (August 1969)	Handok gan ganho yowon hyeopjeong	Handok kan kanho yowŏn hyŏpchŏng	1969	번역 표준 원칙
3910	한독재정차관협정	韓獨財政借款協定	Korea-Germany loan agreement	Handok jaejeong chagwan hyeopjeong	Handok jaejŏng ch'agwan hyŏpchŏng		번역 표준 원칙
3911	한러은행	韓露銀行	Korea-Russia Bank	Hanneo eunhaeng	Hallŏ ŭnhaeng	1898	번역 표준 원칙
3912	한류	韓流	Korean Wave (Hallyu)	Hallyu	Hallyu		번역 표준 원칙

NO	용어	한자	영문	RO	MC	시대 및 연도	출전
3913	한문교과 신설	漢文敎科 新設	introduction of Chinese Characters and Classics into the school curriculum	Hanmun gyogwa sinseol	Hanmun gyokwa sinsŏl	1972	번역 표준 원칙
3914	한미 군사고위회담	韓美 軍事高位會談	ROK-U.S. Military Committee Meeting (MCM)	Hanmi gunsa gowihoedam	Hanmi kunsa kowihoedam		번역 표준 원칙
3915	한미 군사원조회담	韓美 軍事援助會談	ROK-U.S. Military Assistance Talks	Hanmi gunsa wonjohoedam	Hanmi kunsa wŏnjohoedam		번역 표준 원칙
3916	한미 면직물협정	韓美 綿織物協定	Korea-U.S. Agreement on Cotton Textiles (officially, Agreement between the Government of the Republic of	Hanmi myeonjikmul hyeopjeong	Hanmi myŏnjingmul hyŏpchŏng	1971	번역 표준 원칙
3917	한미 쇠고기 협상	韓美 쇠고기 協商	Korea-U.S. beef import negotiations	Hanmi soegogi hyeopsang	Hanmi soegogi hyŏpsang	2008	번역 표준 원칙
3918	한미 투자 공동 관리 위원회	韓美 投資 共同 管理委員會	Korea-U.S. Committee for Joint Investment Management	Hanmi tuja gongdong gwalli wiwonhoe	Hanmi t'uja kongdong kwalli wiwŏnoe		번역 표준 원칙
3919	한미FTA	韓美FTA	Free Trade Agreement (FTA) between ROK and the U.S.	Hanmi FTA	Hanmi FTA	2007	번역 표준 원칙
3920	한미간 재정·재산에 관한 협정	韓美間 財政·財産에 關한 協定	Initial Financial and Property Settlement Agreement between the Government of the Republic of Korea and the Government of the United States of America	Hanmi gan jaejeong·jaesan-e gwanhan hyeopjeong	Hanmi kan chaejŏng·chaesan-e kwanhan hyŏpchŏng	1948	번역 표준 원칙

NO	용어	한자	영문	RO	MC	시대 및 연도	출전
3921	한미간 핵연구 및 훈련기구와 자제의 공여에 관한 협정 서명	韓美間 核硏究 및 訓鍊機構와 資材의 供與에 關한 協定 署名	signing of the agreement on U.S. assistance for the acquisition of certain nuclear research and training equipment and materials for ROK	Hanmigan haegyeongu mit hullyeongiguwa jajeui gongyeoe gwanhan hyeopjeong seomyeong	Hanmigan heagyŏngu mit hullyŏngiguwa chaje ŭi kongyŏ-e kwanan hyŏ pchŏng sŏmyŏng		번역 표준 원칙
3922	한미간 행정권이양	韓美間 行政權移讓	U.S. transfer of administrative authority to ROK	Hanmigan haengjeonggwon iyang	Hanmigan haengjŏngkw ŏn iyang	1948	번역 표준 원칙
3923	한미경제원조협정	韓美經濟援助協定	Comprehensive Agreement regarding Economic Technical Assistance between the Government of Republic of Korea and the Government of the United States of America	Hanmi gyeongje wonjo hyeopjeong	Hanmi kyŏngje wŏnjo hyŏpchŏng	1961	번역 표준 원칙
3924	한미경제협정	韓美經濟協定	Comprehensive Agreement regarding Economic, Technical Assistance between the Government of the Republic of Korea and the Government of the United States of America	Hanmi gyeongje hyeopjeong	Hanmi kyŏngje hyŏpchŏ ng	1961	번역 표준 원칙
3925	한미경제협정반대투쟁	韓美經濟協定反對鬪爭	protests against Korea-U.S. economic agreement	Hanmi gyeongje hyeopjeong bandae tujaeng	Hanmi kyŏngje hyŏpch ŏng pandae t'ujaeng	1961	번역 표준 원칙
3926	한미공조	韓美共助	Korea-U.S. cooperation	Hanmi gongjo	Hanmi kongjo		번역 표준 원칙
3927	한미군사위원회 (MCM)	韓美軍事委員會	ROK-U.S. Military Committee Meeting (MCM)	Hanmi gunsa wiwonhoe (MCM)	Hanmi kunsa wiwŏnhoe (MCM)	1978-	번역 표준 원칙
3928	한미문화협회	韓美文化協會	Korean American Cultural Association	Hanmi munhwa hyeophoe	Hanmi munhwa hyŏ phoe		번역 표준 원칙

NO	용어	한자	영문	RO	MC	시대 및 연도	출전
3929	한미상호방위원조협정	韓美相互防衛援助協定	Mutual Defense Assistance Agreement between the Government of the Republic of Korea and the Government of the United States of America	Hanmi sangho bangwi wonjo hyeopjeong	Hanmi sangho pangwi wŏnjo hyŏpchŏng	1950	번역 표준 원칙
3930	한미상호방위조약	韓美相互防衛條約	ROK-U.S. Mutual Defense Treaty	Hanmi sangho bangwi joyak	Hanmi sangho pangwi choyak	1953	번역 표준 원칙
3931	한미상호방위조약 비준서 교환의 건	韓美相互防衛條約 批准書 交換의 件	Ratification of the ROK-U.S. Mutual Defense Agreement	Hanmi sangho bangwi joyak bijunseo gyohwanui geon	Hanmi sangho pangwi choyak pijunsŏ kyohwan-ŭi kŏn	1954	번역 표준 원칙
3932	한미수교 100주년	韓美修交 100周年	100th anniversary of Korea-U.S. diplomatic relations	Hanmi sugyo 100junyeon	Hanmi sugyo 100junyŏn	1982	번역 표준 원칙
3933	한미안보협력체제	韓美安保協力體制	Korea-U.S. security cooperation	Hanmi anbo hyeomnyeok cheje	Hanmi anbo hyŏmnyŏk ch'eje		번역 표준 원칙
3934	한미야전군사령부 (CFA, ROK/US Combined Field Army)	韓美野戰軍司令部	ROK-U.S. Combined Field Army Command	Hanmi yajeongun saryeongbu (CFA, ROK/US Combined Field Army)	Hanmi yajŏn'gun saryŏngbu (CFA, ROK/US Combined Field Army)	1980-1992	번역 표준 원칙
3935	한미연례안보협의회의(SCM)	韓美年例安保協議會議	ROK-U.S. Security Consultative Meeting (SCM)	Hanmi yeollye anbo hyeobui hoeui (SCM)	Hanmi yŏllye anbo hyŏbŭi hoeŭi (SCM)	1968-?	번역 표준 원칙
3936	한미연합군사령부	韓美聯合軍司令部	ROK-U.S. Combined Forces Command	Hanmi yeonhapgun saryeongbu	Hanmi yŏnhapkun saryŏngbu	1978-	번역 표준 원칙

NO	용어	한자	영문	RO	MC	시대 및 연도	출전
3937	한미연합독수리훈련	韓美聯合독수리訓鍊	ROK-U.S. Combined Foal Eagle Exercise	Hanmi yeonhap doksuri hullyeon	Hanmi yŏnhap toksuri hullyŏn		번역 표준 원칙
3938	한미연합작전	韓美聯合作戰	ROK-U.S. combined operations	Hanmi yeonhap jakjeon	Hanmi yŏnhap chakchŏn		번역 표준 원칙
3939	한미연합항공사령부	韓美聯合航空司領部	ROK-U.S. Combined Aviation Command (CAF)	Hanmi yeonhap hanggong saryeongbu	Hanmi yŏnhap hanggong saryŏngbu		번역 표준 원칙
3940	한미일 삼각안보체제	韓美日 三角安保體制	U.S.-Korea-Japan Security Triangle	Hanmiil samgak anbo cheje	Hanmiil samgak anbo ch'eje		번역 표준 원칙
3941	한미재정재산협정	韓美財政財産協定	Korea-U.S. Financial and Property Settlement	Hanmi jaejeong jaesan hyeopjeong	Hanmi chaejŏng chaesan hyŏpchŏng	1948	번역 표준 원칙
3942	한미전기회사	韓美電氣會社	Korean-American Electric Company	Hanmi jeongi hoesa	Hanmi chŏn'gi hoesa	1904-1911	번역 표준 원칙
3943	한미제1군단	韓美第1軍團	ROK-U.S. I Corps	Hanmi je1 gundan	Hanmi che1 kundan	1971	번역 표준 원칙
3944	한미주둔군지위협정 개정협상	韓美駐屯軍地位協定 改正協商	talks to amend the Korea-U.S. Status of Forces Agreement (SOFA)	Hanmi judungun jiwihyeopjeong gaejeong hyeopsang	Hanmi judungun jiwihyŏ pchŏng kaejŏng hyŏ psang	1991, 2001	번역 표준 원칙

NO	용어	한자	영문	RO	MC	시대 및 연도	출전
3945	한미합동경제위원회	韓美合同經濟委員會	Korean-American Combined Economic Board	Hanmi hapdong gyeongje wiwonhoe	Hanmi haptong kyŏngje wiwŏnhoe	1952-1963	번역 표준 원칙
3946	한미행정협정	韓美行政協定	Status of Forces Agreement (SOFA)	Hanmi haengjeong hyeopjeong	Hanmi haengjŏng hyŏpchŏng	1966 조인 1967 발효	번역 표준 원칙
3947	한미협회	韓美協會	Korean American Council	Hanmi hyeophoe	Hanmi hyŏphoe	1963-?	번역 표준 원칙
3948	한민족말살정책	韓民族抹殺政策	policy for eliminating Korean identity	Hanminjok malsal jeongchaek	Hanminjok malsal chŏngch'aek		번역 표준 원칙
3949	한민족체육대회	韓民族體育大會	World Koreans Festival	Hanminjok cheyukdaehoe	Hanminjok ch'eyuktaehoe		번역 표준 원칙
3950	한민학교	韓民學校	Hanmin School	Hanmin hakgyo	Hanmin hakkyo	1911-1937	번역 표준 원칙
3951	한반도	韓半島	Korean Peninsula	Hanbando	Hanbando		번역 표준 원칙
3952	한반도 비핵화	韓半島 非核化	denuclearization of the Korean Peninsula	Hanbando bihaekhwa	Hanbando pihaekhwa		번역 표준 원칙

NO	용어	한자	영문	RO	MC	시대 및 연도	출전
3953	한반도에너지개발기구	韓半島Energy開發機構	Korean Peninsula Energy Development Organization (KEDO)	Hanbando eneoji gaebal gigu	Hanbando enŏji kaebal kigu	1995-?	번역 표준 원칙
3954	한보사태	韓寶事態	Hanbo Group loan scandal (1997)	Hanbo satae	Hanbo sat'ae	1997	번역 표준 원칙
3955	한복	韓服	*hanbok* (traditional Korean clothing)	Hanbok	Hanbok		번역 표준 원칙
3956	한북흥학회	漢北興學會	Northern Region Association for Promotion of Learning (youth enlightenment movement from Hamgyeongbuk-do Province during	Hanbuk heunghakhoe	Hanbuk hŭnghakhoe	1906	번역 표준 원칙
3957	한불자전	韓佛字典	*Dictionnaire Coréen-Français (Korean-French Dictionary)*	Hanbuljajeon	Hanbuljajŏn	1880	번역 표준 원칙
3958	한비수호통상조약	韓比修好通商條約	Treaty of Amity and Commerce between Korea and Belgium, 1901	Hanbi suho tongsang joyak	Hanbi suho t'ongsang choyak	1901	번역 표준 원칙
3959	한성사범학교	漢城師範學校	Hanseong Teacher Training School (now Seoul National University College of Education)	Hanseong sabeom hakgyo	Hansŏng sabŏm hakkyo	1895-1911	번역 표준 원칙
3960	한성순보	漢城旬報	*Hanseong Sunbo (Seoul Tri-monthly)*	Hanseongsunbo	Hansŏngsunbo	1883-1884	번역 표준 원칙

- 515 -

NO	용어	한자	영문	RO	MC	시대 및 연도	출전
3961	한성외국어학교	漢城外國語學校	Hanseong Foreign Language School	Hanseong oegugeo hakgyo	Hansŏng oegugŏ hakkyo		번역 표준 원칙
3962	한성은행	漢城銀行	Hanseong Bank	Hanseong eunhaeng	Hansŏng ŭnhaeng	1897-1943	번역 표준 원칙
3963	한성전기회사	漢城電氣會社	Hanseong Electric Company	Hanseong jeongi hoesa	Hansŏng chŏn'gi hoesa	1896-?	번역 표준 원칙
3964	한성전보총국	漢城電報總局	Hanseong Telegram Service	Hanseong jeonbo chongguk	Hansŏng chŏnbo ch'ongguk	1885-1894	번역 표준 원칙
3965	한성정부	漢城政府	Hanseong Provisional Government	Hanseong jeongbu	Hansŏng chŏngbu	1919	번역 표준 원칙
3966	한성조약	漢城條約	Hanseong Treaty of 1885	Hanseong joyak	Hansŏng choyak	1885	번역 표준 원칙
3967	한성주보	漢城周報	*Hanseong Jubo* (weekly newspaper published in mixed Chinese and Korean script)	Hanseongjubo	Hansŏngjubo	1886-1888	번역 표준 원칙
3968	한소정상회담	韓蘇頂上會談	Korea-Soviet Union Summit of 1991	Hanso jeongsang hoedam	Hanso ch'ŏngsang hoedam	1990	번역 표준 원칙

NO	용어	한자	영문	RO	MC	시대 및 연도	출전
3969	한약사 제도	韓藥師 制度	licensed Asian Medicine Pharmacist system	Hanyaksa jedo	Hanyaksa chedo	1994	번역 표준 원칙
3970	한영서원	韓英書院	Hanyeong College	Hanyeong seowon	Hanyŏng sŏwon	1906-1917	번역 표준 원칙
3971	한옥	韓屋	*hanok* (traditional Korean house)	Hanok	Hanok		번역 표준 원칙
3972	한은특융	韓銀特融	low-interest central bank loans/ low-interest loans extended by the Bank of Korea	Haneun teugyung	Hanŭn tŭgyung		번역 표준 원칙
3973	한인 빨치산	韓人 Partisan	Korean Partisans	Hanin ppalchisan	Hanin ppalch'Isan		번역 표준 원칙
3974	한인강제이주	韓人强制移住	forced relocation of ethnic Koreans to Central Asia	Hanin gangje iju	Hanin kangje iju	1937	번역 표준 원칙
3975	한인국방경비대 (맹호군)	韓人國防警備隊 (猛虎軍)	California Korean Reserve (Tiger Brigade)	Hanin gukbang gyeongbidae (maenghogun)	Hanin kukpang kyŏngbidae (maenghogun)	1942-?	번역 표준 원칙
3976	한인기독교회	韓人基督教會	Korean Christian Church	Hanin gidokgyohoe	Hanin kidokkyohoe	1918	번역 표준 원칙

- 517 -

NO	용어	한자	영문	RO	MC	시대 및 연도	출전
3977	한인기독학교	韓人基督學校	Korean Christian Institute (in Hawaii)	Hanin gidokhakgyo	Hanin kidokhakkyo	1918	번역 표준 원칙
3978	한인기숙학교	韓人寄宿學校	Korean Compound Boarding School	Hanin gisukhakgyo	Hanin kisukhakkyo	1911	번역 표준 원칙
3979	한인대표회	韓人代表會	Korean Representative Meeting	Hanin daepyohoe	Hanin taep'yohoe		번역 표준 원칙
3980	한인동북의용군	韓人東北義勇軍	Korean Unit of the Northeast Anti-Japanese Allied Forces	Hanin dongbuk uiyonggun	Hanin tongbuk ŭiyonggun		번역 표준 원칙
3981	한인비행대	韓人飛行隊	Korean Aviation Corps	Hanin bihaengdae	Hanin pihaengdae		번역 표준 원칙
3982	한인비행사양성소	韓人飛行士養成所	Korean Aviation School of Willows, California	Hanin bihaengsa yangseongso	Hanin pihaengsa yangsŏngso	1920	번역 표준 원칙
3983	한인사회당	韓人社會黨	Korean People's Socialist Party in Khabarovsk	Hanin sahoedang	Hanin sahoedang	1918-1920	번역 표준 원칙
3984	한인소년기숙학교	韓人少年寄宿學校	Korean Boarding School for Boys	Hanin sonyeon gisuk hakgyo	Hanin sonyŏn kisuk hakkyo		번역 표준 원칙

NO	용어	한자	영문	RO	MC	시대 및 연도	출전
3985	한인소년병학교	韓人少年兵學校	Korean Youth Army School in Nebraska	Hanin sonyeonbyeong hakgyo	Hanin sonyŏnbyŏng hakkyo	1909-?	번역 표준 원칙
3986	한인신보	韓人新報	*Hanin Sinbo* (newspaper published by Koreans in Vladivostok)	Haninsinbo	Haninsinbo	1917-?	번역 표준 원칙
3987	한인애국단	韓人愛國團	Korean Patriot Society	Hanin aegukdan	Hanin aeguktan	1931	한국학중앙연구원, 《영문한국백과》-김구
3988	한인연합협의위원회	韓人聯合協議委員會	Korean United Consultative Committee	Hanin yeonhap hyeobui wiwonhoe	Hanin yŏnhap hyŏbŭi wiwonhoe		번역 표준 원칙
3989	한인자유대회	韓人自由大會	First Korean Congress	Hanin jayudaehoe	Hanin chayudaehoe	1919	번역 표준 원칙
3990	한인중앙학원	韓人中央學院	The Korean Central Institute	Hanin jungang hagwon	Hanin chungang hagwon	1912	번역 표준 원칙
3991	한인촌	韓人村	Koreatown	Haninchon	Haninch'on		번역 표준 원칙
3992	한인합성협회 (하와이)	韓人合成協會 (Hawaii)	United Korean Association of Hawaii	Hanin hapseong hyeophoe (hawai)	Hanin hapsŏng hyŏphoe (hawai)	1907-1909	번역 표준 원칙

NO	용어	한자	영문	RO	MC	시대 및 연도	출전
3993	한일 각료회담	韓日 閣僚會談	Korea-Japan ministerial talks	Hanil gangnyo hoedam	Hanil kangnyo hoedam	1965-?	번역 표준 원칙
3994	한일 경제협의회	韓日 經濟協議會	Korea-Japan Economic Association	Hanil gyeongje hyeobuihoe	Hanil kyŏngje hyŏbŭihoe		번역 표준 원칙
3995	한일 국교정상화	韓日 國交正常化	normalization of diplomatic relations between Korea and Japan	Hanil gukgyo jeongsanghwa	Hanil kukkyo chŏngsanghwa	1965	번역 표준 원칙
3996	한일 국교정상화를 위한 예비회담	韓日 國交正常化를 爲한 豫備會談	preliminary talks for the normalization of diplomatic relations between Korea and Japan	Hanil gukgyo jeongsanghwareul wihan yebi hoedam	Hanil kukkyo chŏngsanghwa-rŭl wihan yebi hoedam	1951	번역 표준 원칙
3997	한일 입어협상	韓日 入漁協商	Korea-Japan fisheries talks	Hanil ibeo hyeopsang	Hanil ibŏ hyŏpsang		번역 표준 원칙
3998	한일경제협력	韓日經濟協力	economic cooperation between Korea and Japan	Hanil gyeongje hyeomnyeok	Hanil kyŏngje hyŏmnyŏk		번역 표준 원칙
3999	한일교섭	韓日交涉	negotiations on normalization of diplomatic relations between Korea and Japan	Hanil gyoseob	Hanil kyosŏp	1965	번역 표준 원칙
4000	한일기본조약	韓日基本條約	Treaty on Basic Relations between the Republic of Korea and Japan	Hanil gibon joyak	Hanil kibon choyak	1965	번역 표준 원칙

NO	용어	한자	영문	RO	MC	시대 및 연도	출전
4001	한일병합	韓日倂合	Japan's annexation of Korea	Hanil byeonghap	Hanil pyŏnghap	1910	번역 표준 원칙
4002	한일수교	韓日修交	normalization pf diplomatic relations between Korea and Japan	Hanil sugyo	Hanil sugyo	1965	번역 표준 원칙
4003	한일의정서	韓日議政書	Korea-Japan Protocol of 1904	Hanil uijeongseo	Hanil ŭijŏngsŏ	1904	번역 표준 원칙
4004	한일청구권자금의 운용 및 관리에 관한 법률	韓日請求權資金의 運用 및 管理에 關한 法律	Law on the Employment and Management of Claim Fund of ROK-Japan	Hanil cheonggugwon jageumui unyong mit gwallie gwanhan beomnyul	Hanil ch'ŏnggukwŏn chagŭm-ŭi unyŏng mit kwalli-e kwanhan pŏmnyul	1966-1982	번역 표준 원칙
4005	한일회담	韓日會談	talks on the normalization of diplomatic relations between Korea and Japan	Hanil hoedam	Hanil hoedam	1951-1965	번역 표준 원칙
4006	한일회담반대투쟁	韓日會談反對鬪爭	June 3 Struggle (protests against talks on normalization of Korea-Japan diplomatic relations)	Hanil hoedam bandae tujaeng	Hanil hoedam pandae t'ujaeng	1964-1965	번역 표준 원칙
4007	한자교육논쟁	漢字敎育論爭	controversy on teaching of Chinese characters at school	Hanja gyoyuknonjaeng	Hancha gyoyuknonjaeng		번역 표준 원칙
4008	한족총연합회	韓族總聯合會	Pan-Korean Ethnic Association	Hanjok chongyeonhaphoe	Hanjok ch'ongyŏnhaphoe	1929-1930	번역 표준 원칙

NO	용어	한자	영문	RO	MC	시대 및 연도	출전
4009	한중문화협회	韓中文化協會	Korea-China Cultural Association	Hanjung munhwa hyeophoe	Hanjung munhwa hyŏphoe	1942-1945	번역 표준 원칙
4010	한중민중동맹	韓中民衆同盟	Sino-Korean People's League	Hanjung minjung dongmaeng	Hanjung minjung tongmaeng		번역 표준 원칙
4011	한중연합전선	韓中聯合戰線	Korea-China United Front (against Japan)	Hanjung yeonhap jeonseon	Hanjung yŏnhap chŏnsŏn		번역 표준 원칙
4012	한중호조사	韓中互助社	Korea-China Cooperated Company	Hanjung hojosa	Hanjung hojosa	1921-?	번역 표준 원칙
4013	한청통상조약	韓淸通商條約	Treaty of Commerce between Korea and China, 1899	Hancheong tongsang joyak	Hanch'ŏng tongsang choyak	1899	번역 표준 원칙
4014	할슈타인 원칙	Hallstein 原則	Hallstein Doctrine	Halsyutain wonchik	Halsyut'ain wŏnch'ik	1955-?	번역 표준 원칙
4015	함평고구마사건	咸平고구마事件	Hampyeong Sweet Potato Incident (farmers' struggle for democratization)	Hampyeong goguma sageon	Hamp'yŏng koguma sakŏn	1976-1978	번역 표준 원칙
4016	함포사격	艦砲射擊	naval bombardment	Hampo sagyeok	Hamp'o sagyŏk		번역 표준 원칙

NO	용어	한자	영문	RO	MC	시대 및 연도	출전
4017	함포외교	艦砲外交	gunboat diplomacy	Hampo oegyo	Hamp'o oegyo		번역 표준 원칙
4018	함흥학생사건	咸興學生事件	arrest of Hamheung students in 1942 (for speaking in Korean on a train)	Hamheung haksaeng sageon	Hamhŭng haksaeng sakŏn	1942	번역 표준 원칙
4019	합동물가단속본부	合同物價團束本部	headquarters for consumer price control	Hapdong mulga dansok bonbu	Haptong mulka dansok ponbu		번역 표준 원칙
4020	합동수사본부	合同搜査本部	Joint Investigation Headquarters	Hapdong susa bonbu	Haptong susa ponbu		번역 표준 원칙
4021	합천학살사건	陝川虐殺事件	Hapcheon Massacre	Hapcheon haksal sageon	Hapch'ŏn haksal sagŏn	1919	번역 표준 원칙
4022	핫팬츠		hot pants	hot pants	Hatpaencheu	Hatp'aench'ŭ	번역 표준 원칙
4023	항만건설	港灣建設	harbor construction	Hangman geonseol	Hangman kŏnsŏl		번역 표준 원칙
4024	항명파동	抗命波動	disobedience scandal in the ROK Military	Hangmyeong padong	Hangmyŏng p'adong		번역 표준 원칙

NO	용어	한자	영문	RO	MC	시대 및 연도	출전
4025	항미원조전쟁	抗米援朝戰爭	war on anti-U.S. Aid to Korea	Hangmi wonjo jeonjaeng	Hangmi wŏnjo chŏnjaeng	1950-1953 (휴전협정)	번역 표준 원칙
4026	항복문서	降伏文書	Instrument of Surrender	Hangbong munseo	Hangbok munsŏ		번역 표준 원칙
4027	항일무장투쟁	抗日武裝鬪爭	armed resistance against Japanese colonial rule	Hangil mujang tujaeng	Hangil mujang t'ujaeng		번역 표준 원칙
4028	항일빨치산	抗日partisan	anti-Japanese partisan	Hangil ppalchisan	Hangil ppalch'isan		번역 표준 원칙
4029	항일빨치산 1세대	抗日partisan 1世代	first generation of the anti-Japanese partisans	Hangil ppalchisan 1sedae	Hangil ppalch'isan 1sedae		번역 표준 원칙
4030	항일빨치산투쟁	抗日partisan鬪爭	anti-Japanese partisan struggle	Hangil ppalchisan tujaeng	Hangil ppalch'isan t'ujaeng		번역 표준 원칙
4031	항일언론운동	抗日言論運動	anti-Japanese journalism movement	Hangil eonnon undong	Hangil ŏllon undong		번역 표준 원칙
4032	항일유격대	抗日遊擊隊	anti-Japanese Korean guerrillas	Hangil yugyeokdae	Hangil yugyŏktae	1967-	번역 표준 원칙

NO	용어	한자	영문	RO	MC	시대 및 연도	출전
4033	해관은행	海關銀行	bank for maritime customs	Haegwan eunhaeng	Haegwan ŭnhaeng		번역 표준 원칙
4034	해군사관학교	海軍士官學校	Korea Naval Academy	Haegun sagwan hakgyo	Haegun sagwan hakkyo	1949-?	번역 표준 원칙
4035	해군성	海軍省	Department of the Navy	Haegunseong	Haegunsŏng		번역 표준 원칙
4036	해군특별지원병령	海軍特別志願兵令	1943 Special Ordinance on Naval Volunteer Force	Haegun teukbyeol jiwon byeongnyeong	Haegun t'ŭkpyŏl chiwŏn byŏngnyŏng	1943	번역 표준 원칙
4037	해방	解放	Liberation (from Japanese colonial rule, 1945)	Haebang	Haebang	1945	번역 표준 원칙
4038	해삼위통상사무	海蔘威通商事務	Great Han Empire's Office of Foreign and Commercial Affairs in Vladivostok	Haesamwi tongsang samu	Haesamwi t'ongsang samu		번역 표준 원칙
4039	해상무역	海上貿易	maritime trade	Haesang muyeok	Haesang muyŏk		번역 표준 원칙
4040	해상침투	海上浸透	marine infiltration	Haesangchimtu	haesangch'imt'u		번역 표준 원칙

NO	용어	한자	영문	RO	MC	시대 및 연도	출전
4041	해성	海星	Haeseong, Korean anti-ship missile	Haeseong	Haesŏng	1996	번역 표준 원칙
4042	해양경찰대	海洋警察隊	National Maritime Police Administration	Haeyang gyeongchaldae	Haeyang kyŏngch'aldae	현대	번역 표준 원칙
4043	해양경찰청	海洋警察廳	Korea Coast Guard	Haeyang gyeongchalcheong	Haeyang kyŏngch'alch'ŏng	1953-?	번역 표준 원칙
4044	해외건설촉진법	海外建設促進法	Overseas Construction Promotion Act	Haeoe geonseol chokjinbeop	Haeoe kŏnsŏl ch'okchinpŏp	2012	송기중, 《한영우리문화용어집》, 지문당, 2001.
4045	해외동포사회	海外同胞社會	Korean communities overseas	Haeoe dongpo sahoe	Haeoe tongp'o sahoe		번역 표준 원칙
4046	해외순방	海外巡訪	overseas trip	Haeoe sunbang	Haeoe sunbang		번역 표준 원칙
4047	해외여행자유화	海外旅行自由化	liberalization of overseas travel in 1989	Haeoe yeohang jayuhwa	Haeoe yŏhaeng chayuhwa	1989	번역 표준 원칙
4048	해외파병실	海外派兵室	Expeditionary Forces Room	Haeoe pabyeongsil	Haeoe p'abyŏngsil	1993	번역 표준 원칙

NO	용어	한자	영문	RO	MC	시대 및 연도	출전
4049	해외한족대회	海外韓族大會	All-Korean Overseas Convention	Haeoe hanjok daehoe	Haeoe hanjok taehoe	1941	번역 표준 원칙
4050	해인사대장경판	海印寺大藏經板	woodblocks for printing the Tripitaka Koreana at Haeinsa Temple	Haeinsa daejanggyeongpan	Haeinsa taejanggyŏngp'an	고려	번역 표준 원칙
4051	해인사장경판전	海印寺藏經板殿	Haeinsa Temple Janggyeong Panjeon (depositories for the Tripitaka Koreana woodblocks)	Haeinsa janggyeongpanjeon	Haeinsa changgyŏngp'anjŏn	고려	번역 표준 원칙
4052	해저 광케이블	海底 光cable	undersea optical cables	Haejeo gwangkeibeul	Haejŏ kwangk'eibŭl		한국학중앙연구원,《영문한국백과》-해인사대장경판
4053	해저터널	海底tunnel	submarine tunnel	Haejeo teoneol	Haejŏ t'ŏnŏl		번역 표준 원칙
4054	해조신문	海朝新聞	*Haejo Sinmun* (newspaper published by Koreans in Vladivostok)	Haejosinmun	Haejosinmun	1908-?	번역 표준 원칙
4055	핵 실험	核 實驗	nuclear test	Haek silheom	Haek silhŏm		번역 표준 원칙
4056	핵 항공모함	核 航空母艦	nuclear aircraft carrier	Haek hanggong moham	Haek hanggong moham		번역 표준 원칙

NO	용어	한자	영문	RO	MC	시대 및 연도	출전
4057	핵 확산금지조약	核 擴散禁止條約	Nuclear Nonproliferation Treaty (NPT)	Haek hwaksan geumji joyak	Haek hwaksan kŭmji choyak	1969-	번역 표준 원칙
4058	핵 확산금지조약 탈퇴	核 擴散禁止條約 脫退	withdrawal from the Nuclear Nonproliferation Treaty	Haek hwaksan geumji joyak Taltoe	Haek hwaksan kŭmji choyak t'alt'oe		번역 표준 원칙
4059	핵가족	核家族	nuclear family	Haekgajok	Haekkajok		번역 표준 원칙
4060	핵개발	核開發	nuclear development	Haek gaebal	Haek kaebal		번역 표준 원칙
4061	핵무기 감축협정	核武器 減縮協定	nuclear arms reduction treaty	Haengmugi gamchuk hyeopjeong	Haekmugi kamch'uk hyŏpchŏng	1991	번역 표준 원칙
4062	핵시설 동결	核施設 凍結	freezing nuclear power plants	Haeksiseol donggyeol	Haeksisŏl tonggyŏl		번역 표준 원칙
4063	핵통제	核統制	nuclear control	Haektongje	Haekt'ongje		번역 표준 원칙
4064	햇볕정책	햇볕政策	Sunshine Policy	Haetbyeot jeongchek	Haetpyŏt chŏngch'aek	1998-2002	번역 표준 원칙

NO	용어	한자	영문	RO	MC	시대 및 연도	출전
4065	행복추구권	幸福追求權	right to pursue happiness	Haengbok chugugwon	Haengbok ch'ugugwŏn		번역 표준 원칙
4066	행정명령	行政命令	administrative order	Haengjeong myeongnyeong	Haengjŏng myŏngnyŏng		번역 표준 원칙
4067	행정수도	行政首都	administrative capital	Haengjeong sudo	Haengjŏng sudo		번역 표준 원칙
4068	행정안전부	行政安全部	Ministry of Public Administration and Security	Haengjeong anjeonbu	Haengjŏng anjŏnbu	2008	번역 표준 원칙
4069	행정전산화 10년 계획	行政電算化 10年 計劃	10-Year Plan for Computerization of Public Administration	Haengjeong jeonsanhwa 10nyeon gyehoek	Haengjŏng jŏnsanhwa 10nyŏn kyehoek	1978	번역 표준 원칙
4070	행정중심복합도시 건설청	行政中心複合都市 建設廳	Multifunctional Administrative City Construction Agency	Haengjeong jungsim bokhap dosi geonseolcheong	Haengjŏng chungsim pokhap tosi kŏnsŏlch'ŏng	2006	번역 표준 원칙
4071	향로봉 전투	香爐峰 戰鬪	Battle of Hyangnobong-Peak	Hyangnobong jeontu	Hyangnobong chŏnt'u	1951	번역 표준 원칙
4072	향토예비군	鄉土豫備軍	homeland reserve forces	Hyangto yebigun	Hyangt'o yebigun	1968-?	번역 표준 원칙

NO	용어	한자	영문	RO	MC	시대 및 연도	출전
4073	허정과도내각	許政過渡內閣	Heo Jeong's interim government	Heo Jeong gwado naegak	Hŏ Chŏng kwado naegak	1960	번역 표준 원칙
4074	헌법	憲法	the Constitution	Heonbeop	Hŏnbŏp		번역 표준 원칙
4075	헌법개정100만인 청원운동	憲法改正100萬人 請願運動	Petition of One Million Signatures for Constitutional Amendment	Heonbeop gaejeong 100man cheongwon undong	Hŏnpŏp kaejŏng 100manin ch'ŏngwŏn undong	1973	번역 표준 원칙
4076	헌법개정청원운동 본부	憲法改正請願運動 本部	Headquarters of the Petition for Constitutional Amendment	Heonbeop gaejeong cheongwon undong bonbu	Hŏnpŏp kaejŏng ch'ŏngwŏn undong ponbu	1973	번역 표준 원칙
4077	헌법공포	憲法公布	promulgation of the Constitution	Heonbeop gongpo	Hŏnpŏp kongp'o	1948	번역 표준 원칙
4078	헌법일부 정지	憲法一部 停止	partial suspension of the Constitution	Heonbeop ilbu jeongji	Hŏnpŏp ilbu chŏngji	1972	번역 표준 원칙
4079	헌법재판소	憲法裁判所	Constitutional Court of Korea	Heonbeop jaepanso	Hŏnpŏp chaep'anso	1988-?	번역 표준 원칙
4080	헌법제정	憲法制定	enactment of the Constitution	Heonbeop jejeong	Hŏnpŏp ch'ejŏng	1948	번역 표준 원칙

NO	용어	한자	영문	RO	MC	시대 및 연도	출전
4081	헌병경찰제도	憲兵警察制度	military police system	Heonbyeong gyeongchal jedo	Hŏnbyŏng kyŏngch'al chedo	1910-1919	번역 표준 원칙
4082	헌병무단통치	憲兵武斷統治	political control by the Japanese Military Police during the Japanese Colonial Period	Heonbyeong mudan tongchi	Hŏnbyŏng mudan t'ongch'i	1910-1919	번역 표준 원칙
4083	헌병사령관	憲兵司令官	Provost Marshal	Heonbyeong saryeonggwan	Hŏnbyŏng saryŏnggwan		번역 표준 원칙
4084	헌의6조	獻議6條	Six Proposals (submitted by the Independence Club)	Heonui6jo	Hŏnŭi6cho	1898	번역 표준 원칙
4085	헌정수호성토대회	憲政守護聲討大會	Rally for Safeguarding Constitutionalism	Heonjeong suho seongto daehoe	Hŏnjŏng suho sŏngt'o taehoe	1968	번역 표준 원칙
4086	헌정연구회	憲政硏究會	Society for the Study of Constitutional Government	Heonjeong yeonguhoe	Hŏnjŏng yŏn'guhoe	1905-1906	번역 표준 원칙
4087	헤이그 만국평화회의	Hague 萬國平和會議	The Hague International Peace Conference of 1907	Heigeu manguk pyeonghwa hoeui	Heigŭ man'guk p'yŏnghwa hoeŭi	1907	번역 표준 원칙
4088	헤이그 특사	Hague 特使	three secret emissaries sent to the Hague International Peace Conference of 1907	Heigeu teuksa	Heigŭ t'ŭksa	1907	번역 표준 원칙

NO	용어	한자	영문	RO	MC	시대 및 연도	출전
4089	혁명공약	革命公約	Revolutionary Pledges	Hyeongmyeong gongyak	Hyŏngmyŏng kongyak	1961	번역 표준 원칙
4090	혁명내각	革命內閣	Revolutionary Cabinet	Hyeongmyeong naegak	Hyŏngmyŏng naegak	1961	번역 표준 원칙
4091	혁명법령집	革命法令集	Legal Codes Proclaimed after the April 19 Revolution	Hyeongmyeong beomnyeongjip	Hyŏngmyŏng pŏmnyŏngjip	1961	번역 표준 원칙
4092	혁명열사릉	革命烈士陵	Mausoleum of Revolutionary Martyrs	Hyeongmyeong yeolsareung	Hyŏngmyŏng yŏlsarŭng	1975	번역 표준 원칙
4093	혁명재판소	革命裁判所	revolutionary court / tribunal	Hyeongmyeong jaepanso	Hyŏngmyŏng chaep'anso	1961-1962	번역 표준 원칙
4094	혁신당	革新黨	Innovation Party	Hyeoksindang	Hyŏksindang	1961	번역 표준 원칙
4095	혁신도시	革新都市	"innovative city"	Hyeoksin dosi	Hyŏksin tosi		번역 표준 원칙
4096	혁신운동	革新運動	North Korea's technological innovation movement	Hyeoksin undong	Hyŏksin undong	1960-1961	번역 표준 원칙

- 532 -

NO	용어	한자	영문	RO	MC	시대 및 연도	출전
4097	현대 포니1	現代 Pony1	Hyundai Pony 1	Hyeondae poni1	Hyŏndae p'oni1	1982	번역 표준 원칙
4098	현대건설	現代建設	Hyundai Engineering and Construction	Hyeondae geonseol	Hyŏndae kŏnsŏl	1947-?	번역 표준 원칙
4099	현대국가	現代國家	modern country	Hyeondae gukga	Hyŏndae kukka		번역 표준 원칙
4100	현대자동차	現代自動車	Hyundai Motor Co.	Hyeondae jadongcha	Hyŏndae chadongch'a	1967-?	번역 표준 원칙
4101	현대중공업	現代重工業	Hyundai Heavy Industries	Hyeondae junggongeop	Hyŏndae chunggongŏp	1973	번역 표준 원칙
4102	현리 전투	縣里 戰鬪	Battle of Hyeon-ri Village	Hyeon-ri jeontu	Hyŏn-ri chŏnt'u	1951	번역 표준 원칙
4103	혈맹	血盟	blood alliance	Hyeolmaeng	Hyŏlmaeng		번역 표준 원칙
4104	혐오시설	嫌惡施設	unpleasant facilities	Hyeomo siseol	Hyŏmo sisŏl		번역 표준 원칙

NO	용어	한자	영문	RO	MC	시대 및 연도	출전
4105	협동농장	協同農場	collective farm	Hyeopdong nongjang	Hyŏptong nongjang	1953-	번역 표준 원칙
4106	협동조합	協同組合	cooperative associations	Hyeopdong johap	Hyŏptong chohap	1920-?	한국학중앙연구원, 《영문한국백과》-협동조합
4107	협력업체	協力業體	partner firms	Hyeomnyeok eopche	Hyŏmnyŏk ŏpch'e		번역 표준 원칙
4108	협상선거법	協商選擧法	Revised Act on the House of Representatives Election	Hyeopsang seongeobeop	Hyŏpsang sŏn'gŏbŏp	1958	번역 표준 원칙
4109	형평사	衡平社	Equal Balance Association	Hyeongpyeongsa	Hyŏngp'yŏngsa	1923-1936	번역 표준 원칙
4110	형평운동	衡平運動	movement to abolish the class system	Hyeongpyeong undong	Hyŏngp'yŏng undong	1923-?	번역 표준 원칙
4111	혜민원	惠民院	Office for Relief Work (Hyeminwon)	Hyeminwon	Hyeminwŏn	1901-1903	번역 표준 원칙
4112	호남고속도로	湖南高速道路	Honam Expressway	Honam gosokdoro	Honam kosoktoro	1973	번역 표준 원칙

NO	용어	한자	영문	RO	MC	시대 및 연도	출전
4113	호남의병	湖南義兵	Righteous Army of Jeolla-do	Honamuibyeong	Honamŭibyŏng		번역 표준 원칙
4114	호남정유 여수공장	湖南精油 麗水工場	Honam Oil Refinery Yeosu Plant (now GS Caltex)	Honam jeongyu yeosu gongjang	Honam jŏngyu yŏsu gongjang	1969	번역 표준 원칙
4115	호남창의소	湖南倡義所	Honam Righteous Army Headquarters in Gobu, Jeollanam-do Province	Honam changuiso	Honam ch'angŭiso	1908	번역 표준 원칙
4116	호남철도주식회사 취지서	湖南鐵道株式會社 趣旨書	Prospectus of Honam Railway Corp.	Honam cheoldo jusik hoesa chwijiseo	Honam ch'ŏlto chusik hoesa ch'wijisŏ	1908	번역 표준 원칙
4117	호남학회	湖南學會	Cholla Educational Association	Honam hakhoe	Honam hakhoe	1907-1910	Ki-baik Lee, translated by Edward W. Wagner, A New History of Korea, Harvard University Press, 1984,
4118	호르무즈 해협 봉쇄	Hormuz 海峽 封鎖	embargo of the Strait of Hormuz	Horeumujeu haehyeop bongswae	Horŭmujŭ haehyŏp pongswae		번역 표준 원칙
4119	호세불납투쟁	戶稅不納鬪爭	protest against household tax	Hose bullap tujaeng	Hose pullap t'ujaeng		번역 표준 원칙
4120	호스티스 영화	hostess 映畵	"hostess movies" (a movie genre featuring the lives of low-class women that became popular in the 1970s as they drew attention to	Hoseutiseu yeonghwa	Hosŭt'isŭ yŏnghwa	1970-?	번역 표준 원칙

- 535 -

NO	용어	한자	영문	RO	MC	시대 및 연도	출전
4121	호적제도	戶籍制度	family registry system	Hojeok jedo	Hojŏk chedo		번역 표준 원칙
4122	호주제	戶主制	male family head system (*hojuje*)	Hojuje	Hojuje	1958-2008	번역 표준 원칙
4123	호주제 폐지	戶主制 廢止	abolishment of the male family head system (*hojuje*)	Hojuje pyeji	Hojuje p'yeji	2008	번역 표준 원칙
4124	호헌동지회	護憲同志會	Association for the Protection of the Constitution	Hoheon dongjihoe	Hohŏn tongjihoe	1954	번역 표준 원칙
4125	호헌철폐	護憲撤廢	"win a constitutional amendment for direct presidential elections"	Hoheon cheolpye	Hohŏn ch'ŏlp'ye	1987	번역 표준 원칙
4126	홈드라마		home drama	TV drama	Hom deurama	Hom tŭrama		번역 표준 원칙
4127	홍구공원의거	虹口公園義擧	bomb set off in Hongkou Park in Shanghai by Martyr Yun Bong-gil (1932)	Honggu gongwon uigeo	Honggu kongwŏn ŭigŏ	1932	번역 표준 원칙
4128	홍범14조	洪範14條	Fourteen-Point Law	Hongbeom14jo	Hongbŏm14cho	1894	번역 표준 원칙

NO	용어	한자	영문	RO	MC	시대 및 연도	출전
4129	홍상어	紅상어	Red Shark, Korean anti-submarine missile	Hongsangeo	Hongsangŏ	2012	번역 표준 원칙
4130	홍익인간의 교육이념	弘益人間의 敎育理念	hongik ingan, educational ideology of "benefit for all humanity"	Hongik inganui gyoyuk inyeom	Hongik in'gan-ŭi kyouk inyŏm	1949	번역 표준 원칙
4131	홍주의병	洪州義兵	Righteous Army in Hongju (now Hongseong)	Hongju uibyeong	Hongju ŭibyŏng	1906	번역 표준 원칙
4132	화랑훈련	花郞訓鍊	Hwarang Exercise	Hwarang hullyeon	Hwarang hullyŏn		번역 표준 원칙
4133	화력발전소	火力發電所	thermoelectric power plant	Hwaryeok baljeonso	Hwaryŏk palchŏnso		번역 표준 원칙
4134	화력지원협조본부	火力支援協調本部	Fire Support Coordination Center (FSCC)	Hwaryeok jiwon hyeopjo bonbu	Hwarŏk chiwŏn hyŏpcho bonbu		번역 표준 원칙
4135	화력진지(Fire base)	火力陣地(Fire base)	fire support base	Hwaryeok jakjeon (Fire base)	Hwaryŏk chinji (Fire base)		번역 표준 원칙
4136	화북조선독립동맹	華北朝鮮獨立同盟	North China Korean Independence League (NCKIL)	Hwabuk joseon dongnip dongmaeng	Hwabuk chosŏn tongnip tongmaeng	1942-1946	Peter H. Lee, Sourcebook of Korean Civilization(Volume 2), Columbia University Press, 1993,

NO	용어	한자	영문	RO	MC	시대 및 연도	출전
4137	화북조선청년연합회	華北朝鮮青年聯合會	North China Korean Youth Federation	Hwabuk joseon cheongnyeon yeonhaphoe	Hwabuk chosŏn ch'ŏngnyŏn yŏnhaphoe	1941-1942	번역 표준 원칙
4138	화생방	化生放	chemical, biological, radiological (CBR) safety and protection	Hwasaengbang	Hwasaengbang		번역 표준 원칙
4139	화석연료	化石燃料	fossil fuel	Hwaseok yeonryo	Hwasŏk yŏllyo		번역 표준 원칙
4140	화요회	火曜會	Tuesday Society (Hwayohoe, Communist group)	Hwayohoe	Hwayohoe	1924-1926	번역 표준 원칙
4141	화의신청	和議申請	application for composition	Hwaui sincheong	Hwaŭi sinch'ŏng		번역 표준 원칙
4142	화이론	華夷論	Sinocentrism	Hwairon	Hwairon		번역 표준 원칙
4143	화이적 명분론	華夷的 名分論	justification based on Sinocentrism	Hwaijeok myeongbunnon	Hwaijŏk myŏngbunnon		번역 표준 원칙
4144	화이체제	華夷體制	Sino-Barbarian dichotomy	Hwaicheje	Hwaich'eje		번역 표준 원칙

NO	용어	한자	영문	RO	MC	시대 및 연도	출전
4145	화전정리사업	火田整理事業	afforestation of slash-and-burn fields	Hwajeon jeongni saeop	Hwajŏn chŏngni saŏp	1967-1979	번역 표준 원칙
4146	화천 전투	華川 戰鬪	Battle of Hwacheon	Hwacheon jeontu	Hwach'ŏn chŏnt'u	1950	번역 표준 원칙
4147	화친조약	和親條約	treaty of peace and amity	Hwachin joyak	Hwach'in choyak		번역 표준 원칙
4148	화폐개혁	貨幣改革	currency reform	Hwapye gaehyeok	Hwap'ye kaehyŏk		번역 표준 원칙
4149	화폐정리사업	貨幣整理事業	reform of the Korean currency (by the Japanese colonial government)	Hwapye jeongni saeop	Hwap'ye chŏngni saŏp	1904-1910	번역 표준 원칙
4150	화학섬유공장	化學纖維工場	chemical textile plant	Hwahak seomyu gongjang	Hwahak sŏmyu kongjang		번역 표준 원칙
4151	확산방지구상	擴散防止構想	Proliferation Security Initiatives (PSI)	Hwaksan bangji gusang	Hwaksan pangji kusang	2003	번역 표준 원칙
4152	환경개선사업	環境改善事業	environment improvement projects	Hwangyeong gaeseon saeop	Hwan'gyŏng kaesŏn saŏp		번역 표준 원칙

NO	용어	한자	영문	RO	MC	시대 및 연도	출전
4153	환경부	環境部	Ministry of Environment	Hwangyeongbu	Hwangyŏngbu	1994	번역 표준 원칙
4154	환경영향평가법	環境影響評價法	Environmental Impact Assessment Act	Hwangyeong yeonghyang pyeonggabeop	Hwan'gyŏng yŏnghyang p'yŏngkapŏp	2012	번역 표준 원칙
4155	환경오염	環境汚染	pollution	Hwangyeong oyeom	Hwan'gyŏng oyŏm		번역 표준 원칙
4156	환경운동연합	環境運動聯合	Korean Federation for Environmental Movement	Hwangyeong undong yeonhap	Hwan'gyŏng undong yŏnhap	1993-	번역 표준 원칙
4157	환곡제도	還穀制度	Government Grain Loan System	Hwangok jedo	Hwan'gok chedo	?-?	번역 표준 원칙
4158	환구단	圜丘壇	Hwangudan Altar	Hwangudan	Hwan'gudan	1897	번역 표준 원칙
4159	환율현실화	換率現實化	rationalization of exchange rates	Hwanyul hyeonsilhwa	Hwanyul hyŏnsirhwa		번역 표준 원칙
4160	환태평양 해군훈련	環太平洋 海軍訓練	Pacific Rim Naval Exercises	Hwantaepyeongyang haegun hullyeon	Hwant'aep'yŏngyang haegun hullyŏn		번역 표준 원칙

NO	용어	한자	영문	RO	MC	시대 및 연도	출전
4161	활빈당	活貧黨	Hwalbindang (bandits robbing from the rich to help the poor)	Hwalbindang	Hwalbindang	1899-1905	번역 표준 원칙
4162	황국신민	皇國臣民	imperial subject	Hwangguk sinmin	Hwangguk sinmin	1937-1945	번역 표준 원칙
4163	황국신민화	皇國臣民化	turning Koreans into the imperial subjects (of Japan)	Hwangguk sinminhwa	Hwangguk sinminhwa	1937-1945	번역 표준 원칙
4164	황국신민화교육	皇國臣民化敎育	education for turning Koreans into the imperial subjects (of Japan)	Hwangguk sinminhwa gyoyuk	Hwangguk sinminhwa kyoyuk	1938	번역 표준 원칙
4165	황국신민화운동 (황민화운동)	皇國臣民化運動	movement to turn Koreans into imperial subjects of Japan	Hwangguk sinminhwa undong (hwangminhwa undong)	Hwangguk sinminhwa undong (hwangminhwa undong)		번역 표준 원칙
4166	황국신민화정책 (황민화정책)	皇國臣民化政策	policy of turning Koreans into the imperial subjects of Japan	Hwangguk sinminhwa jeongchaek (hwangminhwa jeongchaek)	Hwangguk sinminhwa chŏngch'aek (hwangminhwa chŏngch'aek)	1937-1945	번역 표준 원칙
4167	황국협회	皇國協會	Imperial Association	Hwangguk hyeophoe	Hwangguk hyŏphoe	1898-?	Ki-baik Lee, translated by Edward W. Wagner, A New History of Korea, Harvard University Press, 1984,
4168	황궁요배	皇宮遙拜	bowing in the direction of Japan's Imperial Palace	Hwanggungyobae	Hwanggungyobae	1910-1945	번역 표준 원칙

NO	용어	한자	영문	RO	MC	시대 및 연도	출전
4169	황무지개척권	荒蕪地開拓權	right to develop all uncultivated state-owned lands	Hwangmuji gaechokgwon	Hwangmuji kaech'ŏkkwŏn	1904	번역 표준 원칙
4170	황석영 방북	黃晳暎 訪北	novelist Hwang Sok-yong's unauthorized visit to North Korea	Hwang Seok-yeong bangbuk	Hwang Sŏk-yŏng pangbuk	1989	번역 표준 원칙
4171	황성기독교청년회	皇城基督敎靑年會	Hwangseong Young Men's Christian Association	Hwangseong gidokgyo cheongnyeonhoe	Hwangsŏng kidokkyo ch'ŏngnyŏnhoe	1903-1913	번역 표준 원칙
4172	황성신문	皇城新聞	*Hwangseong Shinmun (Capital Gazette)*	Hwangseong sinmun	Hwangsŏng sinmun	1898-1910	번역 표준 원칙
4173	황용주필화사건	黃龍珠筆禍事件	arrest of journalist Hwang Yong-ju over publication of anti-government article	Hwang Yong-ju pilhwa sageon	Hwang Yong-chu p'irhwa sakŏn	1964	번역 표준 원칙
4174	황장엽 망명사건	黃長燁 亡命事件	Hwang Jang-yeop's defection to South Korea	Hwang Jang-yeop mangmyeong sageon	Hwang Chang-yŏp mangmyŏng sakŏn	1997	번역 표준 원칙
4175	황토현 전투	黃土峴 戰鬪	Battle of Hwangto-hyeon	Hwangtohyeon jeontu	Hwangt'ohyŏn chŏnt'u	1894	번역 표준 원칙
4176	황포군관학교	黃浦軍官學校	Military Academy of the Chinese Nationalists (now Huangpu Military Academy)	Hwangpo gungwan hakgyo	Hwangp'o kun'gwan hakkyo	1927-?	번역 표준 원칙

NO	용어	한자	영문	RO	MC	시대 및 연도	출전
4177	황해해전	黃海海戰	Battle of the Yellow Sea	Hwanghae haejeon	Hwanghae haejŏn	1894	번역 표준 원칙
4178	황화론	黃禍論	Yellow Peril	Hwanghwaron	Hwanghwaron	1895	번역 표준 원칙
4179	회사령	會社令	Decree on the Restriction of Corporate Activity	Hoesaryeong	Hoesaryŏng	1910-1920	번역 표준 원칙
4180	횡성 전투	橫城 戰鬪	Battle of Hoengseong	Hoengseong jeontu	Hoengsŏng chŏnt'u	1951	번역 표준 원칙
4181	후계자 문제	後繼者問題	issue of succession	Hugyeja munje	Hugyeja munje		번역 표준 원칙
4182	후방차단	後方遮斷	rear interdiction	Hubangchadan	Hubangch'adan		번역 표준 원칙
4183	후보단일화	候補單一化	selection of a single candidate to run against the leading candidate	Hubo danilhwa	Hubo tanilhwa		번역 표준 원칙
4184	훈련도감	訓鍊都監	Military Training Agency	Hullyeondogam	Hullyŏndogam	1593-1882	James B. Palais, Politics and Policy in Traditional Korea, Harvard University Press, 1991, p.73.

NO	용어	한자	영문	RO	MC	시대 및 연도	출전
4185	훈민정음	訓民正音	Hunmin jeongeum (Correct Sounds for the Instruction of the People)	Hunmin jeongeum	Hunmin chŏngŭm	조선	번역 표준 원칙
4186	훈춘사건	琿春事件	Hunchun Incident	Hunchun sageon	Hunch'un sakŏn	1920	번역 표준 원칙
4187	휘문고등학교	徽文高等學校	Whimoon High School	Hwimun godeunghakgyo	Hwimun kodŭnghakkyo	1904-?	휘문고등학교 사이트 http://www.whimoon.hs.kr/
4188	휴교령	休校令	order for school closures	Hyugyoryeong	Hyugyoryŏng		번역 표준 원칙
4189	휴대용 태양전지	携帶用 太陽電池	portable solar batteries	Hyudaeyong taeyangjeonji	Hyudaeyong t'aeyangjŏnji		번역 표준 원칙
4190	휴대폰	携帶phone	cellular phone / mobile phone	Hyudaepon	Hyudaep'on		번역 표준 원칙
4191	휴전	休戰	truce	Hyujeon	Hyujŏn	1953	번역 표준 원칙
4192	휴전감시위원단	休戰監視委員團	Armistice Commission	Hyujeon gamsi wiwondan	Hyujŏn kamsi wiwŏndan	1953-1954	번역 표준 원칙

NO	용어	한자	영문	RO	MC	시대 및 연도	출전
4193	휴전교섭	休戰交涉	ceasefire negotiations	Hyujeon gyoseop	Hyujŏn kyosŏp		번역 표준 원칙
4194	휴전반대운동	休戰反對運動	anti-truce movement	Hyujeon bandae undong	Hyujŏn pandae undong	1953	번역 표준 원칙
4195	휴전선	休戰線	Military Demarcation Line (MDL)	Hyujeonseon	Hyujŏnsŏn	1953-?	번역 표준 원칙
4196	휴전회담	休戰會談	truce talks	Hyujeon hoedam	Hyujŏn hoedam	1951-1953	번역 표준 원칙
4197	휴전회담과 조인	休戰會談과 調印	truce talks and signing of the armistice	Hyujeon hoedamgwa join	Hyujŏnhoedamgwa Choin	1951-1953	번역 표준 원칙
4198	흑룡강	黑龍江	Amur River	Heungnyonggang	Hŭngnyonggang		번역 표준 원칙
4199	흑룡회	黑龍會	Black Dragon Society (Kokuryukai)	Heungnyonghoe	Hŭngnyonghoe	1901-1946	번역 표준 원칙
4200	흑백투표함	黑白投票函	black and white ballot boxes	Heukbaek tupyoham	Hŭkpaek t'up'yoham	1948-1957	번역 표준 원칙

NO	용어	한자	영문	RO	MC	시대 및 연도	출전
4201	흑색선전	黑色宣傳	malicious propaganda	Heuksaek seonjeon	Hŭksaek sŏnjŏn		번역 표준 원칙
4202	흥경성 전투	興京城 戰鬪	Battle of Xingjingcheng	Heunggyeongseong jeontu	Hŭnggyŏngsŏng chŏnt'u	1933	번역 표준 원칙
4203	흥남철수 작전보고서	興南撤收 作戰報告書	reports on the Heungnam Evacuation Operations	Heungnam cheolsu jakjeon bogoseo	Hŭngnam ch'ŏlsu chakchŏn pogosŏ		번역 표준 원칙
4204	흥남철수작전	興南撤收作戰	Heugnam Evacuation Operations	Heungnam cheolsu jakjeon	Hŭngnam ch'olsu ch'akchŏn	1950	번역 표준 원칙
4205	흥사단	興士團	Young Korean Academy	Heungsadan	Hŭngsadan	1913-?	Robert E. Buswell & Timothy S. Lee. Christianity in Korea, Honolulu: University of Hawaii Press,
4206	흥사단 원동임시 위원부	興士團 遠東臨時 委員部	Far East interim branch of the Young Korean Academy (in Shanghai)	Heungsadan wondong imsi wiwonbu	Hŭngsadan wŏndong imsi wiwŏnbu	1920	번역 표준 원칙
4207	흥업구락부	興業俱樂部	Heungeop Club	Heungeop gurakbu	Hŭngŏp kurakpu	1925	번역 표준 원칙
4208	1·21청와대 기습사건	1·21靑瓦臺 奇襲事件	Cheong Wa Dae Raid (1968)	1·21 cheongwadae giseup sageon	1·21 ch'ŏngwadae kisŭp sakŏn	1968	번역 표준 원칙

NO	용어	한자	영문	RO	MC	시대 및 연도	출전
4209	1·4후퇴	1·4後退	January 4 retreat (second NK occupation of Seoul)	1·4 hutoe	1·4 hut'oe	1951	번역 표준 원칙
4210	10·15선거	10·15選擧	October 15 election (1963)	10·15 seongeo	10·15 sŏngŏ	1963	번역 표준 원칙
4211	10·26박대통령 시해사건	10·26朴大統領 弑害事件	assassination of President Park Chung-hee (Oct. 26)	10·26 bak daetongnyeong sihae sageon	10·26 pak taet'ongnyŏng sihae sakŏn	1979	번역 표준 원칙
4212	10·26사태	10·26事態	assassination of Park Chung-hee	10·26 satae	10·26 sat'ae	1979	번역 표준 원칙
4213	10·2시위	10·2示威	October 2 student demonstrations (1973)	10·2 siwi	10·2 siwi	1973	번역 표준 원칙
4214	10·4남북공동선언	10·4南北共同宣言	October 4 South-North Korea Joint Declaration	10·4 nambuk gongdong seoneon	10·4 nambuk kongdong sŏnŏn	2007	번역 표준 원칙
4215	100억 달러 수출	100億 弗 輸出	10 billion dollars in exports	100eok dalleo suchul	100ŏk tallŏ such'ul	1977	번역 표준 원칙
4216	105인 사건	105人 事件	Case of the 105 Men in 1911	105in sageon	105in sakŏn	1911	번역 표준 원칙

NO	용어	한자	영문	RO	MC	시대 및 연도	출전
4217	10월유신	10月維新	Yushin (Constitutional Amendment of October 1972)	10wol yusin	10wŏl yusin	1972	번역 표준 원칙
4218	11·26총선	11·26總選	November 26 general election (1963)	11·26 chongseon	11·26 ch'ongsŏn	1963	번역 표준 원칙
4219	12·12사태	12·12事態	Military Coup of December 12, 1979	12·12 satae	12·12 sat'ae	1979	번역 표준 원칙
4220	124부대	124部隊	Unit 124 (North Korean special operation forces unit)	124 budae	124 pudae	1968	번역 표준 원칙
4221	12해리영해법	12海里領海法	Act on the Extension of Korea's Territorial Seas to 12 Nautical Miles (enacted in 1977)	12haeri yeonghaebeop	12haeri yŏnghaepŏp	1977	번역 표준 원칙
4222	14개조 평화원칙	14個條 平和原則	Woodrow Wilson's Fourteen Points	14gaejo pyeonghwa wonchik	14kaejo p'yŏnghwa wŏnch'ik	1918	번역 표준 원칙
4223	1987 노동자 대투쟁	1987 勞動者 大鬪爭	Great Labor Struggle of July and August 1987	1987 nodongja daetujaeng	1987 nodongja taet'ujaeng	1987	번역 표준 원칙
4224	1민족, 1국가, 2제도, 2정부	1民族, 1國家, 2制度, 2政府	One Nation, One State, Two Systems and Two Governments	1minjok, 1gukga, 2jedo, 2jeongbu	1minjok, 1kukka, 2chedo, 2chŏngbu		번역 표준 원칙

NO	용어	한자	영문	RO	MC	시대 및 연도	출전
4225	1인당 국민소득	1人當 國民所得	per capita GDP	1indang gungmin sodeuk	1indang kungmin sodŭk		번역 표준 원칙
4226	2·12총선	2·12總選	February 12 general election (1985)	2·12 chongseon	2·12 ch'ongsŏn	1985	번역 표준 원칙
4227	2·7구국투쟁	2·7救國鬪爭	February 7 Incident of 1948 (struggle against the proposed establishment of separate government in South Korea)	2·7 guguk tujaeng	2·7 kuguk t'ujaeng	1948	번역 표준 원칙
4228	2·8독립선언	2·8獨立宣言	Declaration of Independence of February 8, 1919	2·8 dongnip seoneon	2·8 tongnip sŏnŏn	1919	번역 표준 원칙
4229	2·8독립선언서	2·8獨立宣言書	February 8 Declaration of Independence	2·8 dongnip seoneonseo	2·8 tongnip sŏnŏnsŏ	1919	번역 표준 원칙
4230	2·28대구학생의거	2·28大邱學生義擧	February 28 Daegu Student Democratic Movement (1960)	2·28 daegu haksaeng uigeo	2·28 taegu haksaeng ŭigŏ	1960	번역 표준 원칙
4231	2002년 한·일월드컵	2002年 韓·日 World Cup	2002 FIFA World Cup Korea/Japan	2002nyeon han-il woldeuceop	2002nyŏn han-il wŏltŭk'ŏp	2002	번역 표준 원칙
4232	2010년 밴쿠버 올림픽	2010年 Vancouver Olympics	2010 Vancouver Winter Olympics	2010 baenkubeo ollimpik	2010 paenk'ubŏ ollimp'ik	2010	번역 표준 원칙

NO	용어	한자	영문	RO	MC	시대 및 연도	출전
4233	2012년 런던올림픽	2012年 London Olympics	2012 London Olympics	2012 reondeon ollimpik	2012 rŏndŏn ollimp'ik	2012	번역 표준 원칙
4234	2018년 평창동계올림픽	2018年 平昌冬季 Olympics	2018 Pyeongchang Winter Olympics	2018neyon pyeongchang donggye ollimpik	2018nyŏn p'yŏngch'ang t'ongye ollimp'ik	2018	번역 표준 원칙
4235	21개조 요구	21個條 要求	21 Demands (made by Japan to China)	21gaejo yogu	21kaejo yogu	1915	번역 표준 원칙
4236	23부	23府	23 bu (administrative districts)	23bu	23pu	1895-1896	번역 표준 원칙
4237	2대 악법	2大 惡法	Two Bad Laws	2dae akbeop	2tae akpŏp	1961	번역 표준 원칙
4238	2대악법 반대투쟁	2大惡法 反對鬪爭	protest against the Two Bad Laws	2dae akbeop bandae undong	2tae akpŏp pandae undong	1961	번역 표준 원칙
4239	3·15마산의거	3·15馬山義擧	March 15 Masan Democractic Movement (1960)	3·15 masan uigeo	3·15 masan ŭigŏ	1960	번역 표준 원칙
4240	3·15부정선거	3·15不正選擧	fraudulent election of March 15, 1960	3·15 bujeong seongeo	3·15 pujŏng sŏn'gŏ	1960	번역 표준 원칙

NO	용어	한자	영문	RO	MC	시대 및 연도	출전
4241	3·1민주구국선언	3·1民主救國宣言	Declaration for Democracy and Saving the Homeland (March 1, 1976)	3·1 minju guguk seoneon	3·1 minju kuguk sŏnŏn	1976	번역 표준 원칙
4242	3·1운동	3·1運動	March First Independence Movement of 1919	3·1 undong	3·1 undong	1919	번역 표준 원칙
4243	3·1절발포사건	3·1節發砲事件	Shooting Incident of March 1, 1948	3·1jeol balpo sageon	3.1chŏl palp'o sakŏn	1948	번역 표준 원칙
4244	3·24 데모	3·24 示威	March 24 demonstrations (1964)	3·24 demo	3·24 taemo	1964	번역 표준 원칙
4245	351고지 전투	351高地 戰鬪	Battle of Hill 351	351goji jeontu	351koji chŏnt'u	1953	번역 표준 원칙
4246	38선	38線	38th Parallel	38seon	38sŏn	1945-1950	번역 표준 원칙
4247	38선획정	38線劃定	drawing the demarcation line along the 38th Parallel	38seon hoekjeong	38sŏn hoekchŏng	1945	번역 표준 원칙
4248	3개년 대한원조계획	3個年 對韓援助計劃	Three-Year Aid Program for Korea	3gaenyeon daehan wonjo gyehoek	3kaenyŏn taehan wŏnjo kyehoek	1953	번역 표준 원칙

NO	용어	한자	영문	RO	MC	시대 및 연도	출전
4249	3당 대표회담	3黨 代表會談	meeting of the leaders of the three major parties	3dang daepyo hoedam	3tang taepyo hoedam		번역 표준 원칙
4250	3당 합당	3黨 合黨	three-party merger	3dang hapdang	3tang haptang	1990	번역 표준 원칙
4251	3대 기술혁명	3大 技術革命	(North Korea's) three technological revolutions	3dae gisul hyeongmyeong	3tae kisul hyŏngmyŏng	1970	번역 표준 원칙
4252	3대혁명 붉은기 쟁취 운동	3大革命 붉은旗 爭取運動	Three-Revolution Red Flag Movement	3dae hyeongmyeong bulgeungi jaengchwi undong	3tae hyŏngmyŏng pulgŭn'gi chaengch'wi undong	1975-	번역 표준 원칙
4253	3대혁명(사상·기술·문화)	3大革命 (思想·技術·文化)	(North Korea's) Three Revolutions: Ideology, Technology and Culture	3dae hyeongmyeong (sasang·gisul·munhwa)	3tae hyŏngmyŏng (sasang·kisul·munhwa)	1970-?	번역 표준 원칙
4254	3대혁명소조운동	3大革命小組運動	Movement of Three Revolution Cells	3dae hyeongmyeong sojo undong	3tae hyŏngmyŏng sojo undong	1973-	번역 표준 원칙
4255	3대혁명역량	3大革命力量	capability to achieve the Three Revolutions	3dae hyeongmyeong yeongnyang	3tae hyŏngmyŏng yŏngnyang	1964-?	번역 표준 원칙
4256	3백공업	3白工業	three white industries of the 1950s: sugar, cotton yarn, and wheat flour	3baek gongeop	3paek kongŏp	1950년대	번역 표준 원칙

NO	용어	한자	영문	RO	MC	시대 및 연도	출전
4257	3선개헌	3選改憲	constitutional amendment to allow a third presidential term	3seon gaeheon	3sŏn kaehŏn	1969	번역 표준 원칙
4258	3성조정위원회	3省調停委員會	State-War-Navy Coordinating Committee	3seong jojeong wiwonhoe	3sŏng chojŏng wiwŏnhoe		번역 표준 원칙
4259	3세대 화상전화	3世代 畵像電話	video calling on 3G mobile phones	3sedae hwasang jeonhwa	3sedae hwasang jŏnhwa		번역 표준 원칙
4260	3저호황	3低好況	"three lows" driving Korea's economic development: low interest rates, low exchange rates, low oil prices	3jeo hohwang	3jŏ hohwang	1986-1988	번역 표준 원칙
4261	4·19혁명	4·19革命	April 19 Revolution (1960)	4·19 hyeongmyeong	4·19 hyŏngmyŏng	1960	번역 표준 원칙
4262	4·19후의 노동운동	4·19後의 勞動運動	labor movement after the April 19 Revolution	4·19huui nodong undong	4·19huŭi nodong undong	1960 전후	번역 표준 원칙
4263	4·19후의 학생운동	4·19後의 學生運動	student movement after the April 19 Revolution	4·19huui haksaeng undong	4·19huŭi haksaeng undong	1960 전후	번역 표준 원칙
4264	4·19희생자 합동 위령제	4·19犧牲者 合同 慰靈祭	joint memorial service for the victims of the April 19 Revolution	4·19 huisaengja hapdong wiryeongje	4·19 hŭisaengja haptong wiryŏngje		번역 표준 원칙

NO	용어	한자	영문	RO	MC	시대 및 연도	출전
4265	4·26 총선	4·26 總選	April 26 general election (1988)	4·26 chongseon	4·26 ch'ongsŏn	1988	번역 표준 원칙
4266	4·27 선거	4·27 選擧	April 27 election (2011)	4·27 seongeo	4·27 sŏngŏ	2011	번역 표준 원칙
4267	4·3 보궐선거	4·3 補闕選擧	April 3 by-election (1990)	4·3 bogwol seongeo	4·3 pogwŏl sŏngŏ	1990	번역 표준 원칙
4268	4·13호헌조치발표	4·13護憲措置發表	April 13 announcement for the suspension of constitutional debates (1987)	4·13hoheon jochi balpyo	4·13hohŏn choch'I palp'yo	1987	번역 표준 원칙
4269	40대 기수론	40代 旗手論	argument for 40s-generation leadership	40dae gisuron	40tae kisuron	1971	번역 표준 원칙
4270	40대기수	40代旗手	40s-generation leadership	40dae gisu	40tae kisu		번역 표준 원칙
4271	4H운동	4H運動	4-H Movement	4H undong	4H undong	1947-?	번역 표준 원칙
4272	4개국 외무장관회의	4個國 外務長官會議	Four-Nation Foreign Ministers' Conference	4gaeguk oemujanggwan hoeui	4gaeguk oemujanggwan hoeŭi		번역 표준 원칙

NO	용어	한자	영문	RO	MC	시대 및 연도	출전
4273	4대 의혹사건	4大 疑惑事件	Four Great Scandals	4dae uihok sageon	4tae ŭihok sagŏn	1961-1964	번역 표준 원칙
4274	4대강살리기 사업	4大江 살리기 事業	restoration of the four major rivers	4daegang salligi saeop	4taegang salligi saŏp	2008-?	번역 표준 원칙
4275	4대강유역 종합개발	4大江流域 綜合開發	Four Rivers Development Project	4dae gang yuyeok jonghap gaebal	4taegang yuyŏk chonghap kaebal	1966-?	번역 표준 원칙
4276	4대국안전보장론	4大國安全保障論	Theory of Security by the Four Powers	4Daeguk Anjeon Bojangnon	4taeguk anjŏn pojangnon	1971	번역 표준 원칙
4277	4대군사노선	4大軍事路線	Four-point Military Guidelines	4dae gunsa noseon	4tae kunsa nosŏn	1962-?	번역 표준 원칙
4278	4월참변	4月慘變	April Incident of 1920 (massacre of Koreans in Vladivostok's Sinhanchon [New Korean Village] by the Japanese)	4wol chambyeon	4wol ch'ambyŏn	1920	번역 표준 원칙
4279	4월혁명	4月革命	April Revolution of 1960	4wol hyeongmyeong	4wŏl hyŏngmyŏng	1960	번역 표준 원칙
4280	5·10총선거	5·10總選擧	May 10 general election (1948)	5·10 chong seongeo	5·10 ch'ong sŏn'gŏ	1948	번역 표준 원칙

NO	용어	한자	영문	RO	MC	시대 및 연도	출전
4281	5·15서울역시위	5·15Seoul驛示威	May 15 demonstration at Seoul Station (1980)	5·15 seouryeok siwi	5·15 sŏulyŏk siwi	1980	번역 표준 원칙
4282	5·15선거	5·15選舉	May 15 election (1956)	5·15 seongeo	5·15 sŏngŏ	1956	번역 표준 원칙
4283	5·16군사정변	5·16軍事政變	May 16 Coup (1961)	5·16 gunsa jeongbyeon	5·16 kunsa chŏngbyŏn	1961	번역 표준 원칙
4284	5·17쿠데타	5·17Coup	May 17 Coup (1980)	5·17 kudeta	5·17 k'udet'a	1980	번역 표준 원칙
4285	5·18광주민주화운동	5·18光州民主化運動	Gwangju Democratic Uprising of May 18, 1980	5·18 gwangju minjuhwa undong	5·18 kwangju minjuhwa undong	1980.5.	번역 표준 원칙
4286	5·25총선	5·25總選	May 25 general election (1971)	5·25 chongseon	5·25 ch'ongsŏn	1971	번역 표준 원칙
4287	5·3선거	5·3選擧	May 3 election (1986)	5·3 seongeo	5·3 sŏngŏ	1967	번역 표준 원칙
4288	5·3인천항쟁	5·3仁川抗爭	Incheon May 3 protest for constitutional amendment and direct elections	5·3 incheon hangjaeng	5·3 inch'ŏn hangjaeng	1986	번역 표준 원칙

NO	용어	한자	영문	RO	MC	시대 및 연도	출전
4289	5·4운동	5·4運動	May 4th Movement of 1919	5·4 undong	5·4 undong	1919	번역 표준 원칙
4290	518민주화운동 기록물	518民主化運動 記錄物	Human Rights Documentary Heritage 1980 Archives for the May 18th Democratic Uprising against Military Regime, in	518 minjuhwa undong girongmul	518 minjuhwa undong kirokmul		유네스코 http://www.unesco.org/new/en/communication-and-information/flagship-project-activities/mem
4291	5공청문회	5共聽聞會	public hearings on the Fifth Republic	5gong cheongmunhoe	5kong ch'ŏngmunhoe	1988	번역 표준 원칙
4292	5공청산	5共淸算	clearing the legacy of the Fifth Republic	5gong cheongsan	5kong ch'ŏngsan	1988-1989	번역 표준 원칙
4293	5공화국	5共和國	Fifth Republic	5gonghwaguk	5konghwaguk	1981-1988	번역 표준 원칙
4294	5도행정국	5道行政局	Five-Province Administrative Bureau	5do haengjeongguk	5to haengjŏngguk	1945-1946	번역 표준 원칙
4295	5적필화사건	5賊筆禍事件	"Five Thieves" Controversy (arrest of those concerned with the publication of Kim Ji-ha's poem "Five Thieves" in *Sasanggye* [World	5jeok pilhwa sageon	5chŏk p'irhwa sakŏn	1970	번역 표준 원칙
4296	6·10만세운동	6·10萬歲運動	June 10 Independence Movement (1926)	6·10 manse undong	6·10 manse undong	1926	번역 표준 원칙

NO	용어	한자	영문	RO	MC	시대 및 연도	출전
4297	6·10명동성당 시위	6·10明洞聖堂 示威	June 10 demonstration for democracy at Myeong-dong Cathedral (1987)	6·10 myeongdong seongdang siwi	6·10 myŏngdong sŏngdang siwi	1987	번역 표준 원칙
4298	6·15남북공동선언	6·15南北共同宣言	June 15 South-North Joint Declaration	6·15 nambuk gongdong seoneon	6·15 nambuk kongdong sŏnŏn	2000.6.15	번역 표준 원칙
4299	6·23평화통일 외교정책	6·23平和統一 外交政策	June 23 Declaration, or the Special Foreign Policy for Peace and Unification of June 23, 1973	6·23 pyeonghwa tongil oegyo jeongchaek	6·23 p'yŏnghwa t'ongil oegyo chŏngch'aek	1973	번역 표준 원칙
4300	6·23평화통일선언	6·23平和統一宣言	June 23 Declaration of Peaceful Reunification	6·23 pyeonghwa tongil seoneon	6·23 p'yŏnghwa t'ongil sŏnŏn	1973	번역 표준 원칙
4301	6·25납북인사	6·25拉北人士	persons abducted by North Korea during the Korean War	6·25 napbuk insa	6·25 nappuk insa	1951	번역 표준 원칙
4302	6·25전쟁	6·25戰爭	the Korean War	6·25 jeonjaeng	6·25 chŏnjaeng	1950-1953	번역 표준 원칙
4303	6·29민주화선언	6·29民主化宣言	June 29 Declaration	6·29 minjuhwa seoneon	6·29 minjuhwa sŏnŏn	1987	번역 표준 원칙
4304	6·3사태	6·3事態	June 3 Incident	6·3 satae	6·3 sat'ae	1964	번역 표준 원칙

NO	용어	한자	영문	RO	MC	시대 및 연도	출전
4305	6·8부정선거 규탄시위	6·8不正選擧 糾彈示威	protest against June 8 fraudulent elections	6·8 bujeong seongeo gyutan siwi	6·8 pujŏng sŏn'gŏ kyut'an siwi	1967	번역 표준 원칙
4306	6·10항쟁	6·10抗爭	June 10 pro-democracy protests	6·10 hangjaeng	6·10 hangjaeng	1987	번역 표준 원칙
4307	64M D램 개발	64M DRAM 開發	development of 64-mega DRAM chip	64M D-raem gaebal	64M D-raem kaebal	1992	번역 표준 원칙
4308	6개년 경제개발계획	6個年 經濟開發計劃	Six-year Economic Development Plan	6gaenyeon gyeongje gaebal gyehoek	6kaenyŏn kyŏngje kaebal kyehoek		번역 표준 원칙
4309	6월민주항쟁	6月民主抗爭	June Democracy Movement of 1987	6wol minju hangjaeng	6wŏl minju hangjaeng	1987	번역 표준 원칙
4310	6차교육과정	6次敎育課程	Sixth Revised National Curriculum	6cha gyoyuk gwajeong	6ch'a kyoyuk kwajŏng	1995-2000	번역 표준 원칙
4311	7·20선언	7·20宣言	July 20 Declaration	7·20 seoneon	7·20 sŏnŏn	1990	번역 표준 원칙
4312	7·29총선	7·29總選	July 29 general election (1960)	7·29 chongseon	7·29 0=ch'ongsŏn	1960	번역 표준 원칙

NO	용어	한자	영문	RO	MC	시대 및 연도	출전
4313	7·30 교육개혁	7·30 教育改革	July 30 Education Reform	7·30 gyoyuk gaehyeok	7·30 kyoyuk kaehyŏk	1980-1987	번역 표준 원칙
4314	7·4남북공동성명	7·4南北共同聲明	Joint Communique of July 4, 1972 between South and North Korea	7·4 nambuk gongdong seongmyeong	7·4 nambuk kongdong sŏngmyŏng	1972	번역 표준 원칙
4315	7·7특별선언	7·7特別宣言	July 7 Special Declaration for Unification	7·7 teukbyeol seoneon	7·7 t'ŭkpyŏl sŏnŏn	1988	번역 표준 원칙
4316	70년대 리얼리즘문학	70年代 realism 文學	1970s realism literature	70nyeondae rieollijeum munhak	70nyŏndae riŏllisŭm munhak	1970년대	번역 표준 원칙
4317	70년대 소설	70年代 小說	1970s novels	70nyeondae soseol	70nyŏndae sosŏl	1970년대	번역 표준 원칙
4318	70년대 시	70年代 詩	1970s poetry	70nyeondae si	70nyŏndae si	1970년대	번역 표준 원칙
4319	731부대	731部隊	Unit 731 of the Japanese forces	731budae	731pudae	1936-1945	번역 표준 원칙
4320	8·15선언	8·15宣言	August 15 announcement of the Plan for Peaceful Unification	8·15 seoneon	8·15 sŏnŏn	1970	번역 표준 원칙

NO	용어	한자	영문	RO	MC	시대 및 연도	출전
4321	8·15해방	8·15解放	liberation from Japanese colonial rule (August 15, 1945)	8·15 haebang	8·15 haebang	1945	번역 표준 원칙
4322	8·18판문점도끼사건	8·18板門店도끼事件	August 18 Panmunjeom Axe Murder Incident (1976)	8·18 panmunjeom dokki sageon	8·18 p'anmunjŏm tokki sakŏn	1976	번역 표준 원칙
4323	8·3비상경제조치	8·3非常經濟措置	emergency measure of August 3, 1972 to freeze private loan repayments	8·3 bisang gyeongje jochi	8·3 pisang kyŏngje choch'i	1972	번역 표준 원칙
4324	8·15 대통령저격사건	8·15 大統領狙擊事件	assassination attempt on President Park Chung-hee	8·15 daetongnyeong jeogyeok sageon	8·15 taet'ongnyŏng chŏgyŏk sagŏn	1974	번역 표준 원칙
4325	88서울올림픽	88Seoul Olympics	1988 Seoul Olympics	88 seoul ollimpik	88 sŏul ollimp'ik	1988	번역 표준 원칙
4326	88올림픽고속도로	88Olympic高速道路	88 Olympic Expressway	88 ollimpik gosokdoro	88 ollimp'ik kosoktoro	1984	번역 표준 원칙
4327	88특별여단	88特別旅團	88th Special Brigade	88 teukbyeol yeodan	88 t'ŭkpyŏl yŏdan	1942	번역 표준 원칙
4328	8월종파사건	8月宗派事件	August 1956 Incident (Kim Il-sung's purge of pro-Chinese and pro-Soviet factions)	8wol jongpa sageon	8wŏl chongp'a sagŏn	1956	번역 표준 원칙

NO	용어	한자	영문	RO	MC	시대 및 연도	출전
4329	8월테제	8月Thesis	August Thesis	8wol teje	8wŏl t'eje	1945	번역 표준 원칙
4330	8월폭풍작전	8月暴風作戰	Soviet invasion of Manchuria	8wol pokpung jakjeon	8wŏl p'okp'ung chakchŏn	1945	번역 표준 원칙
4331	9·18사변	9·18事變	September 18 Incident (aka Manchurian Incident; Mukden Incident)	9·18 sabyeon	9·18 sabyŏn	1931	번역 표준 원칙
4332	9월총파업	9月總罷業	September General Strike	9wol chongpaeop	9wŏl ch'ongp'aŏp	1946	번역 표준 원칙
4333	AFKN-TV	AFKN-TV	American Forces in Korea Network (AFN)	AFKN-TV	AFKN-TV	1950	번역 표준 원칙
4334	AID원조자금	AID援助資金	Agency for International Development (AID) fund	AID wonjojageum	AID wŏnjojagŭm		번역 표준 원칙
4335	ASTA세계총회 서울개최	ASTA世界總會 Seoul開催	World Congress of the American Society of Travel Agents (ASTA) in Seoul	ASTA segyechonghoe seoul gaechoe	ASTA segyech'onghoe sŏul kaech'oe	1983	번역 표준 원칙
4336	Buy American 정책	Buy American 政策	buy-American policy	Bai Amerikan jeongchaek	Buy American chŏngch'aek	1933	번역 표준 원칙

NO	용어	한자	영문	RO	MC	시대 및 연도	출전
4337	CDMA 서비스상용화	CDMA의 service 商用化	commercialization of CDMA service	CDMA-ui seobiseu sangyonghwa	CDMA-ŭi sŏbisŭ sangyonghwa	1996	번역 표준 원칙
4338	DJP연합	DJP聯合	alliance of two opposition party candidates, Kim Dae-jung and Kim Jong-pil, for the 1997 presidential election	DJP yeonhap	DJP yŏnhap	1996	번역 표준 원칙
4339	DMB	DMB	digital multimedia broadcasting (DMB)	DMB	DMB		번역 표준 원칙
4340	F1코리아그랑프리	F1Korea Grand Prix	2012 F1 Korean Grand Prix	F1 Koria geurangpeuri	F1 Koria kŭrangpŭri	2012	번역 표준 원칙
4341	G20	G20	Group of Twenty Finance Ministers and Central Bank Governors (aka G20)	G20	G20	1999	번역 표준 원칙
4342	G20정상회의	G20頂上會議	G20 Summit	G20 jeongsang hoeui	G20 chŏngsang hoeŭi	2008-?	번역 표준 원칙
4343	GATT 쇠고기수입 제한 철회권고	GATT 쇠고기輸入 制限 撤回勸告	recommendation to lift restrictions on beef imports under the General Agreement on Tariffs and Trade (GATT)	GATT soegogi suip jehan cheolhoe gonggo	GATT soekoki suip chehan ch'ŏrhoe kwŏn'go	1989	번역 표준 원칙
4344	IMF구제금융	IMF救濟金融	IMF bailout	IMF guje geumyung	IMF kuje kŭmyung		번역 표준 원칙

NO	용어	한자	영문	RO	MC	시대 및 연도	출전
4345	IT산업	IT産業	information and technology (IT) industry	IT saneop	IT sanŏp		번역 표준 원칙
4346	JOC (카톨릭 노동청년회)	JOC (Catholic 勞動靑年會)	Young Catholic Workers (Jeunesse Ouvrières Catholiques)	JOC (katollik nodong cheongnyeonhoe)	JOC (k'at'ollik nodong ch'ŏngnyŏnhoe)	1958-1980	번역 표준 원칙
4347	K-11 복합소총	K-11 複合小銃	K-11 Korean Dual Barrel, Air-Burst Weapon	K-11 bokhap sochong	K-11 pokhap soch'ong	2008	번역 표준 원칙
4348	K1A1전차	K1A1戰車	K1A1 Tank	K1A1 jeoncha	K1A1 chŏnch'a	1997-?	번역 표준 원칙
4349	K-200장갑차	K-200裝甲車	K-200 Armored Personnel Carrier (APC)	K-200 janggapcha	K-200 changgapch'a		번역 표준 원칙
4350	KAL007기 피격사건	KAL007機 被擊事件	bombing of Korean Air Flight 007 in 1983	KAL007gi pigyeok sageon	KAL007gi p'igyŏk sakŏn	1983	번역 표준 원칙
4351	KAL858기 피격사건	KAL858機 被擊事件	bombing of Korean Air Flight 858 in 1987	KAL858gi pigyeok sageon	KAL858gi p'igyŏk sakŏn	1987	번역 표준 원칙
4352	KAL기 납북사건	KAL機 拉北事件	hijacking of Korean Air flight to North Korea in 1969	KALgi napbuk sageon	KALgi nappuk sakŏn	1969	번역 표준 원칙

NO	용어	한자	영문	RO	MC	시대 및 연도	출전
4353	KAL빌딩 방화사건	KAL building 放火事件	Korean Air Building Arson Incident of 1971	KAL bilding banghwa sageon	KAL pilding panghwa sakŏn	1971	번역 표준 원칙
4354	KBS 사태	KBS 事態	KBS labor union strike of 1990	KBS satae	KBS sat'ae	1990	번역 표준 원칙
4355	KDX-Ⅱ 구축함	KDX-Ⅱ 驅逐艦	KDX-Ⅱ Destroyer	KDX-Ⅱ guchukham	KDX-Ⅱ kuch'ukham		번역 표준 원칙
4356	KDX-Ⅲ 이지스함	KDX-Ⅲ Aegis艦	KDX-Ⅱ Aegis	KDX-Ⅲ ijiseuham	KDX-Ⅲ ijisŭham		번역 표준 원칙
4357	KOICA-NGO봉사단	KOICA-NGO奉仕團	KOICA-NGO Volunteer Program	KOICA-NGO bongsadan	KOICA-NGO pongsadan		번역 표준 원칙
4358	K-pop 열풍	K-pop 熱風	K-pop fever	K-POP yeolpung	K-pop yŏlp'ung		번역 표준 원칙
4359	KTX	KTX	KTX (Korea Train eXpress) bullet train	KTX	KTX	2004-?	번역 표준 원칙
4360	KT공작계획안	KT工作計劃案	KT Manuvering Plan Proposal	KT gongjak gyehoegan	KT kongjak kyehoegan	1973	번역 표준 원칙

NO	용어	한자	영문	RO	MC	시대 및 연도	출전
4361	K-레이션	K-ration	K-Ration (field ration)	K-reisyeon	K-reisyŏn		번역 표준 원칙
4362	LA폭동	LA暴動	Los Angeles riots of 1992	LA pokdong	LA p'oktong	1992	번역 표준 원칙
4363	Le Petit Parisien	Le Petit Parisien	*Le Petit Parisien*	Le Petit Parisien	Le Petit Parisien	1904	번역 표준 원칙
4364	M-1고지 전투	M-1高地 戰鬪	Battle of M-1 Hill	M-1 goji jeontu	M-1 koji chŏnt'u	1953	번역 표준 원칙
4365	M1탄 일체	M1彈 一體	M1 rifle cartridges	M1tan ilche	M1t'an ilch'e	1950-1953	번역 표준 원칙
4366	MBC강변가요제	MBC江邊歌謠祭	MBC Riverside Song Festival	MBC gangbyeon gayoje	MBC kangbyŏn kayoje	1984, 1985, 1986	번역 표준 원칙
4367	ML파	ML派	Marxist-Leninist Faction	ML pa	ML pa		번역 표준 원칙
4368	MQ-1 프레데터		MQ-1 Predator	Unmanned Aerial Vehicle, MQ-1 Predator	MQ-1 peuredeteo	MQ-1 p'ŭredet'ŏ	1994	번역 표준 원칙

NO	용어	한자	영문	RO	MC	시대 및 연도	출전
4369	OECD 가입	OECD 加入	accession to the Organisation for Economic Co-operation and Development (OECD)	OECD gaip	OECD kaip	1996	번역 표준 원칙
4370	OSS연합작전	OSS聯合作戰	OSS Combined Operations	OSS yeonhap jakjeon	OSS yŏnhap chakchŏn	1944	번역 표준 원칙
4371	PL480원조	PL480援助	food aid program based on Public Law 480	PL480 wonjo	PL480 wŏnjo	1954	번역 표준 원칙
4372	T50	T50	T-50 Golden Eagle	T50	T50		번역 표준 원칙
4373	UN 한국통일결의안	UN 韓國統一決議案	United Nations General Assembly Resolution 195 (The Problem of the Independence of Korea)	UN hanguk tongil gyeoruian	UN han'guk t'ongil kyŏrŭian		번역 표준 원칙
4374	UN군사령부	UN軍司令部	United Nations Command	UNgun saryeongbu	UN'gun saryŏngbu	1950-1978	번역 표준 원칙
4375	UN한국위원단	UN韓國委員團	United Nations Commission on Korea (UNCOK)	UN hanguk wiwondan	UN han'guk wiwŏndan	1948-1950	번역 표준 원칙
4376	UR대책실무위원회	UR對策實務委員會	Working-level Commission to Devise Measures in Preparation for the Uruguay Round	UR daechaek silmu wiwonhoe	UR taech'aek silmu wiwŏnhoe		번역 표준 원칙

NO	용어	한자	영문	RO	MC	시대 및 연도	출전
4377	WTO가입	WTO加入	accession to the World Trade Organization	WTO gaip	WTO kaip	1955	번역 표준 원칙
4378	X-마스고지전투	X-mas高地戰鬪	Battle of Christmas Hill	X-maseu goji jeontu	X-masŭ koji chŏnt'u	1951-1952	번역 표준 원칙
4379	YH무역여공농성사건	YH貿易女工籠城事件	YH Industrial Company Incident of 1979 (sit-in demonstrations by female workers)	YH muyeok yeogong nongseong sageon	YH muyŏk yŏgong nongsŏng sakŏn	1979	번역 표준 원칙
4380	YWCA 위장결혼식 사건	YWCA 僞裝結婚式 事件	YWCA political protest in the guise of a wedding ceremony	YWCA wijang gyeolhonsik sageon	YWCA wijang kyŏrhonsik sagŏn	1979	번역 표준 원칙